Miracle-Gro® Complete Guide to Houseplants

Meredith® Books
Des Moines, Iowa

Miracle-Gro Complete Guide to Houseplants
Editor: Denny Schrock
Contributing Writers: Lynn Steiner, Darrell Trout
Copy Chief: Terri Fredrickson
Copy Editor: Kevin Cox
Publishing Operations Manager: Karen Schirm
Senior Editor, Asset and Information Management: Phillip Morgan
Edit and Design Production Coordinator: Mary Lee Gavin
Art and Editorial Sourcing Coordinator: Jackie Swartz
Editorial Assistant: Susan Ferguson
Book Production Managers: Pam Kvitne, Marjorie J. Schenkelberg, Mark Weaver
Imaging Center Operator: Patricia J. Savage
Contributing Technical Proofreaders: Deborah Brown, Dave Slaybaugh
Contributing Proofreaders: Sara Henderson, Jodie Littleton, Stephanie Petersen, Barb Rothfus
Contributing Prop/Photo Stylists: Brad Ruppert, Sundie Ruppert
Contributing Indexer: Ellen Sherron
Other Contributors: Janet Anderson, Ball Horticultural Company, Benary Seeds, Campania International, DeRoose Plants, Dynamic Design/Ames True Temper, Excelsa Gardens, Greenleaf Plants, Harvey Floral Company, Hermann Engelmann Nurseries

Additional Editorial Contributions from Squarecrow Creative
Designer: Greg Nettles

Meredith® Books
Editor in Chief: Gregory H. Kayko
Executive Director, Design: Matt Strelecki
Managing Editor: Amy Tincher-Durik
Executive Editor: Benjamin W. Allen
Senior Associate Design Director: Tom Wegner
Marketing Product Manager: Brent Wiersma

Executive Director, Marketing and New Business: Kevin Kacere
Director, Marketing and Publicity: Amy Nichols
Executive Director, Sales: Ken Zagor
Director, Operations: George A. Susral
Director, Production: Douglas M. Johnston
Business Director: Jim Leonard

Senior Vice President: Karla Jeffries
Vice President and General Manager: Douglas J. Guendel

Meredith Publishing Group
President: Jack Griffin
Executive Vice President: Doug Olson

Meredith Corporation
Chairman of the Board: William T. Kerr
President and Chief Executive Officer: Stephen M. Lacy

In Memoriam: E.T. Meredith III (1933–2003)

Photographers
(Photographers credited may retain copyright © to the listed photographs.)
B=Bottom, C=Center

David Cavagnaro: 19 Column 4BC
Rosemary Kautzky: 19 Column 1B

All of us at Meredith® Books are dedicated to providing you with the information and ideas you need to enhance your home and garden. We welcome your comments and suggestions about this book. Write to us at:
Meredith Corporation
Meredith Gardening Books
1716 Locust St.
Des Moines, IA 50309–3023

If you would like more information on other Miracle-Gro products, call 800/225-2883 or visit us at: www.miraclegro.com

Note to the Readers: Due to differing conditions, tools, and individual skills, Meredith Corporation assumes no responsibility for any damages, injuries suffered, or losses incurred as a result of following the information published in this book. Before beginning any project, review the instructions carefully, and if any doubts or questions remain, consult local experts or authorities. Because codes and regulations vary greatly, you always should check with authorities to ensure that your project complies with all applicable local codes and regulations. Always read and observe all of the safety precautions provided by manufacturers of any tools, equipment, or supplies, and follow all accepted safety procedures.

Contents

Troubleshooting.....................80

Indoor specialties......................90

Encyclopedia of houseplants 112

The indoor garden

Plants provide cheer with their greenery and colorful flowers, and the process of growing plants indoors makes your life better by giving you daily contact with nature. Having greenery around through the cold gray months is an excellent way to ward off the winter blues.

Foliage plants are the backbone of most houseplant collections. In full form year-round, they provide varied shades of green as well as other colors, a rich variety of textures, and many interesting leaf shapes. There is a houseplant to suit almost any indoor growing location or condition.

Flowering plants provide bright splashes of color and exquisite scents. They are usually more challenging to grow than foliage plants, but the effort is worth it. By matching your preferences and your plants' needs you'll be rewarded with flowering plants that provide stunning color and possibly a sweet fragrance for weeks or even months at a time.

Place indoor plants in your home with all the visual diversity of an outdoor garden. Most people limit themselves to plants they can put on a windowsill or table, but houseplants lend themselves to many other uses. Upright forms grow into indoor trees, trailing types look attractive in hanging baskets or climbing on a trellis, and some plants can be shaped and pruned into interesting forms and topiary shapes. Consider creating a terrarium or an indoor herb garden in the kitchen. The options are almost limitless!

Growing plants indoors provides you with a variety of ways to add to your existing decorative style or create a new focal point. You can use houseplants to provide color and style to highlight your home's best features or to cover up the problem areas you don't want anyone to notice. Almost any room in

◄ Foliage and flowering plants complete the decorating of any room. Durable palms, dracaenas, and peace lilies grow well in less than perfect conditions, soften hard lines, and cheer up owners and visitors. Bromeliads or other flowering plants can add color for several months or be moved to help set the stage for entertaining. This setting is a good use of both tabletop and floor plants.

▲ This bedroom has been turned into a sanctuary from the hustle and bustle of life. The plants help to create a relaxed and comfortable environment. Select plants you love and want to spend time with, from large foliage plants, such as schefflera, ficus, dracaena, and others to small personal favorites, or add a fragrant plant such as an orchid to bring a natural scent to your room.

BRIEF HISTORY OF INDOOR GROWING

Bringing the outdoors in has always been a challenge. Plants were meant to grow outside, under natural conditions, not under an artificial environment inside. Despite this, people have been tending indoor plants since ancient times.

The development of glass and indoor heating were major influences on indoor plant culture. In the 17th century, newly discovered flora arrived in Europe from all over the world aboard the trading vessels that crisscrossed the oceans. Orchids, palms, camellias, aroids, sansevierias, and cactus were among the many plants that found their way into European glasshouses.

By the 1870s, indoor gardening was a full-fledged hobby enjoyed by masses. There was frenzied interest in anything tropical, and all kinds of paraphernalia, including Wardian cases, plant cabinets, misters, and indoor arches were developed. Plants that tolerated low light were especially popular as a way to brighten up dull living quarters, just as they are today.

any home or style of house can be enhanced by the presence of houseplants. Whatever the size your collection of houseplants, their beauty will add a bright new dimension to interiors.

Houseplant trends

Indoor gardeners have moved beyond windowsill gardening and macramé hangers to discover new, exciting ways to use houseplants. Today's houseplant enthusiasts are more inclined to create indoor gardens rather than tend individual plants. Basket gardens are popular, as are floor and tabletop groupings.

Houseplants are also used individually as specimens or accents. Plants with bold foliage or architectural shape provide a living flourish for a room. Plants trained into topiaries and standards have become popular, both as specimens and as a part of groupings. The tropical look is fashionable, both indoors and out. Since many houseplants are tropical in origin, they readily lend themselves to this look.

Prim rows of windowsill pots have given way to indoor trees with branches reaching over sofas and chairs or shrubs filling in large awkward corner spaces. Instead of draperies, today hanging baskets and vining plants are often used to screen windows in homes and apartments.

Along with traditional houseplants, such as pothos, philodendrons, and palms, many gardeners overwinter outdoor plants in sunny windows or sunrooms. Easy-to-grow moth orchids are especially popular because they bloom for many months with minimal care.

▶ Baskets are an attractive way to display or grow plants such as these amaryllises and azaleas. The natural materials blend well with most varieties of foliage or flowering plants. Forced bulbs always look nice; try a range of daffodils or easy-to-grow paperwhites and amaryllis. Add a low growing flowering or foliage plant or use natural-looking moss to give baskets a finished appearance. They also make nice gifts for almost anyone in your life.

Benefits of indoor gardening

▲ Many palms work well in formal room settings. This large one is in scale with the room and the furniture. It helps bring symmetry to the setting and softens the scene. Bring color accents with flowering orchids, bulbs, or other plants into the room for entertaining. Use decorative cache pots to cover less attractive growing containers.

Indoor air pollution

Most people spend a lot of time indoors at the office, home, or school. This lack of fresh air can lead to health problems. Chemicals found in synthetic building materials in homes and offices can lead to sick building syndrome. These unhealthy indoor environments can cause people to suffer from allergies; asthma, eye, nose,

and throat irritations; fatigue; headaches; nervous system disorders; and respiratory ailments and sinus congestion.

Primary sources of poor indoor air quality are tightly built houses that reduce ventilation of outdoor air. Synthetic furnishings and building materials that release toxic chemicals add to the problem. Examples of toxins from building

materials are formaldehyde from carpeting, pressed wood, and foam insulation. Hydrocarbons come from vinyl furniture, detergents, and fabric softeners. Benzene originates in glues, paints, and varnishes. Paint and adhesives also contribute trichloroethylene toxins.

Houseplants go a long way in absorbing these chemicals and helping alleviate sick building syndrome.

According to a U.S. Environmental Protection Agency study, houseplants are a first line of defense against indoor air pollution. Research shows that plants filter chemical toxins from the air, creating a healthier environment. Besides breaking down toxic chemicals in the atmosphere, plant leaves clean the air by trapping dust and other particulates. And in the

NATURAL AIR FILTERS

The following houseplants are high-efficiency indoor air pollution fighters.

Areca palm	Chinese evergreen	Peace lily	Schefflera
Arrowhead vine	Dieffenbachia	Philodendron	Snake plant
Banana	Dracaena	Pothos	Spider plant
Boston fern	English ivy	Pygmy date palm	Weeping fig

Arrowhead vine
(Syngonium podophyllum)

Boston fern
(Nephrolepis exaltata)

Weeping fig
(Ficus benjamina)

Pygmy date palm
(Phoenix roebelinii)

Spider plant
(Chlorophytum comosum 'Vittatum')

Banana
(Musa spp.)

Dieffenbachia
(Dieffenbachia maculata)

Peace lily
(Spathiphyllum wallisii)

Snake plant
(Sansevieria trifasciata laurentii)

Schefflera
(Schefflera actinophylla)

natural process of respiration, plants absorb carbon dioxide and give off oxygen and moisture in return. This increase in room humidity results in better living conditions for you and your plants.

Researchers at the National Space Technology Lab found that houseplants reduced pollutants, particularly nitrogen and formaldehyde. In addition to the filtering action from plant foliage, the soil or media they grow in also serves as a filter to remove pollutants. A single spider plant in an enclosed chamber filled with formaldehyde removed 85 percent of the pollutant in a day. All it takes is one potted plant per 100 square feet to clean the air in an average home or office. As few as 15 houseplants can reduce the pollutants in an average home.

Mental and physical health

Plants make people happy. At home and in public spaces, plants enhance mental, physical, and social health. Scientific research shows that interacting with plants has measurable benefits as well. Working with or near plants and flowers lowers blood pressure, eases stress, and makes people feel better. People who care for plants derive pleasure from their well-being. Such a nurturing relationship fulfills human emotional needs.

Members of the American Horticultural Therapy Association (AHTA) develop indoor and outdoor gardening programs designed to feature the therapeutic and wellness benefits of people-plant relationships. Therapy programs rely on the fact that plants appeal to human beings' senses. Plants elicit a peaceful and serene feeling or evoke pleasant memories helpful to healing. Regular garden walks can help to focus attention and recover strength, and they may reduce depression and negative thoughts.

Hospitals have incorporated plants into patient environments. Research has shown that it speeds recovery. A plant-filled atrium or a healing garden accessible to wheelchairs provides patients and family members moments of serenity and peace.

Positive effects also are evident in commercial settings where the presence of plants raises humidity levels, making the workplace more comfortable. Such oxygen-rich working environments also may suppress airborne microbes that carry disease. Because improved mood and lowered blood pressure can be attributed to working around plants, it is no surprise that workplace productivity increases.

Room by room

Most rooms in any home are improved by houseplants' forms, colors, and fragrances. Each room in a house has a different function, and its practical use combined with growing conditions for those plants determines the sort of environment it can offer to plants.

Complement the features of a room by using houseplants with suitable shapes, sizes, and colors.

Plants should enhance the layout of the room without dominating it. An older home with high ceilings can readily handle a tall-growing palm, but a small bathroom calls for a more diminutive plant.

High ceilings will appear lower if you use hanging baskets and cascading plants, whereas low rooms will appear higher if you use a bold and upright plant. Plants with arching branches and small leaves will give the illusion of added width to a narrow room.

Remember that houseplants are living things that change in size and shape as they grow and require regular tending. Leave ample room behind the plants for air circulation as well as access for routine watering and grooming. Also leave space between plants and wallpaper or artwork. Blooming plants in particular may leave behind traces of pollen or stains from flower petals.

Beyond size and other aesthetic factors, you must consider what these rooms offer your plants. How much

▲ The large weeping fig makes this entryway more welcoming and softens the expanse of wood and stone. The space is large, airy, and sunny and is suited to many large plants, including those that grow into treelike proportions. At least one large scale plant is needed to make a significant visual impact.

available light is there or can you alter the area with supplemental lighting? Also consider humidity. Is there enough there or can you add to it without your walls growing moss or your wallpaper peeling? Think of temperature range in the area you want to use and consider the changes that occur

through the seasons of the year. When heat comes on in cooler climates, it can damage plants and lower humidity. You may want to position plants on a seasonal basis or even on a temporary basis for dinner parties and other events. Later in the book these issues are covered in greater detail.

▶ This grouping of plants has much more impact than would a single plant. Anchor a display with one or two larger plants, such as this majesty palm and English ivy topiary. With those focal points, smaller plants can be added for color and texture. Here they are combined with a small dieffenbachia, a calathea, and an arrowhead vine. Using similar types and styles of pots will unify the design.

Entryways and hallways

Entryways are where visitors get their first impression of the inside of your home. A touch of greenery or splash of blooming color is a great way to say welcome, and the sweet scent of a fragrant flower will greatly enhance the experience.

Unfortunately most entryways and hallways are not conducive to healthy plant growth. Many entryways are subject to blasts of cold air, which can be devastating to some plants, and they are often quite cool at night. Most hallways are narrow and poorly lit, but if you have a large well-lit hallway or entryway, you have an opportunity to create a grand arrangement using bold, beautiful plants.

For best effect choose tough, easy-to-grow plants that fit the space. A large plant in a small hallway will make the area look even smaller. If your entryway or hallway includes stairs, consider using the same type of plant on both levels of the

stairway to tie the two floors together.

If you want to make a splash in your entryway but the conditions are less than satisfactory, use brightly colored disposable gift plants that you can replace as needed. Or alternate between two plants that you can rotate, keeping one in good light and the other in the darker area.

Make sure plants are out of the line of traffic in this often-congested spot. Most plants can tolerate some traffic, but any plant that is constantly brushed against will inevitably become damaged. Plants should not obstruct the stairs or doorway. Avoid spiky or thorny plants that can injure passersby. Soft-leaved ferns and palms are good choices.

Living rooms and family rooms

For most people the living room, family room, or great room is the room in which most entertaining takes place and the area of the house where the family gathers

▲ A Norfolk Island pine is a standout in any room with good light. It has interesting textural qualities. Here it is used as a floor plant to fill the space between a chair and an end table.

most often. It is also a popular spot for indoor plants. The light level is typically good and there is usually ample space.

Living rooms generally contain large furniture and plants should be of an appropriate size to counterbalance them: one or two large plants look much better than a clutter of smaller ones. Avoid scattering a few pots of greenery around the room. Instead look for a few areas in which to focus houseplants as specimen plants or groupings.

In any living area side tables and coffee tables can feature smaller plants, either alone or in groupings. Houseplants should relate to other objects, such as ornaments, books, or lamps, which may in themselves suggest the choice of plants. Although designed expressly for putting things on, shelves and mantelpieces do not usually promote the long-term well-being of plants. These areas are good for temporary display of plants, perhaps something from a basement light cart that is now in flower.

Lack of humidity in winter and low light are the main obstacles to growing houseplants in living rooms. Position plants away from radiators or open fires in an area with adequate light. Make sure you can water them easily. Plants should not be in the way of people moving about—both for your convenience and for the

PLANTS FOR LIVING ROOMS AND FAMILY ROOMS

African milk tree
Asparagus fern
Cactus
Cast-iron plant
China doll
Chinese evergreen
Corn plant
Dieffenbachia
Dracaena
False aralia
Fiddle-leaf fig
Grape ivy
Hibiscus
Homalomena
Madagascar dragontree
Norfolk Island pine
Palms
Peace lily
Peperomia
Philodendrons
Podocarpus
Pothos
Pregnant onion
Schefflera
Screw pine
Snake plant
Spider plant
Succulents
Ti plant
Umbrella plant
Weeping fig

health of the plants. Protect fine furniture from water stains by placing impermeable protectors under all containers and using felt pads to prevent scratches.

▲ This cyclamen adds a color accent to the living room. Diminutive flowering or foliage plants can be moved to suit decorating or entertainment needs even if the location will not be permanent.

▲ This formal parlor is enhanced by symmetrical window treatments and a pair of urns and bold-leaf philodendrons. The room's opulence needs bold plants such as dieffenbachia or philodendron to be noticed. This pair makes a powerful statement and continues the formal balance.

▲ Rosemary is useful and decorative for a kitchen windowsill. Given adequate sun and moisture it will grow well and can be shaped into a ball or tree or be allowed to grow in a more relaxed shape. All plants benefit from pruning or pinching back and will be stronger for it. With organically grown herbs, the trimmings are good for cooking; rosemary pairs well with chicken. Place sprigs under the skin and in the cavity before roasting and you will be rewarded with chicken flavored from your own kitchen windowsill herb garden.

▲ This collection of herbs is well suited for this bright kitchen window. The porous clay containers attractively unify the grouping. They are a good match for these plants that prefer moderately dry soil.

PLANTS FOR KITCHENS

African violet
Aloe
Baby's tears
Begonias
Cuban oregano
English ivy
Ferns
Grape ivy
Herbs
Philodendron
Piggyback plant
Polka-dot plant
Pothos
Queen's tears
Red flame ivy
Scented geranium
Spider plant
Strawberry begonia
Swedish ivy
Sweet bay
Tahitian bridal veil
Wandering Jew
Wax plant

Kitchens

Several factors make the kitchen a good place for houseplants. There is easy access to water, humidity is often higher than in other rooms, and light is usually good. But maybe most importantly it is often the most-used room in the house and a place that houseplants will be regularly enjoyed.

Herbs are a logical choice for kitchens, where the leaves can readily be snipped for cooking. The kitchen is also a great place for plant propagation and a good place for keeping a close eye on ailing plants. Save your fragrant plants for other rooms where their scents can be enjoyed, rather than masked by cooking odors.

A common obstacle to growing houseplants in the kitchen is lack of space. Most kitchens have little available floor or countertop space. Kitchens are also busy places, and plants must be kept out of the way. Effectively display houseplants in kitchens along windowsills or in hanging baskets in front of windows. You might be able to add hooks at the top of windows for small hanging baskets or consider adding a glass shelf in the middle of the window. In large kitchens consider tucking an upright plant into the corners around the eating area. Look for space under counters where you might be able to add supplemental fluorescent lighting. Four tubes are needed for most herbs. Grow them in the center of the lights and place other lower light plants under the ends of the tubes.

Dining rooms

The dining room is often overlooked as a place for houseplants, perhaps because it is often one of the least-used rooms in the house.

▶ This country kitchen has good light suitable for growing a range of herbs and phalaenopsis orchids. Use the herbs for cooking and move the orchids to the dining table for a centerpiece.

This country dining room uses low light plants well. Old favorites like English ivy perform well in the low light of this challenging spot. Some cut flowers make the room ready for guests.

PLANTS FOR DINING ROOMS

African violet
Cyclamen
English ivy
Grape ivy
Lady palm
Oxalis
Peace lily
Peperomia
Philodendrons
Pilea
Pothos
Primrose
Zeezee plant

However dining room decor is often sparse and is an ideal backdrop for the addition of attractive houseplant foliage and colorful flowers.

The two main ways to use houseplants in the dining room are as floor specimens and as tabletop centerpieces. Floor plants are nice in large dining rooms, but remember that the table often hides the lower half of large plants. This can be an advantage, since many large houseplants tend to get leggy as they get older. Any meal will be enhanced by the presence of an arching houseplant that provides a subtle overhead canopy.

The focal point of any dining room is the table. Dining room table centerpieces must be low growing to prevent interference with conversations. They must also be healthy and clean to remain attractive. The last thing your guests want to do is sit down to a meal with a dusty, brown-leaved houseplant in front of them.

One significant challenge to placing plants in dining rooms is space. Many dining rooms are quite small and are filled with large pieces of furniture. Diners must be able to maneuver comfortably around the dining room table. Plants should not make the room into an obstacle course. Plus most plants grow poorly when you regularly brush up against them.

The other major challenge is available light. Many dining rooms are interior rooms with few windows, sometimes none. You may have to use supplemental lighting even for low light foliage plants. If light is low you might have to rotate plants with areas that do get much better lighting. Never hesitate to bring small blooming plants into the room for special events and dinner parties.

As in the kitchen, dining rooms are usually not good places for fragrant plants that can conflict with food aromas. Some plants are only fragrant during the day or in the evening; take that into account also.

This bright dining nook with wonderful light, varied space, and locations to grow plants can support a wide diversity of plants. A large foliage plant, such as this ficus, works well in a big pot on the floor near the window. Place sun lovers close to the window in the brightest light. Grow small flowering and foliage specimens on the tops of tables and other furniture in the room. Shift plants around to display them at their best and to coordinate with decorating or culinary themes. The monkey plant in the foreground needs bright light to bloom while the fern on the dining table will tolerate lower light conditions. A colorful bouquet on the credenza complements the less colorful foliage plants used in the room.

Room by room *(continued)*

Bedrooms

Many people completely overlook bedrooms for displaying houseplants. They may think they are used too little to make the effort and expense worthwhile, and the distance from water sources and grooming tools makes plant care more challenging.

However bedrooms offer the perfect opportunity for you to create your own personal retreat. You don't have to worry as much about style and colors and whether or not the plants match your decor. You can simply grow what you love. Houseplants can contribute a healthy, relaxed feeling to a bedroom; and the increased humidity they provide can enhance sleep. Large houseplants placed in front of a window can buffer outdoor noise.

Bedrooms are often cooler than other rooms of the house and provide the perfect environment for plants like flowering maple, primroses, and cyclamen. Consider fragrant plants such as jasmine and stephanotis so you can drift off with their natural perfume around you.

And don't forget the guest bedroom. This is an excellent location to place colorful gift plants, such as calceolaria, cyclamen, exacum, freesia, or orchid pansy to brighten the room and provide a cozy feeling.

▲ This palm's simple lines complement the bedroom's modern decor. One substantial architectural plant with strong and limited lines is more desirable than a lush foliage plant or a grouping of smaller plants that could look cluttered.

Bathrooms

Bathrooms are often the last place people consider for houseplants. However the high humidity found there makes it one of the best indoor environments for many plants. The moisture bathes plants and deters pests such as spider mites. Most bathroom surfaces resist water and are easily cleaned, and it's handy to water plants that sit inches away from a faucet. A fragrant plant is a good choice for bathrooms, where the scent will be amplified in the small space.

In older homes the major limiting factors in the bathroom are usually light and space. In most bathrooms floor space is

▲ A heartleaf philodendron is a nice addition to a night stand in a corner of a bedroom that does not get bright light. Add an attractive basket like this one or a cache pot to complete the look.

PLANTS FOR BEDROOMS

Arrowhead vine
Asparagus fern
Bloodleaf
Boston fern
Chinese evergreen
Coleus
Corn plant
Cyclamen
Dracaena
Freesia
Grape ivy
Jasmine
Orchid pansy
Oxalis
Pilea
Polka-dot plant
Schefflera
Spider plant
Stephanotis
Streptocarpus

▲ An upright Ming aralia in the corner completes this bedroom's Asian theme. This Asian native is adaptable to a wide range of growing conditions and can be pruned or shaped into a variety of shapes from columnar to mini-tree forms. The finely divided foliage and medium green color provide a subtle contrast to taupe or tan walls.

◀ A Victorian oak bathroom is nicely accented with ferns. They are appropriate to the period because they would have been found in houses of that era. Ferns grow well in the higher humidity that is typical in bathrooms.

▼ Symmetrical plants and containers befit this sunny bathroom alcove. Plants that have been grown for many years will work well and fit the period decor.

PLANTS FOR BATHROOMS

African violet
Alocasia
Anthurium
Areca palm
Baby's tears
Begonias
Bromeliads
Calathea
Coleus
Creeping fig
Croton
English ivy
Episcia
Ferns
Hibiscus
Japanese euonymus
Monkey plant
Nerve plant
Orchids
Peperomia
Polka-dot plant
Prayer plant
Stromanthe
Streptocarpus
Ti plant

lacking and houseplants will be limited to those suitable for hanging baskets or tabletops. A hanging basket placed over the bathtub has a ready-made spot for collecting excess water. In new homes bathroom floor space has expanded and the light pours in. That provides space for large plants on the floor and in other locations. Adding a number of plants to that space can turn a bathroom into a spa.

In many bathrooms ventilation comes from an open window. Be careful about placing houseplants where they will be damaged by chilly drafts. Since many bathroom surfaces are ceramic, plastic pots or wicker baskets are better container choices than ceramic, which can be easily broken if dropped. Lastly avoid placing houseplants where they may be damaged by pore-clogging aerosol sprays, which are commonly used in bathrooms.

▼ The arrowhead vine softens and completes the look of this opulent bathroom. It is placed in a vacant corner that is otherwise difficult to use. Its silvery green foliage adds warmth to the room. Other large-leaf plants, such as dieffenbachia, philodendron, or African mask, would also be appropriate additions. All of these selections will benefit from this high humidity environment.

▲ This bathroom is turned into a spa with the addition of plants. Add scented oils, thick fluffy towels, candles, and soft music and you will be enveloped in serenity. Plants soften angular architectural edges and add to the retreat feeling. Use tropical foliage plants, such as this palm, along with scented flowering plants for an exotic ambiance.

Choosing and displaying houseplants

Buying houseplants

Sources

You have several options for purchasing houseplants. You can buy from a reputable local source or order by mail from a catalog or website. A good place to find specialty plants is at a plant society sale. Ordering plants through the mail always is risky since plants can be damaged in transit by temperatures too high or too low, but sometimes it is the only way to find certain plants. A reputable company will only ship when conditions are right and will guarantee their plants, replacing them if necessary.

What to look for

As with all gardening, it pays to do a little research before you shop. Come up with a list of which plants are suitable for your conditions and your intended level of care. Avoid impulse buying. It's too easy to end up with a plant that looks great in the greenhouse but quickly goes downhill once you get it home. Or you may find that the cute little potted plant you couldn't resist quickly grows up to be a great big plant that is too large for its space.

Examine plants carefully before buying. Foliage plants should be lush and full and have good color. Stems and leaves should be firm, not wilted or distorted, and roughly equal on all sides. New growth should be evident. The foliage should appear natural, not covered with polish or wax. Avoid purchasing plants that look as if they have been heavily pruned. A yellow leaf or two at the base of a plant is nothing to be alarmed about, but if you see many yellow or fallen leaves, the plant is probably stressed and therefore is not a good choice.

Avoid bringing home an insect- or disease-infested plant. Examine plants closely where the branches join the stem and on the bottom sides of leaves. Leaf spots can indicate disease or physical damage. Damaged leaves

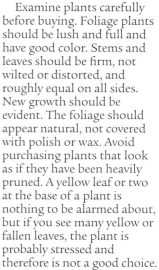

HERE'S A TIP...

Take carpet and paint samples with you when buying houseplants. The samples will help you choose plants that complement or contrast with the room's decor. Also take along some digital photos of the room to refresh your memory of details such as furniture placement and other accessories included in the room.

▲ A plant hunter's joy is a greenhouse and nursery that offers many types of plants from which to choose. Large hanging baskets and other mature plants will give you instant satisfaction. Smaller plants are also available for inclusion in terrariums, dish and basket gardens, or to grow into larger plants.

▲ After making your selections at the garden center, carefully pack your car for the trip home. Nursery-grown plants are often in small pots and will tip over easily; secure them in boxes and plastic flats.

never recover, however. Give the plant a vigorous shake. A plant that's unsteady in its pot may not be well rooted. Shaking the plant also tells you whether the plant has whiteflies because the flies, which resemble dandruff, fly off when you disturb the plant.

When choosing a flowering plant, look for one mostly in bud with just enough open blooms to let you see its eventual color. As with all general rules, there are exceptions. Long-blooming plants such as anthuriums and moth orchids can be purchased in full bloom since their flowers last for several months.

Transporting your plants

Remember that your plant has been growing in a carefully controlled environment and is vulnerable to changes in its surroundings, especially temperature extremes. Make sure the salesperson carefully wraps your plant to protect it from drafts between the store and your home, especially if you're shopping in winter.

Once you get your new plant home, unwrap it and give the soil a thorough soaking by placing the pot in the sink and watering thoroughly from the top until the water has washed

through the holes in the bottom of the container. Let it drain, and then repeat the whole process about 30 minutes later. This not only saturates the soil around roots, it also washes out any salt buildup from plant food applied at the nursery.

Acclimating your plants

Plants often need time to acclimate to their new surroundings. Some plants, such as weeping fig, may shed a few leaves as they settle in. Avoid extremes for the first week or so, including under- or overwatering, high or low temperatures, and intense light. One way to acclimate a plant while keeping it isolated is to place it in a large, transparent plastic bag and set it in bright light but not direct sun. The high humidity inside the bag is just what the plant needs to help it adapt to the lower light of the average home. After two weeks, if no insects are observed, move the plant to a light level closer to what it will ultimately require. Punch a few holes or make a few slits in the bag to allow some air exchange into the bag. After several more days completely remove the bag and move the plant to its permanent location. Even if you move it into lower light, it probably won't drop leaves.

DON'T BUY THESE PLANTS

If your potential houseplant purchases demonstrate any of these symptoms, avoid buying them unless you know that the condition is normal for that plant. Look for other plants that are less likely to transport problems to your home. See pages 82–89 for more detailed descriptions, photos, and solutions to houseplant problems.

● **Weak, spindly growth:** This indicates the plant has been grown in stressful conditions and may never fully recover.
● **Leaves with holes or torn edges:** This may indicate the presence of chewing insects or rough handling by nursery workers.
● **Crawling or flying insects:** Avoid knowingly taking pests home with your plants.
● **Curled or twisted new shoots:** Feeding from aphids, temperature extremes while shoots were in the bud stage, or herbicide injury could be the cause. (Note: some varieties of plants naturally develop curled or twisted shoots.)
● **Oval brown bumps on the stem:** These may be scale insects. Especially note if the stems or leaves below the brown bumps are sticky from the honeydew they secrete.
● **Sticky sap on the leaves:** In addition to scale insects, other insects such as aphids secrete honeydew as they feed.
● **Sunken brown, rotting sections on stems:** This is a sign of fungal disease or root rot.
● **Soft, mushy, dark brown roots:** Gently knock the plant out of its pot to see whether it has healthy white (or creamy tan) roots. Mushy, dark brown roots indicate rot.
● **Circling roots:** If healthy roots circle around the inside of the pot, the plant is potbound. It may have suffered moisture stress, and at the least needs immediate repotting and disentangling of the roots.
● **Root ball shrinking away from pot:** The soil has been allowed to excessively dry. Soaking the root ball may revive the plant, but it has been stressed and may not recover.
● **Sour or rotten odor in the soil:** This is a symptom of poor aeration, usually from overwatering.
● **Many faded flowers:** The plant may be nearing the end of its bloom cycle. Choose one just beginning to bloom instead. Browning blooms may also be a sign of fungal disease.

▲ Isolate new plants from your current collection to give disease or pest problems time to become visible. This prevents problems from spreading to your prized specimens.

▲ Enclose sensitive new plants, such as weeping fig, in a large clear plastic bag to raise humidity and prevent shock from moving them from a greenhouse into dry home air.

Appreciating foliage

Foliage plants present indoor gardeners with a nearly endless assortment of colors, sizes, textures, and shapes to choose from—broadleaf and narrowleaf, upright and spreading, smooth and textured, and many shades of green as well as other colors. They fit a variety of decorating needs, and most provide long-term value and interest year-round. Some are best suited as background plants, while others are showy enough to stand alone as specimens.

Leaf color

Nature provides a mind-boggling array of leaf colors and combinations, including various shades of green and interesting variegation. In most variegated plants the basic green is marked with a pattern of white, gray, silver, cream, gold or yellow, or red and purple. The contrasting color may border leaf edges, follow veins, form a pattern, or be confined to one area, such as the central band of the leaf. The coloring is often enhanced by leaf texture.

Light or brightly colored foliage brightens dim areas while dark leaves stand out best against a lighter background. Create dramatic displays with foliage plants by concentrating on the interplay between two or three colors. A stunning combination includes a multicolored croton complemented by bloodleaf and variegated gold and green ivy.

Most foliage plants with colorful leaves need bright light to bring out the richness of their hues. When given insufficient light, many revert to all green.

▶ This grouping of plants shows some of the diversity available in houseplant leaf color. Shown clockwise from the lower left are: pink and green dotted polka-dot plant; red-edge peperomia; a pink-vein fittonia; a variegated English ivy with cream-color leaf margins; red, cream, and green stromanthe; 'Tricolor' blushing bromeliad; deep pink and green arrowhead vine; and variegated creeping fig in the center. Various leaf textures and shapes add to the differences. Note how the leaves with light variegation brighten dim locations. Most variegation requires bright light for colors to remain true and to prevent leaves from fading to less intense color or reverting to a solid color.

HOUSEPLANTS WITH COLORFUL FOLIAGE

In addition to the plants listed below, many houseplants have species or cultivars with colored or variegated leaves. These are often given a name such as "variegata" (variegated), "aurea" (gold), or "purpurea" (purple) to reflect their leaf color.

Red, pink, or purple leaves
Bloodleaf
Herringbone plant
Madagascar dragontree
Nerve plant
Oxalis
Persian shield
Polka-dot plant
Purple heart
Purple-leaved
  Swedish ivy
Rainbow plant
Red flame ivy
Velvet plant

Polka-dot plant

Nerve plant

Oxalis

Persian shield

Gold or yellow leaves
Dracaenas
Dumb canes
Dwarf schefflera
English ivies
Gold dust dracaena
Showy stromanthe
Snake plant

Gold dust dracaena

Corn plant (dracaena)

Croton 'Super Star'

Snake plant 'Laurentii'

White or cream leaves
African mask
Aralia ivy
Arrowhead vine
Balfour aralia
Chinese evergreen
Crystal anthurium
Cuban oregano
Dracaenas
Dumb canes
English ivies
Japanese euonymus
Nerve plant
Pothos
Sanchezia
Screw pine
Spider plant
Striped inch plant
Zebra plant

'Marble Queen' pothos

Spider plant

Dieffenbachia

English ivy

Silver or gray leaves
Aluminum plant
Beautiful ctenanthe
Chinese evergreen
Chirita
Monkey plant
Nerve plant
Peacock plant
Persian shield
Satin pothos
Strawberry begonia
Watermelon begonia

Chinese evergreen

Silver vase plant

Cathedral windows 'Argentea'

Aluminum plant

Multicolored leaves
Begonias
Bromeliads
Coleus
Copperleaf
Crotons
Flame violet
Prayer plant
Purple false
  eranthemum
Ti plant

Croton

Coleus

'Tricolor' blushing bromeliad

Appreciating foliage *(continued)*

Leaf shape

After color, leaf shape creates the strongest initial impression. The immense variety of leaf shapes and their arrangements on plant stems provide a wide range of options for choosing interesting foliage plants. Leaf shapes fall into groupings, including fan shape, highly divided, feathery, lance or sword shape, oval, heart shape, and even fiddle shape. In addition leaf edges can be gently wavy, finely toothed, lobed, entire (smooth edges) or scalloped.

Leaf Surface Texture

Leaf surface textures are as varied as color and size, ranging from glossy to matte, hairy to wrinkled, and ribbed to quilted. These textural variations add richness and interest to plants, either as specimens or when combined with contrasting textures. Leaf color is often enhanced or modified by texture. The variations in texture result in shades of color from the lighted areas into the shadows. The result is often more a work of art than an act of nature.

► Leaf shapes and textures are nicely varied in this group of plants. Included are two types of dieffenbachias (upper and lower center); deeply textured iron cross begonia and pinwheel pattern 'Escargot' rex begonia (center left); the smoother solid green grape ivy (upper right); succulent, vining wax plant (lower left); and tiny creeping baby's tears (center).

HOUSEPLANTS WITH UNUSUAL LEAF SHAPE

Alocasia	Oxalis
Baby's tears	Piggyback plant
Dwarf papyrus	Ponytail palm
False aralia	Scented geranium
Fiber optic grass	Schefflera
Fishtail palm	Screw pine
House bamboo	Snake plant
Japanese fatsia	Staghorn fern
Ming aralia	Split-leaf
Norfolk Island pine	philodendron

Fishtail palm

Fiber optic grass

False aralia

Alocasia

Piggyback plant

Japanese fatsia

Oxalis

Ming aralia

PLANTS WITH UNUSUAL LEAF TEXTURE

All plant leaves have some texture, even if they are smooth. Here are some that have more interesting textured leaves.

Alocasia	Cuban oregano	Friendship plant	Nerve plant	Red flame ivy
Asparagus fern	Dwarf papyrus	Homalomena	Norfolk Island pine	Rubber tree
Baby's tears	Earth star	Panda plant	Peperomia	Scented geranium
Begonia	Ferns	Maidenhair fern	Purple passion	Strawberry begonia
Cactus	Fiber optic grass			

Asparagus fern

Red flame ivy

Purple passion

'Moon Valley' friendship plant

Ripple peperomia

Norfolk Island pine

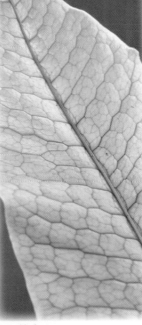

Crocodile fern

Cuban oregano

Flowers & fruits

Foliage plants may form the backbone of the indoor garden, with variegated leaves adding a splash of color, but flowering plants make an indoor garden spectacular. Their bright colors and exquisite scents can make even the longest winter pass a little more pleasantly.

Persuading a plant to bloom indoors is a rewarding activity, building anticipation from the first sign of a bud until the flower shows its full face. What color will the flower be? How large? How long will it take to open? When the blossom actually arrives you feel as though you have personally aided in a small miracle. An even greater reward comes when plants produce fruits in your indoor garden.

Bringing a houseplant into bloom need not be a difficult task. Many houseplants can be coaxed into bloom with a little tender care. Some bloom for a short time; others bloom for weeks or even months if conditions are right. In some plants the true flowers are less notable than the flamboyant bracts that surround them. These bracts often remain long after the flowers have died. Flowers and bracts may work together to provide visual impact.

▶ Exotic hibiscus and blooming geraniums pair with the colorful foliage of coleus to create a tropical feel in this family room. Brilliant reds and intense pinks bring warmth and energy to the grouping.

FRUITING HOUSEPLANTS

It's difficult to get plants to set fruit indoors. Without typical pollinators such as moths, bees, flies, or hummingbirds, you may have to help nature along a bit. Sometimes just gently shaking the mature flowers will produce pollination. Learn to distinguish the stamen, the male portion of the flower, from the stigma, the female portion. Use a small soft brush or a cotton swab to gently move pollen, which often looks like yellow dust, from the male to the female flower parts. With luck your plant will be pollinated and will develop fruit. Allow only a small number of fruits to develop on indoor plants because lower light levels will be unable to sustain heavy crop loads. Support weak fruit-bearing branches if necessary.

Banana
Calamondin orange
Coffee
Coralberry
Lemon
Lime
Natal plum
Orange
Orange-jessamine
Pineapple

Calamondin orange

Banana

Lemon

Ardisia (coralberry)

FLOWERING HOUSEPLANTS

If you have limited space, look for blooming plants that also have attractive foliage when not in bloom (indicated by an *).

African violet*
Anthurium*
Ardisia*
Begonia*
Bromeliads*
Cactus*
Cape lily*
Chenille plant*
Christmas cactus

Cuphea
Clivia
Columnea
Crown-of-thorns*
Episcia*
Flowering maple*
Guppy plant*
Hibiscus*
Hoya*

Ixora
Japanese pittosporum*
Jasmine
Lipstick plant*
Lollipop plant
Monkey plant*
Myrtle*
Orange-jessamine*
Orchids

Osmanthus
Oxalis*
Peace lily*
Scented geranium*
Shrimp plant
Stephanotis*
Streptocarpus
Tahitian bridal veil*
Zebra plant*

African violet

Chenille plant

Flowering maple

Ixora

Shrimp plant

Hibiscus

Anthurium

Clivia

Lipstick plant

Zebra plant

Belleara orchid

Christmas cactus

Placing plants

When deciding how to place plants, think about how you want them to fill space. Do you want one large dramatic plant or a group with contrasting splashes of colors and textures? Do you want your plants to blend into the decor or stand out in a place of prominence?

Balance and scale are important when placing plants in a room. In a long narrow room, a few 4-inch plants on one end of the room would lack impact. Instead place a large upright plant at each end of the room to draw attention. Don't be afraid to move a plant or a group of plants to create a natural harmony or satisfying contrast with surroundings. Try out the effects of plants in conjunction with mirrors and other wall hangings. Sometimes it takes several attempts before you find the right plant or combination for the spot.

Some plants look best standing alone in a place of honor. An orchid or bromeliad in flower or a well-grown croton are usually most effectively displayed as a single specimen. You don't want to lessen the impact of these statements by hiding them in a junglelike setting.

Other plants look best when grouped to create a lush effect. Not only is a grouping nice to look at, it is good for the plants, which enjoy the extra humidity created from proximity to one another. The possibilities for attractive arrangements of compatible plants are endless. They can be large groups of floor plants or small tabletop collections. The only rule is that grouped plants must be compatible in their environmental needs.

Groups can be composed of mixed shapes to get a sense of variety, or you can repeat a basic shape. Generally the greater the three-dimensional

▲ This foliage-filled corner makes a powerful visual statement, a triangle filled with plants: ti plant *(Cordyline)*, Chinese evergreen *(Aglaonema),* rubber plant *(Ficus elastica)* and lesser known narrow-leaf fig *(Ficus binnedijkii)*. This variety of color, texture, and size combines in a significant mass arrangement.

effect you can achieve, the better the grouping will look. Create depth by positioning a conspicuous specimen in front or to the side of the other plants. Vary heights with pedestals, shelves, crates, or platforms. Fabric-covered bricks provide an easy-to-make, attractive elevated platform for pots. Incorporate complementary plant stands to vary heights.

Plant groupings should have symmetry and balance. They can include small tufted plants in front and vines that wend their way though the other plants. Some plants have horizontal growth

▼ This tabletop grouping of ribbon plant, strawberry begonia, and friendship plant produces an attractive display that could work in almost any small area. The close relationship of shape and materials of the pots is useful in pulling the eye to the group even with contrasting leaf colors, textures, and shapes.

▲ A large 30-year-old ponytail palm adds drama to this landing and would be a standout virtually anywhere to create excitement and maximum impact. It has more visual power than a grouping of numerous small plants, even those well grown and attractively displayed.

THESE ARE SOME REPRESENTATIVE PLANTS WITH DISTINCT SHAPES:

COLUMNAR
African milk tree
Cacti, upright
Corn plant
Green dracaena
Heart-leaf philodendron
   (on a pole)
Snake plant
Yucca

Snake plant 'Laurentii'

UPRIGHT ARCHING
Christmas cactus
Dieffenbachia
Fishtail palm
Lemon
Ming aralia
Parlor palm
Schefflera
Silver vase plant
Zeezee plant

Parlor palm

ROSETTE
African violet
Bird's-nest fern
Bird's nest snake plant
Blushing bromeliad
Earth star
Echeveria
Haworthia
Sago palm
Tiger jaws

Blushing bromeliad

SPREADING
Asparagus fern
Cast-iron plant
Episcia
Prayer plant
Red flame ivy
Strawberry begonia
Stromanthe
Walking iris

Stromanthe

TRAILING
Burro's tail
English ivy
Grape ivy
Hoya
Philodendron
Plectranthus
Pothos
Rosary vine
Spider plant
Wandering Jew

English ivy

ROUNDED
Anthurium
Ball cactus
Begonia (many)
Chinese evergreen
Ferns (many)
Fiber optic grass
Golden barrel cactus
Osmanthus
Peace lily
Peperomia (many)

Iron cross begonia

CREEPING
Baby's tears
Creeping charlie pilea
Creeping fig
Fittonia

Creeping fig

WEEPING
Boston fern (on pedestal)
Ponytail palm
Weeping fig

Boston fern

patterns or may be trained that way, while others stand straight and tall. Harmonize plant colors with their neighbors and with the furnishings of the room. Include a tall, arching palm or weeping fig to serve as a canopy for the grouping. Some plants are innocuous enough to be used in almost

any grouping. Pothos, peace lily, and flamingo flower are good for tying a group together, and Japanese aucuba, bay, and Japanese euonymus make good foliage backdrops for groupings, especially when pruned tightly, similar to a hedge.

Some houseplants have strong architectural form

that lends itself to use as a specimen, where it becomes a piece of living sculpture. Other plants are more utilitarian and are best used to help organize a space as a screen or subtle room divider. A plant's form is its general outline. Many plant qualities contribute to form, including the density of growth, the

number of stems and branches, and the way the leaves are arranged. Keep in mind that a plant's shape often changes as it grows, but most plants fall into one of these classifications: columnar, trailing, upright arching, weeping, rosette, rounded, creeping, or spreading.

Plant function

◄ This plant grouping of Chinese fan palm, Madagascar dragontree, and China doll works as a living screen and gives the room two distinct seating areas. Plants are stair stepped nicely using their natural size combined with placement of one on a table to give it more height and substance. Use the same approach to screen part of a room from view.

Houseplants to the rescue! Most furniture is not designed to fit in corners, but many foliage plants bring a deserted corner to life. They perform best when tucked away from traffic. Massed foliage plants give an empty fireplace an elegant look in summer. Because light is often dim near the fireplace, use plants tolerant of low light or rotate plants to a brighter location after several weeks. Use low-growing plants such as pothos or English ivy to hide the bare bottoms of tall plants such as dieffenbachia, areca palm, Norfolk Island pine, and weeping fig.

▲ This schefflera fills a large empty corner in this living room. It provides a visual break between the sofa and the bookshelves.

FLOOR PLANTS

Alocasia
African milk tree
Areca palm
China doll
Chinese fan palm
Corn plant
False aralia
Fiddle-leaf fig
Fishtail palm
Madagascar dragontree
Norfolk Island pine
Podocarpus
Ponytail palm
Pygmy date palm
Sago palm
Schefflera
Screw pine
Snake plant
Split-leaf philodendron
Ti plant
Weeping fig

Functional plants

Houseplants can solve decorating problems. Strategically placed plants can camouflage architectural problems or separate a large room into inviting areas for different activities. Almost every room has two or three areas too small to accommodate a functional piece of furniture and yet too large to be ignored.

Floor plants

Plants that are too large for a grouping or tabletop but sit on the floor produce drama from size alone. Treelike plants such as weeping fig, Norfolk Island pine, and many palms need a spot of prominence. Large-leaf plants

such as alocasia and split-leaf philodendron quickly command a place of honor. Even a few leaves are dramatic. Some can be architectural plants because of distinctive lines. Lucky bamboo and snake plant have distinctive forms even while

► A large palm with architectural foliage and stature produces a striking visual presence and becomes a focal point in the room. Its mass, height, and texture give it the prominence to draw attention to it. The sleek container reflects the room's style and is important in its aesthetic presentation. The living mulch of ivy is beneficial to the plant and softens the lines of the container and room.

◀ The maroon and copper colors of red-leaf philodendron combine well with the metal watering can and cachepot. As the plant grows, it may require a pole for support and eventually will make a good floor plant.

▼ Small sedums or other low growing cacti or succulents make nice tabletop plants for a Southwestern decor. Combine with desert inspired containers or clay pots for an attractive small accent.

young and can be displayed on tabletops. Most, however, develop their interesting shapes and forms when they become large and mature. They usually require a lot of space and look best placed on the floor away from other plants and furniture. Most large palms become architectural plants when they reach full size. Ponytail palm with its large bulbous base and leaves that weep down, tall dracaenas, or columnar cactus become the focal point in a room. To further enhance the beauty of these plants, place a concealed spotlight where it will showcase the unique form at night.

Tabletop plants

Any plant that is low growing and interesting when viewed from above makes a good tabletop plant. Some, such as earth star, are best used as a single specimen. Others, such as nerve plant, striped inch plant, and oxalis, are fine as parts of groupings. These plants make a nice

▲ This communal container of peperomias adds color to an office desktop. Since these plants all need similar growing conditions, they will perform well and look good together when given proper care.

centerpiece because they stay below eye level and don't interfere with dinner guests' sight lines. Use colorful blooming plants alone or as part of a mixed planting. If you group several small plants in one container, cover the pots with sphagnum moss or Spanish moss or repot into the same style and color of pot for a unified and finished look. Consider using a decorative container or a low basket lined with plastic to show off the plants.

TABLETOP PLANTS

African violet
Baby's tears
Begonia
Brake fern
Button fern
Cactus (low-growing types)
Cigar plant
Earth star
Echeveria
English ivy
Episcia
Fittonia
Oxalis
Calathea
Peperomia
Pilea
Polka-dot plant
Prayer plant
Purple passion
Red flame ivy
Streptocarpus

Plant function *(continued)*

▲ This Boston fern is perched on top of a wonderful antique column adapted as a pedestal, allowing the fronds to drape naturally so they will not experience physical damage from contact with hard surfaces. This creative use of salvaged materials benefits the plant and coordinates with many period styles and rooms.

▲ This plant stand raises the grape ivy to a level for easy viewing without having to install any special hardware to hang it on the wall or from the ceiling. The narrow stand allows vines to drape naturally and allows easy access for grooming or rotating the plant for even light exposure and growth. It can easily be shifted to other locations when redecorating or rearranging furniture.

Bookshelf plants

Nothing softens a wall of bookshelves like a cascading houseplant hanging over the edges or the accent of a small flowering plant. Pothos and heart-leaf philodendron are trailing plants that are easy to control. African violets are useful for their flowers; some have variegated leaves that provide color even when the plant is not in bloom. Unfortunately most bookshelves have insufficient light to support houseplants. However it's fairly easy to supplement light by installing fluorescent tubes out of sight under shelving. Place lights 6 to 24 inches away from the upper surface of the plant. Drill an opening in the back of the bookcase

PLANTS FOR PEDESTALS

Asparagus fern
Boston fern
Christmas cactus
Fiber optic grass
Grape ivy
Guppy plant
Philodendron
Pothos
Piggyback plant
Red flame ivy
Spider plant

Pedestal plants

Pedestals are an excellent way to raise plants off the floor without having to drill holes in the wall or ceiling for hanging hardware. Many of the plants that work well in hanging containers are good choices for display on pedestals. A spider plant with all its babies hanging down or a guppy plant with shiny leaves and bright orange flowers looks terrific on a pedestal and takes on a different appearance when viewed from above. Small floor plants take on an entirely different look when they are grown at a level where they can be seen better. Keep pedestal plants out of high-traffic areas and avoid plants with sharp spines that could harm passersby.

◀ Variegated English ivy and heart-leaf philodendron soften the appearance of these bookshelves. Both are easy-to-control vining plants. Calathea completes the triangle.

▼ White shelves reflect light and boost growth of plants some distance from windows. Supplemental lighting can also be added.

BOOKSHELF PLANTS

African violet
Arrowhead vine
Begonia
Creeping fig
Grape ivy
English ivy
Episcia
Peperomia
Philodendron
Pilea
Pothos
Strawberry begonia
Streptocarpus
Striped inch plant
Wandering Jew

to run the electrical cord through. Experiment with how long to keep the lights on, starting with 6 to 8 hours a day up to 14 to 16 hours daily. Add a timer to automatically turn lights on and off.

Vining plants

Vining plants may be used as upright accents or as hanging plants. Some grow more vigorously and require

▲ A heart-leaf philodendron trained on a moss pole creates an upright architectural statement for the room and echoes the vertical lines of the draperies and statuary.

support unless you pinch and prune them often. A well-grown vining plant brings a strong architectural component to a room. Use vines around window or mirror frames or train them

to wrap around pillars or grow up trellises to become a soft room divider. Hoya and jasmine look lovely when their long vines are trained to wrap around wire hoops and formed into living wreaths.

▲ English ivy winding its way through a metal topiary support lends an informal air to this setting.

VINING PLANTS

Bougainvillea
Clerodendrum
Creeping fig
English ivy
Grape ivy
Hoya
Jasmine
Mandevilla
Passionflower
Philodendron
Pothos
Stephanotis
Wax vine

Plant function *(continued)*

◄ This metal plant stand can slide into tight locations, support the plant, and display it a bit above eye level. The 'Brasil' philodendron is able to grow better because it is exposed to more light and the stems do not have to lie on a table or shelf.

HANGING PLANTS

Baby's tears
Boston fern
Burro's tail
Chenille plant
Columnea
English ivy
Episcia
Grape ivy
Fiber optic grass
Guppy plant
Jasmine
Lipstick plant
Monkey plant
Philodendron
Piggyback plant
Plectranthus
Pothos
Rabbit's foot fern
Rattail cactus
Red flame ivy
Rosary vine
Spider plant
Staghorn fern
Strawberry begonia
String of beads
Swedish ivy
Tahitian bridal veil
Teddy bear vine
Wandering Jew

Hanging plants

You may think of hanging plants as an outdoor feature, but some houseplants look best when viewed at eye level or slightly higher, where you can enjoy their trailing stems or dangling flowers. Plants with trailing growth habits also grow better if their stems are not lying on the tabletop or the floor. You can achieve a wide variety of different looks by using plants with diverse textures. A fern can be lacy, draping softly over the side of a container. Burro's tail has plump, overlapping leaves

► Arrowhead vine looks good in a hanging basket. It is durable and easy to grow if given moderate light and humidity. While it is young it may remain rather small and compact; as it ages it will begin to vine more aggressively, filling a large basket with foliage. Remember to turn it regularly to keep color and shape even.

that produce a living sculptural presentation. Another look is the heart-leaf philodendron with its glossy green leaves. Select the textural appearance you desire for the spot with the correct growing conditions for the plant. Hanging plants can save space while allowing you to enjoy them at eye level. (They also remain out of reach of cats and other pets that have a penchant for nibbling or "attacking" plants as prey.) Keep in mind that the hanging mechanism needs to be strong enough to support the weight of the plant, pot, and wet soil. You don't want your plant to come crashing down.

Locate hanging plants where they will not interfere with foot traffic and where people will not bump their heads on the suspended plant. Good locations include corners, in stairways, or over

HERE'S A TIP...

Warning: Plant hangers installed directly in wallboard and gypsum ceiling panels hold much less weight than ones installed in wood. In addition the panels weaken when wet or humid. Never use a decorative screw hook installed into a gypsum ceiling panel alone because only a few threads connect with a rather soft material. A toggle bolt assembly installed through the panels is better. Follow the manufacturer's instructions but take into account potential weakening from moisture. With this type of hanger do not attempt to hang plants weighing more than 5 pounds after they are watered. (The weight difference between dried out pots and ones that have just been watered is significant.)

large permanently placed pieces of furniture.

It is usually easier to take down a hanging plant and carry it to the sink to water it, rather than guessing how much water it needs, spilling water onto the floor or furniture when you misjudge.

LOCATING WALL STUDS AND CEILING JOISTS

Use a stud finder, a specialized tool that lights up when it rolls over the stud or joist, to locate a firm backing. With a pencil lightly mark the edges of the stud. Typically studs and joists are 1½ inches wide and spaced 16 inches on center. Drill pilot holes into the center of the desired stud or joist, then screw the plant hook or wall bracket screws into the pilot holes. In homes with wallboard look for a linear nail head pattern that shows lightly through paint or wallpaper. This pattern will give you the approximate center line of the stud. Before drilling pilot holes you can test whether you have located the stud or joist by driving in a finishing nail. If you nail into wood rather than just drywall, you'll know that you have correctly located the stud or joist.

1 Locate and mark joist or stud.

2 Drill appropriate size pilot hole.

3 Screw plant hook in place.

4 Hang plant from hook.

This decorative toggle ceiling hook is designed for use where a stud or joist is unavailable. It has a 5-pound limit.

1 Locate stud and drill pilot holes for screws.

2 Install screws through bracket.

3 Hang plant of appropriate weight and dimensions.

The same is true for staghorn fern, which is often mounted on a hanging slab that needs to be soaked periodically. Keep in mind that room temperatures near the ceiling are warmer than at floor level. Plants will dry out faster there. Water accordingly.

Ceiling hooks

Use a drill bit that is slightly smaller than the solid shaft of the ceiling or screw hook to drill a pilot hole in the ceiling joist. Start the screw hook by hand and finish turning the hook until all threads are into wood. Use a screwdriver blade, pliers, or other tool to do the turning. For decorative hooks turn the hook by hand or cover the decorative hook with scrap cloth to avoid tool marks from the installation process. If no joist is in the correct place and you have access to the attic directly above the desired location, install a piece of 2×4 between ceiling joists in the attic. Use the pilot hole to guide placement of the new support. If you have no access, you may want to consult a carpenter about installing a decorative wood plate on a portion of the ceiling, then attach the plant hanger to the decorative plate.

Wall brackets

Follow manufacturer's suggestions to stay within suggested weight limitations for wall brackets. Some heavyweight wall brackets are available, but most support only a small plant and container. Wall brackets mount to a wall stud with screws. Locate the stud and place the bracket in the center of the stud at the desired height. Use a level to ensure that it is perpendicular to the floor, then lightly mark the screw holes. Drill pilot holes, align the bracket over the holes, and install screws.

Plants to fit your lifestyle

Consider the level of care you want to provide your plants and the presence of children and pets when selecting houseplants. Are you a plant lover who loves to dote on houseplants, spending time nearly every day looking them over and checking for water and grooming needs? Or are you someone who just wants something green in the corner? Most people fall somewhere in between. Luckily most plants fall somewhere in between too. No houseplant is completely carefree, but some get by on less attention than others. If you have an active lifestyle where you must be away from home frequently for more than a few days, choose plants that tolerate some neglect. These plants are also good choices for offices, where people are sometimes absent for several days at a time and plant maintenance chores are low priority. A large plant in a large pot is a better choice for infrequent care than small plants in small pots that dry more rapidly. Avoid growing poisonous plants until children (or grandchildren who visit frequently) are older and can understand that houseplants are not for tasting. Avoid spiny plants such as cactus, which can easily harm a curious toddler, cats, or hyperactive dogs.

EASY-TO-GROW, DURABLE PLANTS

Aloe	Dracaenas	Hoya	Philodendron	Snake plant
Arrowhead vine	Dieffenbachia	Lady palm	Pothos	Spider plant
Asparagus fern	English ivy	Parlor palm	Ponytail palm	Succulents
Cactus	Ficus	Peace lily	Rubber tree	Swedish ivy
Cast-iron plant	Flamingo flower	Peperomia	Schefflera	Wandering Jew
Chinese evergreen				

Snake plant

Chinese evergreen

Peace lily

Arrowhead vine

Green dracaena

Pothos

Golden barrel cactus

Rubber tree

Dieffenbachia

POISONOUS PLANTS

Amaryllis
Chenille plant
Chinese evergreen
Clivia
Crown-of-thorns
Croton

Dieffenbachia
English ivy
Ficus
Fishtail palm
Flamingo flower
Oleander

Peace lily
Philodendron
Pothos
Pregnant onion
Schefflera
Split-leaf philodendron

PLANTS WITH SPINES OR THORNS:

Blushing bromeliad
Bougainvillea
Cactus
Citrus (some)
Crown-of-thorns
Dyckia
Earth star
Madagascar palm
Pygmy date palm
Sago palm

Heart-leaf philodendron

Croton

Cactus

Clivia

Dieffenbachia

Crown-of-thorns

Oleander

English ivy

Pygmy date palm

Houseplant care

In this chapter you'll learn the best ways to give your plants what they need to survive and thrive in your indoor environment. You'll learn what to do with your new houseplants after you get them home, including choosing an appropriate growing medium and container. This chapter also provides details on proper watering and feeding.

Most houseplants benefit from some grooming from time to time to keep them looking their best. You'll find information on pinching, pruning, and staking. Eventually your houseplants will require repotting to stay vigorous and looking their best. Basic repotting information is also found in this chapter.

At some point you may want to try your hand at propagating new plants from your old ones—either as a way to increase your collection, to share with friends, or as a way to replace older plants that look worn out. This chapter gives basic information on various propagation methods, including when and how to do them successfully.

You'll also learn about what can go wrong with your houseplants. Pests are a part of every indoor gardener's life, but there's no need to let them deter you from growing

▲ Healthy and attractive plants are the result of understanding and supplying the basics for plant growth coupled with good care and grooming. Plants grow well and look good when all the plant's parts are healthy. They have strong roots to anchor the plant and absorb water and nutrients and sturdy stems to transport the food, water, and minerals produced through photosynthesis in the leaves. Prolific flowering is another sign of good health.

▶ Keeping leaves clean helps plants look good and to grow better. Dust buildup not only is unattractive but clogs leaf pores and slows plant growth. Dust on the leaf surface encourages insect infestations and filters light. Use a soft moist cloth to gently wipe dust from shiny-leaf plants or give plants a shower occasionally to wash dust away. Check for pests as you do regular grooming.

and enjoying houseplants. The secret to pest control is to prevent problems by providing the appropriate conditions for good growth—proper light, watering, humidity, and feeding. And by observing your plants regularly, you'll be able to identify problems early while they are still easy to control.

How do plants grow?

Although the to-do list of watering, lighting, feeding, grooming, and propagating may be bewildering at first, these tasks become easy and natural once you understand the basic processes of plant growth. In fact these tasks end up being part of the fun of growing plants rather than being considered work.

Understanding the basic parts of a plant, what each does, and the growth process will make you a better grower.

Plant parts: Roots, stems, leaves, and flowers are the four basic parts of plants. All but flowers are crucial to plant growth and health.

● **Roots** anchor the plant and absorb the water and minerals that nourish it. Most absorption occurs through the root tips and the tiny hairs on young roots. Roots send water and nutrients to the stem, which carries the nourishment to other parts of the plant. The thickened roots of some plants also store food.

● **The stem** transports water, minerals, and food produced through photosynthesis in other parts of the plant to the leaves, buds, and flowers. It also physically supports the plant. In some cases stems store food during a plant's dormant period; in others the stems manufacture food. In some plants stems grow as runners that creep aboveground (stolons) or belowground (rhizomes and tubers).

● **Leaves** The vast majority of plants have clearly defined leaves. Each leaf manufactures food for the plant through photosynthesis, absorbing light over its surface. Its pores absorb and diffuse gases and water vapor during photosynthesis, respiration, and transpiration.

● **The flower** is the sexual reproductive organ of the plant. Most plants flower in their natural environments, but relatively few plants bloom indoors.

Photosynthesis: Like all other living things, plants need food for energy. The basic foods for all living things are sugar and other carbohydrates. Unlike animals, however, plants are able to harness the energy of the sun to manufacture their own sugar.

In photosynthesis light energy, carbon dioxide, and water interact with the green plant pigment chlorophyll to produce plant sugars and oxygen, which is released into the atmosphere. Houseplants get light from the sun, filtered through windows, or from artificial lights. Carbon dioxide is drawn in from the air by the leaves, and the roots supply the water. Photosynthesis supplies most of the oxygen on the planet.

Photosynthesis requires an environment that provides adequate light, warmth, and humidity for plants. No amount of supplemental fertilizer can compensate for an unfavorable growing environment.

Respiration: Sugars created by photosynthesis combine with oxygen to release energy used for plant growth and survival. Respiration produces carbon dioxide, water, and a small amount of heat, which are released into the air.

Transpiration: Sunlight falling on a leaf can heat it well above the temperature of the surrounding air. Through transpiration water vapor leaves the plant from leaf pores (stomata), cooling the leaf. The higher the temperature and the lower the humidity, the faster a plant transpires. If it loses more water than it can absorb through its roots, it wilts, which is why proper watering is so essential to the survival of a houseplant.

▲ Water plants when they need it. Learn your plant's moisture needs and treat it accordingly. Some plants need to go quite dry between waterings, while others need to stay evenly moist. Most should dry slightly between waterings. The soil mix, type of pot, amount of light, and seasonal variations in temperature impact how often you will need to water.

◀ Almost all plants will eventually require renewal, division, significant grooming, pruning, or propagation to look their best and to be maintained within the bounds of their location. Pruning or pinching removes branches or parts of the plant to improve the shape and provides material to produce new plants.

Light

▲ These ball cacti require the most intense light you can give them in order to thrive and look their best. They need full sun much of the day to mimic their habitat in the wild. Place them in a sunny south or west window.

▲ African violet grows well near a window with light filtered through gauze curtains. The flat rosette of leaves and mound of flowers indicates that it is thriving. Direct sun could burn the leaves and lower light would produce few flowers.

Before choosing a houseplant closely evaluate the light, humidity, and temperature levels of the area where the new plant will grow. For best results find houseplants that match your room's growing conditions rather than trying to drastically change the conditions. And keep in mind that light, humidity, and temperature conditions change throughout the year.

Light intensity

The amount of available light is one of the most important factors to consider in the care of houseplants. Without adequate light plants photosynthesize poorly. Their food supplies dwindle and they gradually decline. Improper lighting is one of the most frequently encountered plant problems.

Before choosing an indoor plant evaluate the light level in the location the plant will be placed. Select a plant whose light requirements match what the setting has to offer. Available light is determined both by intensity and by duration. Indoor light levels vary widely. Your home might have intense light, usually a southern exposure that receives sun much of the day. This would also describe a greenhouse or many sunrooms. It could be bright, with direct sunlight hitting the plant for a few hours each day and indirect sunlight during the hottest parts of the day. Bright light also describes the light generated by a four-tube fluorescent fixture located close to plants. Medium light levels are found several feet inside a room with a sunny window or from a two-tube fluorescent fixture with full-spectrum bulbs. Low light describes an interior location away from windows.

South-facing windows receive the most intense light. Heat buildup from direct sun can burn foliage of plants

that don't require high light. Most east- and west-facing windows receive medium light, or about two-thirds of the light available through south-facing windows. Low-light north-facing windows receive about one-fifth the light that south windows do.

You can use your hand to measure home light intensity reasonably well. Pass it over the plant and in front of the light source. If you see a sharp, clear shadow the light is high in intensity. A softer, more diffused shadow means medium light, while a faint or no shadow demonstrates low light.

Factors other than window direction also influence the amount of available light for growing houseplants. Trees and shrubs, nearby buildings, awnings, curtains, and dirt on the window all affect the amount of light available. Also light-colored walls reflect light onto plants, while dark walls absorb light.

Light levels vary with the season. You may need to move some plants away from the strong sunlight that pours in through south-facing windows in summer. However in fall and winter this south window may be ideal. In some cases more sun streams through windows in winter, when the sun is closer to the horizon, than when it is high overhead in summer. These undiffused winter rays can be strong enough to burn foliage.

Duration

Day length also affects available light. Obviously plants receive more light during the longer days of spring, summer, and fall than they do in winter. With light fixtures you can control the duration of light with a timer. Some flowering plants rely on day length for flower bud development. Poinsettia, kalanchoe, and Christmas cactus flower only when day length is less than 12 hours (or more accurately, when the length of the dark night period is longer than 12 hours.)

Phototropism

Houseplants need an even light source. Phototropism is the plant's tendency to grow toward light. If plants are not rotated regularly, they become disfigured. The stems and leaves on the side exposed to more light bend toward the light, leaving the shaded side of the plant sparse. For flowering plants more buds will form to produce more flowers with fewer on the shady side. Turn plants a quarter turn each week or with each watering to maintain fullness on all sides.

PLANTS FOR BRIGHT LIGHT

These plants need 4 or more hours of direct sunlight a day to grow well. Many tolerate lower light levels for short periods.

Bromeliads
Cactus
Cape lily
Chenille plant
Chinese hibiscus
Citrus
Coleus

Croton
Crown-of-thorns
Flowering maple
Heliconia
Ixora
Japanese euonymus
Jasmine

Lollipop plant
Madagascar jasmine
Monkey plant
Orchids
Polka-dot plant
Purple passion
Screw pine

Shrimp plant
Succulents
Sweet bay
Ti plant

Chenille plant

Croton

Calamondin orange (citrus)

Golden barrel cactus

Tiger jaws (succulent)

Flowering maple

Polka-dot plant

Phalaenopsis orchid
'Hakalau Queen'

Light requirements

Plants in this book are described as needing low, medium, bright, or intense light, although some plants thrive in a range of light levels. Plants may tolerate slightly more or less light than is optimal; however too much direct sun causes damage by scorching foliage, and too little light causes plants to become spindly.

● **Low light:** Light shade, a position well back from the nearest window. It provides enough light to read by

HERE'S A TIP...
A decorator's secret
Does your decor call for a houseplant in a spot that is just too dark for even low-light plants to thrive? Don't let that ruin your design ideas! Purchase two identical low-light-tolerant plants, and keep switching them back and forth. Place one in the desired spot for two weeks while the other basks in bright light and high humidity elsewhere in the house, then switch them around. Most foliage plants will thrive for years if they get enough light for just two weeks out of each month.

without too much strain but little or no direct sunlight.
● **Medium light:** A level at which both some foliage and some flowering plants thrive. Medium light is found in a northeast or west window that receives a few hours of early morning or late afternoon sun.
● **Bright light:** Direct sunlight for several hours in early morning or late afternoon, but not the full strength of midday sun. Usually this light is found directly in front of an east or west window or a few feet back from a south window. It is ideal for many flowering plants, herbs, cacti, and succulents, but is too bright for most foliage plants.
● **Intense light:** Four or more hours of direct sunlight daily. An unshaded window facing due south during the summer months receives intense light. A greenhouse, conservatory or sunroom may also provide intense light for plants growing in them.

A few guidelines about light

A sheer curtain lessens the light intensity and heat in a south or west window, making the conditions appropriate for a medium- or bright-light plant.

INCREASING LIGHT

Most indoor settings are darker than they seem to the human eye. In many homes it's difficult to read a newspaper even at midday without extra light. Bright light is often attainable only directly in front of windows. Here are some strategies for increasing the light plants receive:
● **Keep the windows clean.** Dust and grime reduce light considerably.
● **Remove window screens when they're not needed.** Screens cut light by up to 30 percent.
● **Paint walls flat white or pastel shades** and use pale furniture and floor coverings to reflect light. Dark colors absorb light.
● **Hang mirrors strategically to reflect light.**
● **Add artificial lighting.**
● **Keep the foliage clean.** Dust blocks light from reaching chlorophyll in leaves.
● **Replace small windows with larger ones** or add a greenhouse window, bay window, or solarium.

Flowering plants usually need bright to intense light in order to bloom, but some fare well in medium light.

A south window provides direct light farther into the room in winter than in summer, but heat buildup is greater in summer. The intensity of direct light varies according to the season. When the sun is higher in the sky (in the summer in the Northern Hemisphere), the light is hotter and more intense but reaches less distance into the room. In winter the sun is lower in the sky, providing direct light

farther into the room but with less intensity.

Low-light plants usually do well in east, northeast, or north windows, where they get mostly indirect light. A west window is usually hotter than a south window because of the concentrated quality of the sunlight in the late afternoon.

An east window strikes a nice compromise between heat and intensity. It receives full sun in the morning hours when the temperature is still cool. Most flowering plants thrive under such conditions.

▼ Indoor light intensity for plant growth depends on the distance from the window and the direction of exposure.

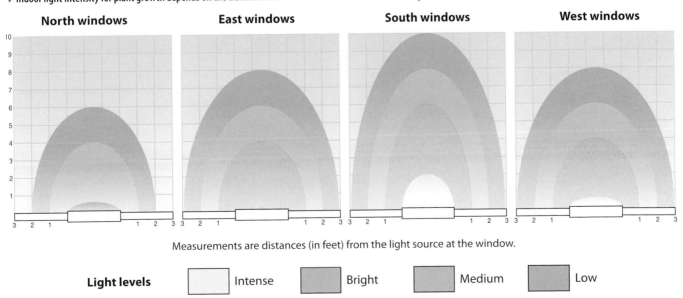

Measurements are distances (in feet) from the light source at the window.

North windows   East windows   South windows   West windows

Light levels   Intense   Bright   Medium   Low

Light *(continued)*

Signs of light stress

It is important to recognize the signs of light stress. Low light levels can lead to a decline in health because insufficient food is produced to replace older leaves as they die, leaving pale, stunted plants. On the other hand plants exposed to too much light may become scorched, bleached, and limp. Houseplants with variegated leaves generally need more light than plants with plain green leaves because they have less chlorophyll, the green pigment that produces energy for the plant through photosynthesis.

PLANTS FOR MEDIUM LIGHT

These plants require good light but not direct sun. An unobstructed east window provides ideal conditions for them.

Alocasia
African violet
Begonia
Boston fern
Button fern
China doll

Dracaena
English ivy
Ficus
Fittonia
Grape ivy
Japanese aucuba

Japanese fatsia
Japanese holly fern
Maidenhair fern
Norfolk Island pine
Peperomia
Piggyback plant

Ponytail palm
Pygmy date palm
Red flame ivy
Schefflera
Spider plant
Swedish ivy

Weeping fig 'Too Little'

English ivy 'Royal Hustler'

African violet

Iron cross begonia

Boston fern

Schefflera

Dracaena 'Lemon Lime'

Fittonia 'Red Anne'

PLANTS FOR LOW LIGHT

Remember that most plants only tolerate low light. They grow best in medium or bright light levels. Flowering gift plants can be maintained for a while in low light.

Bamboo palm	Dieffenbachia	Lady palm	Philodendron	Zeezee plant
Cast-iron plant	Dracaena	Parlor palm	Pothos	
Chinese evergreen	Heart-leaf homalomena	Peace lily	Snake plant	

Heart-leaf philodendron

Peace lily

Cast-iron plant

Snake plant

Chinese evergreen

Parlor palm

Light *(continued)*

Supplementing light

You can use supplemental lighting to improve growth of plants that need a little more light than is available naturally. Artificial lighting can be beneficial in winter when day length and light intensity decrease. Also use it to manipulate day length for plants requiring short or long days to flower. Good supplemental sources provide more light than heat. Plants respond best to the full spectrum of sunlight. There are several ways to get it.

● **Incandescent:** Bulbs commonly found in lamps and ceiling fixtures are not appropriate as the sole source of light for houseplants. Not only are they hot, but they also emit only the red and far-red part of the spectrum, which is too narrow for plants to thrive. Although inefficient they can be used to supplement natural light if placed far enough away from the plants to avoid overheating the leaves.

● **Halogen:** Popular in contemporary interior design, these lights produce a nearly perfect spectrum. However their narrow beams and their extreme heat make them inappropriate for houseplants.

● **Fluorescent:** These lights remain cool to the touch, allowing plants to grow much closer to the tubes without damage. They also cost less and use less electricity than other lights. Cool white tubes have an enhanced blue range and warm white tubes have an enhanced red range. A combination of the two provides a wide, although not full, spectrum that's usually sufficient for most plants. Costlier full-spectrum grow lights are best for plants that require full sun. To be effective, fluorescent lights must be close to the plants, generally from 6 to 12 inches from the tubes. Bright-light plants should be close to the tubes with lower light-requiring plants farther away. Inverted pots can be used to adjust the height of the plants. Rotate plants regularly because the ends of the bulbs provide less intense light than the centers. Or put low-light plants toward the ends and bright-light plants in the middle.

● **High-intensity:** By far the most efficient supplemental lighting, high-intensity lamps work best in large areas. They are more expensive than fluorescent lights but are worth it if you need a great deal of supplemental lighting. If you are serious about providing good-quality light for your houseplants, look into high-intensity metal halide or high-pressure sodium lights.

Metal halide lamps offer the best spectrum for the largest number of plants and are

SIGNS A PLANT MAY NEED MORE LIGHT:

● **Weak, elongated stems and spindly, lanky growth.**
● **Plants have smaller new leaves.**
● **Variegated plants may revert to solid green or become less variegated.**
● **Numerous leaves drop.** (It is normal for older leaves to die.)

● **Pale new leaves.** (Can also be caused by lack of water or nutrients, spider mites, or too much light, which can also fade or bleach out leaves.)
● **Brown leaf tips and margins.** (Usually in combination with overheating, improper watering, or lack of adequate humidity.)

● **Flowering plants fail to produce buds or have reduced or no flowers.** (If the flowering plant is healthy otherwise.)
● **All growth faces or stretches to the nearest available light source.**
● **Little or no growth.** (Some plants go into semi-dormancy in winter.)

This African violet lacks flowers because it is growing in light levels that are too low.

A dark corner led to stretched growth and leaf loss on this plectranthus.

Under low light conditions variegated plants such as this croton may revert to nearly solid green.

▲ Incandescent light used for supplemental lighting must be kept far enough away to avoid overheating leaves. Here incandescent light is used to highlight the blooms of campanula and cyclamen. Ferns that tolerate low light add fine texture.

▲ Consider high-intensity metal halide or high-pressure sodium lamps for flowering plants or intensely colored foliage plants that need bright light.

intense enough to work in areas with limited or no natural light.

High-pressure sodium lamps are good for flowering plants that need extremely bright light.

Low-pressure sodium lamps and mercury discharge lamps are generally used for commercial purposes only.

All types of lights lose effectiveness over time, so replace bulbs regularly, especially fluorescent tubes. Use a permanent marking pen and write the date of installation of a new tube. You will learn the pattern of decline with the tubes you are using and know when to replace them. Fixtures should have white reflectors to make best use of light.

Controlling day length

When almost enough natural light is available, turning on supplemental lighting a few hours each day to extend the day length during the winter months is usually sufficient to ensure healthy growth. Plants grown under lights alone, however, need 8 to 16 hours of lighting every day. Studies show that most plants grow best with 12 to 16 hours of light per day. Put short-day plants such as poinsettia under 10- to 12-hour days for a few months in fall, though, or they won't bloom.

Using a timer ensures plants get the right duration of light. Watch your plants for a few weeks and adjust the timer cycle as needed. Also adjust it as the sun's intensity and duration change over the year. Many indoor gardeners give their plants 14- to 16-hour days during much of the year, then cut back to 12 hours in winter. There is no need to reduce the hours of supplemental lighting in winter. Most plants grow better with longer light duration year round.

▲ Inexpensive fluorescent lights are a good choice to supplement lighting for most plants. They remain cool so plants can be placed close to the tubes for maximum growth and flowering.

Watering

Determining water needs

Overwatering is considered the primary houseplant killer. Excessive water means too little oxygen in the soil. The roots are unable to take in any more water, the top portion of the plant is stressed, root rot results, and the plant dies. It's better to err on the dry side than to water your plants too much.

All plants have slightly different watering requirements depending on how they are grown and changes in plant growth through the seasons. Therefore water on an as-needed basis rather than by the calendar. Learn your plants' water needs. In general plants grown in well-drained soil in an appropriate-size container should be watered when the top ½ to 1 inch of soil feels

◄ This collection of cactus gardens, jade plants, and yucca is well suited for a dry microclimate with bright light. They are located on a plant shelf that is difficult to reach for frequent watering. It is often better to grow what suits your house or a particular location rather than making changes in the environment to suit the plants. Most homes have at least one spot that has bright light and is dry. Select appealing succulents or cacti to grow there.

dry. Measure this by pushing your index finger down into the soil.

You should water thoroughly every time you water even if your schedule is somewhat irregular. Do not water in small frequent amounts. In general flowering plants need more water than foliage plants.

Seasonal variations

A plant's water requirements vary as the seasons change. Watering according to a set schedule—for example once a week—doesn't take into account these variations. Instead check your houseplants frequently and keep in mind all the factors that affect their watering needs.

Plants absorb more water when humidity is low. If your skin is dry, your plants are

probably dry too. However plants grow more slowly in the cooler, shorter days of winter, a sign that they're using less water. So if you compensate for dry air by watering on a schedule suited to the warm days of summer, you'll end up overwatering.

High humidity slows transpiration, which reduces moisture uptake by roots. Unless the plant is in a breezy area where wind moves moisture away from the leaves, you'll need to water less often.

Light affects water uptake

too. Overcast skies in spring and fall slow plant growth and reduce water requirements. Plants exposed to bright light use more water than those in low light, depending on humidity.

As plants grow and their root ball enlarges they will dry more rapidly. Once repotted they will require less frequent watering.

Each variation in soil mix produces variation in watering needs. The lightest mixes will need watering far more often than a heavier organic mix.

REDUCING WATERING NEEDS

If watering every four or five days is too frequent for your schedule, there are a few ways you can keep plants moist a bit longer.

Larger pots: Repot plants that dry out too quickly into larger pots. Rapid drying and a constant need for water might indicate a need to repot anyway. Soil acts as a water reservoir, so a larger pot holds more water than a smaller pot.

Double pots: Another easy method of reducing watering needs for plants in clay pots is to double pot. Place the clay pot inside a larger cachepot, adding peat moss, sphagnum moss, Spanish moss, or perlite to fill the void around the inner pot. When you water, moisten the filler material as well as the soil. Water will slowly filter through the porous clay walls into the potting mix.

Self-watering pots: These may cut your watering chores to once every few weeks.

▶ Use your fingers to determine the soil's moisture level to decide if the plant needs to be watered. By touching the surface, or pushing a bit deeper, you can learn more than by just looking at the plant. Moist soil will feel cool and damp; potting mix that requires watering will feel warmer and drier to the touch.

◀ Moisture meters are helpful in determining water needs for a plant in a large pot. A touch to the soil surface of small pots provides a good measure of the plant's water needs. But for larger and deeper pots, the meter's long metal probe can give you a more accurate idea of how much moisture is in the lower levels of the pot.

Plants in clay pots dry out more rapidly than those in plastic. Those mounted on slabs dry even faster.

When to water

You will eventually get to a point where you know your plants well enough to lift a pot and judge from its weight whether to water. You will learn which plants dry out most quickly because of the reasons above. Over time adjusting your watering to accommodate your plants will become second nature. The secret lies in learning to recognize the individual signals each plant gives. You will eventually be able to see subtle differences in appearance of the plant that suggests it needs water.

Look at your plant. A well-watered plant looks healthy. Its tissues are firm because all the cells are filled with water, and its leaves are glossy. Many plants show signs of decline before wilting entirely: Their leaves have lost their sheen and are slightly limp and pale. Such flagging is a sure sign that a plant needs water. If you catch a plant at this point, before it actually wilts, you can prevent permanent damage. Once a plant has completely wilted, it seldom fully recovers. It may perk up after being watered, but it will suffer from brown edges and poor growth.

Underwatering and overwatering surprisingly can cause the same symptoms. Consistently overwatering plants saturates the soil, which causes the plant's tiny root hairs to rot and die. A plant without root hairs can't absorb water, so it wilts even though the soil is saturated. More water will not reverse the wilting or save the plant.

Moisture meters

Small pots less than 8 inches in diameter are easy enough to water: When the soil at the top is dry, the rest of the root ball is probably fairly dry as well. In big pots, especially 12-inch standard pots and larger, the same may not hold true. The mix may be dry on the top, yet still wet at the bottom. That bottom layer needs to dry out before you water again, or stagnation, a precursor to rot, can set in. For such pots it's wise to use an inexpensive water meter, a gadget made up of a long metal probe with an easy-to-read gauge on top. Insert the meter deep into the root mass and water when it reads "dry." Replace the meter once

▶ The curled and dry leaves indicate this plant has dried out. The lower leaves are already falling off. Avoid letting your plant get this dry by checking the soil on a regular basis. Water this plant immediately, soaking the entire root ball if it has pulled away from the pot.

a year, because meters tend to give false readings after a while.

Another type of water meter "sings" when plants need water. Usually shaped like a bird (although you can also find cow meters that moo, frog meters that croak, and green thumbs that sing "How Dry I Am"), it's designed to be inserted permanently into the soil of a plant, rather than being moved from plant to plant as with traditional meters. When the soil dries out too much, its vocal warning reminds you that it's time to water. Most models also have a photoelectric eye so they won't sound off in the middle of the night. Although these meters may seem like a gimmick, many gardeners find them helpful. Use one per room in the plant that always seems to dry out first. When the meter sings it's time to water that plant and check the others as well.

Home microclimates

You'll soon learn which microclimates in your home cause plants to dry out quicker, and which ones permit plants to go longer between waterings.

- **Windows:** A south window can become too hot and cause plants to dry out quickly. A north-facing room may stay quite cool in winter, decreasing the need for watering of plants located there.
- **Vents:** The areas around heat registers and air-conditioning vents often are too dry or drafty for many houseplants. Plants native to arid climates tolerate these conditions, but many tropical plants cannot.
- **Fireplaces:** The space above a fireplace is hotter and drier than it looks. An English ivy gracing the mantel may turn crisp and brown with the first fire of the season.
- **Bathrooms and kitchens:** Rooms with running water naturally are more humid than the rest of the house. You can take advantage of these locations with plants that need the almost constant humidity of the rain forest, such as ferns.
- **Plant shelves and hanging baskets:** Plants in places close to the ceiling will dry out faster than those at lower levels because temperatures are warmer close to the ceiling.

Watering *(continued)*

▲ Top watering is a standard technique to give plants needed moisture. Apply tepid water slowly until it runs freely out the drainage holes. This action also leaches out excess salts. Never allow plants to sit in water in a saucer or cachepot for more than 30 minutes. Excess moisture can lead to root rot.

▲ Soaking a plant's root ball for 30 minutes by submersion watering is a useful way to hydrate soil that has completely dried out. Fill a sink or tub with enough water to wet the entire root ball and plunge the plant in, pot and all. You may need to hold the pot under water until it soaks up some moisture.

The best way to water

For most plants the best and easiest way to water is to pour water on the soil surface. Apply water until it runs freely out the drainage holes, an action that also leaches excess salts from the soil. The goal is to thoroughly moisten the growing mix. If the soil is so dry that it has pulled away from the sides of the pot and water runs down the sides without wetting the soil, immerse the entire pot in a bucket of tepid water. Let the root ball soak for about 30 minutes, then drain. This technique, called submersion watering, is also useful for plants that need a great deal of water, such as blooming plants or florist's hydrangea and other gift plants that dry out quickly.

A few plants, such as African violet and episcia, benefit from bottom watering because water droplets mark their leaves. Place the pot in a saucer of tepid water and allow capillary action to draw water into the soil. This method takes longer than top watering, but it keeps water off leaves.

Whichever watering method you choose, prevent the plant from sitting in water a long time. After about 30 minutes empty the saucer.

◀ Capillary matting is a good material to use to bottom water plants. This non-woven material wicks water up to the soil mix through the bottom of the pot. The matting works well in large trays with or without a water reservoir and raises the humidity around all the plants. This tray has a water reservoir under the capillary matting, permitting less frequent watering.

If the plant is too heavy to lift, remove the excess water with an old turkey baster or towel. On the other hand, semiaquatic plants, such as dwarf papyrus *(Cyperus)* and fiber optic grass *(Isolepis),* prefer to have their pots sitting in water at all times. Place them in a cachepot that's 2 inches wider than their pot and keep adding water as the level drops. You can even submerge the entire root ball under an inch or so of water if you prefer. These plants also put up with regular watering, but only if they're kept quite moist and thoroughly watered before their root ball dries out.

Wick watering systems and self-watering pots and capillary mats are other methods to bottom water houseplants. All three forms of watering operate on the principle of capillary action. In the same way that water moves upward to moisten an entire towel when just one corner dips into the sink, water moves from a reservoir into the potting mix above. All that's needed is an absorbent link—a physical connection of some sort—between the water and the growing medium.

These methods work well for plants that need to stay evenly moist. You can purchase wicking material from specialty dealers including growers who sell African violets. Or make your own using yarn or pieces of nylon stockings. The material should be absorbent but resist rot. Most natural fibers rot quickly. Thread the wick through a drainage hole so that it extends about halfway into a pot with about the same length hanging out the bottom. Add potting soil and the plant. Water well and set aside to drain. Insert the other end of the wick into a large saucer or container filled with gravel mounded in the middle. This container will hold water and keep the bottom of the pot raised and out of the water, but with the wick in the water.

Self-watering pots have a water reservoir that needs attention only when it gets low, usually every couple of weeks. Since plant food is typically added to the water at the same time, you feed and water twice a month instead of every few days. Meanwhile the pot delivers water at the rate the plant uses it, adjusting to changes in light, humidity, or temperature. Plants in self-watering pots are usually more evenly watered than plants in conventional pots, but since the soil is kept constantly moist, plants that need to dry out between waterings don't perform well in them. The same is true for plants on capillary matting or in self-watering pots.

▲ African violets and other fuzzy-leaf plants that are susceptible to water spotting can be bottom watered. This cachepot is designed for bottom watering. Place the inner pot in the cachepot filled with tepid water.

▲ Adding mulch to the top of your pots will help the plant retain moisture longer. This practice reduces maintenance time, soil temperature fluctuations, and drying. As a bonus it also looks attractive.

Many types of self-watering containers are available. Some have built-in reservoirs. Others are actually two pots: a grow pot and an outer pot or cachepot that fits around the grow pot like a reservoir.

Self-watering pots have different ways of indicating when the reservoir is empty. Some pots show the water level with a float, often colored red for maximum visibility. Others have a clear plastic gauge along one side of the reservoir. In still others the entire reservoir is made of a transparent material so you can see the water level even from a distance. The disadvantage of the latter is that the water is exposed to light, which encourages the growth of unsightly algae. Most containers have an opening in the side or on the top into which you can pour the water. Always wait until the reservoir is empty before watering again. These pots work particularly well for hanging pots or others in difficult-to-reach locations.

Capillary matting looks a bit like nonwoven carpet padding. It is ideal to use in large trays filled with plants. The matting can be cut to fit inside the tray. The matting is then watered often enough to stay moist. Another approach is to cut one end of the matting so it drapes over the end of the tray into a reservoir filled with water.

The matting wicks water along its length. Plants sitting on the matting with their soil mix touching the matting can draw water up as needed. Place the pot on the matting and water well from the top to ensure that the soil mix comes into contact with the matting. Clean the matting occasionally to prevent algae from growing on it.

An occasional trip to the shower is also an effective way to water plants. At the same time you can rinse dust, dirt, and minor insect infestations from the leaves and leach the soil of excess mineral salts. Use tepid water and a gentle flow to prevent the soil from washing out of the container. Use a bathtub or shower year round. Or if weather permits and outdoor tap water is not too cold, take plants outside and rinse them with a garden hose.

▶ Wick watering is a simple method of watering plants that need to stay evenly moist. This wicking system has an external reservoir that contains water. The water moves by capillary action through the narrow tube into a ceramic base that is inserted into the pot's soil. As the soil dries, additional water wicks into the pot.

While you're away

If you're going to be away for a few days and can't find someone to care for your plants, you can easily set up a simple self-watering system. Line a sink or bathtub with old towels, newspapers, or other thick, absorbent material. Set pots with drainage holes directly on the absorbent material or matting. Remember the growing media must contact the absorbent material. Soak the matting well and leave the faucet dripping on it. The plants will draw up moisture as needed. You can also use wick watering on a temporary basis. This works fine for a few plants but is impractical as a long-term solution. Consider changing your collection over to wick watering over time. When you go away just fill the plants' water reservoirs.

As another option remove dead and fading leaves and flowers from plants, water them well, and seal them inside large, transparent plastic bags. Place them out of direct sun to prevent overheating. Water can't escape through the plastic bags, so your plants can go for several weeks without additional water.

Watering *(continued)*

◄ Many bromeliads, such as this blushing bromeliad, need constant water in their central cup. Water them by filling the cup rather than watering the soil. Although the roots anchor the plant in place, in the wild the roots attach the plant to a tree and have little function in water absorption. Most of the bromeliad's nutrients and water enter the plant through the central cup.

What kind of water?

To avoid shock and possible root damage from extreme temperatures, use tepid water when watering. Many gardeners let water stand overnight to reach "room temperature," but standing water actually can be considerably colder than room temperature.

Tap water is fine for houseplants unless the plant is sensitive to hard or softened water. Unless your municipal water supplier issues a treatment warning or your water has a strong chemical smell, there is generally no need to let tap water stand for 24 hours before using it. The small amount of chlorine it normally contains is not dangerous to most plants. It also can be helpful to use water from the hot water tap. Heating can dissipate some chemicals.

If your tap water is hard (alkaline) and you're growing plants that require an acid soil, such as azaleas and hydrangeas, you'll need to amend the soil. Alkaline conditions make it difficult for plants to absorb iron and other trace elements. Regular applications of iron chelate, included in some fertilizers, help keep foliage green. When the new foliage on acid-loving plants is yellow, it's a sign that the plant may need extra iron chelate fertilizer. Regularly repotting in a growing mix with added acidic soil amendments, such as peat moss, provides the acidity needed to release nutrients. You can also use plant food formulated to retain soil acidity while nourishing the plant.

Softened water contains salts that may accumulate in the soil and harm plants. If your home has a water softener, use an outdoor tap for plant water or install a bypass tap in the water line before it enters the softener so you'll have a source of hard water for plants. If this

◄ Terrariums have special watering requirements. Because they are closed systems, humidity stays high and watering must be done carefully to avoid overwatering. Add water a small amount at a time and check back several hours later to see if it was enough. If the inside glass stays covered with moisture, leave the lid partially open to allow some to escape.

WATERING EQUIPMENT

Watering cans come in a wide variety of sizes and shapes. They may be plastic or metal with short or long spouts. You may want several kinds for different purposes, including one with a long spout to reach into challenging spots. Some come with a swiveling spout that folds against the can to save on storage space or to fit more easily into a sink for filling. Use a large-capacity can, but one that you can lift easily, for greater efficiency. A watering can with a capacity of a gallon or two will need refilling less frequently.

Indoor gardening hoses are available with a watering wand attachment. They usually thread onto the waterspout in a sink (check to see that they are the right size for your sink's spout). You can water plants within reach of the length of the hose with no need to carry a bulky watering can. Some watering wands convert to a mist setting, which is good for plants on slabs.

Misters can be simple plastic bottles with a squeeze handle. The water output is adjustable, from a stream to a mist of water. Fancier ones have plungers that are used to create pressure within the bottle and a handle to release the water or mist. Keep several of the inexpensive types. Use one for plain water and others to dilute plant food for foliar feeding.

A squeeze bottle may be the same type as used for misting, but with a curved plastic spout for watering. Purchase the bottles with the same size screw-on opening for misting and watering so that the bottles can be interchanged if necessary.

This colorful watering can has a swivel spout that makes storage when not in use more convenient.

A coiled watering hose that attaches to the kitchen sink faucet allows a drip-free watering method.

This mister bottle has a plunger to create pressure in the bottle and an adjustable spray nozzle.

is not possible, draw water just before the softener cycle, when the salt content is at its lowest level.

Special watering needs

Not all plants have the same watering needs, of course. Here are a few that require special attention.

● **Hanging baskets:** A hanging container may need more frequent watering than a pot set on the ground or on a windowsill. Exposed to air on all sides, it quickly loses water to evaporation. Give the soil a thorough soaking whenever you water it or water it sparingly several times in one day until the mix is evenly moist. Even better take down the container and submerge it in a bucket or sink of tepid water for half an hour, then drain carefully before hanging it up again. You can water hanging planters easily using a squeeze-type plastic watering bottle designed especially for the purpose. Gardeners with many plants may prefer to use a hose with a wand to water hanging baskets. A squeeze bottle or water wand acts like an extension of your arm, letting you reach a plant well above your head. You can also purchase commercial pulley systems that allow you to lower the pot to chest level for watering, then raise it up again with little effort.

● **Wood slabs:** Some plants, notably staghorn fern, bromeliads, and some orchids, are grown fixed to slabs of wood, cork, or osmunda fiber. This allows them the air circulation they prefer but makes watering more challenging. You can water by spraying or misting the plant, but you may need to mist frequently. It is far easier to soak the slab in tepid water for 20 to 30 minutes. Plants grown on slabs dry out even more quickly than those in hanging baskets. As with other plants be sure to soak them as soon as their leaves begin to flag.

● **Orchids:** Most orchids are grown in light soil mixtures that retain little moisture. This means that they can dry out quickly. This is especially true at warmer temperatures and where there is a lot of air movement. Water orchids in such conditions lightly but more frequently.

● **Bromeliads:** Most bromeliads have a central cup that should be kept filled with water. Air plants (*Tillandsia* spp.) absorb water only through their leaves and need to be soaked or misted.

● **Terrariums:** With their glass walls, terrariums maintain extremely high humidity and therefore must be watered with care. Remember that terrariums are closed systems with little water evaporation, so add water in small increments. For small terrariums use an eye dropper, adding only a few drops of water at a time. It is easy to overwater and almost impossible to remedy the problem in terrariums with a narrow opening.

Humidity

Consider relative humidity in your selection of indoor plants. Relative humidity describes the degree of moisture in the air compared to how much it can hold at a given temperature. It tends to be highest in summer, although air-conditioning lowers indoor humidity dramatically. Relative humidity is lowest (often desert-dry) in winter, when the home heating system dries out the air. Generally the colder the air outside, the drier the air indoors.

The relative humidity in the native habitat of many tropical and subtropical plants reaches about 80 percent; most houses average between 35 and 50 percent relative humidity and sometimes fall below 20 percent in winter. Although many plants have adapted to lower humidity levels, most do better when the relative humidity is at least 50 percent. Most plants, excluding cacti, succulents, or other desert plants, grow better with additional moisture in the air.

Too much humidity is much less likely to occur in your home, but if humidity is too high, plants become susceptible to rot, mold and mildew. The best way to address this is to increase ventilation or move the plant to another room with drier air or better air circulation.

If the relative humidity in a room is too low, plants may lose water faster through their leaves than they can replace it through their roots. Brown leaf tips, yellow leaf margins, flower bud drop, and wilting are characteristic symptoms of this problem. Low humidity is most common during winter, when indoor air is dry from central heating.

Here are some ways to raise the humidity around your houseplants:

● **Group plants together.** Each plant benefits from evaporation from its own damp soil and the moisture emitted from its neighbors' soil. As the plants transpire water from their leaves, the grouping of foliage is more likely to trap moisture, creating higher humidity around the plants than in the rest of the room. Use capillary matting in a tray under the plants to add additional humidity.

● **Humidify the air.** Install humidifiers in individual rooms on the heating system to humidify the entire home. Keep them filled with clean water and you and your plants will benefit.

● **Use a gravel tray.** Place 1 inch of gravel in a 2-inch-deep waterproof tray. Fill the tray with water to just below the top of the gravel. Place your plants on top of the gravel. As water evaporates from the surface of the stones, it creates a more humid microclimate around the plants. Be certain the pots sit above the water line to prevent root rot from waterlogged soil.

● **Use evaporating water.** Place a shallow glass or decorative container of water near the plant. As the water evaporates it provides some additional humidity for your houseplant. If the container isn't decorative, hide it behind the plant. You can even use large containers, like a bucket with towels wicking the water up and allowing it to evaporate into the room. This is unattractive but effective. You can also place containers of water directly on radiators in winter to increase the amount of evaportion.

● **Mist plants.** Use a mister bottle to spray water on the plant foliage. Use room temperature water. This is a temporary solution, and some experts think it does

INCREASING RELATIVE HUMIDITY

Action	Result
Install a humidifier on your furnace	Most efficient method to raise humidity yet watch for variation by room
Use a room humidifier	Provides localized moisture control in the air
Group plants	Each plant gives off a considerable amount of moisture through transpiration; raises humidity nearby
Place a pebble tray under plants	Water in the tray evaporates, increasing humidity around those plants
Double-pot the plant	Water in filler material between pots evaporates, and raises humidity
Grow the plant in an enclosed environment (terrarium or small greenhouse)	Transpired water recycles in the enclosed space creating a humid microclimate
Mist plants	Creates temporary increase in humidity; may also increase disease incidence

A pebble tray increases the humidity around these violets.

A room humidifier adds moisture to the plant room.

PLANTS THAT TOLERATE LOW HUMIDITY

Aloe	Crown-of-thorns	Sago palm
Cactus	Kalanchoe	Snake plant
Cast-iron plant	Peace lily	Succulents
Clivia	Ponytail palm	Sweet bay

Clivia

Aloe

Crown-of-thorns

Panda plant

Brain cactus

Snake plant 'Laurentii'

PLANTS THAT REQUIRE HIGH HUMIDITY

Alocasia	Calathea	Lollipop plant
Areca palm	Crepe ginger	Monkey plant
Baby's tears	Ferns	Orchids
Beautiful ctenanthe	Fittonia	Prayer plant

Alocasia

Baby's tears

Boston fern

Maidenhair fern

Cretan brake fern

Fittonia

Orchid 'Goldenzelle Lemon Chiffon'

Prayer plant

more harm than good. Misting the foliage of plants with water is apt to cause disease problems and often creates water spots on furniture, carpeting, or drapes. Misting and high humidity do help reduce problems from spider mites.

● **Provide good growing conditions.** Water plants carefully whenever they need moisture. Cool temperatures and a good soil mix that holds water can help overcome the negative effects of low humidity.

● **Select a good site.** Keep plants away from radiators and drafty locations. Moving air picks up water vapor. Place plants in areas that are naturally higher in humidity: for example, near the kitchen sink, above an aquarium, or in the bathroom, provided they receive enough light.

● **Grow under glass.** Put especially sensitive plants in terrariums or other enclosures, where you can control the environment more easily. Place a glass cloche over a plant to maintain a higher level of humidity around its leaves. If you have many humidity-sensitive plants, a small greenhouse may be a good investment.

● **Double pot.** Place your potted houseplant in a second larger pot and fill the gap between the pots with moist sphagnum moss. Keep the moss moist by watering it. Evaporation of water from the sphagnum moss increases the humidity around the double-potted plant.

Temperature

◄ Ferns respond well to typical bathroom conditions, which tend to be more humid than other rooms. This fern is growing close to the floor, which is the coolest section of the room, another condition it prefers. If light levels are low, rotate the fern to a brighter location occasionally.

You know your home and its idiosyncrasies better than anyone else, so you are the perfect person to find the best places for your indoor garden. Once you know your home's microclimates, you can map out areas in your home where houseplants will thrive.

When choosing a location for you plant, consider humidity, temperature, and air circulation as well as light. Avoid extremely hot, intensely sunny areas or dark locations where success with most plants will be limited. Indoor microclimates change with the season and the weather, so plants may be ideally situated in winter but need relocation in summer. Move plants as needed to find the best growing conditions. You'll know in a week or so whether a change has improved a plant's health.

Take advantage of differences in temperature microclimates by choosing plants that can profit from them. Since cool air sinks, the air near the floor is cooler than the air in the rest of the room. This is a great place to put plants such as ferns that need less heat. Hot air rises so watch for signs of drying in plants on top of bookshelves or cabinets.

In the warmest areas around fireplaces, incandescent lights, and sunny summer windows, grow cacti and succulents that can best use warmth and low humidity. Where conditions are both hot and humid, near a dishwasher, clothes dryer, or humidifier, try thin-leaved species, such as schefflera, China doll, and bougainvillea. Avoid areas where rapid temperature changes may occur. Cold drafts or hot air blasts near

Temperature is not as critical as light, but it is important. Most foliage houseplants grow best when temperatures are 70–80°F during the daytime and 60–68°F at night, which falls within the range maintained in most homes. Flowering houseplants grow well with the same daytime temperatures but a night temperature of 55–60°F,

which prolongs the bloom period. As a rule of thumb provide night temperatures 10 to 15 degrees lower than day temperatures to trigger bloom in azaleas, orchids, flowering maples, and other blooming plants.

Most houseplants dislike temperature extremes. Keep them away from drafts, such as near an outside door that you open frequently, a leaky

window, or an air-conditioner duct. Avoid heat sources that can quickly dry out plants. Heat ducts, radiators, appliances that generate heat, such as television sets, or fireplaces are potential trouble spots. These extremes may cause foliage damage or loss, and even plant death. Buds on flowering plants are especially sensitive to sudden temperature changes.

PLANTS FOR COOL PLACES

As long as you maintain an indoor temperature that is comfortable you'll likely be successful with most houseplants. However some plants require cooler temperatures to do their best or to set flowers. Many gift plants need cooler temperatures, especially at night, to keep flowers blooming a long time.

Asparagus fern
Cactus
Cape lily
Christmas cactus

Clivia
Coralberry
Cyclamen
Geranium

Japanese aucuba
Japanese euonymus
Japanese holly fern
Japanese pittosporum

Jasmine
Myrtle
Orange-jessamine
Osmanthus

Streptocarpus
Sweet bay
Table fern

Clivia

Cretan brake fern

Boston fern

Christmas cactus

Cape lily

Cyclamen

windows and entrances can make some plants wilt.

Use a maximum/minimum thermometer to determine cool spots and warm corners in your home. Leave it in one place for 24 hours to record the low and high temperatures during the period. Do this in several rooms and in different locations within a room. Make a note of the temperature variations and place plants accordingly.

Air circulation

Plants grouped close together may look attractive, but overcrowding can harm plant health. Air movement around each plant is necessary to remove moisture from the leaves and can help prevent disease problems. Regular air movement around leaves and stems produces sturdier, denser plants that grow continuously at a steady rate.

Open a window in mild weather to increase air movement. A ceiling or table fan also keeps the air moving. Consider adding small whisper fans on light stands, in bookcases, or in any other location where air is stagnant.

Growing media

A houseplant needs an "anchor" to hold it in place and provide nutrients. Some plant roots can thrive in water only, but most need soil or potting mix to grow well. Plant roots require air and water for health, so the mixture in which the roots reside must provide plenty of both. It must also retain nutrients for the plant's use.

Growing mix

Garden soils are generally too heavy for use in containers and bring with them the problems of disease and insects. Many potting mixes for indoor plants are soilless. You can customize them according to individual plant needs if you want, but commercial mixes available at your local garden store are adequate for most plants. If you grow in a soilless mix that contains no fertilizer, use a plant food that contains trace elements. These minor elements are needed in very small quantities by plants for good growth. In garden soils the trace elements come from the soil. In soilless mixes you may need to add them in the plant food you use.

Most commercial soilless mixes are composed of peat moss or decomposed bark and vermiculite or perlite in

INDIVIDUAL POTTING MIX INGREDIENTS

Ingredient	Description	Features	Uses
Calcined clay	Clay heated and pulverized	Most commonly available as unscented cat litter	Adds weight, drainage, and aeration
Charcoal	Heated & processed wood	Use only horticultural grade	Absorbs salts and by-products of plant decay; removes impurities; removes acidity
Coir	Coconut husk fibers	Substitute for peat moss	Moisture and nutrient retentive
Leaf mold	Decayed leaves	Excellent organic additive	Adds moisture retention; some nutrients
Peat moss	Partially decayed plant material from the middle and bottom of peat bogs	Acid pH; no nutritive value	Retains moisture in mix
Perlite	Expanded volcanic rock	Moisture and nutrient retentive; lightweight	Improves drainage and aeration
Sand	Naturally occurring	Coarse, round river sand is best; beach sand may contain harmful salts; avoid sharp sand	Adds drainage and weight
Shredded bark	Finely shredded or ground bark	Almost no nutritive value	Adds moisture holding ability to mix
Sphagnum moss	Plant matter harvested from the top of peat bogs	Fibers longer than those of peat moss; decomposes slowly	Used mainly to line baskets and in orchid mixes; rarely used in regular potting mixes
Vermiculite	Mica expanded by heating	Moisture and nutrient retentive	Increases moisture holding capacity

Calcined clay

Charcoal

Coir

Leaf mold

Peat moss

Perlite

Sand

Shredded bark

Sphagnum moss

Vermiculite

various proportions. They are free of pests, diseases, and weed seeds. They are also affordable, simple to use, and widely available. Some mixes contain slow release plant food that provides nutrients for several months. Just remember not to feed again during those months.

Beware of inexpensive potting soils. They are often dark in color because they contain large amounts of decomposed organic matter. These mixes compact readily and retain too much moisture.

If you need a potting mix with other ingredients, you can mix your own or purchase a ready-made specialty mix. Wear a dust mask when handling dry ingredients. It is better to work with them when slightly moist. Commercial potting blends for flowering plants contain more organic materials that retain moisture, such as shredded bark or compost, because flower buds are sensitive to water loss. Cacti and other succulents need a mix that has sand or calcined clay for extremely good drainage. Bromeliads and orchids need a coarse mix of bark chips, which provide plenty of air for the roots.

When choosing a growing mix look for one that is of medium weight. Those that are too light, such as straight peat moss, may not adequately anchor a plant. Too heavy a mix, such as sterilized topsoil, causes drainage problems. You can also adjust according to a plant's needs; simply add perlite to lighten it a bit or add humus or commercial sterilized topsoil for a heavier mix.

Measuring acidity and alkalinity

An important factor in the composition of any growing medium is its acidity or alkalinity, which is measured in terms of pH. The pH scale ranges from 0 to 14, with 7 being neutral. A pH reading higher than 7 is alkaline, and one lower than 7 is acidic.

SPECIALIZED MIXES

Some houseplants require special potting media to grow well.

● **African violets, florist's gloxinias, streptocarpus, and other gesneriads** prefer a slightly acidic soil mix that retains moisture and is equal parts sand, peat moss, sterilized topsoil, and leaf mold or a commercial mix specially formulated for African violets. Some growers prefer a soilless mix and feed regularly.

● **Bromeliads, orchids, and other epiphytes** need a lot of air around their roots. Use equal parts sphagnum moss, coarse bark, and coarse perlite or a commercial orchid mix. Add gravel for weight to bromeliad mix to improve the stability of the pot. Some orchids do well growing in bark, osmunda fiber, and sphagnum moss in mixture or alone.

● **Cactus, succulents, and many palms** need a well-drained mix that is one part coarse sand, two parts sterilized potting soil, and one part calcined clay or a commercial cactus mix.

● **Ferns** like a well-drained soil high in organic matter. Mix three parts peat moss-based potting mix, two parts perlite, and three parts leaf mold.

An all-purpose potting mix works well for most plants. Some include an additive that allows you to water less often.

African violets and their relatives prefer a soil mix that retains moisture well and is slightly acidic.

Cacti and succulents need a mix that drains well. Most citrus and palms will grow well in the same type of mix.

Orchids and many bromeliads need a moisture-retentive mix that also drains well.

Highly acid mixes cause yellowing and leaf drop. Alkaline soil causes stunted growth and dull green, yellowish, or purplish leaf color. If plants start showing those symptoms, have your soil tested to see if your mix has a pH close to 7. Most packaged potting mixes are slightly acid and most houseplants prefer that. The mixes have a pH of about 6.5 to 6.8, which is ideal for most plants. For acid-loving plants such as azaleas, gardenias, and citrus, prepare the mix with extra peat moss. Use dolomitic lime to raise the pH for plants such as cacti and succulents that prefer a neutral or slightly alkaline soil.

Repotting

◄ When it's time to repot a plant with multiple stems, such as this English ivy, take the opportunity to divide the large plant and make several new ones to expand your collection or share with friends. Make certain that each division has healthy roots and shoots.

Eventually most houseplants need repotting. The main reasons to repot a plant are to encourage more rapid growth, to replace poor or compacted soil, or to reduce watering needs. Or maybe you just want a more attractive container for your plant.

Repotting is stressful to plants. Avoid doing it unless a plant needs it. Some plants, such as clivia, citrus, and fishtail palm, actually grow best with pot-bound conditions. The best time to repot is usually in spring, when the plant begins active growth and recovers quickly. If necessary repot flowering plants right after they finish blooming.

Some signs that could indicate that your plant needs repotting are a top-heavy plant; decreasing leaf size on new growth; wilting soon after watering; roots at the soil surface or protruding through the drainage holes; and lower leaves turning yellow. To determine whether

a plant needs repotting, tap it out of its pot and look at the root system. If the roots are spread out with few (or none) growing through the drainage holes, repotting may not be necessary. However if the root ball is such a mass of roots that virtually no soil is left, the time has come to repot. That condition indicates the plant should have been repotted earlier.

With a plant that has outgrown its pot, you have the option of putting it into a bigger container or pruning the root ball and putting the plant back into its original pot. If you want the plant to grow bigger, give it a larger pot. Generally you should increase large pots by only 1 or 2 inches larger in diameter, smaller pots by ½ to 1 inch larger. If you choose a pot that is too large, it will hold more soil and therefore more water than the plant can use. That could lead to root rot.

To maintain the plant's size, tap it out of its pot and slice off about an inch all around the root ball,

including underneath, with a sharp knife. When you disturb the root system this way, the plant may drop some of its foliage in response to losing a portion of its roots.

When a plant looks as if it needs feeding but doesn't respond to fertilizer, it's probably time to replace all or part of the soil. For partial replacement remove the plant from its pot and knock off some of the old soil; tease out the roots a bit to encourage them to grow into the new soil; and then repot the plant. Another option is to topdress the plant, or scrape off the top inch or so of soil and add new soil. Topdressing is the easiest way to replace soil for plants that should not have their roots disturbed, such as amaryllis.

If the soil is completely depleted or is infested with insects, remove as much of the soil around the roots as possible. Tap off loose soil, and then wash the roots with warm water. Examine the roots for any problems, prune out diseased or damaged

areas and repot. This can result in leaf loss. Do it only if absolutely necessary.

It is never necessary to add a drainage layer of gravel or potshards when repotting. Studies have shown that such layers actually hinder proper drainage and waste valuable root space. If you're worried that the potting mix will run out the drainage hole or holes, place a piece of newspaper, paper towel, metal screening, or one small shard across the bottom of the empty pot.

Dividing

While you're repotting you can divide overgrown plants that have multiple stems or crowns (the base of the plant where the roots and stems join). Doing so rejuvenates plants that have outgrown their pots and provides you with new plants.

Remove the plant from its pot and slice through the root ball with a sharp knife or spade. You may need to saw some plants apart, but others gently break apart by hand. Make sure each division includes some of the main root and stem system. Plant the divisions immediately in potting mix in permanent containers and then water thoroughly. Keep the pots in bright light but out of direct sun, watering frequently until the plants root. You also can put the potted divisions inside clear plastic bags to reduce moisture loss. When they appear upright and healthy, gradually acclimate them to room conditions, then place them in a permanent location and care for them as you would mature plants.

STEPS FOR POTTING OR REPOTTING

1. Thoroughly water the plant several hours or a day before repotting.
2. Gather needed supplies such as a pot and saucer, screening material to cover drainage holes, newspaper to cover your work surface, and potting mix.
3. Moisten the potting mix by adding warm water and mixing it in with a spoon to make it easier and safer to handle. Potting soil is hard to wet once it's in the pot.
4. Loosen the plant by running a knife around the inside edge of the pot or by tapping the pot on the edge of a table. Slip out the plant. Hold the top of a small plant between your fingers,

supporting the root ball in your palm. Remove a larger plant by laying the pot on its side and sliding out the plant or the pot away from the plant.
5. Unwind circling roots and cut off any that look rotted. If the plant is pot-bound, make shallow cuts every few inches from the top to the bottom of the root ball with a sharp knife. Cut off an inch or so of the root ball if you intend to put the plant back into the same container.
6. Pour some potting mix into the new pot. Make a custom-sized space for your plant by placing the empty old pot on top of the potting soil base in the center

of the new pot. Make sure that the plant is at the same depth as it was planted before. Then fill in more mix around the roots.
7. Tamp the soil lightly with your fingers as you work; pressing too hard will compact the growing mix. Water the plant well. For plants where drainage is critical, fill the pot with mix and pick it up and tap it on the counter a few times. Watering will then settle the soil as much as required.
8. If you pruned the roots substantially, cut back the top of the plant accordingly.

1 Browning fronds are a sign that this fern is pot-bound and needs repotting. Thoroughly water the plant several hours or a day before repotting to counteract the shock of transplanting.

2 Tip the pot upside down and tap the rim on the edge of a bench or counter to remove the plant. If the plant doesn't budge, loosen the root ball by running a knife along the inside edge of the pot.

3 Loosen the root ball with your fingers. Tease apart the roots so they will readily grow into the new soil. If the plant is pot-bound make vertical cuts in the root ball to force new root growth.

4 Unwind and remove circling roots. Cut off excessively long ones or any roots that appear damaged.

5 Place potting mix in the bottom of the new pot. Center the plant on top of the soil base. Fill in around the plant with soil mix, keeping the soil an inch or so beneath the pot rim to provide space for watering.

This fern completely fills its container with a mass of roots and fronds. It's a good candidate for repotting and division.

Choosing a container

▲ Clay pots insulate root zones from rapid temperature fluctuations. They are porous; the soil in them will dry out more quickly than that in plastic or ceramic containers. They are heavier and more stable than plastic pots, which is good for top-heavy plants. Their rustic look is good for casual rooms and country kitchens, and works well with cacti and succulents.

▲ Plastic pots are available in many shapes, sizes, and colors. They hold moisture well, are lightweight, and are easy to keep clean. Use plastic pots if you tend to underwater or for plants such as ferns that should be kept evenly moist.

▲ Fired ceramic containers often have decorative designs and finishes. They are strong but are subject to breakage if dropped on hard surfaces. Coordinate colors and designs with room décor. They are easy to clean and keep looking fresh. Glazed ceramic holds moisture well and works well for plants that prefer to stay moist.

Containers are the indoor version of the outdoor gardener's hardscape. They come in a wide array of colors and styles, which makes choosing a container almost as much fun as choosing a plant. However you must also be practical and follow certain guidelines when selecting an appropriate container.

Most containers are made of plastic, ceramic, or clay. Which is better for houseplants? It depends on several factors, including the type of plant and your watering habits.

Unglazed clay (terra-cotta) pots are porous, so the soil dries out quicker than in plastic or ceramic pots. On the other hand clay insulates better and shields the root zone against rapid temperature shifts. Clay pots are best for plants with lower water needs or if you tend to overwater. They also weigh more and can make top-heavy plants more stable. They can be readily moved outside for the summer. Clay pots will break if dropped. Their casual, rustic style looks nice in a country kitchen or sunroom, but they are usually not the best choice for formal settings. It's a good idea to soak clay pots in water for a couple hours before planting.

Plastic and ceramic pots retain water longer and transmit temperature changes faster than clay pots. Use them if you tend to underwater or if you need to keep plants moist. Plastic pots are generally less expensive than clay or ceramic pots and weigh less. They do not shatter if dropped on the floor. Ceramic pots come in a wide array of colors and designs that become an important part of a room's decor.

Whatever container you choose it is important to use the correct size. Containers too small or too large present an unbalanced appearance. An appropriate container should provide room for soil and roots, allow sufficient top room for proper watering, and be attractive without competing with the plant. Top-heavy plants must have sturdy, weighted containers so they don't tip over. A good design principle to keep in mind is that the pot should be no taller than one-third of the height of the plant/container combination. Thus a 9-inch-tall pot supports an 18-inch-tall plant (top growth) with a total height of 27 inches.

Standard pots—those in which the depth is equal to the diameter of the pot—were once the usual format for both clay and plastic pots. Azalea pots—those in which the depth is equal to three-quarters the diameter—now are a widely used shape for plastic pots since the mix stays more evenly moist in a squatter pot. If you want better drainage, use standard pots or try the "long Tom" pot, which has a diameter about one-half its height.

Self-watering pots, which allow you to water less frequently, are discussed on pages 46–47.

New plant purchases need not be potted into a different container right away. If the nursery pot is of adequate size and the plant isn't root-bound, it can stay in that pot for a while. In some cases it is better for the plant to avoid the risk of transplant shock. Place the nursery pot in a basket or cachepot to make it more attractive. Lift the plastic containers out of the pots and water them in the sink as needed. "Double potting" is a good option for many plants, especially when you want to reduce watering needs. Place a plant in its nursery pot in a larger decorative cachepot that may or may not have drainage holes, filling the space between the two pots with sphagnum moss or perlite. To water moisten the filler material as well as the soil. Double potting also helps increase the humidity around a plant.

ONE PLANT, THREE LOOKS

When philodendron 'Brasil' is trained to a pole in a tall, narrow container, it creates a formal vertical accent.

The same plant grown in a wide, shallow bowl has a more informal, rounded appearance.

For yet another option, try growing it at eye level in a hanging basket with stems trailing over the pot's edge.

Drainage

Good drainage is imperative. No matter what type of plant you are growing, the pot must have drainage holes, unless it is a self-watering pot. If you want to use a decorative pot that doesn't have drainage holes, use it as a cachepot (see page 60) or drill drainage holes in its bottom. Regardless of the type every pot must have good drainage and a saucer underneath to catch excess water and protect your floor or table. Plants that sit for long periods with their roots in saturated soil are susceptible to root rot.

A common myth says that if you put a layer of stones in the bottom of a nondraining pot, it will give the water somewhere to drain. In actuality excess water does not move into the gravel unless the soil above it is saturated. The plant's roots will soak in the soil's water, stagnate, and rot. There is no substitute for a pot that drains well.

▲ The removable drain plug in this polystyrene pot may be left in for use as a cachepot or removed for drainage.

▲ Resin and polystyrene pots are durable and look much like high-end ceramic or decorative clay pots. They are generally less costly than ceramic and are less subject to breakage. They may be used as cachepots or if they have a drainage hole, may be used as a growing container with a saucer underneath to catch drips.

▲ Molded concrete containers provide a classic but rugged appearance. Most are gray, but colored concrete containers are also available. Their heaviness makes them unwieldy to move around but prevents top-heavy plants from tipping over.

Choosing a container *(continued)*

Cachepots

Ideally a cachepot should be about 2 inches wider than the grow pot so that you can insert and remove the latter readily and easily see any standing water in the bottom. You can convert a cachepot into a double pot (see page 51) by filling the space around and under the grow pot with peat moss, sphagnum moss, Spanish moss, or perlite, or by covering the potting mix and pot edge with decorative mulch. If the grow pot is too low for the cachepot, raise it on an inverted pot or saucer placed in the bottom of the cachepot. You can also use a layer of gravel on the bottom of the cachepot. This will raise the inner pot level and keep the bottom out of water.

Be careful when watering plants in cachepots. Even with a gravel layer or inverted pots, excess water may sit in the bottom or in the saucer inside, leaving the bottom of the plant sitting in water. Half an hour after you water, check the cachepot and drain it if necessary. You can siphon off extra water with a turkey baster.

Any ornamental container that can hide a grow pot is a cachepot. It may be ceramic, plastic, metal, wood, or any other material, and it needn't have drainage holes, although it can have them as long as you place a waterproof saucer either inside or underneath. It needn't even be a dedicated plant container: Old watering cans, washbasins, teakettles, and other items are often used as cachepots. You also can find cachepots sold for this purpose from gardening product retailers.

Woven baskets make wonderful homes for plants but must be used as cachepots due to their tendency to rot when they contact moisture. Either carefully line them with plastic before inserting the grow pot or put a saucer in the bottom. In case water accidentally seeps through, place baskets on plastic mats or cork pads. As with other cachepots you can use Spanish moss or some other mulch to hide the grow pot.

Window boxes and wood planters made of rot-resistant redwood or cypress fill a decorative niche. Because their construction may not be as watertight as that of plastic, clay, or ceramic containers, they are probably best used as cachepots. Line them with plastic and conceal the grow pots and drainage trays inside. You also can opt for waterproof plastic and metal window boxes.

Mulches

Mulching helps preserve moisture in the soil just as it does in the outdoor garden. Traditional and natural mulches work well with clay pots and include various sizes of bark chips, shredded bark, long fibered sphagnum moss and Spanish moss. Many people like to use small stones, crushed shells, sand, chicken grit, pea gravel, or white or colored pebbles, either with a natural finish or polished. These work well with cacti and succulents. You can be more creative in matching mulches to other kinds of decorative pots. Think about using small or large buttons, coins, metal washers, glass rock, small seashells, or starfish. You can blend or contrast colors; have

▲ This dwarf schefflera growing in a plastic pot with drainage holes is placed inside a decorative ceramic pot. Long fibered sphagnum moss is used to disguise the lip of the less attractive growing container and to reduce watering needs.

▲ You can display plants grown in small individual pots in a larger basket to create a unified appearance. Here fittonia, house bamboo, and aluminum plant combine in an informal grouping. Line the basket with plastic to prevent damage to furniture.

▼ 'Tiki' dieffenbachia growing in a functional pot with drainage holes is displayed in a decorative metal cachepot. Do not let water accumulate in the cachepot because roots standing in water will rot.

DECORATIVE MULCHES AND TRIMS

Spanish moss

Dried sphagnum moss

Excelsior

Fine gravel

Decorative stones

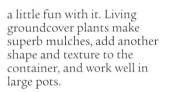
Crushed seashells

a little fun with it. Living groundcover plants make superb mulches, add another shape and texture to the container, and work well in large pots.

Saucers and surface protectors

Place all pots with drainage holes on a saucer or tray of some sort. Even cachepots are best placed on saucers, especially if they are made of unglazed clay. Sooner or later water may seep through or condense on the pot's side and drip down and damage furniture or floors. To do a good job the saucer must be at least as wide as the pot's upper diameter and also deep enough to hold excess water that may flow through the pot during watering.

Clear plastic saucers are widely available and inexpensive. You also can recycle old plates as saucers or purchase ones that match or complement the plant's pot. Beware of unglazed clay saucers, because they are porous and can stain the surface they sit on. Some terra-cotta saucers have an unglazed outer surface but are glazed inside so water won't flow through. You also can paint the inside of an unglazed saucer with waterproof varnish or enamel or place it on a round of cork. For a more natural look place saucers that match pots inside clear plastic ones. The plastic saucers virtually disappear from view but protect surfaces from moisture damage.

New absorptive mats are available that protect surfaces and absorb some excess

▲ This cork round will protect furniture from scratching but is limited in the amount of water it can absorb.

moisture. They have a soft vinyl side that is placed on surfaces that could be damaged. The absorptive side, a nonwoven mat, absorbs moisture.

◄ A variety of ceramic and plastic saucers can be used to protect surfaces from water. Treat unglazed clay saucers with waterproof varnish or enamel or place them inside a clear plastic saucer or on an absorbent mat.

Feeding

▲ Miracle-Gro® Pour & Feed Liquid Plant Food is premixed for convenience. Apply it directly to the soil of houseplants and container plants according to label directions.

Miracle-Gro® Water Soluble All Purpose Plant Food 24-8-16

GUARANTEED ANALYSIS — F 1198

Total Nitrogen (N) 24%
   3.5% Ammoniacal Nitrogen
   20.5% Urea Nitrogen
Available Phosphate (P_2O_5) 8%
Soluble Potash (K_2O) 16%
Boron (B) 0.02%
Copper (Cu) 0.07%
   0.07% Water Soluble Copper (Cu)
Iron (Fe) 0.15%
   0.15% Chelated Iron (Fe)
Manganese (Mn) 0.05%
   0.05% Chelated Manganese (Mn)
Molybdenum (Mo) 0.0005%
Zinc (Zn) 0.06%
   0.06% Water Soluble Zinc (Zn)

Derived from Ammonium Sulfate, Potassium Phosphate, Potassium Chloride, Urea, Urea Phosphate, Boric Acid, Copper Sulfate, Iron EDTA, Manganese EDTA, Sodium Molybdate, and Zinc Sulfate. Information regarding the contents and levels of metals in this product is available on the internet at: http://www.regulatory-info-sc.com.

KEEP OUT OF REACH OF CHILDREN
MANTENER FUERA DEL ALCANCE DE LOS NIÑOS

Scotts Miracle-Gro Products, Inc.
14111 Scottslawn Road
Marysville, OH 43041

Miracle-Gro® Plant Food
was developed by the trusted experts of Miracle-Gro® branded products to provide plants with the ideal mix of nutrients to thrive. Plants grow bigger and more beautiful, helping gardens fill in quickly so you can enjoy them sooner. Give your entire garden the ultimate

▲ Miracle-Gro® Water Soluble All Purpose Plant Food has an analysis of 24-8-16. The numbers represent the percentage of nitrogen (24), phosphorous (8) and potassium (16). This plant food is considered complete because is contains all three elements.

▲ Miracle-Gro® African Violet Food is formulated to provide the balance of nitrogen, phosphorous, and potassium African violets need for growth and flowering. Use it whether you top or bottom water.

Types of plant food

All plants require certain essential elements for proper growth. Plant foods provide the soil with the nutrients and minerals plants need to remain healthy.

A complete plant food (one that contains nitrogen, phosphorous, and potassium) is a good choice for most houseplants. Nitrogen primarily enriches the greenness of the foliage and promotes stem and leaf growth. Phosphorus encourages flowering and root growth. Potassium contributes to stem strength, root growth, and disease resistance. Plant foods formulated for flowering plants usually contain less nitrogen and more phosphorus and potassium. Those designed for foliage plants tend to have higher nitrogen content and less phosphorus and potassium. If you grow many different types of plants, it may be easier to apply a good all-purpose fertilizer or to alternate between a flowering plant fertilizer and one for foliage. A typical all-purpose food would be 8-7-6, where the numbers representing the percentages by weight of nitrogen, phosphorus, and potassium, respectively, are nearly equal. Some plants require more specialized plant foods such as those for orchids or African violets. Orchids growing in bark will need regular applications of higher nitrogen formulas to promote foliage growth. Rotate that with high phosphorous formulas for flowering plants. Feed acid-loving plants like gardenias, azaleas, and citrus with an acid-based plant food. Because cacti are slow growers, they prefer a low-nitrogen plant food.

In addition to the three major nutrients, plants need smaller quantities of sulfur, calcium, and magnesium, as well as the micronutrients iron, manganese, zinc, copper, chlorine, boron and molybdenum. This is particularly true for plants growing in soilless mixes. A lack of these micronutrients causes hard-to-diagnose symptoms such as stunted growth and yellowing or reddening of leaves. If you suspect a deficiency, apply a soluble plant food rich in micronutrients.

Application methods

Plant foods come in several forms. Water-soluble granular, crystalline, or liquid plant foods are convenient because the dilute solutions reduce the potential for fertilizer burn. Slow-release formulas are generally designed for a single yearly application and last for six to nine months under normal growing conditions. Many indoor gardeners find them practical. Apply time-release fertilizers according to instructions on the label. Some are tablets or sticks you insert into the soil. Others are pellets that are mixed into the growing media.

When applying plant food always read the label first and follow the directions carefully.

Apply plant food to moist soil only. Never exceed the recommended application amount. Often applications should be even more dilute than recommended since label recommendations are based on ideal growing conditions.

Frequency of application

The need to feed houseplants is determined by the plant's growth rate and age, your desire for new plant growth, and the season. Avoid feeding when a plant is under stress or not in active growth.

Plant food applications should be more frequent when the plant is ready to put on a growth spurt. This is usually in the spring and summer when sunlight intensity increases and the days are warmer and longer. Frequency of feeding can vary from every 2 weeks to every several months during the

growing season. A general rule for application is to feed according to label directions from March to September. During the short days of winter, many houseplants that receive little or no supplemental light enter a resting stage and do not require feeding.

Of course there are exceptions to every rule. Sometimes plants may grow more in winter, getting more light because of leafless trees and reflected light off snow. If you see increased growth and flowering, then feed. Or if leaves are uniformly and generally becoming yellow, plants probably need feeding. African violets and other flowering houseplants that grow and flower nonstop benefit from monthly feeding year-round. Feed flowering plants when in bud and flower. Plants growing under fluorescent lights grow year round. Growth usually slows in winter, however, so use a bit less food.

Plants growing in soilless mixes require more frequent feeding. Some gardeners feed with dilute plant food at every watering during the growth season. Others use continuous feed forms of plant food. Make certain the plant food includes micronutrients.

Leaching

If you accidentally overfeed a plant, leach it thoroughly several times with tepid water and discard the drainage water. In mild weather you can do this outdoors using a garden hose. Leaching also helps wash out accumulated mineral salts, which can build up and harm the plant. Salt buildup shows up as a whitish deposit on pot surfaces or as salt burn on the edges of leaves. You may have to leach weekly for several weeks to alleviate it.

◀ Miracle-Gro® Indoor Plant Food Spikes are easy to use. Use the aerator to make an opening in the soil before inserting the spike. Each spike continuously feeds and provides micronutrients for about 60 days.

▲ Miracle-Gro® Liquid All Purpose Houseplant Food is in an easy-to-use liquid form. You can add a few drops of plant food to water for each watering or use a stronger concentration at longer intervals.

▲ Osmocote® Smart-Release Plant Food can be incorporated into dry soil mix prior to planting or applied to the soil surface of container plants. Plant food is released over approximately 4 months every time the plant is watered.

Grooming

Plants with soft stems, such as this aluminum plant, can be pinched back with just your fingertips. You could also use sharp pruning shears. Cut or pinch just above a node. Removal of stem tips encourages new vigorous growth and results in a more compact and aesthetically desirable specimen.

Almost all houseplants need some regular grooming to look and do their best. Not only does it make your plants look and grow better, it also keeps you in touch with your plants, providing an opportunity to observe them for signs of problems or abnormalities.

Basic grooming includes deadheading spent flowers and removing dead leaves from plants and soil. Completely yellow or brown leaves won't green up again; pull or cut them off with clean, sharp scissors or a razor blade craft knife. The best time to pinch or prune houseplants is during the spring and summer growing season so that new growth will cover the pruning wound. Make the pruning cut or pinch just above a node, the point where a new leaf or branches can readily develop.

Pruning and pinching

Pruning and pinching can be rewarding—both for you and for your plants. It's a good way to keep your green thumb active in late winter and early spring, and it acts as a tonic for plants, encouraging new growth. Although many houseplants grow an entire lifetime with no need for pruning or pinching, for plants that respond well to pruning, the result is a bushier, denser plant with a more appealing shape or size. Pruning encourages and directs growth and corrects structural problems. In some cases pruning is essential to remove diseased or damaged wood and nonflowering stems. It also can adjust a plant's height and width and shape it to your needs or liking.

Pruning tools

Prune using sharp bypass pruning shears or houseplant grooming shears, sharp scissors, or a razor blade craft knife. Anvil-type pruners crush the stem rather than slice it off. The type of plant will dictate the tool. Some plants are woody and hard to cut; some have soft stems that can be pinched with your fingernails. Even with soft tissue it's best to use a sharp clean tool to avoid smashing tissue.

▲ Prune plants with woody stems with sharp, clean bypass pruners. Remove side branches or stems at the point of attachment to the main trunk or shoot. Cut just outside the branch collar (swelling at the base), but don't leave a stub.

► This striped inch plant has become leggy. Its growth is stretched out with bare, open stems. Cut most of the stems back to a lower node to encourage new bushy growth. Many plants can be cut back to close to the soil line. Use the shoots you remove to propagate and grow new plants.

Pruning goals

The main reason for pruning is to make the plant look better. Think of the results before making a cut. If you lop off a major stem accidentally, you may have to wait a long time for another stem to replace it. Work slowly and step back often to get an overview of the plant. If in doubt about removing a stem or branch, use a piece of paper to block the view of that stem and get a visual reading of what the plant would look like with it removed. It also is helpful to place the plant on a revolving turntable so you can rotate the plant and work around the plant rather than on one side at a time. To rejuvenate an overgrown plant, prune the plant back 6 to 8 inches from the soil. New growth usually appears within a few weeks. Within a few months you will have an attractive houseplant once again.

Trailing plants, such as Swedish ivy and pothos, produce new leaves on the ends of long stems. Regular snipping forces new leaves to grow along the stem. Cut a stem just above a node, or leaf joint. Clip the stems at different lengths to keep the plant looking natural. Other plants, such as ming aralia and fishtail palm, have naturally irregular shapes, so you need only remove an occasional unhealthy leaf. Always keep the natural shape of the plant in mind when pruning.

Some plants, such as philodendrons and figs, have sap that can irritate your skin. Wear gloves when working with these plants.

Pinching

Pinching is often done with fingernails rather than pruners. Pinch out the tip of a stem and its topmost leaves to promote growth of the side buds. Pinching is a great way to keep shrubby plants full. On some plants such as coleus, pinching flower spikes encourages development of more attractive foliage. Fittonia, polka-dot plant, coleus, and purple passion are a few plants that require frequent pinching to look their best.

Some plants, such as African violet and peperomia, send up leaves from a flat crown in a symmetrical shape called a rosette. Prune them to maintain an even shape. Remove older leaves from the underside of the rosette, pinching off the leaf and petiole close to the base. Those areas are often difficult to get to with fingers, so consider using a razor blade craft knife to cut near the stem.

Removing diseased plant parts

To remove diseased tissue, prune into healthy tissue, keeping in mind the overall shape of the plant. Dispose of the prunings immediately and sterilize pruners between cuts with rubbing alcohol or a solution of 1 part household bleach to 9 parts water to avoid spreading disease.

Root pruning

Pruning roots stimulates new growth. Use severe root pruning to keep a plant in a small pot, although there are limits to how much of the root system you can remove without hurting the plant. A reduction in the number of roots means less moisture and nutrient uptake. Adjust watering and feeding during the recovery period after root pruning. Remove any damaged, dead, or diseased roots at the same time.

▲ Root pruning stimulates growth of plants. Use it to regulate the size of a plant and to keep it in a small pot rather than moving it into a larger pot when repotting. Water less after root pruning because fewer roots will use less water.

▲ Deadheading (removing spent flowers) will improve the appearance of this cyclamen and keep it from producing seed. Energy a plant uses for seed production cannot be used for foliar or flower growth, which most houseplant growers prefer. Dying flowers are unattractive and provide a good place for fungal diseases to start. Pinch off the old flowers with your fingers or use sharp, pointed scissors in order to reach deep inside a plant without damaging it.

Deadheading

Unless the plant develops attractive fruits, such as citrus, Jerusalem cherry, or ornamental pepper, keep fading flowers clipped off to maintain plant health and promote rebloom. Removing spent flowers is called deadheading. Not only are dying flowers unattractive, they also provide a good place for fungal diseases to gain a foothold. Keep the plant tidy for better visual effect. Even ornamental seedpods are an energy drain. Decide which is more important to you, the energy that could be used by the plant or the ornamental value of the seedpod.

Removing leaves

Remove yellow, brown, or withered leaves to keep the plant looking its best. Use a narrow-blade hand pruner or sharp scissors to make a clean cut without tearing the plant. Leaves that are pale green or yellow-green may green up again after feeding, so hold off on trimming them. If the leaves are large and have only brown tips or edges, trim them rather than removing them. The remaining green part of the leaf continues to photosynthesize and adds to

▲ Dust plants with hairy leaves, such as those of African violet, with a soft bristle brush. Cosmetic brushes work well. Brush the top and the bottom surfaces of leaves, keeping an eye out for pests and diseases at the same time.

▲ Use a soft damp cloth to wash leaves of glossy and waxy leafed plants such as this rubber plant. Dust clogs leaf pores and is detrimental to plant health. Rinse small plants in a sink using the hand rinse nozzle and tepid water. Large plants can be moved outdoors or into the tub to be given a shower.

▲ Plants look their best when brown, yellow, or withered leaves are removed. Use a razor knife, sharp scissors, or bypass pruners to remove them. If only a portion of the leaf is affected, rather than removing the entire leaf, trim the damaged section following the natural shape of the leaf.

the plant's health. Avoid cutting straight across the leaf but shape it to look like a small version of the same leaf. The cut leaf will blend with other leaves and the plant will look much better. While you are grooming the leaves, rotate each pot a quarter turn. This lets all parts of the plant have equal access to the light and ensures even growth.

Dusting and washing

Dust buildup on leaves not only looks bad but also clogs leaf pores (stomata), preventing transpiration and blocking light. Dust plants with hairy leaves with a soft cosmetic brush.

Spray small-leaf plants with water to wash off the dust or gently shake the plant to dislodge the dust. To dust shiny large-leaf plants, carefully wipe the top and bottom of each leaf with a soft damp cloth while you support each leaf with your other hand. If the dust is greasy, use a solution of one teaspoon of dish detergent to one gallon of water to clean the leaf. A damp cloth is also useful to remove white mineral deposits from foliage.

Plants with small, ridged leaves, such as ripple peperomia, benefit from a quick rinse with tepid water. Rinse plants in the kitchen or laundry room sink with a hand rinse nozzle. Or clean small plants in a sink full of tepid soapy water. Place your hand over the soil to keep the potting mix in place, invert the pot, and swish the leaves around in the soapy water. Rinse with plain water and allow to air dry. Take large plants to the shower and rinse with tepid water. In good weather you can also take them outside in the shade and rinse them with the gentle spray from a hose. Enclose the pot in a plastic bag, tied at the top to prevent soil from being washed away.

Avoid leaf shine products containing wax that can build up on the leaf surface and clog pores. Once you clear away the dust, a leaf's natural shine will come through on its own.

Providing support

◀ Pinning the stems of this English ivy to a moss pole will encourage the plant to send roots into the pole where it comes in contact with moist moss. Plants that use aerial roots to cling, such as philodendrons and pothos, root easily and adapt well to being grown on a moss pole. The additional roots in the pole will encourage new foliage growth and help the moss pole to fill in quickly.

is an excellent sturdy support and particularly suitable for climbing plants.

You can buy ready-made moss poles but they are also easy to make. Build your own moss pole out of chicken wire or ½-inch mesh hardware cloth. Roll the chicken wire or hardware cloth into a tube 3 to 4 inches in diameter. Place the tube into a pot that is half full of potting mix. Fill the tube with pre-moistened long fibered sphagnum moss. Use a stick to press the moss down to eliminate air spaces.

Creating a topiary

Topiary is the art of fashioning living plants into ornamental shapes. A bunny-shape planting nestled amid a grouping of foliage plants adds a whimsical nature to your indoor garden. Indoor topiaries consist of a wire form packed with long fibered sphagnum moss and covered with small-leaf houseplants that respond well to regular snipping and pruning. If you are artistic you can create your own forms out of chicken wire, but a wide array of designs and sizes are available from specialty nurseries. They are made of heavy gauge wire, often coated with epoxy for long life. Larger topiary forms are hinged to make stuffing easier.

Cover the entire form with a single type of plant or use a variety of plants for various parts of the topiary. The extremities of the form will dry more rapidly than the body, so you may want to select plants that tolerate more drying for those locations. Good choices

▲ This heart-leaf philodendron has been trained on a moss pole. This produces a lush concentration of foliage instead of a loose and open growth pattern. It also gives a strong vertical appearance to a vine that would normally drape or sprawl.

Climbing plants need some type of support to grow upright.

When choosing a stake or support system, use one that is at least as thick as the stem to be supported. Thin stakes bend and break, especially as the plant top gets heavier with new foliage. You can, however, use thin flexible branches such as willow or dogwood in arches rather than as straight sticks. Driftwood also makes an artistic decorative support. Stakes made of natural materials or painted natural colors, such as green or brown, will disappear when engulfed with foliage.

Staking and training works best if you start with young plants. The stems of older plants bend less easily, while young plants are more pliable. You also can prune young plants to cover their support system as they grow.

Choose wire or plastic ties, naturally colored materials such as twine and raffia, or dark green twist ties or plastic tape to hold the plant in place without scarring the stem. The wider or softer a tie, the less chance it will injure the plant stem. Make the shape of a figure eight with your tie, with one loop around the stake and one loop around the plant stem. This allows the plant a little movement and reduces the chances of stem breakage. Tie loosely so the expanding stem has plenty of room for growth. Secure the plant in several places for greater stability.

In some cases a stake is necessary to temporarily correct a problem. Once the plant has started growing well, remove the stake. In other cases a stake is an integral part of the plant-pot combination and the overall look for the plant.

Training to a moss pole

Plants that use aerial roots to climb such as philodendrons and pothos grow well on a constantly moist medium. A pole made out of wire netting stuffed with sphagnum moss

CREATING A ROSEMARY TOPIARY

Begin with a 2-year-old rosemary plant with one well-developed sturdy stem. Tie the stem loosely to a stake with figure-eight twist ties at several intervals.

When the plant reaches the desired height, pinch the growing tip to force side shoots to sprout. This will become the main head of the topiary.

As side shoots develop, prune them to achieve the shape you want. It may be possible at some point to remove the stake if the plant can stand on its own.

1 Select a small plant with a strong single upright-growing stem.

2 Loosely tie the stem to a stake inserted in the soil.

3 Pinch the growing tip and side shoots to create the shape you desire.

4 This nearly finished topiary will have two globes of foliage once it is completed.

▶ An English ivy topiary adds an air of formality and elegance to this table setting. Its rounded ball shape echoes the form of the container. Loosely vining shoots draping over the pot's edge soften the effect.

include English ivy, Japanese euonymus, creeping fig, myrtle and rosemary.

Treat the topiary form much as you would a moss pole. Start by placing the form in a pot that is half filled with growing mix. Use moistened long fiber sphagnum moss for forms that are designed to be filled with planting medium.

(Some houseplant topiaries are created by training a vine directly onto the wire frame with no growing mix inside the frame.) Make shallow indentations in the moss with your fingers or a spoon and place plants in the indentations. Once the topiary is fully planted, water it well. Use a mister or the hose attachment on your

watering can to produce a gentle flow of water to keep the moss moist. A shower or dip in the sink can be quick ways to remoisten the topiary.

A standard is a specific topiary form with a single treelike stem in which all growth is concentrated in a sheared crown of foliage in a lollipop form. Standards

work best with plants that have strong woody stems. These include coleus, flowering maple, geranium, myrtle, sweet bay, citrus, calamondin orange, and Ming aralia. Shrubby herbs are common for making topiaries, with rosemary, sweet bay, and lavender being top choices.

Making more plants

Propagation

Some plants are easy to propagate at home; others are more challenging. The keys to success are starting with healthy plants, choosing the proper propagation method, and providing a suitable environment for propagation.

Plant diseases and insect pests can be propagated along with plants, so start with healthy plant parts or disease-free seed. Portions of healthy, vigorously growing plants are more likely to establish roots and begin to grow on their own. Spring and summer are the best times to propagate most plants since that is when most are putting on new growth.

Seeds and cuttings need high humidity, a moist growing medium, and warm temperatures for quick germination and successful root development. High humidity reduces water loss from leaves so that new

▶ Cuttings are one of the easiest propagation techniques for starting new houseplants. Beginning with healthy, disease-free plants, make a clean cut just below a node with pruning shears or a razor type-craft knife. Remove lower leaves from the cutting and place it in a moist rooting medium. Expanded peat pellets, water, vermiculite, perlite, or potting soil may serve as the rooting medium. Difficult-to-root plants may need rooting hormone applied to the base of the cutting. Keep the rooting medium moist and the cuttings in a humid environment or enclosed in plastic out of direct sun. You'll soon have new rooted plants to pot up.

plants don't wilt and dry out before they develop a good root system. Moist air keeps the growing medium from drying out so quickly.

Use a loose, sterile propagation medium free of disease organisms. Likewise clean and sanitize containers before use. Any shallow container will do, as long as it allows excess water to drain out. A clear plastic (plastic wrap or polyethylene) cover keeps the air around plants moist and lets in light. It also makes it easy to check for emerging seedlings, wilting, or other signs of trouble.

Division

Division is an excellent way to rejuvenate a plant that has overgrown its pot. It's also a wonderful way to end up with more than one plant. Plants with fibrous root systems are easily divided by removing the plant from its pot and cutting the root ball into as many sections as size dictates. Make sure that each division has some of the main root and stem system. Multistem or spreading plants such as ferns and snake plant can be multiplied using this method. Other plants develop suckers or bulblets (pregnant onion and oxalis, for example) at their base that can be gently pulled apart and replanted. A good time to do this is when you repot the plant.

PROPAGATION TECHNIQUES

Plant	Techniques	Difficulty
African violet	Leaf cuttings, division	Easy
Aloe	Offsets	Easy
Asparagus fern	Division	Easy
Begonia	Division, leaf cuttings	Moderately easy (needs humidity)
Bird's nest fern	Division	Easy
Boston fern	Division	Easy
Calathea	Division	Moderately easy (needs humidity)
Cast-iron plant	Division	Easy
Chenille plant	Tip cuttings	Moderately easy (needs humidity)
Chinese evergreen	Division, stem tip cuttings	Easy
Coleus	Tip cuttings	Easy
Crown-of-thorns	Tip cuttings	Moderately easy
Dracaena	Division	Easy
Earth star	Offsets	Easy
Episcia	Stolons, stem cuttings	Moderately easy (needs high humidity)
Ficus	Air layering	Difficult
Flowering maple	Tip cuttings, seed	Moderately easy (needs high humidity)
Guppy plant	Tip cuttings	Moderately easy (needs humidity)
Hoya	Tip cuttings	Difficult
Lipstick plant	Tip cuttings	Moderately easy (needs high humidity)
Maidenhair fern	Division	Easy
Philodendron	Tip cuttings, layering	Easy
Pothos	Tip cuttings, layering	Easy
Prayer plant	Division	Moderately easy (needs humidity)
Purple passion	Tip cuttings	Difficult
Queen's tears	Offsets	Easy
Snake plant	Division, leaf cuttings	Easy to moderately easy
Spider plant	Offsets	Easy
Streptocarpus	Division, leaf cutting	Easy

DIVISION

1 To divide a fibrous rooted plant such as Chinese evergreen, remove it from its container. Remove any damaged or diseased leaves and roots.

2 Use a sharp knife to cut through the root ball, making as many divisions as desired. Make certain that each division has healthy roots and at least one shoot.

3 Plant each division at the same depth it previously grew. Fill the new container with fresh growing media. Firm the soil around the roots and water in.

Propagation *(continued)*

◀ Spider plants produce miniature plants (plantlets) on shoots from the mother plant. It is ideal to root these prior to removing them from the parent plant. Plantlets may be rooted in containers of water or pinned to soil to develop new roots. When they are well rooted, remove the plantlets from the mother plant and pot them into their new containers.

Plantlets

Several common houseplants reproduce by sending out miniature new plants on runners or shoots. These include spider plant, episcia, strawberry begonia, and many varieties of Boston fern. It is best to root plantlets before removing them from the parent plant. To do this pin the plantlets down to soil with a paper clip, usually in a second pot. After roots form—in about 3 to 4 weeks— snip and remove each plantlet from the parent plant and repot. Some plants produce plantlets on leaves, such as piggyback plant and mother-of-thousands. Any of these plantlets can be removed from the parent plant and rooted, similar to cuttings.

Offsets

Small new plants that form at the base of an old plant and remain attached to it are known as offsets. You can cut or break them off and plant them just as you would divisions. Detach offsets only when they are mature enough to survive on their own, usually when they have taken on the look of the mature plant and have some established root system. You can propagate screwpine and many bromeliads using this method. Although it's best to remove offsets that have already developed roots, in some cases, such as African violets, plants have offsets that can be rooted similar to cuttings. Plant unrooted offsets in moist growing mix until they are well rooted.

▲ Pin down the plantlets of strawberry begonias using a paper clip to keep the plantlet anchored to the potting soil. Keep the rooting media moist and the plantlet will soon develop roots of its own. It can then be severed from the mother plant and grown on in the rooting container.

OFFSETS

1 After flowering this silver vase plant grew offsets, called pups. To remove the pups and start new plants, pull the entire plant out of its pot. Slice through the root system between the old stem and the pup.

2 Place the newly severed pup into an individual pot filled with bromeliad mix. Keep the soil barely moist and the vase of the bromeliad filled with water until new roots expand into the potting mix.

Layering

Layering is a technique similar to rooting cuttings, except that the part of the plant (usually a branch) to be rooted remains attached to the parent plant. The great advantage of layering is that the parent plant supplies the new plant with water and nutrients while its roots form. Daily maintenance is therefore unnecessary. For plants slow to root this is a distinct advantage. There is one disadvantage: New plants develop more slowly from layering than from cuttings.

A suitable plant for soil layering has a branch or stem that's low enough for you to bend into contact with the growing mix. Creeping and trailing plants are ideal subjects for the technique. Note that many plants self-layer wherever they touch the soil. In this case simply detach the rooted branch and transplant it into a new pot.

LAYERING

1 Pin a node of vining stems of arrowhead vine to rooting media in individual pots. Use paper clips or bent pieces of wire to hold stems in place. Keep the media moist.

2 When roots have developed, cut the stem between the rooted cutting and the mother plant.

3 Combine several rooted cuttings together in a hanging basket or standard pot to produce a large plant quickly.

Cuttings

▲ A heating mat will speed rooting of most types of cuttings. Gentle bottom heat encourages new roots to grow. Place individual pots or flats with stem, cane, or root cuttings on the mat.

Growing houseplants from cuttings is the most popular method of vegetative propagation. It is an easy way to duplicate the attractive features of the original plant. The new plant is an exact genetic copy of the original.

Depending on the plant you can take cuttings from stems, leaves, or roots. Stem cuttings usually include a portion of the stem with some leaves and are 3 to 6 inches long. Each stem cutting should have two to six nodes. The tip end of the stem provides fastest results.

To take a stem cutting, make a clean cut. Remove excess leaves, allowing two or three to remain. Remove flowers, flower buds, or seeds to direct all energy into producing roots rather than blooms or seeds. Remove any damaged leaves or those below the soil line. To speed rooting dip the cutting in rooting hormone and insert the base of the cutting 1 to 3 inches deep into the propagation mix. Although some gardeners routinely dip all cuttings in rooting hormone before planting, this step is not necessary for all plants and may inhibit fast rooting plants such as coleus and Swedish ivy. Plants with slightly woody stems, such as miniature rose, are more likely to benefit from use of a rooting hormone. You can buy extra-strength rooting hormone for woody cuttings that are especially difficult to root.

Adding bottom heat from heating cables may be useful for some difficult-to-root cuttings. When propagating succulents, cacti, and ficus, allow the cut surface to air dry before sticking the cutting. This allows callous tissue to form on the cut end and helps prevent diseases.

Cuttings will root in a variety of media: in commercial rooting mix, in vermiculite, in soilless potting mix, or in water. Most plants require constantly moist mix for rooting. Plants that need to dry out need a rooting mix that is kept barely moist.

Most cuttings benefit from a high humidity environment. You can use a professional propagating unit. Most have a plastic tray with a clear plastic dome cover. Often the cover has air vents so you can adjust humidity levels. Fill the tray about three-fourths full with moist rooting medium. Add cuttings in rows or in specific areas of the tray. You can incorporate a small

CUTTINGS IN WATER

1 Remove a 4- to 6-inch-long stem tip cutting from Japanese peperomia. Use a clean sharp knife or bypass pruner to make the cut just below a node. Remove lower leaves, and any buds, flowers, or seeds.

2 Place cuttings in water. If necessary, use a section of aluminum foil to create a support for the cuttings. (Place the foil over the container of water, poke holes through the foil, and stick the stems through the holes into water.) Place the container with cuttings in an area with good light but out of direct sun. Monitor water level and refill as necessary. When roots develop on the cuttings, plant them into potting soil.

3 Stems with new turgid white roots are ready for potting into their own pots. Use a growing medium that suits the specific plant. You may find it helpful to use a pencil to open space in the medium for the cutting so you do not damage tender new roots. Place the cutting in media, lightly firm soil around it, and water.

CUTTINGS IN POTTING MIX

1 Propagate plants by taking 4- to 6-inch-long stem tip cuttings. Use a sharp clean knife or bypass pruners to cut just below a node.

2 Remove lower leaves from the cutting and dip the base of the cutting in rooting hormone. Make a hole in the rooting medium with a pencil, insert the cutting, and firm the medium around the stem.

3 Keep potted cuttings in a high humidity enclosure such as this propagator made from a wire frame covered in polyethylene. A clear plastic zipper enclosure bag works well for an individual pot.

propagation heating cable. Keep the propagator in an area with bright light but no direct sun. Clear plastic sweater boxes make a low budget propagator or you can use deli containers with clear plastic tops to fashion a homemade propagator.

You can also place cuttings in individual pots containing moistened rooting media. You can keep the entire pot enclosed in a plastic bag and out of sun until cuttings start to grow. Acclimate rooted cuttings to room conditions by opening the plastic bag gradually.

Compressed peat pellets are another option for starting cuttings. Moisten the pellets prior to use. They will expand when water is added. Use an ice pick, pencil, or other tool to make a hole slightly larger in diameter than the stem cutting. Place the cutting into the hole and squeeze the pot a bit to firm the cutting in place. Enclose the pellets and cuttings in a propagating box until roots develop. After rooting pot the cutting and pellet into growing medium. This prevents transplant shock.

Start easy-to-root plants, such as pothos and wandering Jew, by placing

4-to 6-inch-long tip cuttings in a glass of water. If necessary use a section of aluminum foil to hold the cutting in place. Once roots form transfer the cuttings to soil. Few root hairs develop on cuttings rooted in water. Some experts suggest this delays formation of a typical root system and that you are better off propagating plants in a soilless rooting medium.

Cane cuttings

Some plants, such as dieffenbachia and dracaena, can be propagated from cane cuttings. Place 3- to 6-inch-long cut sections of the cane vertically or horizontally in premoistened rooting media. Be sure that each cane section has at least two nodes. Keep the rooting medium moist and cover the container with plastic to increase humidity. It will take several weeks to several months for new growth to develop. Bottom heat speeds development of new roots and shoots. When the cutting grows roots about 1 inch long, plant them into pots for growing on. Acclimate rooted cuttings to their new location because they are coming out of a high humidity environment.

CANE CUTTINGS

1 Cut bare stems of dieffenbachia into 3- to 6-inch sections. The leafy top could be treated as a stem tip cutting.

2 Place cane cuttings horizontally onto premoistened rooting media. Each cane section should have at least two nodes contacting the media.

3 After cane sections develop strong roots, pot the sections into appropriate growing media. Slowly acclimate the potted cuttings to typical humidity.

▲ Take leaf cuttings or leaf petiole cuttings (include the stem that attaches the leaf to the main stem) of African violets. Cut a healthy leaf from a parent plant using a clean sharp knife. Use a leaf of medium size and age. Begonias, peperomias, florist gloxinias, sedums, kalanchoes, echeverias, and jade plants also can be grown from leaf cuttings. Leaf petiole cuttings work with rex and rhizomatous begonias, episcia, gloxinia, hoya, peperomia, and steptocarpus.

Leaf cuttings

Only a few plants reproduce from leaf cuttings, including African violets, some begonias and peperomias, florist gloxinia, sedum, kalanchoe, echeveria, and jade plant. To take a leaf cutting simply cut a healthy leaf from the parent plant and stick the leaf in moist rooting medium. Firm the medium around the base of the leaf. For succulent leaves allow the cut end to dry (callus) for a day or so before sticking the cutting. A leaf cutting must initiate both roots and shoots and usually takes longer to develop a mature plant than does a stem cutting.

Some plants can grow a new plant from the leaf petiole, the short stem that attaches the leaf to the main stem. These include African violet, rex and rhizomatous begonias, episcia, gloxinia, hoya, peperomia, and streptocarpus. Cut a medium-size and medium-age leaf with petiole attached and place the petiole in rooting medium. Florist gloxinia and other sinningias take a long time to propagate this way because they must produce a tuber before new roots and shoots develop.

Certain plants, such as snake plant, streptocarpus, gloxinia, African violet, and some begonias, produce a new plant from a section of leaf. To propagate snake plant from cuttings, cut the long leaf blades into 3- to 4-inch-long sections. Orient the sections in the same direction they grew on the original plant. To avoid confusion notch the upper end of each leaf section. Insert the cuttings, notch-end up, into barely moist rooting media. After the new plant forms, cut away and discard the old leaf section. For streptocarpus and rex and fibrous begonias you can cut along the leaf midrib, removing it. Place the remaining leaf half cut end down in rooting media. Each

▲ Use rooting hormone powder or liquid hormone solution to speed root development. Dip the cut end of the leaf in the powder or liquid. Make a hole in the rooting medium with a pencil before inserting the hormone-treated leaf. Keep the cutting in high humidity until it forms new roots.

◄ You may use sections of snake plant leaves for propagation. Maintain the correct orientation of the leaf cuttings by notching the top of each 3- to 4-inch-long section.

◄ Place sections with the notch up into pots containing barely moist growing media, then firm the medium around each section. Keep pots in bright light out of direct sun, and keep the soil barely moist until new shoots and roots develop.

LEAF CUTTINGS

1
Each burro's tail leaf can grow into a new plant. Remove individual leaves from the plant and allow them to dry for a day. Place each leaf stem side down into potting soil. Keep the soil barely moist and the pots in bright light but not direct sun.

2
New shoots soon emerge from each leaf. Allow shoots to grow until a small clump of leaves develops. Transplant them into a larger pot.

3
This burro's tail plant has begun to arch over the edge of the pot. It was produced from a single leaf placed into one pot. Place several together for quicker results.

vein along that leaf may produce a new plant.

Root cuttings

A few plants, such as ti plant, propagate from latent buds in their roots. To propagate a plant from a root cutting, place 2-inch-long sections of thick root horizontally in rooting medium, similar to the process described for cane cuttings (see page 75). When a plantlet forms transplant it as you would other cuttings that have rooted.

Air layering

Air layering works well for some plants, such as dieffenbachia, dracaena, and ficus, that develop thick woody stems that may not respond well to stem cutting. The technique is especially useful for salvaging leggy plants or mature specimens that have lost most of their lower leaves.
1. Use a sharp knife to scar two sides of the trunk at the desired height, usually just below the remaining leaves, or cut an open lip of stem on both sides and keep open with a thin piece of wood or wooden match stick.
2. Sprinkle a pinch of rooting hormone onto a couple handfuls of moist sphagnum moss and place the moss around the two cut scars, holding it in place with a piece of clean polyethylene.
3. Secure the polyethylene by tying a twist tie at each end (top and bottom), keeping the interior as airtight as possible, and check occasionally that it is still moist.
4. Once the new roots begin to grow in the moss (you'll be able to see them through the poly), cut off the top of the plant just below the new roots, creating a new plant.
5. Pot up the air-layered cutting in new soil and care for it as you would the parent plant. New shoots may sprout on the old stem as well, so don't discard it.

AIR LAYERING

1
To air layer a leggy woody plant first scar the stem with a sharp knife.

2
Surround the scarred stem with moist long-fiber sphagnum moss.

3
Wrap the moss in plastic and secure with a twist tie at the top and bottom.

4
Keep the moss moist and watch for new root development.

5
Cut the rooted section from the stem and pot it up.

Seeds and spores

Many houseplants may be started from seeds in the same way as garden plants. Collect seed from your own plants or purchase from seed retailers, garden centers, and mail-order nurseries. Many plant societies have seed exchanges with seeds available of rare species and plants recently collected from the wild. Remember that seeds from hybrid plants will not be an exact copy of their parent plant. Look for seed packets with descriptions of cultural needs. Check the fine print for special instructions on light and sowing depth.

Seed starting

To start seeds fill a tray or shallow pot with slightly moist sterile seed-starting mix. Dust the top of the mix with milled sphagnum moss. The sphagnum is helpful in preventing damping off, a fungal disease that quickly kills seedlings. Use an index card or other stiff paper folded in half to sow seeds in a regular pattern on the mix. Put the seedling tray in a warm (70–75°F) room with bright, indirect light and readily available water. Bottom heat from cables or mats will speed germination.

SEED STARTING

1 Most houseplant seeds are small and take a long time to germinate. Sow them on the surface of a seed starting mix. Add a thin layer of milled sphagnum moss to help prevent damping off. Moisten the seeds and potting mix, and enclose them in a plastic bag or cover with plastic wrap to hold in moisture. Place the flat in bright light out of direct sun and keep the media moist.

2 As seedlings emerge remove the plastic covering and move the container into brighter light. Once they sprout, seedlings require full-spectrum light such as that from the sun or from fluorescent tubes hung several inches above the seedlings. These begonia seedlings are compact and healthy, indicating that they are receiving adequate light.

3 When true leaves appear transplant seedlings to individual pots. Use a pencil to pry seedlings from the seed starting container without damaging the seedlings' fragile roots. You can also use the pencil to create a shallow planting hole in the new pot. Keep the seedlings moist and begin feeding when they are two to three weeks old.

For greater success with seeds, remember that large, hard seeds (including those of palms if they appear dry) should be soaked in tepid water overnight before sowing. Cover large seeds to a depth twice their diameter, firming the growing mix around each seed by pressing gently on the soil surface.

Scatter tiny seeds such as those of primrose, cyclamen, streptocarpus, and florist gloxinia on top of moist growing mix and leave them uncovered. Sow medium-size seeds such as those of ornamental pepper and coleus on the growing mix and cover them with a thin layer of seedling mix or milled sphagnum moss. Water lightly to settle the seed in place by misting the mix. Then slip the seed tray or pot into a clear plastic bag or cover it with glass, plastic, or a clear lid.

When seedlings emerge remove the covering and move the container into brighter light. Once they sprout, seedlings require full-spectrum light such as that provided by the sun or a fluorescent grow light. A greenhouse is an ideal place to grow seedlings. But a light stand with adjustable fluorescent tubes hung several inches above the top of the seedlings works well too. Raise the light gradually as seedlings grow in order to produce sturdy plants.

When true leaves appear thin the plants or pot individual seedlings. Keep the seedlings moist and begin feeding them when they are two to three weeks old.

Spores

Unlike most other plants, ferns produce spores, not seeds. You will need plenty of patience to propagate ferns from their dustlike spores.

Spores are similar to seeds but are smaller and much slower to sprout and grow. Sow spores on damp seeding mix as you would other fine seeds. Dust with a coating of milled sphagnum moss and mist frequently. Cover with clear plastic to keep the humidity high in the germination tray. Keep spores constantly moist; they can take months to sprout. After sprouting they can remain enclosed in the high-humidity chamber much longer. Wait until the small ferns approach transplanting size before removing the plastic lid.

STARTING A FERN FROM SPORES

1 Ferns produce spores rather than seeds. Spores are much smaller than most seeds. To collect spores place a mature fern frond on a piece of smooth white paper in a dry, wind-free area. Ripe spore cases will shed black, brown, or yellow powder, that is a mixture of spores and fragments of the cases.

2 Carefully crease the paper and collect the spores in the center. Have a container ready with an inch or two of sterile moistened growing mix. Sparsely sprinkle the spores on the surface of the mix. Mist the mix and keep it moist.

3 Cover the container with clear plastic to keep the humidity high in the germination tray. Spores will take 2 to 8 weeks to germinate. Keep the tray enclosed until small ferns develop and approach transplanting size.

Troubleshooting

▲ Give your plants a thorough examination regularly. Use a magnifying glass for a closer look. Some pests are tiny and hard to detect. Catching a problem early can prevent it from getting out of control and spreading to other plants in your collection. Isolate problem plants while you take steps to control the pest.

In an ideal world you would bring your new healthy plant home, give it the perfect spot where the growing conditions are just right and with basic care the plant would thrive. However conditions aren't perfect, life gets busy, and you forget to water and feed your plants. Stressed and neglected plants are susceptible to diseases and insect infestations. All of these problems are much easier to correct if caught early. Make it a habit to really look at your plants each time you water. Look for obvious problems and subtle clues of insects or diseases. Immediately isolate any problem plant and work to control the problem. Check the plants in the area to make sure the problem has not spread; check them again a few days later. Use the information in this chapter to identify and fix the problem. With diligence and a little know-how, you will keep your plants healthy and attractive.

LEAF PROBLEMS

Symptom	Potential Cause	Action Steps
Leaves curl	Aphids	Remove aphids with forceful water spray; wipe leaves with a cotton swab dipped in rubbing alcohol; spray with indoor oil spray or other insecticide
Leaves curl & drop	Cold draft; underwatering	Check growing area to confirm its suitability for lack of drafts; check growing media for dryness or shrinkage away from pot's edge; repot if required and improve watering regime
Leaf drop, sudden & severe	Shock from moving	Increase humidity; water when soil mix dries out; wait for new growth
Leaf drop, lower leaves	Temperature too high	Check plant growth requirements & move to more suitable location if necessary
Leaf drop, lower leaves	Not enough light	Check plant growth requirements & move to more suitable location if necessary
Leaves lose sheen, lack normal color	Mealybugs and/or spider mites	Apply rubbing alcohol with cotton swab or spray 50/50 alcohol & water for mealybugs; spray insecticidal soap, indoor oil spray or commercial insecticide for either
Leaves lose sheen, lack normal color	Too much light	Move plant to lower light
Leaves develop brown tips or leaf margins	Low humidity; underwatering	Increase humidity by grouping plants, place on a pebble tray with water, or use a humidifier; water more frequently and more thoroughly
Variegated leaves turn green	Insufficient light; excess nitrogen	Move plant to brighter light; use plant food with lower level of nitrogen
Leaves wilt	Under- or overwatering	Improve watering pattern; repot if pot-bound or unsuitable growing mix

FLOWER PROBLEMS

Symptom	Potential Cause	Action Steps
Buds turn brown, don't open, fall off	Bud blast	Increase humidity; maintain adequate moisture in soil mix; move plant to area with lower temperatures
Plant does not produce buds and flowers	Insufficient light	Improve duration and intensity of light
Plant does not produce buds and flowers	Wrong day length	Confirm day length requirements; alter pattern for long- or short-day plant
Plant does not produce buds and flowers	Temperature drop needed	Provide 10–15°F night time temperature drop
Plant does not produce buds and flowers	Dormant period required	Provide adequate dormant, cool period
Flowers fade quickly	Temperature too high	Keep at lower temperature
Flowers fade quickly	Low humidity	Improve humidity with pebble tray or humidifier
Flowers fade quickly	Underwatering	Improve watering pattern

WHOLE PLANT PROBLEMS

Symptom	Potential Cause	Action Steps
Slow growth	Pot-bound plant	Check for roots growing out of or massed in pot; repot if required
Slow growth	Cultural challenges	Confirm plant's needs; improve soil mix, watering, feeding, light, and humidity if less than ideal
Slow growth	Natural dormant/slow growth period	Wait for season change; reduce watering until active growth resumes
Small lumps on stems or leaves; loss of vigor	Scale	Wash plant in soapy water; spray with indoor oil or commercial insecticide
Gray-white coating on leaves, stems	Powdery mildew	Isolate plant; remove infected areas; improve growing conditions; spray with commercial fungicide

Pests

Check your plants for signs of insects or disease every time you water them to find pests before they become a severe problem. Move infected or infested plants away from others and check nearby plants to make sure the problem has not already spread. Use the information provided here to diagnose and fix the problem. Always use the least toxic effective control method available. For example you may be able to control small populations of sucking insects by washing plants in warm soapy water, then rinsing plants with clean water. If you use an insect control product or disease control product, check the label to make sure that your plant's pest is listed and follow the instructions carefully.

Aphids

Aphids on bloodleaf

Problem: New leaves are curled, discolored, and smaller than normal. A shiny or sticky substance may coat them. Small (⅛ inch) soft-bodied green, pink, yellow, black, brown, or gray insects cluster on buds, young stems, and leaves. Aphids are extremely prolific and reproduce rapidly. Damage results when they suck sap from leaves and stems. They excrete excess sugar in a fluid called honeydew, which often drops onto leaves or surfaces below.

Solution: Rinse the foliage under the faucet every several days or take infested plants outdoors and knock off the aphids with a strong stream of water. Wipe off aphids with cotton swabs dipped in rubbing alcohol. Spray weekly with insecticidal soap or an insect control product.

Cyclamen mites

Cyclamen mite damage to African violet

Problem: The stem tips or new growth in the plant center becomes severely stunted. Leaves become brittle, stay small, and may be cupped or curved; their color may change to bronze, gray, or tan. Flower buds fail to develop properly and do not open.

Solution: Spray infested plants several times with an insecticidal soap or a miticide and then isolate them. Discard heavily infested plants. Scour the pots and wash the area where the pots were sitting with a solution of 1 part household bleach to 9 parts water. Observe nearby plants so you can spray if symptoms appear. Avoid touching infested plants and then touching healthy plants.

Fungus gnats

Adult fungus gnat

Problem: Small (⅛ inch) slender, dark insects fly around when plants are disturbed. They frequently run across the foliage and soil and may be found on windows. Fungus gnats are small flies that do little damage. They lay their eggs in soil that contains decaying organic material. After a week the eggs hatch and the larvae crawl through the upper layer of the soil. The larvae are white, ¼ inch long, and have black heads. When present in large numbers, larvae feed on the roots of some plants, killing seedlings.

Solution: Place yellow sticky traps directly on potting soil to catch adults. Let potting mix dry more between waterings. Larvae cannot survive in dry soil. Apply *Bacillus thuringiensis israelensis* to the soil.

Mealybugs

Mealybugs on cycad leaf

Problem: White cottony or waxy insects in small clusters on the undersides of leaves, on stems, and in the leaf joints. Egg masses also may be present. Honeydew, a sticky excretion, may cover the leaves or drop onto surfaces below. Leaves may be spotted or deformed. Infested plants are unsightly, do not grow well, and may die.

Solution: Control is difficult. Wipe off pests with a damp cloth or use cotton swabs dipped in rubbing alcohol. Also wipe off any egg sacs under the rims or on the bottoms of pots. For serious infestations spray stems and both sides of leaves with a solution of 50% rubbing alcohol and water. After a few minutes wash the plant in warm soapy water and rinse. You can also thoroughly spray the soil, stems, and both sides of the leaves with an insect control product or insecticidal soap.

Scale

Scale insects on palm

Problem: Nodes, stems, and leaves or fronds are covered with cottony white masses, crusty brown bumps, or clusters of flattened reddish gray or brown scaly bumps that can be soft or hard. A sticky excretion called honeydew may cover the plant parts and drip on surfaces below. Leaves or fronds turn yellow and may drop. The young, called crawlers, are small (about 1/10 inch) and soft bodied. They feed on the sap. Eventually their legs disappear, but the scales remain in place.

Solution: Wash the plant in warm soapy water. Pick off scales by hand or use a soft toothbrush to remove them. The young can hide under adult shells, so remove all scales as soon as possible. Insecticidal soap or indoor horticultural oil is most effective on crawlers; oil can work on both.

Spider mites

Problem: Leaves are stippled, yellow, dirty looking, and lose their sheen; they may dry out and drop. There may be webbing over flower buds, between leaves, or on the lower surfaces of the leaves. Tap a leaf or stem sharply over a sheet of white paper. Minute specks will drop to the paper and crawl around. Spider mites multiply rapidly. They are visible through a magnifying lens. By the time you see webbing, the infestation is severe. Spider mites cause damage by sucking sap from the undersides of leaves.

Solution: Rinse infested plants in the shower or with a hose every few days or spray them weekly with an insect control product, insecticidal soap, or indoor horticultural oil. Discard badly infested plants. Increased humidity discourages reproduction.

Spider mites on dracaena

Thrips

Thrips damage on chrysanthemum

Problem: Flowers and leaves are abnormally mottled or streaked with silver. Young leaves and flowers may be distorted. Pollen sacs on African violets spill open, leaving yellow powder on the flowers. Dusty black droppings collect on leaves or flowers. Tiny (up to 1/16 inch) dark insects scuttle away when you breathe on the plant. Both adult and immature thrips damage plant surfaces with their rasping mouths. They hide in crevices between stems and flowers and lay eggs inside plant tissues or in the potting mix.

Solution: Thrips reproduce many times each year, so remove heavily damaged leaves and flowers to reduce infestation. Use blue sticky cards or blue stiff paper coated with petroleum jelly for low-level control. Apply an insect control product or insecticidal soap to affected plants and potting mix weekly.

Whiteflies

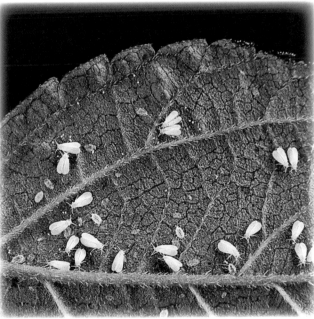

Whitefly adults and larvae

Problem: Tiny (1/16 inch) winged white insects flutter around the plant when you touch it. Translucent scalelike larvae are present under leaves. Leaves may be mottled and yellow. Whiteflies excrete excess sap, which coats the leaves and may drop from the plant.

Solution: Isolate infested plants. Use yellow sticky cards to catch adults. Wipe off larvae with a damp cloth or cotton swab soaked in rubbing alcohol, or shake the plant and vacuum up the cloud of flies. Spray severe infestations weekly with insecticidal soap, an insect control product, or indoor horticultural oil.

Diseases

Bacterial spot

Bacterial spot on heart-leaf philodendron

Problem: Leaves, stems, or both develop many spots that look dark and wet and are sometimes circled by a yellow halo. Wet and crowded conditions cause bacterial spot.

Solution: Remove the diseased plant parts, dipping your shears in a solution of 1 part household bleach to 9 parts water or wiping the blades with rubbing alcohol after each cut. Avoid wetting foliage and water less frequently until plants recover and begin new growth. To prevent recurrence put the plants in a warmer location, increase air circulation around each pot, and do not mist susceptible plants.

Bacterial stem blight

Bacterial stem blight on dwarf schefflera

Problem: Soft, sunken areas with water-soaked margins appear on the stems. Affected areas sometimes crack. Lower leaves may turn yellow and wilt. The stem may rot through so the top of the plant breaks off. Inner stem tissue is brown. Bacterial stem blight is caused by the bacterium *Erwinia chrysanthemi.*

Solution: No cure exists. Discard infected plants. If some stems are still healthy, cut them off above the diseased area and root them. Do not root any stems that have brown streaks. Propagate in an isolated area to ensure only clean material is used. To prevent bacterial stem blight, use a well-drained potting mix and avoid splashing leaves with water. Avoid wetting the plant when watering. Discard excess water after 30 minutes. Increase air circulation around the plant.

Botrytis

Botrytis on begonia

Problem: A grayish mold covers the affected surfaces. Light brown patches on leaves, stems, or flowers gradually darken and turn soft and moist. Infected plant parts curl up and fall off. Botrytis, or gray mold, is a common airborne fungal disease that spreads quickly and is common during periods of high humidity, cool temperatures, and inside closed containers, such as terrariums, where the problem is most common. When the plant stem is infected, the entire plant may rot away.

Solution: Remove infected plant parts and isolate the plant in an area with improved air circulation and low humidity. Bottom water only and do not mist susceptible plants.

If this does not solve the problem, spray the rest of the plant with a disease control product or fungicidal soap. Discard badly infected plants.

Crown, stem, and root rot

Crown, stem, and root rot on orchid

Problem: Plants fail to grow. Leaves appear dull, then turn black. Lower ones may turn yellow and drop. Leaves in the center of the plant turn dark green, then black. When the condition is severe, all the roots are rotted and the plant may wilt and die. Rot is caused by soil-dwelling fungi *(Pythium)* or water molds, that attack the roots. It usually indicates that the plant has been watered too frequently or that the soil mix does not drain well.

Solution: Let the soil dry between waterings or transplant into a fast draining potting mix in a container that drains freely. Discard severely infected plants and soil. Soak empty pots in a mixture of 1 part household bleach to 9 parts water for 30 minutes. Then rinse with water and dry thoroughly before reuse. Wash your hands before touching healthy plants.

Leaf spot

Problem: Circular reddish brown spots surrounded by yellow margins appear on the leaves. Several spots may form a blotch. Badly spotted leaves may turn yellow and die. Leaf spot is caused by one of several fungi, including *Septoria*. Spotting is unsightly but not always fatal.

Leaf spot on red-edge peperomia

Solution: Clip off badly spotted leaves. Bottom water to avoid leaf splash and keep the foliage dry to help prevent the spread of the fungus. This is usually enough to control the problem. If spotting continues, spray the plant with a disease control product or fungicidal soap.

Powdery mildew

Powdery mildew on grape ivy

Problem: White or gray powdery patches develop on the surface of leaves, stems, and flowers, usually appearing first on older leaves and the upper surfaces of leaves. Tissue under the powdery growth may turn yellow or brown. Affected leaves may drop. The powdery patches are fungus strands and spores. Windborne spores can reach nearby plants and infect them. The disease favors low light, dry soil, and warm days with cool nights.

Solution: Isolate an infected plant in a location with more light and better air circulation. Allow soil mix to dry out more. Remove infected leaves. If this fails to control the problem, spray plants with a disease control product or fungicidal soap weekly until the disease is gone.

Sooty mold

Sooty mold on dwarf schefflera

Problem: This black coating on leaf surfaces can easily be rubbed or washed off. Several different fungi present in air and water produce sooty mold, which often reappears a few weeks after it is removed. The coating blocks the leaf pores and slows down or stops photosynthesis.

Solution: Physically removing sooty mold is the first step, but it is a sign of a serious insect infestation. Aphids, whiteflies, mealybugs, and scale insects are the most common houseplant insects that excrete a sticky fluid called honeydew after they pierce and suck plant tissues. This creates an ideal environment for the growth of sooty mold. Identify and control the insects to prevent the return of sooty mold.

Virus

Problem: Plants grow slowly and without vigor. Leaves are lightly mottled or streaked with yellow; they also may show ringed yellow spots. Leaves can be distorted. Viruses are carried from plant to plant by insects, people, or on infected tools.

Solution: No cure exists for infected plants. Destroy them. To prevent viruses control insects through preventive treatment. When pruning dip tools into rubbing alcohol or a solution of 1 part household bleach to 9 parts water between each cut.

Geranim crinkle virus

Cultural problems

Bud blast

Bud blast on hibiscus

Problem: Flower buds form but fail to open. They may turn yellow or brown shortly after forming or attain nearly full size before discoloration appears. Sometimes they simply drop off. Dry air is the most common cause. Other causes are air pollution, excessive heat or cold, too much fertilizer, too little or too much water, and fungal disease. Bud blast is common in young houseplants and others, such as gardenia. It also occurs with plants moved suddenly from a greenhouse to a home environment.
Solution: As the plant nears its flowering cycle, place it on a humidity tray (see page 50) or in a room with a humidifier to increase humidity. Use a large dry cleaner bag to create a temporary greenhouse. Gradually acclimate the plant to ambient room humidity by making holes in the bag. Move plants out of direct sunlight and away from air-conditioning and heating vents. Provide cooler night temperatures.

Cold injury

Cold injury to baby's tears

Problem: Plants fail to grow and are stunted. Leaves may turn silvery or brown, especially on the part of the plant closest to the source of cold, such as a window. Sensitive plants may lose leaves suddenly. Edema or root rot may develop.
Solution: Keep cold-sensitive plants away from windows and air-conditioning ducts. Move them to a warmer location or place a barrier such as an insulated curtain between the plant and the source of cold. Reduce frequency of watering and feeding at cool temperatures.

Dry soil

Dry soil effects on red flame ivy

Problem: Leaves are small; the plant fails to grow well and may be stunted. Plant parts or the whole plant wilts. The edges of broad leaves or the tips of narrow leaves may dry out and become brittle, but they retain a dull green color. Bleached areas may occur between the veins. Leaf tissues may die and remain bleached or turn tan or brown. The plant may die.
Solution: Water the plant thoroughly. If the soil is completely dry, soak the entire pot in water for a couple of hours. Repot in a more appropriate soil mix or if the plant is pot-bound.

Edema

Edema on the leaf underside of peperomia 'Jayde'

Problem: Brown corky patches appear on stems or leaves. Scratching off the patches reveals underlying healthy cells. Too much water, especially during humid weather, is usually the cause of edema. Cells swell up with moisture and burst, then scab tissue forms as the plant heals, leading to a corky appearance. Sucking insects, such as spider mites, may also cause edema on some plants, notably succulents.
Solution: Cut away badly damaged tissues. Prevent edema by watering less frequently, especially when the air is humid and light levels are low. Also check for and control spider mites and other insects. Increase air movement with fans.

Failure to bloom

Problem: The plant fails to flower during its blooming season. No signs of insects or diseases are visible.

Solution: The plant may be too immature to flower. The three most common causes of failure to bloom in mature plants are lack of light, insufficient humidity, and improper temperature. Move the plant to

Failure to bloom in African violet

a brighter spot, place it on a humidity tray (see page 50), and check its temperature requirements. A lack of minerals or an excess of nitrogen could be the cause; give the plant a flowering plant food. Check for insect infestation.

Guttation

Guttation on the leaf underside of homalomena

Problem: Drops of water or sap collect on the tips or the undersides of leaves. They may blacken or form translucent crystals as they dry. Excess soil moisture is the most common cause of guttation. The plant absorbs more water than it can use, causing it to secrete the excess through its leaves. A small amount of guttation is normal in some plants such as dieffenbachia.

Solution: Reduce watering so the plant does not absorb excessive amounts of moisture. Increase light and air circulation and lower humidity so any moisture exuded evaporates rapidly.

High temperature injury

High temperature injury to cyclamen

Problem: Outer leaves turn yellow, then brown, and may die. Stems become soft. The plant stops flowering. High temperatures cause problems for cool-weather plants, which tolerate warm days as long as nights are cool (below 60°F).

Solution: Grow cool-weather plants in a cool room with as much light as possible. If a cool room is not available, put the plants near a window at night. When temperatures are not below freezing, putting the plants outside at night will promote flowering. Keep plants adequately watered and fed. Increase air circulation.

Iron deficiency

Iron deficiency in calamondin orange

Problem: The newest leaves are yellow at the edges. The yellowing progresses inward; in advanced stages the last tissues to lose their green color are the veins. In severe cases the entire leaf is yellow and small, and the plant may be stunted. Iron deficiency is a common problem in acid-loving plants. When the soil pH is 7.5 or higher (alkaline), iron is chemically unavailable to some plants.

Solution: Spray the foliage with a solution containing chelated iron and drench the soil in the pot. Use an acid-based plant food for the plant's regular feeding. When planting or transplanting acid-loving plants, use an acidic growing mix that contains at least 50 percent peat moss. Do not add lime or dolomite.

Cultural problems *(continued)*

Leaf drop

Leaf drop on weeping fig

Problem: After you move the plant to a new location, numerous leaves first turn yellow and then drop off.

Solution: Purchase plants that have been acclimated to local conditions rather than shipped directly from a field or greenhouse to the store and sold immediately. Put plants in the brightest light possible and increase humidity. Cover new plants with a clear plastic bag to temporarily increase humidity while the plants adjust to lower light and humidity. Keep plants away from cold drafts.

Low light

Low light discoloration on 'Florida Beauty' gold dust dracaena

Problem: The plant fails to grow well. Stems and leafstalks may elongate and grow spindly and weak. Leaves may be lighter green and smaller than normal. Typical leaf shape, lobes, and openings in mature leaves may not develop. Lower leaves may yellow and drop. The plant bends toward a light source. A flowering plant fails to produce flowers, and a plant with colorful foliage becomes pale. A variegated plant may lose its variegation.

Solution: Gradually move the plant to a brighter location. Close sheer curtains when the sun shines directly on the plant. If necessary provide supplemental lighting.

Low humidity

Problem: Growth is slow and leaves tend to curl downward. The plant wilts rapidly and needs frequent watering. Flower buds and new leaves wither or fail to develop properly. Leaf edges and tips may turn brown and dry up.

Solution: Place the plant on a humidity tray (see page 50) or keep it in a room with a humidifier. Water as soon as the potting mix is dry just below the top inch. Group plants so the moisture given off by transpiration increases the air humidity around them all. Move the affected plant to a cooler, less sunny spot.

Low humidity effects on fern

Nitrogen deficiency

Nitrogen deficiency in ribbon plant

Problem: The oldest leaves, usually the lower ones, turn yellow and may drop. Yellowing starts at the leaf edges and progresses inward. Growth is slow, new leaves are small, and the whole plant may be stunted. Nitrogen is easily leached from soil during regular watering.

Solution: Spray the leaves with a foliar plant food. Fee the plant with a soluble plant food rich in nitrogen. If there is room in the pot, topdress the soil with pasteurized organic material. Apply a continuous-feed plant food to prevent reoccurrence of nitrogen deficiency.

Overwatering

Problem: The plant fails to grow and may wilt. Leaves lose their glossiness and may become light green or yellow. Roots are mushy and brown. The soil in the bottom of the pot may be soggy and have a foul odor. The plant may die.

Solution: Discard a severely wilted plant or one with brown, mushy roots. For a plant that is less severely affected, do not water again until the soil is almost dry (barely moist). Cut away damaged roots and repot. Prevent the problem by using a lightweight potting mix with good drainage and watering less frequently.

Yellow foliage from overwatering fiddle-leaf fig

Sunburn or leaf scorch

Sunburn or leaf scorch on wax plant

Problem: White, tan, or brown dead patches develop on leaves exposed to direct sunlight. Leaf tissues may lighten or turn gray. In some cases the plant remains green but growth is stunted. Damage is most severe when the plant is allowed to dry out. Sunburn or leaf scorch occurs when a plant is exposed to more intense sunlight than it can tolerate. A plant that is grown in low light burns easily if it is suddenly moved to a sunny location.

Solution: Move the plant to a shaded spot or close the curtains when the plant is exposed to direct sunlight. Prune off badly damaged leaves or trim away damaged leaf areas to improve the appearance of the plant. Keep the plant properly watered.

Salt damage

Salt damage to leaf tips of spider plant

Problem: Leaf edges of plants with broad leaves or the leaf tips of plants with long, narrow leaves turn brown and brittle. This browning occurs on the older leaves first; when the condition is severe, new leaves also are affected. On some plants the older leaves may yellow and die. Salt damage is a common problem found on container-grown plants.

Solution: Leach excess salts from the soil by regular flushing with water. Never let a plant stand in the drainage water. If the plant is too large to lift, empty the saucer with a turkey baster. Do not overfeed. Trim off dead stem tips with sharp scissors.

Water spots

Water spots on leaves of false African violet

Problem: White, yellow, or tan blotches in various patterns occur on older leaves. Small islands of green may be left between the discolored areas. Brown spots sometimes appear within the discolored areas. Water spots are a common problem on fuzzy-leaf plants. They occur most commonly when cold water is splashed on the leaves while the plant is being watered.

Solution: Avoid getting cold water on leaves when watering. Bottom water or use tepid water, which will not cause spotting if it touches the leaves. Spotted leaves will not recover. Remove them if they are unsightly.

Indoor specialties

◀ This colorful grouping of houseplants includes florist's cyclamen *(Cyclamen persicum)*, gardenia *(Gardenia augusta)*, cineraria *(Pericallis ×hybridus)*, and peace lily *(Spathiphyllum wallisii)*. Gardenias are among the most fragrant houseplants and present a rewarding challenge. Some growers specialize in growing fragrant plants, herbs, or small plants for terrariums, dish gardens, or basket gardens. Others force bulbs into flower for beauty and fragrance.

HERBS TO GROW INDOORS

The best herbs for indoor gardens are those grown for their foliage rather than their seeds. Purchase potted plants at garden centers in spring or start plants from cuttings or seed the rest of the year.

Easy:
Basil
Chives
Cuban oregano
Marjoram
Mint
Oregano
Parsley
Sage
Sweet bay
Thyme

Challenging:
Catnip
Chamomile
Cilantro
Lavender
Lemongrass
Lemon verbena
Myrtle
Rosemary
Tarragon
Winter savory

There are a number of nontraditional ways to use houseplants that can add to your growing pleasure. Often this is the case of using durable and basic plants in atypical ways. Combine plants in baskets, terrariums, or group them in dish gardens. These efforts can be large or small, complex or simple. Consider a small herb garden for the kitchen. There is nothing as satisfying and tasty as growing and cooking with fresh herbs. Try forcing some bulbs. It is fun, easy, and you can have color and fragrance in the cold, dreary months of the year.

Each of these efforts requires a bit more care and knowledge than growing a single plant and is a natural extension of love of houseplants. It may take some skill and careful attention to keep a basket or dish garden looking its best, but think what a wonderful accent it can be in your home or as a gift for a friend.

Perhaps the ultimate desire for the average houseplant grower is a greenhouse or conservatory. Many dream

▶ Rosemary *(Rosmarinus officinalis)* is a wonderful herb with a delightful resinous fragrance and a distinctive flavor. It is a bit of a challenge to grow indoors but is happy in bright light. Water it only when the top of the soil starts to dry.

▶ Basil (*Ocimum basilicum*) is easy to grow from seed. Sow a small amount of seed to grow a few plants at a time. It is an annual outdoors but can be maintained longer inside. Keep it in bright light, water it well, and snip leaves for cooking.

of walking into a warm miniparadise filled with lush tropical plants. If your current budget doesn't permit a greenhouse, enjoy some of the readily available indoor plant specialties.

Herbal delights

An indoor herb garden combines beauty with practicality. Herbs provide attractive foliage and fragrance and are useful in the kitchen. Most herbs grown indoors are for culinary use, but don't overlook cosmetic herbs in the bathroom, where they can be clipped and added to bathwater.

All good cooks know that fresh herbs are more flavorful than dried, so find a spot on a sunny windowsill, preferably in the kitchen, to grow a few pots. Herbs need at least 6 hours of sunlight a day or they become leggy and

disappointing. If you have no south or west window, use a fluorescent light placed 4 to 6 inches above the plants to enhance growth. Keep the light on for 12 to 16 hours a day. Move perennial woody herbs such as sage, thyme, and rosemary outdoors in summer.

Frequent harvesting of herbs not only benefits the cook, it also helps the plants by encouraging bushy new growth. Make harvesting cuts just above a leaf node or bud. Avoid removing more than one-third of the leaves from a plant at a time. A strong pruning can severely set back a potted plant. If you use large quantities of fresh herbs, keep backup plants on hand to make sure you have an ample supply. For fast growing ones, such as basil, regularly start new plants from seed.

Average room temperatures are fine for

herbs. Most should dry out a bit between waterings. Water the plants thoroughly when the soil dries down a half-inch or so. Use a well-drained soil mix and a container with

a drainage hole so that the roots do not sit in water. Most herbs look attractive in terra-cotta pots, but you can also grow them in ceramic or plastic pots. Aim for medium to high humidity and keep plants away from gas fumes and cold drafts. The essential oils that provide flavor and aroma in herbs are most prevalent when the plants are kept on the "lean" side. Feed infrequently.

Prevent pest problems by making sure plants receive adequate sunlight, proper watering, and good air circulation. Locate herbs where there is good air movement or provide them with a small fan. The most common insects found on herbs are spider mites and aphids. Wash or spray the foliage with water to minimize insect pests. Do not use chemical insect controls if you plan to use the herbs for cooking.

◀ Snip chive leaves when you need them for cooking or as a garnish. The fresh leaves add a mild oniony flavor to any dish. The bright green color of fresh chives adds zest and life to recipes that call for the herb.

Basket gardens

Basket gardens are a hot trend in indoor gardening. Walk into any garden center or florist shop and you'll see an array of artfully arranged wicker baskets brimming with indoor plants. They are a nice alternative to cut flowers, and they make especially nice housewarming gifts, since the new homeowner ends up with several plants instead of just one. Most last for weeks or even months with little care.

Basket gardens differ from dish gardens in that the plants may remain in their individual containers and are set on moist peat. The individual plants grow into each other and show each other off. Choose plants based on color, shape, texture, and size. Plants may be all of the same kind (several foliage begonias), or they may be a mix of flowering and foliage plants with similar light and temperature requirements.

The basket lends some clues for the types of plants to use. A rush basket calls for bold plants. A dark-color basket looks nice with light-color and variegated foliage and white flowers. Light-color baskets look best with deep green foliage and hot-color flowers. Tall baskets call for tall or trailing plants. Fill the basket to the brim with plants and have leaves or branches cascading over the edges.

When choosing plants keep in mind that most of the plants will eventually need to be potted up and moved to conditions better suited to their long-term health. If your home (or the home of the recipient of a gift basket) is lacking in areas with good bright light, choose plants that can get by on less light.

Basket gardens need careful attention to watering. The peat moss and proximity of plants help reduce watering needs. However, because individual containers are small, check plants daily for water needs. Keep an eye out for pest problems, which can quickly escalate when plants are grown in such tight proximity. Remove yellowing foliage and faded flowers as they appear.

▲ Combine foliage and blooming houseplants in a basket for fun and pleasure. This combination of moth orchid, dieffenbachia, house bamboo, red-edge peperomia, and balfour aralia will eventually outgrow this basket.

▲ This sturdy and attractive basket calls for strong foliage plants, such as patterned calathea, variegated arrowhead vine, and shiny pothos. Finer-textured 'Tricolor' Madagascar dragontree and a small areca palm add a nice foil. The pink blooming cyclamen is a standout and combines well with the foliage plants. Combine your favorite plants in a variety of ways. Try moving them around in the basket until you achieve the overall look you desire. Add or remove plants later to vary the appearance and freshen the arrangement.

PLANTS FOR BASKET GARDENS

African violet
Arrowhead vine
Begonia
Bloodleaf
Chinese evergreen
Dieffenbachia
Dracaena
English ivy
Fittonia
Heart-leaf philodendron
Japanese euonymus
Oxalis
Peperomia
Polka-dot plant
Prayer plant
Primrose
Purple passion
Streptocarpus
Zebra plant

◀ Baskets can be used as a centerpiece for a festive occasion. They also make a nice gift when visiting or having dinner with friends. Plants can remain in their growing containers with pots covered with decorative mulch. Tuck in some cut flowers in a small vase for added color. Here white daisies and purple statice complement gold dust dracaena, wax cissus, variegated peperomia, purple heart, false aralia, and aluminum plant.

ASSEMBLING A BASKET GARDEN

A successful basket garden is the result of choosing an appropriate basket and then selecting five to seven plants with similar light requirements that will look nice together in the basket.

1 Place a piece of heavy plastic such as a trash can liner or 6-mil clear polyethylene in the basket to form a watertight skin. Cut it to shape, allowing a small overhang, which will eventually be tucked in.

2 Cover the base of the basket with 1 to 2 inches of damp sphagum moss or a peat-based potting soil.

3 Put the taller plants at the back or in the middle, poking moss around the pots as you go, and then add smaller plants and trailing plants to soften the overall shape.

4 Make sure that all of the plants are standing upright and that pot rims are covered with moss. Then water as needed. To keep the display looking fresh, snip off individual flowers as they fade and remove any yellowing leaves.

Dish gardens

► This sculpted container has variegated English ivy, button fern, and peperomia, along with a small rock and a zebra figurine. Search flea markets and garage sales for inexpensive unusual containers and decorative objects to add to your dish garden.

▲ This attractive round dish garden makes good use of English ivy, spider plant, arrowhead vine, and baby's tears. The spider plant will soon outgrow its space but is a nice short-term addition.

PLANTS FOR DESERT DISH GARDENS

Agave
Aloe
Cactus
Crown-of-thorns
Echeveria
Graptopetalum
Haworthia
Jade plant
Kalanchoe
Ox tongue
Snake plant (dwarf varieties)

PLANTS FOR OTHER DISH GARDENS

African violet
Button fern
Creeping fig
Fittonia
Flame violet
Oxalis
Peperomias
Polka-dot plant
Prayer plant
Red flame ivy
Snake plant (dwarf varieties)
Streptocarpus

A dish garden is a miniature landscape created by planting small, low-growing plants together in a shallow container. To create a dish garden remove plants from their individual pots and plant together in one larger container.

The best plants for dish gardens are those that are interesting when viewed from above or the side. Keep in mind where the garden will be placed.

Potential containers for dish gardens are limited only by your imagination. A traditional approach is to use a large terra-cotta saucer for a desert garden; almost any shallow container can work. Look for containers at flea markets, garage sales, secondhand stores, or your own attic. Shallow troughs, ceramic containers, bowls, and coffee and soup mugs might work. If the container drains or moisture may seep

► Hypertufa troughs work well with a variety of plants but are particularly suited for cactus and succulent gardens. This variety of cactus and rocks produces a mini desert garden. The light color gravel mulch adds a finishing touch.

through, use an absorbent mat to protect surfaces.

Cacti and succulents are natural complements to a terra-cotta saucer. They are well suited for dish gardens because they tolerate dry conditions and tend to have shallow root systems. Many spread to form attractive clumps. Use a variety of slow-growing stemless globes, rosettes, mat-forming clumps, and squat and columnar forms to make your garden interesting.

You can create successful dish gardens with tropicals too. The best plants to use are low-growing or dwarf versions of foliage plants, but you can also incorporate miniature flowering plants. Choose plants with similar light, temperature, and humidity requirements. Pinch and prune regularly to keep the plants compact and in scale with their setting. The plantings do not have to

be permanent. Often great looking gardens are only practical for several months, after which plants need to be removed or replaced.

Mound the soil or create contours if you have a large enough container. Such sculpting provides the opportunity to include somewhat larger plants and create more three-dimensional designs.

Place the finished dish garden where it will get the correct amount of light for the selected plants. Keep in mind that a shallow container will dry rapidly in a warm, sunny spot. If you cannot give it constant attention compromise with a bit less light. Let the soil in the dish garden get almost dry, then add water a small amount at a time. Feed your garden rarely. Most plants will be removed after several months and you don't want to encourage excess growth.

ASSEMBLING A DESERT DISH GARDEN

A desert dish garden is a low-maintenance, easy-care indoor garden that lends a Southwestern feel to any room.

1 Use a container that is at least 2 inches deep. Large terra-cotta saucers are good choices for these gardens. Fill the container to within ¼ inch of the rim with a sandy well-drained cactus potting mix.

2 With the plants still in their pots, experiment with the design. Try placing taller plants at the rear of a garden to be viewed from one side only, or in the middle of a dish garden that will be seen from all sides.

3 Scoop out soil as needed to accommodate plants' roots and plant cacti with care. Wear sturdy gloves to protect against cactus spines.

4 Cover the soil with pebbles or gravel to emulate the natural look of desert. Add small pieces of wood, rocks, or figurines, if desired.

Terrariums

In addition to preserving humidity and moisture, enclosed gardens also bring beauty and interest to indoor gardening. They are a good option for people with dusty or dry homes or for people who neglect plants. Enclosed gardens are a way to create the specific microclimates required by hard-to-grow or rare plants.

The keys to success with enclosed gardens are choosing an appropriate watertight structure and using compatible plants. A terrarium can be most any clear glass container. It may be completely enclosed or have an open top, such as a brandy snifter or an aquarium. A Wardian case has hinged lids and removable glass panels that can be opened for air circulation. If you decide to use a bottle as a terrarium, use only clear glass so that plants inside get the full spectrum of light. The neck must be narrow enough to be tightly sealed but wide enough so you can get your hands or houseplant gardening tools inside it.

▲ This bottle garden shows a nice proportion of height of plants to the container. For the best appearance of terrarium plantings, relate plant selection to all dimensions, including the vertical. A miniature sinningia and African violet add flowers to the mix.

▲ This fine example of a Wardian case holds a collection of ferns that will do well in the humid enclosure. Moss, rocks, and weathered wood are good accessories to add.

PLANTS FOR TERRARIUMS

Aluminum plant
Baby's tears
Bromeliads (small)
Button fern
Club moss
Creeping fig
English ivies (small-leaved types)
Episcia
Fittonia
Irish moss
Japanese euonymus
Maidenhair fern
Miniature African violet
Miniature sinningia
Peperomia
Polka-dot plant
Parlor palm*
Prayer plant
Rex begonia
Strawberry begonia*

*Young plants only

Give careful thought to plant selection for enclosed gardens. Dwarf and slow-growing plants that thrive in warm, moist air work best. Think twice about using flowering plants. Their appeal is usually temporary, and fallen petals can lead to rot. Make your enclosed garden more interesting by including ornamental accessories: Small pebbles turn into rocks and boulders, and small branches and moss will give your garden a natural look.

Site your terrarium where it will get enough light to satisfy the plants' needs, but keep it out of direct sun. Direct sunlight will overheat the garden. Check moisture levels periodically. Plants must not dry out, but they should not be overwatered either. If spots of mold or mildew appear, your garden has too much moisture. Remove or partially open the lid for two or three days to improve air circulation. Prune plants to keep them from overgrowing their neighbors. Remove dead plants and plant parts as they appear. Apply water-soluble plant food monthly according to package directions.

▶ Some bigger plants are being incorporated into this large Wardian case. Button fern, aluminum plant, Boston fern, asparagus fern, and false African violet provide a variety of leaf textures and colors. Variegated leaves draw the eye into the design and brighten dimly lit areas. Use them selectively or they will overpower what should be a serene woodland scene. Moss and weathered wood blend nicely into natural settings.

PLANTING A TERRARIUM

1

Lay down a 2- to 3-inch layer of drainage material, such as pea gravel, followed by charcoal chips, which act as a soil filter. If the container opening is too narrow for your hands, use a rolled up piece of newspaper or a funnel to get the growing medium into the bottle.

2

Layer 2 to 6 inches of a sterile peat-based potting mix over the gravel base. Create a slope or change in elevation to mimic a natural landscape.

3

Gently tap plants out of their pots. Trim rampant roots to encourage plants to grow more slowly and to more easily fit them into the shallow, restricted root zone in the container.

4

Place plants in holes and firm soil gently around the roots. Use small long-handle tools if necessary to avoid damaging other plants.

5

Add finishing touches such as moss and rocks. Mist with clear water to settle the roots and to clean the plant leaves and the glass.

Water gardens

Several houseplants can be grown without soil in water gardens. By contrasting the clean lines of a clear container with glossy or textured leaves, twisty stems, and delicate roots or bulky rhizomes, you end up with an instant living sculpture. For greatest effect place your sculpture on an uncluttered tabletop in a spot where moderate sunlight can play off the water and glass.

Any nonporous container that holds water can become an indoor water garden. Line the container with about an inch of washed pebbles. Add a layer of charcoal to keep the water sweet. Fill the container two-thirds full with pebbles. Add enough watering solution to fill the container one-third full.

Place plants inside the container and trickle an anchoring material such as pebbles, sea glass, or glass marbles around the roots up to the plant's former soil level. A decorative layer of polished Japanese mini-stones can be used on top. Add an interesting rock to support leaning plants.

Make the watering solution by mixing one-fourth the recommended amount of liquid plant food into the water. Maintain the solution at half the upper level of pebbles. Every 6 weeks or so, change the solution, rinse the roots, and clean the container. Avoid abrasive cleansers and soap, and always rinse the container thoroughly to remove all residue.

▲ This peace lily is in proportion to its tall glass container. If necessary trim roots before planting to fit them into the container. Remove no more than one-third of the roots. Stabilize the plant with glass marbles and maintain the water level so that the roots are always bathed in the solution.

PLANTS FOR WATER GARDENS

Arrowhead vine
Chinese evergreen
Coleus
Croton
Dieffenbachia
Dwarf papyrus
Dwarf schefflera
English ivy
Fiber optic grass
Lucky bamboo
Parlor palm
Peace lily
Philodendron
Striped inch plant
Ti plant
Wandering Jew

▲ Fiber optic grass adapts well to growing in water without soil. The spiky leaves contrast with the glass container and marbles. Wash all the soil off the roots and position them inside the container, keeping the crown (juncture of roots and top) at the same level it was when the plant grew in soil. Add decorative glass beads or polished stones around the roots to a level of the former soil line. You can also use pebbles or sea glass to anchor the roots. Maintain the plant by keeping the water solution to about half the height of the decorative marbles.

▲ Variegated English ivy drapes over a large glass container in this water garden. Silver-white marbles echo the lighter edge of the ivy leaves and the chair frame. Change the solution and rinse the plant's roots every six weeks. Clean the container with nonabrasive cleaners and soap.

Bonsai

Bonsai is the art of growing miniaturized trees and landscapes in a small pot or tray. True bonsai is done with woody plants that need to be grown outdoors, where they receive ample bright light and can go through their required cold dormancy period. These plants can usually be cultivated indoors for a year or two but are hard to keep alive beyond that. Although some bonsai specimens are several centuries old, it is quite possible to create an acceptable young bonsai from a houseplant in only a few years. These are much easier to grow than traditional bonsai and can grow indoors year-round. Choose plants with naturally small leaves, flowers, and fruits. Look for plants that respond well to pruning and produce rough, aged-looking bark from the time they are young. You can buy partially formed bonsai or start your own from small plants or cuttings. Don't overlook badly treated plants at nurseries. They may be missing stems and leaves but with a bit of imagination can be shaped into an attractive bonsai. However, only purchase healthy plants for this purpose.

Depending on its natural shape, you can form your plant into one of many different bonsai styles: formal upright, slanting, cascade, or forest. Select a low, shallow container that will bring visual harmony between plant and pot. By pruning branches and using copper wire to gently bend and hold branches where you want them, you can train the plant to resemble a small tree. The end result will be a unique specimen that lends an Asian feel to any room.

Caring for a bonsai partly depends on the plant grown. Some need intense light, but others adapt to bright or even moderate light. Since they have little root space, watering must be done with utmost care. When the mix begins to feel slightly dry, set the pot in tepid water and let it soak up what it needs. The frequency of watering depends on many factors, including the light level and the season. Bonsai plants require less feeding than similar plants grown conventionally, since you want them to grow slowly.

▲ This satsuki azalea has been trained with horizontal branching structure and appears quite old. The stem has grown into a wide, trunklike form that adds to the appearance of maturity. Branches, leaves, and plant form balance the container.

HOUSEPLANTS ADAPTABLE TO BONSAI

Citrus
Dwarf pomegranate
Jade plant
Japanese euonymus
Japanese pittosporum
Lady palm
Ming aralia
Myrtle
Orange-jessamine
Podocarpus
Weeping fig

◀ Prune a woody houseplant into a bonsai form. Here dwarf schefflera is kept small by pruning and limiting the root zone. Use sharp clean bypass pruners or bonsai scissors to remove unwanted shoots and roots. This low, shallow container adds harmony to the project with the moss adding a natural touch. The exposed roots give this plant an aged appearance.

Greenhouses and conservatories

An even wider array of interesting indoor plants awaits those fortunate enough to have a greenhouse or conservatory. The increased light, greater humidity, and temperature controlled environment of a greenhouse allows you to grow a wider range of plants than a typical home interior can sustain.

A greenhouse environment is a great place to grow plants to a level of perfection that's difficult to achieve in typical homes. Once the plant is in flower or is fruiting, take it into another room to be enjoyed. A greenhouse is also a great environment for overwintering tender landscape tropical plants that you would normally discard at the end of the growing season.

The plants you can grow in your conservatory or greenhouse depend on the minimum winter temperature maintained in the greenhouse. In attached structures day temperatures are generally maintained at 60 to 70°F and some heating ensures nighttime temperatures remain relatively stable. This is a good place for keeping houseplants that require

▲ This attached greenhouse supports a wide variety of plants that are grown to a higher level of perfection than can be done in most homes and windowsills. Plants needing the most light can be grown on tables or hung from the roof. Lower light plants and those that prefer cooler conditions, such as ferns and clivias, can be grown on the floor and under benches.

◀ A greenhouse can support a riot of color from bulbs and flowering plants. Amaryllis, hyacinths, cyclamen, orchids, and other plants fill all available space. A cool greenhouse keeps blooms fresh longer than warm room conditions.

▲ Tropical vines such as mandevilla grow well in a home greenhouse with much less effort than it takes to keep them thriving indoors. Boston fern, browallia, and spider plant also enjoy the conditions in this greenhouse.

better light levels in the winter than are available in the house such as orchids and hibiscus.

Cool greenhouses (minimum 50°F) are suitable for houseplants that tolerate cool temperatures such as plumbago, Madagascar jasmine, stephanotis, citrus, camellia, and bougainvillea. Use a greenhouse with little or no heating to overwinter tender garden plants such as garden geraniums and wax begonias, as long as you maintain a minimum temperature of 40°F or warmer.

The needs of greenhouse plants are similar to those of other houseplants. Use the same growing media, perhaps with some additional perlite for drainage. The same types of plant foods can also be used. But remember that when plants grow slowly at cool temperatures, they need less fertilizer. Watering needs may vary, since greenhouse plants may grow faster and larger than their indoor counterparts. Humidity is usually higher, so these conditions are not suitable for cacti and many succulents unless you have a separate low-humidity structure for them. Be sure to take full advantage of all available greenhouse space by growing plants at all levels, from floor to ceiling. Grow shade-tolerant plants under benches and suspend hanging plants from the roof.

◀ This banana thrives in the intense light and humidity of a greenhouse. Calamondin orange, angel's trumpet, and geraniums also grow well here.

PLANTS FOR A GREENHOUSE OR CONSERVATORY

If you don't have a greenhouse or conservatory, you can grow many of the plants on this list in a window greenhouse, a solarium, or a sunroom. The key is providing adequate light, appropriate temperatures, and high humidity.

Banana
Bougainvillea
Brazilian plume
Bromeliads
Camellia
Cape lily
Citrus
Coffee plant
Flowering maple
Heliconia
Hibiscus
Ixora
Jasmine
Mandevilla
Miniature rose
Monkey plant
Olive
Orchids
Passionflower
Persian shield
Plumbago
Tree fern
Zebra plant

Forcing bulbs

There is no better way to hasten spring's arrival than with a pot or two of cheery spring-flowering bulbs. A pot of tulips on the windowsill in February can renew a winter-worn gardener's desire to survive the winter. The process of forcing bulbs to bloom indoors is satisfying and uncomplicated—it only requires an investment in time and materials and some planning ahead.

Don't wait until winter hits to think about forcing spring-flowering bulbs. Purchase bulbs in fall for winter bloom and provide their required cold period. Once in flower place these showy focal points in your most-used room so you can readily enjoy their temporary blooms.

Be sure to purchase good-quality bulbs in adequate quantities. Most bulbs look best in odd-numbered groups of five, seven, or more, but some, such as hyacinth, make a handsome statement when planted singly, or in groups of three. Make dense plantings of small bulbs, such as snowdrops, scilla, and glory-of-the-snow. Discard the forced bulbs after they finish blooming.

▲ These forced tulips, daffodils, crocuses, and hyacinths add a cheerful spring look to this casual table setting. Display your plants and bulbs in attractive ways. The painted wooden crates pull the look together, echoing the color of the tableware and napkins. Plan ahead, order plenty of bulbs for forcing, give them the required cold period, and enjoy color indoors all winter long.

SPRING BULBS FOR INDOOR FORCING:

Crocus
Daffodil
Dutch iris
Glory-of-the-snow
Grape hyacinth
Hyacinth
Lily of the valley
Paperwhite narcissus
Scilla
Snowdrop
Tulip

▶ This basket garden of forced bulbs exudes a rainbow of color, texture, and scent. The combination makes a great accent for kitchen or dining room. Use it as a centerpiece for a dinner party, to brighten a bedroom or bath, or to give as a gift to some lucky friend.

STEP-BY-STEP FORCING BULBS

For best results choose top-quality, good-sized bulbs recommended for forcing. Plant a single variety in each pot. Or create a bulb garden by planting several different species of bulbs in a large container.

1 Pot bulbs in a clean, shallow container close together with their noses exposed above the soil, leaving ½ inch of headroom for watering. Fill spaces between bulbs with a peaty potting mix. Give the bulbs a good soaking. Label the container and note the planting date on your calendar.

2 Bulbs need a cold temperature treatment of 35 to 48°F for 12 to 14 weeks. Place bulbs in a cold frame, unheated garage, or refrigerator. Do not allow the bulbs to freeze. Check weekly and water as needed to keep the soil from drying out. You also can purchase prechilled bulbs.

3 After bulbs develop about 2 inches of growth place the container in a sunny, cool (50 to 60°F) location until the shoots and leaves begin to expand and turn green. Then move the container to a warmer location for display, but avoid direct sunlight. The bulbs will flower in 3 to 4 weeks.

Move the blooming plants to a cool location each night to prolong the life of the flowers. Small pots of crocus can even be placed in your refrigerator overnight. Keep the soil evenly moist and stake plants if needed. Discard forced bulbs after they are done blooming. As tempting as it is to save them and plant them outdoors, the results are rarely worth the effort. A forced bulb rarely flowers again outside, and if it does, it goes through several years of just producing leaves before it regenerates enough energy to flower.

FORCING BULBS IN WATER

A hyacinth forcing glass holds the base of the bulb just above the water line. Roots grow into the water.

You can force hyacinths, autumn crocus, and paperwhite narcissus in water alone without a cold treatment. Special glass vases that support the bulbs above a water reservoir are available for hyacinths and autumn crocus. Fill the container so the base of the bulb is just above the water. Put the vase in a cool, dark room (preferably under 50°F) for 4 to 8 weeks until the root system develops and the top elongates. Then move it to a bright window, where the plant soon will bloom. Replenish water as needed to keep the roots in water.

Some narcissus, such as paperwhite and 'Soleil d'Or', can be grown in shallow pans of water filled with crushed rocks or pebbles. Place the bulbs deep enough in the pebbles so that each bulb's base is in contact with the water. Keep pots in a cool, dark room for several weeks to ensure root growth and then place in a sunny location and wait for the flower stems bearing many tiny blossoms.

HERE'S A TIP...

To prevent your paperwhites from getting tall and floppy, give them a good stiff drink. Paperwhites grown in water with a 5% concentration of alcohol bloom beautifully on stems one-third shorter than teatotaling paperwhites. Since most liquors are about 40% alcohol, that works out to 1 part alcoholic beverage to 7 parts water.

TIPS FOR FORCING BULBS

Bulb	Weeks of Cold	Minimum Temperature	Comments
Crocus	8–12	45°F	Keep barely moist until mature, then evenly moist
Daffodil	12–16	45°F	Keep under 65°F when in flower
Dutch iris	8–12	45°F	Keep at 60–65°F when in flower
Grape hyacinth	8–12	45°F	Grow in odd numbers, 7, 9, or 11 to container
Hyacinth	8–12	45°F	Easy; can be forced in soil or water
Paperwhite narcissus	None needed	NA	Ready-to-bloom bulbs, easy, grow in pebbles in shallow bowl or soil
Snowdrop	10–14	45°F	Keep at 60°F or less while in flower
Tulip	12–16	45°F	Plant bulbs ½ inch deep, grow in bright light, discard after bloom

Some varieties suited for forcing (when in doubt, select early blooming types):
Crocus: 'Peter Pan', 'Pickwick', 'Purpurea Grandiflora'
Hyacinth: 'Amethyst', 'Blue Jacket', 'Pink Pearl', 'Hollyhock', 'Gypsy Queen'
Tulip: 'Apricot Beauty', 'Bing Crosby', 'Yokohama', 'Jingle Bells', 'White Swallow'
Grape hyacinth: 'Blue Spike', 'Early Giant'
Daffodil: 'Barrett Browning', 'Dutch Master', 'Ice Follies', 'Salome', 'Pink Charm', 'Tete-a-Tete', 'Cheerfulness'
Paperwhite narcissus: 'Ziva'

Crocus

Daffodil

Reticulate iris

Glory-of-the-snow

Grape hyacinth

Hyacinth

Lily of the valley

Paperwhite narcissus

Tulip

Gift plants

Walk through any greenhouse a few weeks before a major holiday and you'll see a wide array of showy flowering plants. These temporary color accents are forced into bloom and offered for sale, usually around the holidays but often all year-round. While sometimes listed as houseplants, most are best treated as a good alternative to cut flowers. Enjoy them for the weeks or months while in flower and then toss them. Gift plants usually require exacting temperature and light conditions to rebloom, and for most people it's just not worth the effort.

To get the most for your money, choose a gift plant with lots of unopened flower buds and healthy, insect-free foliage. Because they are usually growing in a well-drained, lightweight soilless mix and are slightly pot-bound, which encourages blooming, these plants dry out quickly. Check the soil daily. Most require watering when the top ½ inch of soil feels dry to the touch. Water thoroughly, allow plants to sit for about 15 minutes, and then pour out any water remaining in the saucer.

For best and longest flowering, most gift plants require bright, indirect light and cool nighttime temperatures, conditions not always easily satisfied in the normal home. The extra effort of moving a plant to a spot with cooler nighttime temperatures pays off in longer bloom time and more abundant flowers. Most can be brought out into the living area or set on a table for a few days and then moved back to better conditions without any serious setbacks.

Most of these plants don't need feeding. The rigorous feeding program they received in the greenhouse will carry most of them through their temporary time in your home.

▲ Combine gift plants such as these, an azalea, hydrangea, and kalanchoe, with foliage plants such as dieffenbachia, calathea, and Algerian ivy for an instant colorful arrangement for any occasion. Most gift plants require bright, indirect light and cool nighttime temperatures.

▲ Select gift plants with many buds yet to open. This cineraria has some flowers open but also has many buds that will open slowly over time, providing many weeks of color if they receive ample light. Check the soil daily to make sure the plant does not dry out. Water when the top ½ inch of soil feels dry to the touch.

▲ These roses put on an impressive show of color. The coordinating decorative wrapping adds to their appearance and makes them a more dramatic gift. Slice through the base of the wrapping and place the pot on a saucer to ensure proper watering. Excess water sometimes collects in the base of plastic-coated wraps, leading to root rot. Conversely if the potting soil dries too much, the entire pot may need to be immersed in water to rehydrate the peaty soil mix.

Azalea *(Rhododendron indica* hybrids)

Azalea

Description: The florist azalea is an evergreen shrub up to 2 feet tall and wide. It has abundant funnel-shape flowers up to 3 inches across in white or shades of pink, salmon, crimson, magenta, and orange, as well as bicolor. It is available year-round, most plentifully during winter and spring holidays. Look for bushy plants with many unopened flower buds. **Care:** Provide 4 hours of bright to intense light each day. Water thoroughly when the top layer of soil feels dry; soak the pot if necessary. Maintain daytime temperatures around 68°F. Provide cool nighttime temperatures of 45 to 55°F, such as in a cool entryway or enclosed porch.

Caladium *(Caladium bicolor* cultivars)

Caladium

Description: This exotic-looking plant has showy multicolor leaves in combinations of red, pink, silver, orange, white, and green. They are arrow shape, up to 24 inches long, on stalks up to 18 inches tall. Plants are available spring and early summer and stay looking nice for several months. Purchase plants with plenty of unopened leaves. **Care:** Caladium likes bright indirect light and warm temperatures. Nighttime temperatures should be 60 to 70°F. Water thoroughly when the top layer of soil feels dry. Plants rot if overwatered. Feed plants weekly with a high-nitrogen plant food. When the foliage wanes, gradually allow the rootball to dry out. Plants grow from corms. Store corms in the pot until spring temperatures warm. With spring warmth corms will sprout. Gradually increase watering and grow in medium to bright light.

Calceolaria *(Calceolaria ×herbeohybrida)*

Calceolaria

Description: Unusual pouchlike flowers are held above the slightly hairy leaves in stunning bouquets on plants usually less than 1 foot tall. The 2-inch flowers come in shades of red, pink, maroon, bronze, and yellow, often speckled with brown, purple, or red. Calceolaria is available late winter into spring. It is also called pocketbook plant. **Care:** Calceolaria likes bright indirect light but no direct sun. It needs night temperatures down to 40 to 45°F and daytime temperatures of 55 to 60°F for prolonged bloom. Water when the top layer of soil feels dry. Avoid splashing water on foliage and flowers.

Calla lily *(Zantedeschia* hybrids)

Calla lily

Description: This 12-inch bushy plant has elegant cupped blossoms in white or shades of pink, yellow, and orange, with bicolors also available. The slightly fragrant flowers usually last 4 to 6 weeks, and many varieties have interesting speckled foliage, making them ornamental for 2 to 3 months after blooming. Plants are most abundant around Easter. **Care:** Provide bright light and temperatures in the 60 to 75°F range. Keep the soil evenly moist and maintain high humidity. Clip off stems as flowers fade.

Campanula (*Campanula isophylla*)

Campanula 'Blue Wonder in Sorbet'

Description: Small but numerous star-shape flower clusters adorn this spreading plant. They are usually pale blue but sometimes white or mauve. Plants grow about 9 inches tall with trailing stems 12 to 18 inches long. Plants are available in spring to early summer with blooms continuing for several weeks. **Care:** Provide a minimum of 4 hours of bright indirect light each day. Campanula does best in temperatures between 50 and 70°F. Water as needed to keep the soil evenly moist. Feed every 2 weeks with balanced houseplant food. Grow on a pebble tray to increase humidity. Plant in the garden after its initial flush of bloom to enjoy additional cycles of flowers.

Chrysanthemum (*Chrysanthemum ×grandiflorum*)

Chrysanthemum

Description: Chrysanthemum bears showy 3- to 4-inch blooms in white, yellow, pink, orange, lavender, or red, with bicolor forms available on bushy plants growing about 30 inches tall. Numerous flower forms from daisy to quill, spider, anemone, or cushion types are available year-round, with the greatest quantities and selection in fall. **Care:** Provide at least 4 hours of bright indirect light each day but keep out of direct sun. Chrysanthemum likes cool nights, down to 45 to 55°F, and daytime temperatures below 68°F. Water when the top layer of soil feels dry. Flowers can last 3 to 4 weeks.

Cineraria (*Pericallis ×hybridus*)

Cineraria

Description: Glorious masses of richly colored daisylike flowers rise above the hairy leaves, which are green on top and gray-purple underneath. Plants grow about 1 foot tall and wide. Flowers may be white, shades of pink, red, or blue to violet, often with contrasting white centers. Cineraria is available late winter into spring. **Care:** Provide bright indirect light in a cool spot, but avoid direct sun. Night temperatures should be 40 to 45°F with day temperatures 55 to 60°F. Water when the top layer of soil feels dry. Prevent the plant from wilting; it may not recover even if watered. Avoid splashing water on the foliage.

Cyclamen (*Cyclamen persicum*)

Cyclamen

Description: Exquisite flowers in white or shades of pink, red, or lavender rise above heart-shape leaves decorated with silvery or light green markings. Plants have a long bloom period, often up to 5 months. Cyclamen is most readily available December through February. Choose plants with lots of buds hidden down among the leaves. **Care:** Give plants as much light as possible. Cyclamen does best with night temperatures of 40 to 50°F and daytime temperatures less than 68°F. Water to keep evenly moist. Feed every 2 weeks with a water-soluble plant food high in phosphorus. You can grow cyclamen long term if you can give it cool and bright conditions.

Freesia *(Freesia corymbosa)*

Freesia

Description: This bulbous plant has fragrant single or double flowers in white, yellow, mauve, pink, red, or orange. Stems grow to 18 inches. Flowers last a long time and make good cut flowers. Freesia is available as a potted plant in late winter.
Care: Freesia prefers bright indirect or filtered light and temperatures of 55 to 65°F. Keep the soil lightly moist but avoid overwatering, which can cause bulb rot. Stems may need staking, especially on double-flower types.

Fuchsia *(Fuchsia ×hybrida)*

Fuchsia

Description: Bushy plants generally 1 to 2 feet tall and wide support pendant flowers with brightly hued sepals that flare open to reveal petals often in contrasting colors. Flower colors range from white to pink, red, lavender, violet, and purple. Many selections have double flowers. Fuchsia is excellent as a hanging basket. Plants are available in spring, with blooms lasting into fall if temperatures remain cool enough.
Care: Fuchsia prefers bright light to full sun indoors and temperatures in the 50 to 70°F range. Allow soil to dry out slightly between waterings. Feed every 2 to 4 weeks with a balanced plant food.

Gardenia *(Gardenia augusta)*

Gardenia

Description: An attractive glossy-leaf plant sets off the richly scented, waxy white flowers that grow up to 3 inches or more across. Flowers turn cream colored after a few days and then brown. Gardenia is available year-round but is most plentiful around major winter and spring holidays. Look for healthy leaves, good branching and many unopened flower buds.
Care: This plant needs as much light as possible indoors. Soil must be constantly moist at all times. Gardenia prefers night temperatures of about 60°F, but no higher than 65°F, and day temperatures of 68 to 75°F. It needs high humidity to prevent bud blast. Feed monthly using an acidic plant food. Gardenia can be a challenge to grow long term, but performs best if it can be summered outdoors.

Gloxinia *(Sinningia speciosa hybrids)*

Description: Bell-shape 3-inch flowers in rich shades of purple, red, lavender, pink, or white rise on stiff stalks above velvety leaves. Petals are often marked with contrasting bands or speckles. Gloxinia is most plentiful in late winter and early spring. Choose plants with numerous unopened flower buds.

Gloxinia

Care: Provide at least four hours of bright indirect light daily; it does well under fluorescent lights. Keep the soil evenly moist; avoid splashing water on leaves. Use a pebble tray to raise humidity. Gloxinia prefers daytime temperatures around 75°F, dropping to as low as 55°F at night. Allow the plant to go dormant after flowering, as described for *Sinningia cardinalis*, see page 204.

Heather (Erica spp.)

Heather

Description: This subtropical species has masses of bell shape to tubular flowers in white and various shades of pink, mauve, and red. They are usually quite fragrant. Plants are dense and bushy, growing 8 to 24 inches tall with tiny, narrow, needlelike leaves. Mainly available in fall and winter months. Look for plants with flowers just beginning to open.
Care: Plants need bright light and cool to cold temperatures, somewhere in the 40 to 60°F range, to retain leaves and flowers. Keep the soil evenly moist and increase humidity with pebble trays and misting.

Hydrangea (Hydrangea macrophylla)

Hydrangea

Description: Woody stems 18 to 24 inches long support showy, snowball-like blossoms in white and shades of pink or blue. Clusters can be 5 to 10 inches in diameter. Flower color is determined by variety and soil pH, with blue flowers in acidic soils and pink flowers in alkaline soil. White-flower types are not affected by pH. Hydrangea is most readily available in spring.
Care: Provide bright indirect light; flowers droop if light is too intense. Blooming hydrangea plants are often pot-bound. Water thoroughly when the top layer of soil begins to feel dry. Check daily and soak the root ball if necessary to rewet dried soil. Hydrangea prefers daytime temperatures around 70°F, dropping to 55 to 60°F at night.

Jerusalem cherry (Solanum pseudocapsicum)

Jerusalem cherry

Description: Valued for its spectacular marble-size, bright orange or yellow fruits, which last for 6 to 10 weeks, Jerusalem cherry is not a real cherry. Instead it is closely related to potato, and the fruits are poisonous. Keep them away from children. Plants are most popular from autumn through the holiday season. Look for plants with fruits in various stages of development.
Care: Jerusalem cherry does best with at least 4 hours of direct sunlight. Provide night temperatures of 50 to 55°F and day temperatures around 70°F. Water when the top layer of soil feels dry. Feed monthly with a balanced houseplant food.

Kalanchoe (Kalanchoe blossfeldiana hybrids)

Description: An attractive clump of succulent, scallop-edge leaves supports a dense canopy of bright red, orange, yellow, pink, or salmon flowers. Plants grow 6 inches to 1 foot tall, depending on variety. Kalanchoe is available year-round, with greatest availability autumn through late winter. Choose compact plants with most flower buds still unopened. The glossy green foliage is attractive even when the plant is out of bloom.
Care: Provide a minimum of 4 hours of bright sunshine each day. Keep it at night temperatures of 50 to 60°F and day temperatures of 65 to 70°F. Kalanchoe is a succulent and likes its soil to be on the dry side; overwatering causes stem rot. The plant needs a bit more moisture when in flower.

Kalanchoe

Lily *(Lilium* spp.)

Description: Potted lilies have leafy stems 1 to 3 feet tall topped with sweetly scented funnel-shape flowers ranging from pure white Easter lilies to red, yellow, orange, pink, or maroon hybrids. Pollen-laden anthers add interest but are often removed to prevent yellow stains on petals. Available from winter through spring, lilies may be enjoyed in the home while in bloom and transplanted to the garden for a repeat performance in subsequent years. Select a plant with one or two lower flowers open and plentiful upper buds just beginning to show color.
Care: Keep potted lilies in bright, indirect light and at night temperatures of 45 to

Easter Lily

60°F and day temperatures of 68°F or lower. Keep evenly moist but not soggy; too much water causes bulb rot. Transplant to a well-drained site in the garden after danger of freezing has passed.

Marguerite daisy *(Argyranthemum frutescens)*

Description: Marguerite daisy forms mounding plants 18 to 24 inches tall and wide with daisylike flowers in white, pink, or yellow. Leaves have a silvery look and a medicinal fragrance. Look for plants with many buds yet to open.
Care: Give marguerite daisy a minimum of 4 hours of bright light to full sun each day. Keep the soil evenly moist in bright light; allow it to dry more in lower light. Maintain daytime temperatures of 70 to 75°F with 50 to 60°F at night. Regularly remove spent flowers to keep it blooming. It likes to move to a sunny spot outdoors for the summer. Combine it with flowering annuals or perennials for a bold splash of container color.

Marguerite daisy

Orchid pansy *(Achimenes* hybrids)

Orchid pansy

Description: This African violet relative forms mounding plants 12 to 18 inches tall and wide with trumpet-shape flowers in white and shades of pink, red, purple, salmon, orange, and yellow, often with spotted or netted throats. It is spectacular in a hanging basket at eye level. The shiny leaves often have bronze hues. It blooms summer through fall.
Care: Provide a minimum of 4 hours of bright indirect light each day. Keep evenly moist and feed monthly with African violet food. Temperatures of 70 to 75°F are best. Orchid pansy likes average to high humidity. In late fall gradually withhold water to induce dormancy. Once dormant, store it in the pot in a cool, dry location (but do not allow corms to desiccate). With spring warmth rhizomes will sprout. Repot and grow in bright light and keep evenly moist.

Ornamental pepper *(Capsicum annuum)*

Description: Spectacular fruits start out green, then turn yellow, purple, red, or orange, often with several colors on one plant. Plants usually stay in fruit 6 to 10 weeks. Ornamental peppers are edible but extremely hot. Fruiting plants are available autumn through Christmas. Look for fruits in various stages of development. Look for immature plants in garden centers in springtime. Ornamental pepper is also sold as an outdoor bedding plant in spring.
Care: Provide a minimum of 4 hours of bright indirect light each day. It prefers night temperatures of 60 to 65°F and day temperatures of 70 to 80°F. Water when the top layer of soil feels dry. Feed monthly with a balanced houseplant food.

Ornamental pepper

Persian violet (*Exacum affine*)

Persian violet

Description: This neat, mounding plant rarely grows more than 12 inches tall and wide. Flowers are lightly fragrant, bell-shape, and violet-blue, with some selections white or deep purple. Persian violet is available winter through spring. Choose plants with buds just beginning to open. Plants bloom for a long time in small pots.

Care: Persian violet prefers bright light and temperatures of 65 to 75°F. Keep soil constantly moist. Feed every 2 weeks with a balanced houseplant food. Mist to boost humidity. Pinch off faded blossoms to encourage more blooms. Cutting plants back severely sometimes produces another flush of blooms.

Poinsettia (*Euphorbia pulcherrima*)

Poinsettia

Description: This familiar gift plant traditionally has red bracts surrounding tiny yellowish green flowers, but numerous selections are available with pink- or cream-color bracts as well as mauve, orange, and bicolor. Blooming plants are available November through Christmas; some selections hold their color for months. Look for plants with good bract coloration and unopened central yellow flowers.

Care: Poinsettia prefers 3 to 4 hours of direct sunlight but does fine with less intense light. It prefers night temperatures of 60 to 65°F and day temperatures of 65 to 70°F. Avoid drafts and cold windowpanes. Water when the top layer of soil feels dry to the touch.

Primrose (*Primula* spp.)

Primrose

Description: Primrose forms rosettes of bright green, rough-texture leaves topped by dainty flowers in a wide range of colors, including white, yellow, pink, red, apricot, and purple. Look for plants in flower January through early spring. Choose a plant with plenty of buds left to open. Create a tabletop garden by placing several plants in a basket and filling the space around the pots with sphagnum moss.

Care: Provide bright indirect light and night temperatures of 40 to 50°F and daytime temperatures of 68°F or lower. Plants decline quickly in high temperatures. Keep soil evenly moist.

Rose, miniature (*Rosa chinensis* hybrids)

Description: Miniature roses reach 12 to 18 inches tall and bear abundant, sometimes fragrant flowers in shades of red, pink, yellow, and white, often blooming 4 to 6 weeks indoors. Blooming plants are available late winter through early summer as small bushes and sometimes as standards. Purchase a plant with many buds remaining to open.

Care: Provide as much bright light or sun as possible and maintain temperatures between 60 and 75°F. Feed monthly with a balanced plant food. Allow the soil surface to dry to about ½ inch between waterings. Miniature rose needs high humidity. It is quite susceptible to spider mites so wash leaves frequently. Miniature rose makes a challenging houseplant; consider transplanting it to the garden after its first flush of bloom has ended.

Miniature rose

Encyclopedia of houseplants

Houseplants can make your home or office a delightful place to spend time. Not only do they add to the decor, they also provide a year-round outlet for gardeners. Many also improve indoor air quality.

In previous chapters you've seen how you can use houseplants effectively to create your own personal style and how to match plants to the specific conditions found in your home. You've learned about the different cultural requirements houseplants have and how to meet their needs to keep them growing strong and healthy.

Now it's time to use this encyclopedia section to look at specific plants and select the ones that are best suited to your conditions and your lifestyle, as well as to your room furnishings and your own personal taste.

To help you decide which ones to choose, look at the key facts about the plant at the top of each entry, including the primary characteristics such as size, light, temperature, and water needs along with significant aesthetic features. Each plant includes a detailed description of its appearance, guidance on watering and feeding, along with some tips and idiosyncrasies. The following key to definitions will guide you in your selections.

Light

While every plant needs light to grow and thrive, and some need more than others. If you can provide the ideal amount of light for each plant, you stand a very good chance of growing a healthy plant.

Low light means an interior location away from a window or supplemental light source. It is usually a northern or eastern exposure with little or no direct sun. This is enough light to easily read a newspaper.

Medium light is common in most homes where there is indirect sunlight all day. It may also describe a location where direct sunlight is available for a few hours in early morning from an east window, or in the afternoon from a west window. It is found several feet inside a room with a sunny window. It can also be provided by a standard two-tube fluorescent fixture hung several inches above the plant.

Bright light is provided by a south or west exposure where plants get at least two hours of direct sunlight part of the day, but indirect sunlight during the hottest part of the day. A four-tube fluorescent fixture suspended directly over the plant can also provide bright light.

Intense light is available in a southern exposure that receives full sun for much of the day or in a sunroom or greenhouse that receives bright diffused light all day from the south, east, or west.

Temperature

Most plants do well in typical home temperatures. Some may have seasonal preferences or require lower conditions at night; most do well with a 10-degree drop in nighttime temperatures. Specific guidelines are noted for each plant.

Water

Maintaining the correct moisture levels for your plants is significant for their health. Know your plants and water when they need it, not on a preset schedule. Be mindful of seasonal, soil mix, and temperature variations and learn the subtleties of each plant's needs.

Moderately dry soil is for plants that must not stay wet. This can only be achieved with a soil mix that drains well and does not hold much moisture. For large plants the mix should be dry a few inches down before watering.

Barely moist is for plants that need more moisture. For small plants water when the surface starts to dry, for large pots when it is dry ½ to 1 inch down.

Evenly moist is for plants that want constant moisture though not soggy soil. The surface should not be allowed to dry out completely.

▶ Healthy, well-grown houseplants look stunning and add to the enjoyment of your home. This collection of plants includes dieffenbachia, fishtail palm, chrysanthemum, song of India dracaena, and regal geranium. Give plants their required amounts of light and water and grow them in an acceptable temperature ranges for them to do well. If your plants fail to thrive, try moving them around your house to find the right light conditions. Carefully monitor the growing media to maintain the right moisture levels, feed with a quality plant food, and you will soon have beautiful houseplants.

Abutilon (see Flowering maple)
Acalypha hispida (see Chenille plant)
Acalypha wilkesiana (see Copperleaf)
Adenium obesum (see Desert rose)
Adiantum pedatum (see Fern, maidenhair)

Aechmea fasciata (see Silver vase plant)
Aeonium arboreum (see Pinwheel plant)
Aeschynanthus radicans (see Lipstick plant)
African mask (see Alocasia)

African milk tree

(Euphorbia trigona)

Features: Cactuslike stemmed succulent
Size: 1–8'H × 1–3'W
Light: Bright to intense
Temperature: 65–75°F; 50–65°F in winter
Water: Moderately dry

Description and uses: This interesting plant has thick triangular branched stems with a silvery center and spiny edges. Clusters of bright green deciduous leaves appear on new growth, eventually dropping off and leaving the stems bare, resulting in a plant that looks much like a cactus. African milk tree is great by a sunny south or west window. It can tolerate the neglect often found in offices. The sap can cause skin irritation in some people.
Care: Give African milk tree lots of light. It will grow okay in lower light but will flower less. It tolerates temperatures from 50 to 90°F and it thrives in dry air. Feed in summer using a balanced all-purpose plant food. Allow the soil to dry to within 1 inch of the surface between waterings. Keep it cooler and drier in winter. In cold conditions leaves will turn red, providing a clue to this plant's close relation to poinsettia.
Propagation: Propagate from stem tip cuttings. Dip them in warm water to stop the latex sap from bleeding and allow them to dry for 24 hours before planting.
Pests: No major pest problems affect African milk tree.
Recommendations: **'Red'** is a popular cultivar with pink to red stems in high light. **'Purpurea'** has purple-tinted stems and leaves.

African milk tree
(*Euphorbia trigona*)

African violet *(Saintpaulia ionantha)*

Features: Flower clusters above a rosette of foliage
Size: 2–8"H × 3–16"W
Light: Medium to bright
Temperature: 65–75°F
Water: Evenly moist

Description and uses: African violets are among the easiest to grow and most rewarding of all indoor plants. They thrive with lower light than most blooming houseplants and they bloom year-round with little effort.

African violet (*Saintpaulia ionantha*)

Flowers may be white or shades of purple, lavender, wine, pink, rose, bicolor, or with a picotee edge. Flower form can be single, double, ruffled, or bell- or star-shape. All have handsome rosettes of fuzzy leaves, some with wonderful variegation. A single plant in a ceramic pot is a lovely desktop or tabletop accent. They are often included in mixed baskets.

Care: African violets like an east-, west-, or even south-facing window during fall and winter and a north or east window in summer. They perform well under fluorescent lights. They thrive in warm conditions, 70°F days or warmer and a minimum of 65°F degrees at night. Newer varieties may cope with cooler temperatures, but they don't like cold drafts. Keep leaves from touching cold window glass. Water thoroughly when the soil surface feels dry to the touch. Discard excess water because saturated soil leads to root rot. Avoid wetting foliage when watering. Use tepid water because cold water can cause leaf spot. Keep humidity up by placing plants on a pebble tray. Feed regularly with an African violet plant food. Refresh the soil once a year using an African violet or soilless mix, but keep plants in small pots. Remove old, lower leaves, trim off up to one-third of the roots, and set the plant slightly deeper in the pot. Clean leaves with a soft, dry brush. Turn plants regularly to keep them symmetrical. Remove damaged leaves along with their stalks and spent flowers. Remove side shoots (suckers) as they develop to maintain a uniform plant shape.
Propagation: Root healthy, medium-sized leaves with 1 to 2 inches of leaf stalk attached.
Pests: Cyclamen mites, thrips, mealybugs, and aphids can be problems as can crown rot and powdery mildew.
Recommendations: Hundreds of cultivars are available in a wide range of plant forms, leaf shapes, variegations, flower forms, and colors. Standard types form rosettes 8 to 16 inches in diameter. Miniature varieties have rosettes from 3 to 6 inches in diameter and are wonderful in terrariums. Trailing varieties have numerous stems that arch outward and hang down. They look best in hanging baskets.

African violet (*Saintpaulia ionantha* 'Rebel's Rosia Purple')

African violet
(*Saintpaulia ionantha* 'Ever Love')

Miniature African violets (*Saintpaulia ionantha* hybrids)

Agave (*Agave* spp.)

Features: Sculptural pointed leaves
Size: 12–18"H × 12–18"W
Light: Bright to intense
Temperature: 65–75°F, not below 50°F
Water: Barely moist; moderately dry in winter

Description and uses: Agaves grow slowly. They may take 20 years or more to flower before the central mother plant dies. Each leaf is placed in a regular arrangement from the center. Leaf markings or white lines accent the geometry. Most agaves are armed with black thorns on the end of each leaf. Keep them away from children and soft fabrics.

Painted century plant (*Agave victoriae-reginae*)

Care: Provide full sun or bright conditions year-round. Agaves benefit from summering outdoors. Water plants regularly during the growing season. Feed monthly with a balanced plant food. Reduce water and cease feeding in winter. In early spring repot using cactus soil. Water sparingly for a few weeks and gradually resume normal watering.

American agave (*Agave americana*)

Propagation: Remove side shoots before the flowering plant dies. Pot offshoots in cactus soil or sow seeds in early spring.
Pests: Scale, mealy bug, and root aphids are possible problems.
Recommendations: *Agave victoriae-reginae* (painted century plant, royal agave) is a small, to about 12 inches tall and wide, decorative plant with streaks of white on sculptured leaves in a tight rosette.

A. americana (American agave, century plant) becomes a large plant with gray-green leaves up to 5 feet long. It is a dramatic choice for large sunny spaces. It has long, fishhook-shape thorns.

A. filifera (thread agave) grows to 2 feet wide.

A. parviflora (little princess agave) is an attractive small plant to about 12 inches wide.

Aglaonema (*see Chinese evergreen*)
Air plant (*see Kalanchoe, Tillandsia*)
Algerian ivy (*see English ivy*)

Alocasia (*Alocasia ×amazonica*)

Features: White-veined, tropical-looking leaves
Size: 2'H × 3'W
Light: Medium to bright
Temperature: 60–75°F
Water: Evenly moist

Alocasia (*Alocasia ×amazonica* 'Polly')

Description and uses: This dramatic foliage plant boasts striking color, texture, and form. The glossy green leaves, shaped like arrowheads, can grow up to 1 foot wide and 2 feet long. Leaves have prominent veins of silver and narrow white margins. New selections are becoming available in a range of shades from dark green to near black. Alocasia is a striking specimen plant and a good candidate for inclusion in groupings. Place it where it will receive high humidity but protect it from cold drafts.
Care: Alocasia likes warmth and high humidity. If you want to grow it in drier conditions, set it on a pebble tray. It likes bright to medium light in winter and indirect medium light in summer. It should not receive direct sun at any time. Leaves drop and plants may go dormant if it gets chilled or if the soil dries out completely. New leaves develop once the problem is corrected. Keep the soil slightly moist at all times during growing season but keep drier in winter. Overwatered plants can develop root rot. Feed once a month during growing season with balanced foliage plant food. Do not feed in winter. To maintain attractiveness keep leaves clean of dust. Repot annually.
Propagation: Divide when repotting, making sure each division has several pieces of fleshy rhizome and new shoots. Or propagate plants by removing suckers with roots attached or by cutting rhizomes into pieces for rooting.
Pests: Spider mites, mealybugs, and scale may infest stressed plants.
Recommendations: 'Hilo Beauty' has leaves with a beautiful mosaic of green, creamy white, and yellow. 'Polly' is a vigorous selection with dark green leaves that set off bright silvery veins.

A. lowii is a vigorous grower with grayish metallic leaves with silver veins and purplish undersides.

A. corozon is a dwarf species with waxy pewter-toned leaves and dark veins. It can be grown in a tall terrarium.

A. cucullata has heart-shape leaves with prominent veins and upturned margins.

Aloe (Aloe spp.)

Features: Spiky green leaves; medicinal sap
Size: 3'H × 3'W
Light: Bright
Temperature: 65–75°F
Water: Moderately dry

Aloe (Aloe vera)

Description and uses: *Aloe vera* is an easy-care succulent with elongated leaves that fan out in a vase shape from a central base. Put a small plant on a sunny kitchen window where it will be readily available for use on burns and skin irritations. For serious burns seek medical attention. The sooner gel from *Aloe vera* leaves is applied to a burn, the quicker it heals. Aloes are good in dish gardens and in rooms with Southwestern decor. Keep the spiky leaves away from high-traffic areas. It was formerly classified as *A. barbadensis*.
Care: Aloe tolerates low humidity and winter temperatures down to 50°F. Grow it in any good potting soil or cactus mix. Feed plants monthly spring through fall with a balanced plant food. Do not feed in winter. Keep soil slightly moist spring through fall. Water less in winter but do not allow soil to dry completely. Provide good drainage. Plants will rot if sitting in water. Aloes can stay in the same pot a long time, although plants often become top heavy. Repot every other year in spring or as needed. Avoid injuring or breaking leaves, because the scars will show forever. Gradually move aloe outdoors for summer. Plants sunburn if moved to bright sun too quickly. Similarly plants do not like to go directly from warm sunny conditions to a dim room in fall when the plant is returned indoors. Aloe rarely blooms when grown indoors, but outdoor plants may bloom.

Aloe (A. vera) in bloom

Propagation: Remove offsets that form at the base of the plant in spring or early summer. Allow the cut roots to dry for a day before potting.
Pests: Mealybugs can be a problem.
Recommendations: Partridge-breasted aloe (*A. variegata*) forms a tight rosette of beautifully patterned leaves and only grows 6 inches tall.

Lace aloe (*A. aristata*) has dense, 4-inch-long dark gray-green leaves and threadlike leaf tips. It forms offsets freely.

A. haworthioides has thin, dark green leaves with white spines and grows to only 4 inches.

Spider aloe (*A. humilis*) grows to 8 inches with narrow, spiny leaves.

Partridge-breasted aloe (A. variegata)

Alpinia (see Shell ginger, variegated)

Amaryllis (Hippeastrum hybrids)

Features: Bell-shape colorful flowers
Size: 1–2'H × 1'W
Light: Bright
Temperature: 70–75°F; 65°F in flower
Water: Evenly moist; dry when dormant

Amaryllis (Hippeastrum hybrid)

Description and uses: Amaryllis is an easy bulb to grow. Dramatic bell- or trumpet-shape flowers bloom in winter or spring, often before leaves emerge. Amaryllis comes in shades of red, white, pink, salmon, and patterns. Plants may bloom for up to 6 weeks. The larger the bulb the more flower stems and flowers will develop.
Care: Place a mature bulb one-half to two-thirds into potting soil in a relatively small pot, leaving no more than 1 inch between the bulb and the edge of the pot. Moisten the soil and place the potted bulb in a warm, 70–75°F, bright area. Keep barely moist until top growth begins, then maintain moist, never soggy, conditions during active growth. When the flower stem is about 6 inches tall start using low-nitrogen plant food every 2 weeks. Increase watering while in flower. To prolong bloom keep at 65°F when flowers begin to open. Remove flowers as they fade. Pull out the flower stalk after it yellows. Grow the straplike leaves several months in bright light to build strength for flowering the next year. After several months of foliage growth, withhold water. Leaves will stop growing and die back. Cut them off near the bulb. Store the bulb in a cool, dry, dark location. After two to three months dormancy water the plant to begin the cycle again. Blooming plants are top heavy. A heavy pot or small stake may be useful to counterbalance the bloom stalk.

HERE'S A TIP...
Start bulbs 2 weeks apart for a succession of bloom.

Propagation: Remove offsets with their own roots and plant in potting soil. It may take 3 years for offsets to reach blooming size.
Pests: Thrips, aphids, mealybugs, and spider mites are occasional problems.
Recommendations: Several cultivars are available. Select large bulbs in your choice of flower colors.

American agave (see Agave)
Ananas (see Pineapple)

Anthurium *(Anthurium andraeanum)*

Features: Heart-shape flowers
Size: 2–3'H × 2'W
Light: Medium to bright
Temperature: 65–80°F
Water: Evenly moist; barely moist fall and winter

Description and uses:
Anthurium, also known as flamingo flower, has showy flowering bracts that often last for 8 weeks or more. The waxy bracts are often used in cut flower arrangements. Most are red, but hybrids are available in shades of pink, lavender, white, and even green. The heart-shape, shiny green leaves are also attractive. Select a container that will coordinate with the bloom color.

Anthurium *(Anthurium andraeanum)*

Care: Flamingo flower needs bright to moderate light with no direct sun. It survives as a foliage plant with less light, but fails to bloom. Feed monthly spring through late summer. In fall and winter feed every 6 weeks with a balanced plant food. Anthurium needs moderate to high humidity. Grow plants on pebble trays or in a room with a humidifier if necessary. Use a peaty soil mix, such as African violet mix. Repot every year or so in spring, moving up only slightly in pot size. Clean the leaves regularly with a sponge and tepid water. Leaves contain toxic sap, so make sure pets and children do not ingest them.

Pigtail anthurium *(A. scherzerianum)*

Propagation: Separate new crowns that appear more than an inch away from the main stem. Root stem tip cuttings at temperatures over 75°F.
Pests: Fungus gnats, spider mites, or fungal leaf blight can be problems.
Recommendations: Crystal anthurium *(A. crystallinum)* has striking, velvety dark green leaves with white veins. Leaves are pink-bronze when young. They can reach 12 inches across and 20 inches long.
    Pigtail anthurium *(A. scherzerianum)* is

> **HERE'S A TIP...**
> Anthurium flower blossoms make superb cut flowers because they last a long time. Cut and enjoy the blooms in cut flower arrangements.

a smaller, easier-to-grow plant with thicker lance-shape leaves, a curled spadix (central spike on the flower), and orange-red bracts. It is more tolerant of dry air and is usually longer lived than other anthuriums.

Aphelandra *(see Zebra plant)*
Aporocactus *(see Cactus, rattail)*
Apostle plant *(see Walking iris)*

Aralia *(Polyscias spp.)*

Features: Lacy foliage
Size: 1–10'H × 1–3'W
Light: Medium to bright
Temperature: 65–85°F
Water: Evenly moist

Description and uses:
Ming aralia *(Polyscias fruticosa)* is an upright woody plant with a treelike appearance. Deeply cut lacy leaves give it a fine texture. Stems grow in zigzag fashion and older plants develop a beautiful corky, gnarled trunk. It can be trained as a bonsai. Set Ming aralia against a light-colored wall to set off the fine foliage and to increase light levels.

Ming aralia *(Polyscias fruticosa)*

Care: Aralias need warm temperatures away from cool drafts, and bright light without direct sunlight. They require high humidity and careful attention to watering. Dry slightly between thorough soakings but never allow soil to dry completely. Overwatering leads to root and stem rot.

Aralias are not heavy feeders; three applications of a foliage plant food in summer is sufficient. Repot only when roots fill the pot. Sudden leaf drop can signal the need to repot. Plants seldom need drastic pruning, but regular pinching will keep them shapely.

Balfour aralia *(Polyscias scutellaria 'Balfourii')*

Propagation: Take stem cuttings in late spring when temperatures are above 75°F. Use rooting hormone. Air layering also is effective.
Pests: Possible insect pests include scale, mealybugs, and spider mites.
Recommendations: 'Elegans' is a smaller selection with extremely dense, curled leaves. It is often called parsley aralia.
    Balfour aralia *(P. scutellaria 'Balfourii')* has glossy green, rounded scalloped leaflets with white margins. Leaves pucker on older plants. 'Marginata' is another cultivar with leaves edged in white. 'Pennockii' has slightly larger leaflets variegated creamy white.

Geranium-leaf aralia (*P. guilfoylei*) grows quite large. It has shiny, medium green leaflets with deep lobes and white margins. **'Victoriae'** is a popular selection that usually stays under 3 feet tall. Its gray-green leaves are notably larger and more divided.

Araucaria (*see Norfolk Island pine*)
Arboricola (*see Schefflera*)

Ardisia (*Ardisia* spp.)

Features: Dark green leaves; bright red berries
Size: 1–3'H × 1–2'W
Light: Bright
Temperature: 55–70°F
Water: Evenly moist; barely moist in winter

Description and uses: Ardisia (*A. crenata*), is a handsome, slow-growing, single-stemmed evergreen shrub. Its leaves are oval and glossy with scalloped edges. Clusters of small white or pale pink, slightly fragrant flowers appear in summer and last for months. Glossy red berries that appear in fall and remain for several months are the source of one common name, coralberry. It is one of the few houseplants that successfully fruits indoors. This Asian native, often sold as *A. crispa*, is a landscape plant in warm climates. In some areas it has become invasive.

Ardisia (*Ardisia crenata*) with berries

Care: Provide bright light year-round. For better berry production use a small brush to transfer pollen from one flower to another. Ardisia prefers cool temperatures and high humidity. Keep it away from drafts. Keep soil evenly moist. Feed with bloom-enhancing plant food monthly in summer. Prune back in early spring. Place ardisia outside for summer but bring it back in before temperatures dip below 50°F. Repot only if necessary in spring. Discard older plants that no longer flower and fruit well.

Propagation: Take semihardwood stem cuttings in spring or summer. Sow seeds from shriveled berries in early spring.

Pests: Spider mites can be a problem, especially in low humidity and at temperatures above 70°F. Small nodules that form along leaf edges are normal and should be disregarded.

Japanese marlberry (*Ardisia japonica* 'Midgee')

Recommendations: Japanese marlberry (*A. japonica*) is lower growing, rarely getting taller than 12 inches. It is often used as a groundcover in warm climates.

Areca palm (*see Palm, areca*)
Aroid palm (*see Zeezee plant*)

Arrowhead vine (*Syngonium podophyllum*)

Features: Variegated arrowhead-shape leaves
Size: 6–36"H × 6–36"W
Light: Low to medium
Temperature: 60–75°F
Water: Evenly moist

Description and uses: This lush foliage plant is one of few variegated plants that retain variegation in low light. The species is a vine with dark green leaves marked with white along the veins. Newer cultivars have compact growth and showier leaves in varying shades of green and bronze with more pronounced variegation. Most remain about 15 inches in height and need no support when young. They revert to their vining heritage as they age. Use small plants in mixed baskets and with other foliage plants in tabletop gardens.

Arrowhead vine (*Syngonium podophyllum*)

Train vining types to an upright form on a moss pole. Arrowhead vine does well in the artificial light or low light conditions of offices. It is excellent for improving indoor air quality. The sap contains calcium oxalate crystals that can irritate skin and are toxic. It is

Arrowhead vine (*Syngonium podophyllum*)

sometime sold as *Nephthytis*, an outdated name.

Care: Arrowhead vine tolerates low light but may become leggy. Pinch back stems to make it bushier. Leaves turn pale and limp in direct sun. Keep plants away from cold drafts. Keep soil slightly moist at all times during the growing season but drier in winter. Arrowhead vine likes average to high humidity. Repot every 2 years or so. When older plants begin to vine, tie them to a pillar or cut them back. Clean leaves regularly.

Propagation: Create new plants by layering stem tips or by taking stem cuttings.

Pests: Possible pests include mealybugs, scale, aphids, and spider mites.

Recommendations: 'Arrow' is compact with leaves suffused with creamy variegation. **'Emerald Gem'** is a well-known form with short leafstalks and crinkled leaves. **'Pixie'** has white marbled leaves and stays about 1 foot tall and wide.

Artillery plant (*see Pilea*)

Asparagus fern (Asparagus densiflorus)

Features: Fernlike foliage
Size: 10–36"H × 12–36"W
Light: Medium to bright
Temperature: 60–75°F
Water: Evenly moist

Asparagus fern (Asparagus densiflorus 'Sprengeri')

Description and uses: This subtropical relative of asparagus is not a true fern, and the foliage is needlelike. Asparagus fern stems shoot upward and outward, making it a good hanging basket plant. Small white flowers half hidden among needles turn into bright red berries, but neither are prominent enough to be ornamental. The berries are poisonous and should be kept away from children and pets. All ornamental asparagus plants have sparse but sharp thorns.

Care: Asparagus fern likes average to high humidity. Needles turn brown and fall off when humidity is too low. It likes evenly moist soil. The tuberous root ball dries out quickly, so plants need regular monitoring. Feed with all-purpose plant food during the growing season. Prune back long, ungainly growth. Asparagus fern loves to be summered outdoors in a shady location.

Foxtail fern (A. densiflorus 'Myers')

Remove some of the potatolike tubers when repotting. Needles turn yellow and drop if the soil is too wet or too dry or if plants are moved suddenly to low light.

Propagation: Divide crowns of established plants with a sharp knife or saw or propagate new plants from seed.

Pests: Spider mites can be a problem, and aphids are attracted to tender young shoots of asparagus fern.

Recommendations: '**Sprengeri**', the most widely available cultivar, has arching stems sparsely covered with flat, dark green,

Plumose fern (A. setaceus)

1-inch needles, giving plants an open, frothy appearance.

Foxtail fern (*A. densiflorus* 'Myers') is more upright, with densely needled, bright green 2-foot stems. It looks better as a tabletop plant than in a hanging basket.

Plumose fern (*A. setaceus*) looks the most like a true fern. The spreading, layered stems are covered with tiny needles. Young bushy plants can be used in terrariums, hanging baskets, and tabletop groupings. Older plants can have stems up to 10 feet long, which can be trained up a trellis or cut back to promote denser growth. '**Nanus**' is a compact, nonclimbing selection.

Aspidistra (*see Cast-iron plant*)
Asplenium (*see Fern, bird's nest*)
Astrophytum (*see Cactus, bishop's cap*)

HERE'S A TIP...

Asparagus fern fills its pot quickly with fleshy roots and may need division every year. Slip the plant out of its pot and slice cleanly through the root ball with a sharp knife. Repot the pieces in fresh potting soil.

Aucuba, Japanese (Aucuba japonica)

Features: Green leaves often flecked yellow
Size: 1–5'H × 1–5'W
Light: Medium to bright
Temperature: 60–75°F; cooler in winter
Water: Barely moist

Japanese aucuba (Aucuba japonica)

Description and uses: Japanese aucuba is a rounded evergreen shrub that is commonly used as a landscape plant in warm climates. It is fast growing and has shiny dark green, leathery leaves. Many cultivars have variegation ranging from small spots to large blotches that cover most of the leaf. Because it tolerates cool drafts it can be used in entryways.

Care: Give this plant average to high humidity. It tolerates a wide range of light, from medium-low to bright. Full sun in summer will bleach leaves. Site it where nighttime winter temperatures are 50–65°F. Allow the soil to dry between waterings. Excess soil moisture leads to root rot. Japanese aucuba is a light feeder. Use a balanced plant food several times during the growing season. Prune it regularly to keep the plant dense and less than 3 feet tall. Repot annually. Japanese aucuba loves to spend the summer outdoors in a semishady spot.

Propagation: Take semihardwood stem cuttings in mid- to late summer; a rooting hormone will speed root formation.
Pests: Spider mites can be a problem in high light and low humidity. Scale may develop if conditions are too warm.
Recommendations: Gold dust plant (*A. japonica* 'Variegata') is the classic cultivar. Its leaves are lightly sprinkled with yellow spots. **'Crotonifolia'** has larger, more abundant gold and white patterns similar to croton coloration. **'Picturata'** has yellow-centered leaves surrounded by yellow spots.

Australian maidenhair *(see Fern, maidenhair)*

Avocado *(Persea americana)*

Features: Glossy leaves
Size: 1–6'H × 1–4'W
Light: Bright
Temperature: 65–75°F; 65°F in winter
Water: Evenly moist; barely moist in winter

Description and uses: Avocado is an attractive foliage plant with glossy leaves, 4 to 6 inches long and 2 to 3 inches wide. It's a great conversation piece. Show it off as you pass the guacamole. It also is a great project to get kids interested in gardening by starting a plant from a discarded avocado pit.
Care: Grow the plant in fertile potting mix in bright light. It adapts to less light but will be leggy. Keep soil moist during the growing season but allow it to dry a bit in winter. Repot in spring if necessary. Many avocado plants do well for about 3 years then decline. Others may grow well for 10 years or more. Pinching the stem seldom induces desired branching, but give it a try if your avocado becomes too tall. Avocados need cool night temperatures to bloom and fruit. It's best to consider the plant an attractive foliage plant and conversation piece. Leave fruit production to commercial growers. Pets and birds should not be allowed to chew or peck at the leaves.
Propagation: Start avocado from seed. Use the seed (pit) of a green skinned fruit because it will germinate better than seed from a black fruit. Wash the pit, soak it overnight, and scrape off the papery covering. Place the pit into soil with the pointed end just out of the soil. Use a 6-inch pot and rich potting soil. Place at 70°F, water well, and keep moist until the pit sprouts. Germination can take several months.
Pests: Spider mites can be a problem in low humidity.
Recommendations: Named varieties such as **'Brogdin'**, **'Hass'**, and **'Kahaluu'** are available in commercial avocado production areas, but most homeowners who grow this plant enjoy growing it from a pit.

Avocado *(Persea americana)*

Baby's tears *(Soleirolia soleirolii)*

Features: Mat-forming foliage
Size: 1"H × 3–12"W
Light: Medium to bright
Temperature: 55–75°F
Water: Evenly moist

Baby's tears *(Soleirolia soleirolii)* with regular green, chartreuse, and silvery blue foliage

Description and uses: Baby's tears is a creeping plant with thin stems and tiny round leaves. Many people mistake it for moss. Its delicate appearance is best displayed in a shallow pot or hanging basket where it can cascade over the sides of the container. It makes a nice groundcover in terrariums or surrounding larger plants that require high soil moisture. It is also known as Corsican mint and Irish moss.
Care: Baby's tears grows best in bright, indirect light but tolerates medium light. It likes cool temperatures and high humidity. Never allow the soil to dry out completely or the plants will collapse and die. On the other hand roots will rot if the soil is consistently wet. Feed plants every 2 to 3 weeks with a half-strength high nitrogen plant food. This fast grower needs repotting frequently. Prune or pinch back plants regularly to keep them attractive.
Propagation: Start new plants every year from divisions. Rather than rooting individual fine-textured stems, remove a section of the plant and lay it on moist soil. Roots will soon form.
Pests: Possible pests include whiteflies and aphids.
Recommendations: **'Aurea'** has bright green foliage with a golden cast. **'Variegata'** has silver-edge leaves.

Baby's tears *(see Pilea)*
Ball cactus *(see Cactus, ball)*

Bamboo, dwarf *(Pleioblastus pygmaeus)*

Features: Delicate grassy foliage
Size: 1–2'H × spreading
Light: Bright
Temperature: 65–75°F
Water: Evenly moist; barely moist in winter

Description and uses: This small bamboo can reach 2 feet tall but is often shorter. The delicate-appearing leaves and structure lend themselves to Asian décor. It is a tough, quick growing plant.
Care: Grow dwarf bamboo in a good quality potting soil. Keep it moist during active growth, but provide less moisture in winter. In good conditions it might need to be divided a couple of times during the year. Use balanced plant

food every few weeks during the summer. It tolerates dry conditions and less light but quality is reduced. To keep the plant small crowd the roots in a container. In such conditions you'll need to water the plant carefully. Occasionally lift the plant, prune the roots and shoots, add fresh potting soil, and return to the same size container. Trim and shape any time the plant is growing well.

Propagation: Divide plants in spring.

Pests: Few pests affect dwarf bamboo, but aphids, mealybug, scale, and spider mites may appear.

Recommendations: **'Distichus'** is a small, dense, quick growing deep green form with fernlike foliage, to 1 foot.

Dwarf bamboo (*Pleioblastus pygmaeus* 'Dwarf Whitestripe')

Bamboo palm (*see Palm, parlor; Palm, areca*)
Bamburanta (*see Ctenanthe*)

Banana, dwarf (*Musa acuminata*)

Features: Tropical foliage
Size: 3–10'H × 3–6'W
Light: Bright
Temperature: 65–80°F
Water: Evenly moist

Description and uses: If you have the right conditions, dwarf banana's huge paddle-shape leaves bring a strong tropical feel to an indoor setting. Average homes are too cool and too dry for bananas to set fruit indoors. Grow one of the dwarf varieties, and even then it will require a large, well-lit spot with good humidity. This novelty is better suited to a greenhouse than to most living spaces. Banana leaves have a high transpiration rate. It is a good plant for improving indoor air quality. Dwarf banana benefits from summering outdoors in a protected site out of the wind that can shred leaves.

Dwarf banana (*Musa acuminata* 'Tiny Tiny')

Care: Banana needs bright light and high humidity for best foliage color. If possible give it bright light with some direct sun. It needs average to high temperatures (never below 60°F) and should not be exposed to cold drafts. Cold drafts and dry air cause burnt leaf edges on this tropical plant.

Plants will not bloom in low light or low temperatures. Keep the soil damp, but not soggy, at all times. Use an all-purpose plant food during the growing season. Repot as needed using a peaty soil mix.

Propagation: Propagate banana from offsets produced at the base of the plant.

Pests: Spider mites, aphids, and mealybugs are possible pests. Banana is susceptible to anthracnose and wilt.

Recommendations: **'Novak'** rarely grows more than 4 to 5 feet in height. Its foliage may be solid green or bear red spots, especially under strong light. It produces yellow, seedless, edible bananas if it fruits. **'Dwarf Cavendish'** is a compact variety that usually grows to only about 6 feet. **'Super Dwarf Cavendish'** is even smaller, growing 2 to 4 feet tall. **'Sumatrana'** makes a striking foliage plant with green leaves stained with burgundy-brown. It grows to 6 feet.

Bear's paw fern (*see Fern, rabbit's foot*)
Beaucarnea (*see Ponytail palm*)
Beefsteak plant (*see Copperleaf*)

Begonia spp. (*Begonia* species and hybrids)

Features: Showy flowers, foliage, or both
Size: 6–72"H × 6–36"W
Light: Medium to bright
Temperature: 65–75°F
Water: Evenly moist

Angel-wing begonia (*Begonia coccinea* hybrid)

Description and uses: Most houseplant begonias come from tropical regions. Some are selected for their showy flower clusters. Others are prized for their interesting leaf shapes and colors. All have fleshy stems and lopsided leaves, with one side of the leaf larger than the other. The most popular houseplant begonias are angel-wing begonias, fancy-leaf begonias, and winter-blooming begonias. Wax begonia (*B. semperflorens*) is a popular outdoor bedding plant that is often brought inside in fall, offering colorful temporary blooms into early winter, but it grows poorly indoors without bright light and good air circulation.

Angel-wing and fancy-leaf begonias are showy year-round. Place them where they can be enjoyed at all times. Small fancy-leaf begonias are good terrarium specimens. Winter-blooming types are often used as temporary color accents for winter windowsills. Create a showy grouping by growing

Iron cross begonia *(Begonia masoniana)*

Eyelash begonia *(B. boweri 'Bull's Eye')*

are *B. coccinea* and *B. ×corallina*. Many cultivars are available. **'Bubbles'** is a small selection with reddish pink flowers set off by dark green spotted leaves. **'Cracklin' Rosie'** has dark green leaves speckled pink with reddish undersides. **'Looking Glass'** has pink flowers and metallic silver leaves with olive green veins and red undersides. **'Lucerna'** has silver-spotted leaves and salmon-colored flowers year-round. **'Orange Rubra'** has pendulous mandarin orange flowers and is a good choice for hanging baskets. **'Orococo'** is another good choice for hanging baskets. It has white flowers and ivy-shape green-gold leaves edged in dark red. **'Sophie Cecile'** is more upright and has deeply cut green leaves speckled with white and red undersides. Flowers are rose-pink.

Fancy-leaf begonias are more challenging to grow but worth the effort. They produce large showy leaves dramatically marked with shades of silver, green, pink, and red. They tolerate less light than flowering types. They sometimes go dormant in winter, shedding leaves. Trim

Star begonia *(B. heracleifolia 'Benitochiba')*

off dead leaves, allow the soil to become almost dry, and keep the plant at about 60°F until new growth appears, usually in 6 to 10 weeks. **Eyelash begonia** *(B. bowerii)* is a small begonia with hairy leaves and stems. A good choice for terrariums is **Beefsteak begonia** *(B. erythrophylla)*, an old-fashioned begonia with thick rhizomes and large, round, shiny bronze leaves. **Star begonia** *(B. heracleifolia)* is a large begonia with palmate (hand-shape) leaves that are deeply cut. **Iron cross begonia** *(B. masoniana)* has

begonias with other high-humidity flowering houseplants, such as orchids and bromeliads, offset by a backdrop of fern foiage.

Care: Flowering and foliage begonias require bright light year-round to do their best. They do well in average home temperatures but can be damaged by temperatures below 55°F. Feed actively growing flowering plants every 2 to 3 weeks with a high-phosphorus plant food. Feed leafy types every 2 weeks from spring through fall with balanced food, monthly in winter. Water begonias well, then allow them to dry a bit before the next watering. All types require moderate to high humidity. Pebble trays are a good source of extra humidity in dry winter homes. Avoid misting, which can cause powdery mildew. Pot begonias in a peaty, well-drained soilless mix such as African violet mix. Most begonias like to be slightly pot-bound. Overwatering can cause leaves to turn yellow or brown and fall off. Excess light leads to pale, brittle leaves on fancy-leaf types.

Propagation: All begonias can be propagated from stem cuttings. Fancy-leaf types can be propagated from leaf cuttings. Some types can be grown from seed.

Pests: Begonias are susceptible to a variety of insect and disease problems including leaf spots, powdery mildew, thrips, mites, and mealybugs.

Recommendations: Angel-wing begonias are easy to grow and have both showy leaves and attractive flowers. The leaves are often splotched with spots. Flowers hang in elegant pendant clusters. Bloom time varies, with most blooming in late winter and spring. They are among the largest begonias, some reaching up to 6 feet

Rex begonia *(B. Rex Cultorum 'Escargot')*

in height if left unpruned. However pinch or prune to keep them bushier. The two most popular species in this group

Wax begonia *(B. Semperflorens Cultorum)*

Rieger begonia (B. ×hiemalis hybrid)

heavily textured, apple green leaves marked with a dark brown cross. **Rex begonia** (*B. Rex Cultorum* hybrids) is usually grown for its foliage but bears pink or white blooms if given enough light. Most grow horizontally across the soil surface, spreading by rhizomes that root where they touch the soil. Hundreds of cultivars are available, selected for leaf color, shape, and plant size. **'China Curl'** has deeply twisted leaves with a center band of silver on chocolate brown leaves. **'Raspberry Swirl'** has raspberry-color leaves with silver and green edges. **'Fireworks'** has silvery leaves nearly covered by ruby red veins.

Winter-blooming begonias are the result of crosses involving semituberous or tuberous begonias. They have fibrous roots and swollen tuber-like bases. They are usually available in early winter. The bushy, pendulous growth makes it a good choice for hanging baskets. Deadheading helps prolong flowering time. Winter-blooming begonias are best enjoyed while in flower and then discarded. The two main types are **Lorraine** or **Christmas begonias** (*B. ×cheimantha*) and **Reiger** or **elatior begonias** (*B. ×hiemalis*). Lorraine begonias have pink or white single flowers. Rieger begonias have numerous camellia-like blossoms to 2 inches wide in shades of red, pink, salmon, orange, or yellow.

HERE'S A TIP...

Begonias propagate readily from leaf cuttings. Remove a leaf with part of its petiole attached. Make slits across the major veins and lay the leaf on sterile potting soil and pin it to the soil with a hairpin. New plants will form at the slits in the veins.

Beloperone (see Shrimp plant)
Billbergia (see Queen's tears)
Bird's nest anthurium (see Anthurium)
Bird's nest fern (see Fern, bird's nest)
Bishop's cap cactus (see Cactus, bishop's cap)

Black pepper vine (Piper nigrum)

Features: Vine with shiny black-green leaves
Size: 5'H × trailing
Light: Bright
Temperature: 65–85°F
Water: Evenly moist

Description and uses: Black pepper vine is a strong grower with oval solid black-green, leathery leaves. It is grown as a foliage plant or novelty. Unless it is grown in a greenhouse or conservatory it is highly unlikely to produce flowers and set seed. Berries are green, changing to red and then black. They are then dried and used as peppercorns.

Lacquered black pepper vine
(Piper magnificum)

Care: Grow black pepper vine as a hanging basket or trained on a totem in bright light and high humidity. Soil should be a fertile potting mix kept moist during the growing season. Use balanced plant food every two months during growth.
Propagation: Take stem tip cuttings and enclose in plastic to maintain high humidity. Keep the temperature above 70°F.
Pests: Aphids are occasional pests.
Recommendations: **Saffron pepper** (*P. crocatum*) has highly textured metallic white and green leaves with rose-red patches. **Lacquered black pepper vine** (*P. magnificum*) has glossy large dark green crinkled leaves.

Blechnum (see Tree fern, miniature)
Bleeding heart glorybower (see Clerodendrum)

Blood leaf (Iresine herbstii)

Features: Colored heart-shape leaves
Size: 1–2'H × 1'W
Light: Bright
Temperature: 60–75°F
Water: Evenly moist; barely moist in winter

Description and uses:
Use blood leaf where you want a splash of intense color. The heart-shape leaves are brilliant maroon with wide arching pinkish red veins. The succulent stems are also red. Its other common name, chicken gizzard plant, comes from the leaf shape. This accent plant becomes a focal point wherever it is used. Make it part of mixed baskets and foliage groupings.

Blood leaf (Iresine herbstii)

Care: Blood leaf needs bright light to develop good leaf color. Normal room temperatures are good for growth. Plants tolerate 55°F in winter. Blood leaf needs average to high humidity. Water as needed to keep the soil evenly moist. During winter water only enough to keep the mixture from drying out. To encourage bushy growth, pinch out the growing tips at 2- to 3-month intervals.
Propagation: Take stem tip cuttings in winter or spring. Divide plants with multiple stems.
Pests: Spider mites and aphids are the main pest problems.
Recommendations: Bloodleaf is also used outdoors as bedding plant. **'Aureoreticulata'** has green leaves with yellow veins and red stems. **'Brilliantissima'** has crimson foliage with pink-red veins.
   Blood leaf (*I. lindenii*) has black-red foliage shaped like willow leaves.

Blood flower (*see Blood lily*)

Blood lily (*Scadoxus multiflorus*)

Features: Powder puff red flowers
Size: 18–24"H × 12–18"W
Light: Bright
Temperature: 65–75°F; 55–65°F in winter
Water: Evenly moist; moderately dry during dormancy

Blood lily (*Scadoxus multiflorus*)

Description and uses: Blood lily (also known as *Haemanthus multiflorus*) sends up broad lance-shape to oval, nearly stemless leaves that form an arching rosette, followed by a thick leafless flower stalk often marbled with maroon spots. A large ball of bright red flowers to 6 inches across forms at the stem tip. Although each bloom has six colorful petals, long scarlet stamens dominate the flower, giving the entire flower head the appearance of a giant red powder puff.
Care: Blood lily grows from a bulb that has alternating growth and rest periods. Plant the bulb with the tip protruding from the soil. New leaves form after flowering. Water and feed regularly when the plant is in active growth. When the bulb goes dormant in winter, withhold water. Remove faded foliage and store the bulb in its pot in a cool basement or similar spot. Repot infrequently as pot-bound plants bloom better. Use a 50:50 mix of regular potting soil and cactus mix. Soggy soil will rot the bulb. All parts of the plant include toxins. Do not allow children and pets to chew on them.
Propagation: Start new plants from offsets or seed.
Pests: Blood lily has no significant pests.
Recommendations: *S.m. katherinae* is an upright growing form of blood lily.

Boat lily (*see Tradescantia*)
Boston fern (*see Fern, Boston*)

Bougainvillea (*Bougainvillea* spp.)

Features: Spectacular flowering bracts
Size: 2–8'H × 2–8'W
Light: Bright to intense
Temperature: 65–75°F; 50–55°F in winter
Water: Evenly moist; moderately dry in winter

Description and uses: Bougainvillea is a popular climber. You also can prune its spiny, woody stems into a shrublike form or allow them to cascade from a hanging basket. In summer it produces masses of bracts in shades of pink, purple, red, orange, or white. It may bloom in winter under ideal conditions. Bracts are long lasting but the tiny tubular white flowers they enclose are ephemeral.

Bougainvillea (*Bougainvillea* 'Orange Fiesta')

Care: Some sun is needed for bougainvillea to flower well. It grows best in a greenhouse, sunroom, or atrium. Keep well watered while in active growth but use less in winter. Never allow it to dry completely. Feed once a week in summer. Bougainvillea blooms on one-year-old wood, so prune hard after flowering to encourage new growth that will bloom the following year. Plants benefit from summering outdoors. Repot in spring. To control size lift the plant from the pot, shave a few inches off the root ball, add new potting soil, and return to the same size pot.
Propagation: Start new plants from stem cuttings dipped in rooting hormone.
Pests: Spider mites, whiteflies, and mealybugs are possible pests.
Recommendations: *B. glabra* **hybrids** are vigorous vines. Standard, dwarf, and variegated cultivars are available. *B. ×buttiana* **'Mrs. Butt'** has scarlet bracts.

Brake fern (*see Fern, brake*)
Brassia (*see Orchid, spider*)
Brazilian edelweiss (*see Sinningia*)

Brazilian fireworks (*Porphyrocoma pohliana*)

Features: Silver and green foliage; flowers
Size: 8–12"H × 8–24"W
Light: Medium to bright
Temperature: 65–80°F
Water: Evenly moist

Description and uses: This South American native is equally at home growing in a bright location indoors or as a container plant or shade-loving bedding plant outdoors. Avoid exposure to direct sun which can cause leaf puckering.

Brazilian fireworks (*Porphyrocoma pohliana* 'Maracas')

From late spring through summer under the right conditions, the plant develops spikes of red bracts from which purple flowers emerge, creating the fireworks display alluded to in the plant's common name. Another reason for the common name is the plant's habit of shooting its mature seeds up to 10 feet away from the plant.
Care: Brazilian fireworks prefers a bright indoor location. It tolerates medium light but may not flower under those conditions. Because the silver-splashed foliage is attractive in its own right, this may not be a concern. It requires warm conditions. Avoid exposure to cool temperatures and drafts, which can cause foliage to pucker and turn yellow. Keep soil evenly moist; avoid excessive watering or drought conditions. Do not allow the plant to wilt. Feed with blooming plant food from spring through summer. Use a slightly acidic, peaty potting mix.
Propagation: Plants reach blooming size in 3 to 4 months from seed. Germination is better in the dark.
Pests: Brazilian fireworks has no significant pests.
Recommendations: 'Maracas' is the primary cultivar available. Deep red bracts (flower spikes) emerge from green leaves marked in silver along the leaf veins.

Brazilian plume (*Justicia carnea*)

Features: Pink, red, purple, or white flowers
Size: 2–4'H × 1–4'W
Light: Bright
Temperature: 60–75°F
Water: Evenly moist

Brazilian plume (*Justicia carnea*)

Description and uses: Brazilian plume is an upright shrub with abundant dark green, slightly hairy leaves. The true flowers are white and protrude from the showy bracts, resulting in unusual blossoms. Brazilian plume is a fast grower that responds well to a hard pruning. Leaves can be 8 inches long. The 5-inch-long flower spikes are produced summer into fall. It is best suited to growing in a conservatory or greenhouse.
Care: Brazilian plume tolerates average room temperatures but likes summer warmth and humidity. It requires bright light with some direct sunlight for good bloom. Keep moist during the growing season and feed with an all-purpose plant food every 2 weeks. To keep plants shapely and less than 3 feet tall, cut away up to half the top growth in early spring and repot in peaty potting soil. Pinch regularly to maintain a uniform shape. Low light causes spindly growth and poor bloom. Leaves can yellow with too little water.
Propagation: Softwood cuttings taken in spring root easily.
Pests: Spider mites and whiteflies can be pests.
Recommendations: 'Huntington Form' has outstanding salmon-rose pink flowers and deep green foliage backed in red. 'Alba' is a pure white flowering form.

Bromeliad *(see individual plant entries)*

Browallia (*Browallia speciosa*)

Features: Trumpet-shape blue-violet flowers
Size: 10–20"H × 10–12"W
Light: Medium to bright
Temperature: 65 75°F
Water: Evenly moist

Description and uses: Browallia is a shrubby plant with many delicate trumpet-shape blue-violet flowers with a white throat. The plant flowers readily in medium light with high humidity. It is often used as an annual bedding plant. Browallia may not last long as a houseplant but it is easily grown from seed. Discard after peak flowering and start new plants.
Care: Purchase browallia in flower or grow from seed. It will take about 4 months to produce flowers from seed. Pinch the plant regularly to keep it compact. Browallia prefers a cool room and bright light but

Browallia (*Browallia speciosa*)

adapts to less than ideal conditions. Remove spent flowers to prolong bloom. Keep evenly moist and feed every 2 weeks when the plant is actively growing. For multiyear use, renew the plant in spring by cutting back one-half of the top growth, root-prune, and repot in fertile potting soil. Summer browallia outdoors in a shady spot.

Propagation: Sow seed and germinate at 70°F. Or start new plants from stem tip cuttings.
Pests: Aphids can be a problem.
Recommendations: 'Major' has larger flowers than the species. 'Alba' bears white flowers.

Bryophyllum *(see Kalanchoe)*
Buddhist pine *(see Podocarpus)*
Bunny ear cactus *(see Cactus, bunny ear)*

Burro's tail *(Sedum morganianum)*

Features: Hanging plant with taillike stems
Size: 4–6"H × trailing
Light: Bright to intense
Temperature: 60–80°F
Water: Moderately dry

Description and uses: Burro's tail is a distinctive plant with succulent, soft green overlapping leaves that form tubular tails. It is a dramatic decorative plant.
Care: Grow burro's tail in bright light in summer in a hanging basket or on a pedestal out of traffic areas. Leaves are fragile; even a slight bump can knock them off the plant. New stems constantly emerge. Grow in well-drained cactus mix but keep the plant adequately watered during summer growth. Overwatering is the most common cause of death. Feed no more than once a month during growth. Give burro's tail as much bright light as possible. It grows best with winter rest and a drop in temperatures.

Burro's tail *(Sedum morganianum)*

Propagation: Start new plants from tip cuttings. Remove the leaves from the cut end of the stem and allow to dry for 24 hours. Plant in barely moist cactus soil and slowly resume watering. Single leaves also root but take a long time to develop into a full-size plant.

Rosy sedum *(Sedum furfuraceum)*

Pests: Burro's tail is generally pest free, but spider mites, mealybugs, and aphids may appear.
Recommendations: Rosy sedum *(S. furfuraceum)* is upright.

Butterfly palm *(see Palm, areca)*
Button fern *(see Fern, button)*
Buttonhole orchid *(see Orchid, buttonhole)*

Cactus, ball *(Notocactus crassigibbus)*

Features: Ball shape; flowers well
Size: 3"H × 3"W
Light: Bright
Temperature: 65–75°F; 50°F minimum winter
Water: Moderately dry

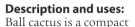
Ball cactus *(Notocactus crassigibbus)*

Description and uses: Ball cactus is a compact ribbed cactus for the windowsill or cactus gardens. It has woolly areoles (small visible bumps from which spines grow).
Care: Grow ball cactus in bright light without direct sun. Water well during the growing season but sparingly in winter when temperatures are lower. Use cactus food about three times a summer. Spines can be painful, so handle plants with care. Keep children and pets away. Repot in spring.
Propagation: Remove and plant offsets when they develop or start new plants from seed.
Pests: Root rot, root mealybugs, and scale may be problems.
Recommendations: Tom Thumb cactus *(N. mammulosus)*, also called *Parodia mammulosa*, has white spines. **Silver ball cactus** *(N. scopa)* has white spines with reddish central spines.

Cactus, ball *(Parodia* spp.)

Features: Ball shape; ribs and thorns
Size: 8"H × 6"W
Light: Bright to intense
Temperature: 65–75°F; 50°F in winter
Water: Moderately dry

Description and uses: Ball cactus is usually round, and generally small, but can become cylindrical with age. It bears yellow or red cup-shape flowers in spring.
Care: Water moderately during spring and summer growth, but allow to dry between waterings. Keeping the soil wet in winter will cause rot. Give it cactus food three times during the growing season. Its thorns are decorative but can be painful. Keep out of traffic areas and away from children and pets.
Propagation: Offsets are the quickest method

Ball cactus *(Parodia* spp.)

of starting new plants. You may also start ball cactus from seed.

Pests: Root rot, mealybugs, root mealybugs, and spider mites may affect ball cactus.

Recommendations: Tufted parodia (*P. penicillata*) bears decorative white thorns. *P. schwebsiana* has orange flowers and white thorns. *P. subterranea* develops brown-black thorns, bears red flowers, and grows to 5 inches in diameter.

Cactus, bishop's cap (Astrophytum myriostigma)

Features: Star-shape vertical spineless ribs
Size: 4–40"H × 2–6"W
Light: Bright to intense
Temperature: 65–75°F; 40–65°F fall and winter
Water: Moderately dry

Description and uses:
With its generally smooth, spineless ribs, bishop's cap cactus resembles a living rock. It has a definite star shape when young, becoming more cylindrical as it ages. Mature plants produce 2-inch yellow flowers, sometimes with a red or orange accented base. Pollinated flowers produce decorative hairy red fruit.

Bishop's cap cactus (*Astrophytum myriostigma*)

Care: Grow bishop's cap in cactus mix in a small clay pot. Give it bright light, such as in a sunny south window. Typical room temperatures are fine for bishop's cap while it is in growth. It tolerates low winter temperatures if kept dry. Give bishop's cap two or three feedings of cactus food during the growing season, but cease feeding in winter.

Propagation: Plants started from seed will take about 6 years to flower.

Pests: Root rot, spider mites, mealybugs, and scale may affect bishop's cap cactus.

Recommendations: Sea urchin cactus (*A. asterias*) is nearly spineless. **'Super Kabuto'** is a highly spotted white clone.

Cactus, bunny ear (Opuntia microdasys)

Features: Branched flat pads
Size: 6–24"H × 4–30"W
Light: Bright to intense
Temperature: 65–75°F; 50°F in winter
Water: Moderately dry

Description and uses:
Thornless flat pads extend up and out from the center of the plant. Glochids, small, round barbed hairy structures on the pads, can cause skin irritation. They easily attach to skin if brushed by accident. Mist plants prior to moving or working with them to reduce irritation. It also helps to use gloves when

Bunny ear cactus (*Opuntia microdasys*)

handling the plant. Bunny ear produces 1½–2-inch lemon yellow flowers in the spring followed by red fruits.

Care: Grow bunny ears in bright to intense light in cactus mix. During growth water well and feed once a month with a balanced plant food. Allow plants to dry before watering again. In winter water just enough to keep plants from shriveling. Cool temperatures, to 50°F, and dry winter conditions encourage spring flowering. Keep out of traffic areas, away from children and pets.

Propagation: Take cuttings of one to several pads. Allow the cut surface to dry 24 hours. Then plant in barely moist cactus mix.

Pests: Possible problems include root rot, spider mites, mealybugs, and scale.

Recommendations: 'Albata' has clusters of smaller pads covered with snow-white glochids. *O. rufida* is a closely related species with reddish brown glochids.

Cactus, chin (Gymnocalycium spp.)

Features: Round with "chins" between areoles
Size: 2–8"H × 2–12"W
Light: Bright
Temperature: 65–75°F; 50°F winter
Water: Moderately dry

Description and uses:
Chin cactus is round and ribbed with distinctive chins or bumps between each areole. Spines curve back toward plant. It bears off-white to red flowers in spring.

Grafted form of ruby ball cactus (*Gymnocalycium mihanovichii* 'Hibotan')

Care: Water well during growth and feed three times during summer. Provide bright light. Give it a cool, dry period in winter. High humidity and soggy soil will cause root rot. Grow in cactus mix. Repot in spring when plant is as large in diameter as the pot in which it is growing.

Propagation: Graft offsets of the colorful types with no chlorophyll onto a green chlorophyll-producing rootstock. Other types may be started from seed or by removing offsets and rooting.

Pests: Root rot, soil mealybug, mealybug, and scale may affect chin cactus.

Recommendations: Dwarf chin cactus (*G. baldianum*) is a green ball to 3 inches in diameter. It can produce red, white, pink, or orange flowers one year from sowing.

Ruby ball cactus (*G. mihanovichii* 'Hibotan') develops into a dramatic ruby-red ball, but must be grafted on various root stocks because the ball can not produce chlorophyll on its own. *G. andreae* has yellow flowers. *G. mihanovichii* is 2 inches in diameter. Its ball shape has pointed ribs with white banding. *G. tillianum* is 5 inches in diameter and bears orange flowers that turn carmine with age. *G. uruguayensis* has yellow flowers.

Cactus, Christmas (Schlumbergera ×buckleyi)

Features: Arching habit; brilliant flowers
Size: 8–12"H × 6–18"W
Light: Bright
Temperature: 70–80°F; 55°F in fall
Water: Moderately dry

Description and uses:

This tree-dwelling cactus has dark green flat stems that are segmented at 1- to 2-inch intervals. The leaf margins are slightly scalloped. Whorls of satiny flowers dangle at the ends of the stems, giving the plant a graceful arching appearance. There are hundreds of cultivars available with flower colors in

Christmas cactus (Schlumbergera ×buckleyi)

lilac, deep rose, salmon, red-orange, and white. Plants usually bloom mid- to late December and are popular holiday decorations.
Care: Christmas cactus is a short-day plant, blooming when subjected to 14 hours of uninterrupted darkness starting about the middle of October. Place the plant in total darkness each night for 6 to 8 weeks or until buds form. It needs bright light during the day. It also can be forced into bloom by providing cool nighttime temperatures, somewhere around 55°F, for 6 to 8 weeks. Keep the plant in

Thanksgiving cactus (Schlumbergera truncata 'Thor Alise')

a sunny indoor location during winter months, moving it outdoors for the summer if possible. Avoid changing its environment once it starts setting buds. If placed in a drafty location or if the lighting is changed, it readily aborts the newly formed buds. Allow the soil to dry between waterings. Feed monthly after flowering when plants start new growth in spring. It rarely needs repotting. When it does use a well-drained soil.

After blooming is finished, prune by pinching or using a sharp knife to cut off several sections. This encourages the plant to branch, creating a fuller plant with more blossoms.
Propagation: Take stem cuttings as new growth begins in spring. Allow the cuttings to callus before potting them.
Pests: Possible pests include stem rot, scale, spider mites, and aphids.
Recommendations: Thanksgiving cactus (*S. truncata*) has two to four pointy teeth along the margins of the stem segments. Three-inch flowers in white and shades of red are borne at the stem tips about a month before Christmas cactus. It is also sometimes called crab cactus.

Cactus, cob (Lobivia spp.)

Features: Starfish-shape thorns
Size: 1–6"H × 1–4"W
Light: Bright
Temperature: 60–70°F; 40°F in winter
Water: Moderately dry

Description and uses:

This small ribbed spherical or cylindrical cactus with yellow or red flowers is native to Bolivia, where it is found at high elevation.
Care: Cob cactus can be treated as an alpine in a frost-free greenhouse. It needs a distinct cool period to

Cob cactus (Lobivia spp.)

flower. Water it well during the growing season, sparingly in winter. Wet soil in winter will cause root rot and death. Provide cactus food three times during growth. Repot in spring in cactus soil when the plant fills its pot.
Propagation: Start cob cactus from seed. Remove and repot offsets when they appear.
Pests: Root rot, mealybugs, soil mealybugs, and scale may affect cob cactus.
Recommendations: *Lobivia boliviensis* (*Echinopsis pentlandii*) is a clumping cactus of variable size. Flowers are red, pink, orange, or yellow, up to 2½ inches in diameter.
    Lobivia caespitosa (*Echinopsis maximiliana*) is a mat-forming cactus, to 8 inches tall. It has yellow flowers with a red throat.
    Lobivia cinnabarina (*Echinopsis cinnabarina*), with red flowers, develops a flattened shape to 6 inches in diameter.
    Lobivia wrightiana (*Echinopsis backebergii*) grows to 3 inches tall and 2 inches in diameter. It has medium purple flowers.

Cactus, crown (Rebutia spp.)

Features: Flattened spherical stems; colorful flowers
Size: 2–6"H × 2–6"W
Light: Bright
Temperature: 60–70°F; 40°F in winter
Water: Moderately dry

Description and uses:

Generally growing into a small cluster of flattened spherical stems, crown cactus is a good choice for cactus dish gardens. Bright red, pink, yellow, white, or orange-red flowers arise from the base of the stem. In some years flowers may cover the plant.

Crown cactus (Rebutia spp.)

Care: Water well during growth and provide cactus food once a month. Give crown cactus little water and no food during its winter rest. The plant requires a drop in winter temperatures for good bloom. Grow in well-drained cactus soil. Repot in spring.

Propagation: Propagate from seed or offsets.

Pests: Crown cactus may develop root rot, soil mealybugs, mealybugs, or scale.

Recommendations: *R. marsoneri* has clumping heads 1½ inches tall and 1 inch wide. *R. minuscula* produces large red flowers at a young age on pale green clumping stems. *R. m. violaciflora* has purple flowers. *R. muscula* has whitish clumping stems about 1½ inches in diameter. It is 2½ inches tall and bears orange flowers. *R. narvaecensis* is 2½ inches tall with pink flowers.

Cactus, Easter lily *(Echinopsis multiplex)*

Features: Spherical plant; flowers
Size: 8"H × 5"W
Light: Bright
Temperature: 65–75°F; 45–55°F winter
Water: Moderately dry

Description and uses: Easter lily cactus makes an attractive small, clumping plant that flowers well. Grow it on a windowsill or in a cactus garden with other plants with low water needs.

Care: Easter lily cactus stores water aboveground rather than in its small root zone. Water moderately spring to fall. Keep it moderately dry in winter and place in a cool spot. Grow in well-drained soil or cactus mix. Use cactus food once a

Easter lily cactus *(Echinopsis multiplex)*

month in spring and summer. Flowers develop best on the shaded side of the plant. Turn the plant regularly to provide uniform light exposure, but avoid moving as flowers are opening.

Propagation: Start Easter lily cactus from seed or offsets.

Pests: Root rot, mealybugs, and scale may affect Easter lily cactus.

Recommendations: *E. eyriesii* is ribbed with brown spines and greenish white scented flowers.

Cactus, Easter *(Hatiora gaertneri)*

Features: Flattened stems; bell-shape flowers
Size: 12–18"H × 12–30"W
Light: Bright
Temperature: 65–75°F; 50–60°F winter
Water: Moderately dry

Description and uses: Easter cactus develops dark green segmented, flattened stems with dramatic many-petaled bell-shape scarlet flowers in spring. Some white, pink or

Easter cactus *(Hatiora gaertneri)*

purple forms are available. It is also known as *Rhipsalidopsis gaertneri* and *Schlumbergera gaertneri*.

Care: Grow it in bright light but out of direct summer sun. As an epiphyte it requires well-drained soil. Water well during active growth and feed every few weeks. It needs cool winter temperatures for good flowering. During the cool period provide only enough water to prevent shriveling. Do not move plant once buds are set.

Propagation: Take stem segment cuttings of one to four segments. Allow cuttings to dry 24 hours before sticking in rooting medium. After rooting, pot and pinch to two segments to encourage branching. Easter cactus may also be started from seed.

Pests: Root rot, mealybugs, and scale are potential pests.

Recommendations: Drunkard's dream (*H. salicornioides*) is a spineless hanging cactus. The 18-inch-long stems have bottle-shape segments.

Cactus, golden barrel *(Echinocactus grusonii)*

Features: Spherical cactus with golden ribs
Size: 2–30"H × 2–30"W
Light: Bright to intense
Temperature: 65–75°F; 45°F winter
Water: Moderately dry

Description and uses: Golden barrel is a popular landscape cactus that is spherical to cylindrical in shape, becoming more oblong with age. As a houseplant it rarely grows larger than 12 inches in height or diameter. The plant has decorative but

Golden barrel cactus *(Echinocactus grusonii)*

brutal golden spines with creamy wool on top of its barrel. Juvenile plants lack a distinct rib structure and thus appear quite different from mature specimens. Golden barrel cactus grows extremely slowly. Mature plants grown in full sun may bear small yellow flowers.

Care: Provide golden barrel cactus with as much bright light or sun as possible. Water thoroughly but allow soil to dry between waterings. Use cactus food several times during the growing season. Water sparingly in winter and withhold plant food. Keep the plant in cool conditions through the winter months. Repot rarely to avoid root damage; use cactus mix. Keep children and pets away from spines.

Propagation: Seed requires stratification (moist cold, such as in a refrigerator) for 1 year before it will germinate.

Pests: Golden barrel cactus may develop root and crown rot, mealybugs, spider mites, or scale.

Recommendations: A rare white ribbed form of golden barrel cactus is occasionally available.

Cactus, hedgehog (Echinocereus spp.)

Features: Columnar or spherical with thorns or hairs
Size: 4–12"H × 4–36"W
Light: Bright to intense
Temperature: 65–75°F; 50–55°F in winter
Water: Moderately dry

Description and uses: Hedgehog cactus branches readily, over time making mounds up to 3 feet in diameter and 1 foot tall, somewhat resembling a hedgehog. Various species of *Echinocereus* have a range of flower colors from green to yellow, pink, orange, and red. Flowers are goblet shape and stay open day and night. Showy red fruits follow the blooms.

Hedgehog cactus (Echinocereus spp.)

Care: Larger species take full sun; smaller ones adapt to bright light. Allow to dry between waterings. Use cactus food once a month during active growth. Keep moderately dry most of the year, and even drier in winter. Repot only when it outgrows its pot, using cactus mix.

Propagation: Cuttings of side shoots root in cactus mix. Hedgehog cactus may also be started from seed.

Pests: Watch for root rot, mealybugs, spider mites, and scale.

Recommendations: Berlander's hedgehog cactus (*E. berlandieri*) has 1-inch-diameter, dark green stems to 12 inches long with yellow-brown spines and purple-pink flowers. *E. pectinatus* has clumping, 4–8 inch tall cylindrical stems and deep pink flowers. **Black lace cactus** (*E. reichenbackii albertii*) has white spines with dark purple tips that look like teeth in a comb. Stems are 1–6 inches tall. *E. reichenbackii fitchii* (*E. fitchii*) has 4–6-inch-long stems with yellowish areoles (hairs around the spines). *E. subinermis* has pale blue-green stems up to 8 inches long.

Cactus, mistletoe (Rhipsalis spp.)

Features: Pencillike leafless stems; berries
Size: 1–3'H × 1–2'W
Light: Medium to bright
Temperature: 65–75°F
Water: Moderately dry

Description and uses: *Rhipsalis* is an interesting leafless genus with round or flat stems that do not look like a cactus. Long pendant stems produce nice hanging baskets or pedestal plants. Under the right conditions, bright, small flowers produce small decorative berries from which the plant gets its common name.

Oriental pencil cactus (Rhipsalis cribata)

Care: Give bright light and regular watering during growth, less in winter. Feed with cactus food several times during the growing season. Mistletoe cactus rarely needs repotting. When it does use cactus mix. Prune lightly to shape and remove damaged stems.

Propagation: Stem cuttings are the easiest method of propagation. Adventurous gardeners may try starting them from seed.

Pests: Mealybugs are occasional pests of mistletoe cactus.

Recommendations: Mistletoe cactus (*R. baccifera*) has stems that hang down. **Oriental pencil cactus** (*R. cribata*) is similar but with pencil-thin stems.

Cactus, old man (Cephalocereus senilis)

Features: Long white stiff hairs
Size: 4–36"H × 2–8"W
Light: Bright to intense
Temperature: 65–75°F; 55°F in winter
Water: Moderately dry

Description and uses: Old man cactus is grown for its woolly long white hairs. These are produced in nature to protect the plant from sun. As a houseplant give it as much sun as possible to produce the hairs that cover sharp yellow spines. Stems are columnar and grow in clumps. In nature it grows over 20 feet tall; in the house rarely more than 3 feet tall. It is slow growing.

Old man cactus (Cephalocereus senilis)

Care: Grow in full sun or as bright a location as possible. Grow in cactus mix. Soak the soil, then allow it to dry between waterings. In winter keep it even drier because old man cactus is sensitive to overwatering. Apply cactus food infrequently during the growing season.

Propagation: Offsets from the main stem may be separated and potted up. Plants started from seed will take many years to reach several inches in height.

Pests: Root rot, mealybugs, and soil mealybugs are potential pests on old man cactus.

Recommendations: No named cultivars are available.

Cactus, peanut (Echinopsis chamaecereus)

Features: Cluster of stems with peanutlike offsets
Size: 2–6"H × 1–12"W
Light: Bright to intense
Temperature: 65–75°F; 45–50°F in winter
Water: Moderately dry

Description and uses:

Peanut cactus (Echinopsis chamaecereus)

Stems of peanut cactus grow up to 6 inches long and can be upright or prostrate. The name comes from the peanutlike offsets that form along many stems. Orange flowers 1½ inches in diameter may develop in spring. Some references list peanut cactus as *Chamaecereus sylvestrii*.

Care: Give peanut cactus as much indoor sun as possible; however outdoors protect the plant from direct summer sun. The plant needs a winter rest period at low temperatures to produce numerous flowers. Provide moderate water during its growth cycle, but keep drier in winter. Use cactus food once a month during active growth.

Propagation: Remove and plant the peanutlike offsets or start new plants from seed.

Pests: Watch for development of root rot, mealybugs, and soil mealybugs.

Recommendations: No cultivars are readily available.

Cactus, pincushion (Mammillaria spp.)

Features: Flowers; compact form
Size: 1–20"H × 1–20"W
Light: Bright to intense
Temperature: 65–75°F; 45–55°F in winter
Water: Moderately dry

Description and uses: Pincushion cacti are small to medium-size plants. They may form solitary columns or cylinders or develop a multistemmed clump. Stems have no ribs but areoles grow in spirals. Yellow, white, red, or pink flowers are produced on the previous year's growth.

Care: The genus *Mammillaria* includes some of the easiest cacti to grow. Provide the brightest light possible. Water thoroughly but allow the soil to dry between waterings. Apply cactus food occasionally during the growing season. Repot young plants each spring in cactus mix. Older plants require repotting less frequently.

Propagation: Pincushion cactus readily develops offsets that may be separated and potted up, or start new plants from seed.

Pests: Root rot, mealybugs, and soil mealybugs may attack pincushion cactus.

Recommendations: Snowball cactus (*M. bocasana bocasana*) forms a small round cluster with many white hairlike spines. It is easy to grow. **Silken pincushion cactus** (*M. bombycina*) is

Snowball cactus (Mammillaria bocasana bocasana)

Silken pincushion cactus (Mammillaria bombycina)

another easy-to-grow cactus that forms large clumps of cylindrical white, woolly stems to 5 inches tall. **Snowball pincushion** (*M. candida*) develops solitary or clumping cylinders with white spines to 12 inches tall. **Lady finger cactus** (*M. elongata*) forms clusters of many-stemmed plants. **Old lady cactus** (*M. hahniana*) forms green clumps to 3½ inches high, frequently with white spines. **Owl's eye pincushion** (*M. parkinsonia*) forms tight clumps with stems bearing white spines and wool. **Feather cactus** (*M. plumosa*) forms whitish mounds to 16 inches wide. **Little candles** (*M. prolifera*) forms large hairy clumps to 3½ inches tall. **Pincushion cactus** (*M. sphaerica*) forms slightly woolly clumps to 20 inches wide. **Spiny pincushion cactus** (*M. spinosissima*) has blue-green solitary stems, to 20 inches, with bristlelike spines. **Rose pincushion cactus** (*M. zeilmanniana*) is a solitary or clumping cactus to 2½ inches tall with bristly white spines.

Lady finger cactus (Mammillaria elongata)

Cactus, rattail *(Disocactus flagelliformis)*

Features: Spiny stems; pink flowers
Size: 4–48"H × 4–48"W, trailing
Light: Bright to intense
Temperature: 65–75°F; 55–65°F winter
Water: Barely moist; moderately dry in winter

Description and uses: Rattail cactus is fast growing. It has creeping or trailing stems to 4 feet long. Showy pink flowers grow along the stems and can last for up to 2 months. To produce fruit indoors you will probably have to hand pollinate the flowers. Hummingbirds pollinate plants outdoors. Display rattail cactus in a hanging basket or on a pedestal out of traffic areas. It is also often sold as *Aporocactus flagelliformis.*

Rattail cactus *(Disocactus flagelliformis)*

Care: Use well drained regular potting soil and keep moist during the growing season. Allow soil to dry slightly in winter. Use balanced plant food once a month during spring and summer. Because rattail cactus has dense growth, regularly inspect the plant for pests. Grow in bright light. Full morning sun is ideal. Keep plants away from children and pets.
Propagation: Take stem cuttings in summer. Allow cut stems to dry a couple of days, then stick them in regular potting mix.
Pests: Watch for development of mealybugs and scale.
Recomendations: *D. nelsonii* is a similar, related species.

Calamondin orange *(×Citrofortunella microcarpa)*

Features: White flowers; edible fruits
Size: 1–4'H × 1–2'W
Light: Bright to intense
Temperature: 65–80°F; 55–65°F winter
Water: Evenly moist

Description and uses: This upright woody shrub is a cross between mandarin orange and kumquat. It sports showy 1-inch bright orange fruits almost constantly beginning in its second year. The white flowers are lightly fragrant. The showy fruits can remain on the plants for weeks. They

Calamondin orange *(×Citrofortunella microcarpa)*

can be used like lemons or made into marmalade.
Care: Calamondin orange needs full sun, ideally from a south-facing window. Plants can grow cooler in winter—down to 55°F—and warmer in summer—up to 80°F, but if temperatures are too warm the plant may not set fruit. Feed every 2 weeks in spring and summer using a balanced plant food that includes micronutrients. Overfeeding can lead to reduced flowering. Plants prefer high humidity but tolerate lower levels. If the air is dry while plants are blooming, flowers will drop without setting fruit. Keep soil evenly moist spring through summer, allowing it to dry a bit between waterings in fall and winter. Repot young plants every 2 years using cactus, palm, and citrus potting soil. Older plants can go longer between repotting. Prune young plants in late spring to encourage branching and keep plants compact. Best fruit production comes from cutting-grown plants rather than seed-grown ones. Lack of flowering can come from too much nitrogen or a plant grown in too large a pot. To ensure good fruit set, dab flowers with a dry paintbrush to distribute pollen among the flowers.
Propagation: Calamondin orange starts easily from stem cuttings taken in early summer.
Pests: Scale is the major insect pest, but aphids, mealybugs, and spider mites can be problems if humidity is low.
Recommendations: Variegated calamondin is much like the species, but has cream and light green leaf markings.

Calathea *(Calathea spp.)*

Features: Leaves marked silver and green
Size: 12–18"H × 12–18"W
Light: Medium to bright
Temperature: 70–85°F
Water: Evenly moist

Peacock plant *(Calathea makoyana)*

Description and uses: This prayer plant *(Maranta)* relative is a beautiful addition to any houseplant collection, provided you give it the necessary conditions. The velvetlike leaves have showy markings in shades of green and silver. Most selections have a distinct reddish color on the leaf undersides. Some selections have narrow, lance-shape leaves and others are oval. New leaves are curled when they emerge. Small specimens are great for terrariums, where humidity is high. Calathea is a good candidate for a humid bathroom.

Calathea (*Calathea* hybrids 'Helen Kennedy')

Care: Do everything you can to increase calathea's humidity level, especially in winter. Give it bright, indirect light but no direct sun. Leaves shrivel and die when exposed to excess light. From spring through summer, feed with a high-nitrogen foliage plant food. Use a fast draining potting soil that contains peat and perlite. Repot annually in spring using fresh soil and a clean container. Individual plants typically live 5 to 8 years. Plants are sensitive to fluoride and salts, so use rainwater or distilled water for watering. Plants enjoy frequent warm showers year-round. Low humidity causes brown leaf tips and edges. Lighter green new leaves could indicate lack of nitrogen or iron. Remove damaged or unattractive leaves.

Propagation: Mature plants can be divided, but it's not easy and plants take a long time to recover. Stem cuttings can be rooted under warm, moist conditions.

Pests: Spider mites, thrips, and mealybugs can be problems.

Recommendations: Many named varieties are available. **'Corona'** is among the most popular. **'Helen Kennedy'** has brushstroke markings on the leaves.

Cathedral windows (*C. picturata*) gets its name from the beautiful veining and striping on its leaves. Leaves of **'Argentea'** have a central silver stripe with a green border and wine-red undersides.

Lance-leafed calathea (*C. rufibarba*) is less showy but is easier to grow.

Peacock plant (*C. makoyana*) has decorative leaves with diagonal green and white stripes, somewhat like a peacock's tail, with an underside with purple stripes.

Ornate calathea (*C. ornata*) has dark green leaves with pink stripes and magenta reverse.

Zebra calathea (*C. zebrina*) has wide zebralike yellow and green stripes.

Cape ivy (*see Wax vine*)
Cape leadwort (*see Plumbago*)

Cape lily (*Veltheimia bracteata*)

Features: Attractive foliage; pink flowers
Size: 2–3'H × 1–2'W
Light: Bright
Temperature: 40–75°F
Water: Barely moist

Description and uses: This showy bulbous plant thrives in a pot. It has leaves up to 15 inches long and 4 inches wide. They are shiny green with slight undulations along the edges. The tubular flowers are pinkish purple and faintly speckled with yellow and last for several weeks. The best place for cape lily is a greenhouse or conservatory, but if you can provide it with the cool, sunny conditions it needs, it makes an outstanding houseplant. It is the same plant as *V. viridifolia*.

Cape lily (*Veltheimia bracteata*)

Care: Plant the large, onionlike bulb in early fall. Set the pot in a spot with sun for at least half the day and night temperatures in the 40–60°F range. It will not flourish if temperatures rise above 60°F during fall and winter. The foliage appears first, followed by the flower spike. Move the plant out of direct sun when in flower to extend bloom life. In late spring leaves turn yellow and the bulb goes dormant. A few months later new growth begins again. Water newly planted bulbs sparingly—only enough to make the entire potting mixture barely moist—until some growth appears above the soil surface. Gradually increase the amount of water, but always let the top half-inch of the mixture dry out between waterings. When the foliage begins to yellow, gradually reduce the amount. Once all leaves have died off, let the dormant bulb remain completely dry in its pot until new growth appears. Apply a high-potassium plant food at half strength once a month from the time leaves are well developed until they start to yellow. Cape lily does not need repotting until it fills its pot with offsets. Use a fast draining mix.

Propagation: In late summer detach offsets and pot them.

Pests: There are no significant pests to watch out for.

Recommendations: 'Rose-alba' has creamy white flowers, without speckles, flushed rosy pink at the base.

Cape primrose (*see Streptocarpus*)
Cardinal flower (*see Sinningia*)
Carludovica (*see Panama hat plant*)

Carrion flower (*Stapelia* spp.)

Features: Star-shape flowers
Size: 4–12"H × 4–24"W
Light: Bright to intense
Temperature: 65–75°F; 50–65°F in winter
Water: Moderately dry

Description and uses: Carrion flower is an unusual spreading succulent with upright, generally spineless stems. The smallest are a few inches tall with 1-inch flowers. Some are 12 inches tall with 8 inch hairy red, purple, or yellow star-shape flowers that smell

Carrion flower (*Stapelia* spp.)

Carrion flower (S. huernia)

like rotten meat. The smell attracts fly pollinators. When in bloom you may want to place the plant outdoors where you won't smell it. *Stapelia* is a challenging plant to grow indoors. A greenhouse or conservatory is best, but a sunny window can work if you provide careful attention to watering.
Care: When in doubt do not water carrion flower. The plant rarely dies from lack of water but certainly will rot with too much. Growing media and pots must have perfect drainage. In warm weather water well then allow to dry before watering again. Cease watering when temperatures are below 60°F. Winter cool temperatures are required to produce next season's flowers. If you repot carrion flower annually it needs no supplemental plant food.
Propagation: Take stem cuttings during periods of active growth. Allow cuttings to callus 1 to 3 weeks, then plant in a cactus potting mix.
Pests: Root rot, mealybugs, and soil mealybugs are potential pests of carrion flower.
Recommendations: Giant starfish flower (*S. gigantea*) can be 12 inches tall and spread to 2 feet. Its flowers are 8 inches wide and pale yellow with crimson striations.

Large flowered carrion flower, (*S. grandiflora*) has hairy star-shape cream flowers. Stems are red-purple to purple.

Hairy carrion flower, (*S. hirsuta*) has red-purple hairy star-shape flowers, occasionally marked with wavy lines.

Caryota (see Palm, fishtail)

Cast-iron plant (Aspidistra elatior)

Features: Deep green foliage
Size: 1–2'H × 1–2'W
Light: Low
Temperature: 45–85°F
Water: Evenly moist; barely moist in fall and winter

Description and uses: Slow growing cast-iron plant lives up to its name. It is almost indestructible, withstanding neglect, low light, low humidity, and a wide range of temperatures. It is the perfect plant to provide greenery in a dark corner. It can tolerate low temperatures, down to 40°F. Cast-iron

Cast-iron plant (Aspidistra elatior)

plant has smooth upright leaves. Start with large plants since plants grow slowly.
Care: Although this workhorse houseplant can get by with little care, it responds nicely when given appropriate conditions. Water in spring and early summer to keep soil evenly moist. Allow soil to dry out in fall and winter. Excess soil moisture can lead to root rot. From late spring to early fall, feed every 2 to 3 weeks with a balanced plant food. Repot in spring as needed; every 3 years is usually sufficient. Wash leaves occasionally to remove dust.
Propagation: Divide plants every 5 years by pulling apart crowded clumps and repotting. Several divisions can be potted in one container to make a large plant.
Pests: Spider mites and scale can be problems.
Recommendations: There are several named varieties, many with speckled or striped foliage. **'Milky Way'** has white spots. **'Variegata'** has yellow stripes. **'Goldspike'** is a rare selection with narrow upright leaves with yellow stripes. **'Stars and Stripes'** has yellow-green stripes and white spots on medium-width leaves.

Cathedral windows (see Calathea)
Cattleya orchid (see Orchid, cattleya)
Century plant (see Agave)
Cephalocereus (see Cactus, old man)

Ceropegia (see Rosary vine)
Chamaecereus (see Cactus, peanut)
Chamaedorea (see Palm, parlor)
Chandelier plant (see Kalanchoe)

Chenille plant (Acalypha hispida)

Features: Drooping tassels of red flowers
Size: 1–3'H × 1–3'W
Light: Bright to intense
Temperature: 70–75°F
Water: Evenly moist

Description and uses: Chenille plant is an upright growing woody shrub that adapts well to pot culture. Its showiest feature is the spectacular spikes of bright red flowers that can reach 12 to 18 inches in length and up to an inch wide.

Chenille plant (Acalypha hispida)

Children love the soft pink and red "caterpillars." When this plant is out of bloom, it has attractive foliage. It can be trained into a standard for a truly amazing specimen plant.

Care: Chenille plant blooms best when given full sun in winter and bright, indirect light in summer. Direct sun causes leaves to fade and reduces flower life. It tolerates lower light but won't bloom as well. Chenille plant likes warm temperatures and high humidity. Feed plants through summer with a balanced plant food. Repot small plants annually. Use regular potting soil. Cut plants back by about one-third in early spring to keep them shrubbier and more attractive in bloom. Avoid excess pinching and pruning, which can delay flower bud set. The sap can irritate skin and is slightly poisonous if ingested. Wear gloves when working with plants and do not allow children or pets to chew plant parts.

Propagation: Take semihardwood cuttings every 2 years to propagate new plants.

Pests: Spider mites, whiteflies, mealybugs, and downy mildew may affect chenille plant.

Recommendations: 'Alba' is a selection with fuzzy creamy white flowers.

Flying foxtail (*A. repens*) is a low growing trailing form with dangling red flowers similar to chenille plant. It's great for hanging baskets.

China doll (*Radermachera sinica*)

Features: Compound leaves
Size: 1–4'H × 1–3'W
Light: Medium to bright
Temperature: 60–75°F
Water: Evenly moist

China doll (*Radermachera sinica*)

Description and uses: With careful attention to pinching and pruning, China doll can be kept to 4 feet or so indoors. Young plants usually have a single vertical stem with a leafy crown of leaves. When the plant matures it becomes more branched. Younger plants have smaller, less divided leaves in a lustrous green color. Mature plants have glossy, doubly compound leaves with prominent veins. Each leaf measures up to 2 feet long with numerous pointed leaflets. China doll is great in a foliage plant grouping or as a backdrop for a blooming plant.

Care: China doll grows well with average temperatures, but can take 55°F in winter. It needs medium to bright light but must be shielded from direct sun. Plants become leggy and unattractive in lower light. It likes medium to high humidity but tolerates low humidity. Water as needed to keep the soil evenly moist. Leaves yellow if the plant is too dry. They turn brown on the edges and fall if too wet. Repot young plants annually in spring. Once plants reach the desired size, continue repotting annually but root prune to limit size and return to the same pot. Feed through the summer with foliage plant food. Pinch the stem tips often. Remove faded leaflets and give plants a shower once a month.

Propagation: Take stem tip cuttings in summer. Use a rooting hormone and bottom heat.

Pests: Possible problems include spider mites, whiteflies, and mealybugs.

Recommendations: 'Crystal Doll' is a variegated form with golden-edged leaves. It does best in bright light.

Chin cactus (*see Cactus, chin*)

Chinese evergreen (*Aglaonema commutatum*)

Features: Arching, often variegated leaves
Size: 1–3'H × 1–3'W
Light: Low to medium
Temperature: 60–75°F
Water: Evenly moist

Chinese evergreen (*Aglaonema commutatum*)

Description and uses: Chinese evergreen is an excellent foliage plant for low to medium light. It is slow growing and can live for 10 years or more. Its standout feature is its lance-shape leaves, which are usually variegated with silver, gray, or shades of green. Variegated forms need brighter light than green forms. Smaller plants are good for tabletops in living rooms and offices. Combine larger plants with other low-light foliage plants such as pothos or sansevieria. Growers often plant several plants in a container for a bushier appearance.

Chinese evergreen (*Aglaonema commutatum* 'Silver Queen')

Chinese evergreen *(Aglaonema commutatum)*

Care: Grow in any good potting soil. Keep soil evenly moist. Overwatering can lead to rot and dry soil causes leaves to droop. Chinese evergreen tolerates drier air better than many houseplants, but it benefits from daily misting in winter. It needs temperatures above 60°F at all times. Feed monthly spring through summer with a balanced plant food; in winter cut back feeding to every 6 weeks. Clean leaves regularly. Plants like to be slightly root-bound, but usually need repotting about every 2 years. If stems become bare at the bottom, cut off the bottom of the root ball and repot, covering base of the stems. New roots will form on the buried plants. The biggest problem this tropical plant faces is cold air. Keep it away from doorways and windows in winter. Plants get gray, greasy splotches that turn yellow if the air is too cold. Brown leaf edges can indicate a buildup of mineral salts in the soil. The sap contains oxalic acid, which causes irritation if ingested.
Propagation: Older, root-bound plants can be divided or air-layered. When plants grow too tall, cut off 6- to 8-inch tip cuttings and root.
Pests: Scale and mealybugs are possible pests; red spider mites may be present in hot, low-humidity conditions.
Recommendations: 'Silver Queen', the most popular cultivar, has leaves with silvery striping and flecking. 'Emerald Beauty' has dark green leaves splashed with chartreuse. 'Silver King' has almost completely white leaves with green flecks. Newer varieties are less likely to be injured by temperatures below 50°F. These include 'Emerald Star', with white speckles on bright green leaves, and 'Silver Bay', with leaf centers generously splashed with cream.

Chinese fan palm *(see Palm, Chinese fan)*
Chlorophytum *(see Spider plant)*
Christmas cactus *(see Cactus, Christmas)*
Chrysalidocarpus *(see Palm, areca)*

Cigar plant *(Cuphea ignea)*

Features: Cigar-shape blooms
Size: 1–2'H × 1'W
Light: Bright
Temperature: 65–75°F; 50–60°F in winter
Water: Evenly moist; moderately dry in winter

Description and uses: This small shrub has slender stems, tiny dark green needle-like leaves, and 1-inch flowers. Its numerous tubular red, pink, or white flowers, often tipped in white, bloom spring through fall and sometimes into winter. Flowers resemble tiny cigars with ashes at their tips. Cigar plant can be moved outside in

Cigar plant *(Cuphea ignea)*

summer or divided into small plants and grown as a tender garden or container plant. It is also known as *Cuphea platycentra*.
Care: Grow cigar plant in a bright location. Use a fertile potting mix. Keep moist during the growing season and feed weekly with balanced plant food. Allow soil to dry during the cool winter season. Plants bloom best when slightly pot-bound. In spring cut back the plant by half. Pinch several times during the season to promote branching.
Propagation: Divide large plants in spring or early summer. Stem tip cuttings taken at the same time root well.
Pests: Whitefly and aphids are the most common pests.
Recommendations: No named cultivars are available.

Cissus *(Cissus spp.)*

Features: Easy-to-grow vine
Size: 1'H × 2–6'W, trailing
Light: Medium
Temperature: 65–80°F
Water: Evenly moist

Description and uses: *Cissus rhombifolia*, commonly known as grape ivy or oakleaf ivy, is the most widely grown species in this genus. This easy-to-grow vine has shiny deep green leaves that are often deeply cut. It has hairy brown stems with curling tendrils that easily cling to a stake, post, or trellis. Most plants can be kept to less than 24 inches with regular pruning. It is a great hanging-basket or pedestal plant, and when trained up a moss pole, it is an excellent choice for filling narrow spaces. Grape ivy is a good office plant and it ranks high for cleaning the air of indoor pollutants.
Care: Grape ivy likes medium light but adapts well to lower light and fluorescent lighting. Water frequently in spring and

Grape ivy *(Cissus rhombifolia)*

Oakleaf ivy (*Cissus rhombifolia* 'Ellen Danica')

summer to keep soil lightly moist at all times. Allow soil to dry to within 1 inch of the surface in fall and winter. Avoid overwatering, which can lead to shriveled leaves and leaf drop. Average humidity is fine. Feed with a half-strength foliage plant food during the growing season. Overfeeding can lead to leaf burn. Repot annually in early summer using a porous fast draining mix. Plants trained to grow upward need a heavy pot to prevent toppling. Pinch plants frequently to keep them compact. Cut back lanky plants to about 6 inches in early spring to rejuvenate them. Leaf tips may turn brown if the soil or air is too dry.

Propagation: Take stem tip cuttings in early summer.

Pests: Possible problems include powdery mildew, aphids, whiteflies, and spider mites.

Recommendations: 'Ellen Danica' is a popular compact cultivar with deeply lobed leaves. 'Mandiana Compacta' is a dwarf leafy selection that can be easily trained to a short pole.

Kangaroo vine (*C. antarctica*) is coarser and more vigorous.

Begonia cissus (*C. discolor*) has rich green silver-patterned leaves that are red underneath and resemble fancy-leaved begonia. It requires constant warmth and high humidity, making it more of a challenge to grow.

Wax cissus (*Cissus rotundifolia*)

Wax cissus (*C. rotundifolia*) has almost round, fleshy, waxy, deep green leaves. Because it has succulent leaves, it needs less water than other cissus. It climbs on forms with help.

Begonia cissus (*Cissus discolor*)

Citrofortunella (see Calamondin orange)
Citrus (see Lemon; Orange)
Clamshell orchid (see Orchid, clamshell)

Clerodendrum (*Clerodendrum thomsoniae*)

Features: Vining foliage; red and white flowers
Size: 1–6'H × 1–2'W
Light: Bright
Temperature: 65–75°F during growth, 55–60°F winter
Water: Well during growth, sparingly in winter

Description and uses: From a large genus of trees, shrubs, and vines, only *C. thomsoniae* is suited to indoor culture. It is a vine that, unchecked, can grow to 15 feet long, but is usually smaller indoors. Grow it in a hanging basket or train it on a totem. Large 5-inch, dark green, heart-shape leaves contrast nicely with red and white summer flowers. Each decorative white calyx persists for weeks. It is also called bleeding heart glorybower.

Care: Keep clerodendrum well watered during its growth cycle. Allow the soil to dry more in winter. Feed weekly with high-phosphorus plant food. It appreciates high humidity. After a winter rest period, repot in fertile potting mix. After it finishes flowering, cut back stems by about one-half to keep growth in bounds.

Propagation: Start new plants from softwood cuttings taken in early summer.

Pests: Overwatering causes crown rot. Whiteflies, mealybugs, and aphids are possible pests.

Recommendations: *C. thompsoniae* 'Variegatum' has wonderful creamy white and pale green variegation that make the plant look attractive even without flowers.

Clerodendrum (*Clerodendrum thomsoniae*)

Clivia (*Clivia miniata*)

Features: Straplike leaves; orange, red, or yellow blooms
Size: 1–2'H × 1–2'W
Light: Medium
Temperature: 60–75°F; 50–55°F winter
Water: Barely moist; moderately dry in winter

Description and uses: Although technically a summer-blooming tuberous root, clivia earns its place as a houseplant with its attractive foliage. The dark green vase-shape leaves are the perfect backdrop for the exotic orange or red flowers that appear in February or March. Plants 3 years old or more bear showy clusters of 10 to 20 tubular flowers in shades of orange, salmon, or red, or occasionally

Clivia *(Clivia miniata)*

Coffee plant *(Coffea arabica)*

Features: Glossy green leaves; white flowers; showy fruits
Size: 6–48"H × 6–36"W
Light: Medium to bright
Temperature: 60–75°F
Water: Evenly moist

Coffee plant *(Coffea arabica)*

white or yellow. When in flower this blooming accent plant deserves a place of prominence in the home.

Care: Clivia's spectacular flowers are produced only when the plant has been exposed to cool, dry conditions. It requires 5 weeks of temperatures between 50 and 55°F. The easiest way to satisfy this is to grow clivia outdoors in dappled shade in summer, bringing it back indoors before the first threat of frost in fall. Once indoors give it moderate light all day. Average room temperatures and humidity levels are fine. The fleshy roots store water, and plants easily rot if the soil remains moist too long. It is better to err on the dry side, watering only enough to keep the leaves from wilting. Gradually increase water as bloom time approaches. Spring through fall feed plants with a balanced plant food. The best bloom comes on older, pot-bound plants. When plants eventually outgrow their containers (every 5 to 7 years or so), repot using a well-drained mix such as orchid mix. Use a broad, heavy pot to prevent toppling. To propagate clivia cut off the flower stalk at the base when the blossoms shrivel and carefully divide the old plant, repotting the youngest crowns. Keep plants attractive by removing yellowing lower leaves and cleaning leaves regularly with a damp cloth.

HERE'S A TIP...

As clivia grows the bottom leaves turn yellow. Remove these by hand to keep the plant attractive.

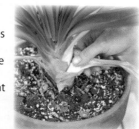

Propagation: Remove offsets with at least 4 leaves after the plant has flowered. Keep barely moist until young plants are in growth.

Pests: Possible problems include scale and mealybugs.

Recommendations: **'Golden Dragon'** and **'Citrina'** are less common selections with yellow blooms. Watch for new double flowered and variegated leaf varieties. They are rare and expensive.

Club foot *(see Madagascar palm)*
Cob cactus *(see Cactus, cob)*
Codiaeum *(see Croton)*
Coffea *(see Coffee plant)*

Description and uses: This upright shrub is usually single stemmed when young, though plants are often sold with several seedlings in the pot. The plant gradually becomes bushy as it ages. Its shiny dark green leaves rank it high as a foliage plant. Although it is the source of coffee beans when grown outdoors in the tropics, without the warmth, light, and humidity of a greenhouse or conservatory, it will seldom be more than a foliage plant indoors. If you want flowers and coffee beans, it's best to purchase a mature specimen already in flower. Flowering generally occurs in midsummer or early fall on plants at least 3 years old.

Care: Coffee plant likes warm temperatures and high humidity. It drops its lower leaves if temperatures fall below 55°F for any length of time, and the leaf tips turn brown if the air is too dry. Keep soil thoroughly moist during the growing period, keeping it barely moist during winter rest. Apply liquid plant food every two weeks from early spring to early fall. Move plants into pots one size larger every spring using regular potting mix. Plants seldom exceed 4 feet indoors. Pinch out the growing tips to help maintain a shrubbier form. Coffee plant enjoys spending the summer outdoors in a shady spot, but be sure to bring it indoors before nighttime temperatures reach 55°F.

Propagation: Cuttings are difficult to root. Use rooting hormone, bottom heat, and enclose in plastic. The best way to propagate coffee plant is from fresh seed sown in spring. Get ripe red berries, remove the pulp, and plant in sterile potting mix.

Pests: Spider mites can be a problem in dry conditions. Look for scale on the undersides of leaves.

Recommendations: **'Nana'** is a dwarf form that may begin to bear flowers and fruit when only 18 inches tall.

Coleus *(Solenostemon scutellarioides)*

Features: Colorful leaves
Size: 10–36"H × 10–36"W
Light: Bright to intense
Temperature: 60–75°F
Water: Evenly moist

Description and uses: This old-fashioned plant has garnered renewed interest in recent years—both as a garden plant and indoors. The result has been many new cultivars in a multitude of leaf colors and shapes. Older varieties needed regular pinching to look nice. Newer cultivars are self-branching and bushier, with square stems that are usually upright but can also be creeping or trailing. The scalloped-edge leaves often have toothed or fringed margins. Some are deeply cut or even lacy. Leaf color can be combinations of red, pink, white, green, orange, or dark purple. Dark blue or white flowers appear in late summer but they detract from the foliage and are usually pruned off. Plants can be trained to a standard or indoor tree. It was formerly classified as *Coleus ×hybridus* or *C. blumei*.
Care: Coleus needs bright to intense light to look good indoors. Low light causes spindly growth. Light needs vary with leaf color. Dark shades need bright light and some direct sun, but pale-colored plants burn in too much sun. Average temperatures and average to high humidity are best. Leaves will die back if the air is too dry. Keep the soil evenly moist. Use an all-purpose plant food every 2 weeks during the growing season. Remove flower spikes as they appear. Plants decline after blooming.
Propagation: Propagate coleus by stem cuttings. It can also be grown from seed, but seedlings will vary from the parent type.
Pests: Whiteflies, spider mites, mealybugs, and scale are possible pests.
Recommendations: Thousands of coleus cultivars are available at garden centers and nurseries. For indoor use choose a small growing variety that complements the decor in your room.

Two varieties of coleus *(Solenostemon scutellarioides)*

Columnea *(Columnea gloriosa)*

Features: Orange-red tubular flowers
Size: 6–12"H × 6–36"W
Light: Medium to bright
Temperature: 65–75°F
Water: Evenly moist; moderately dry in winter

Columnea *(Columnea gloriosa)*

Description and uses: This African violet relative's main feature is its dazzling tubular blossoms, which resemble leaping fish. Its arching form and purplish fuzzy leaves are attractive in their own right. The leafy stems typically rise about 12 inches above the plant before cascading downward, making this an ideal plant for a hanging basket. The showy orange-red flowers are most abundant in spring and summer, but newer hybrids are almost constantly in flower if plants receive ample light. It is also known as goldfish plant.
Care: Columnea likes medium light, such as from an east window. It also does well under fluorescent lights. Keep it away from direct sun and away from cold windows, which can cause leaf drop. Feed plants from spring through summer with a high-phosphorous plant food. Keep soil evenly moist from spring through summer but never soggy. Allow the soil to dry between watering in winter to promote heavier flowering, but take care that the soil never dries out completely. Avoid wetting plants when watering because this can promote stem rot. Plants like moderate to high humidity. Repot as needed in spring, using an African violet mix. Stems can grow to 3 feet long, but pinching them back to 18 inches or less encourages bushy growth. Keep plants inside in summer. High temperatures or excess light can cause leaves to turn brown. Remove yellowed leaves and faded flowers.
Propagation: Stem cuttings taken in spring or summer root readily.
Pests: Possible problems of columnea include spider mites, aphids, and mealybugs.
Recommendations: There are many species and hybrids of columnea available, offering variation in leaf form and color. Many have smooth, shiny leaves and some have variegated foliage. **'Early Bird'** is almost always in bloom with orange flowers streaked with yellow. **'Superba'** has large bright red flowers. **'Frosty Hills'** has waxy white leaves flushed pink and pale green. Large red flowers appear in spring.
   C. microphylla is a more vigorous species, with trailing stems up to 8 feet long. However it is easy to maintain at smaller size.

Cordyline *(see Ti plant)*

Copperleaf (Acalypha wilkesiana)

Features: Mottled red, copper, and pink leaves
Size: 1–4'H × 1–3'W
Light: Bright to intense
Temperature: 65–75°F
Water: Evenly moist; barely moist in winter

Copperleaf (Acalypha wilkesiana)

Description and uses: Copperleaf is a robust plant grown for its wide selection of oval variegated metallic red, copper, and pink leaves up to 6 inches long.
Care: Keep plants moist during growth but never soggy. Allow soil to dry in cooler winter temperatures. Apply plant food each week during spring and summer. Pinch new growth frequently to keep the plant compact. Repot and remove all but 8 inches of top growth early each spring. Give it bright light for the best leaf color. If leaves are mostly green, move the plant into better light. Bleached or faded leaves are a sign of excess sun; move the plant into lower light.
Propagation: Take softwood cuttings in spring or early summer. Use rooting hormone.
Pests: Aphids, spider mites, and scale are occasional problems on copperleaf.
Recommendations: 'Cypress Elf' has wavy, weeping reddish chocolate leaves with a coral edge. Leaves are 4 inches long and ½-inch wide. 'Macafeana' has heart-shape orange-red to creamy pink variegation with copper-bronze flecking. Leaves can be 10 inches wide.

Coralberry (see Ardisia)	**Crassula** (see Jade plant)
Coral cactus (see Cactus, mistletoe)	**Creeping charley** (see Pilea)
Corn plant (see Dracaena)	**Creeping Charlie** (see Pilea)
Crab cactus (see Cactus, Christmas)	**Creeping fig** (see Ficus)

Crossandra (Crossandra infundibuliformis)

Features: Salmon-color flowers; glossy green foliage
Size: 12–24"H × 12–24"W
Light: Medium to bright
Temperature: 65–80°F
Water: Evenly moist

Description and uses: Crossandra is also known as firecracker plant for its spikes of showy flowers in shades of orange and red. Plants often begin to bloom when only a few inches tall and are rarely out of flower once they start. The species is salmon-colored with a yellow eye, but selections are available in orange, red, and coral. Leaves are glossy, waxy, and dark green. This dense, low growing plant rarely gets over a foot tall indoors. It's a great tabletop plant and it does well in groupings where the humidity is higher.
Care: Give firecracker plant medium light during the active growth period, with some direct sunlight in short-day winter months. It does not like temperatures below 65°F. Increase

Crossandra (Crossandra infundibuliformis 'Orange Marmalade')

humidity around plants as needed. While the plant is actively growing, water frequently enough to keep the soil evenly moist. Plants should dry down a bit between winter waterings. Feed with a standard houseplant food during spring and summer. Repot young plants in early spring if root bound. Root prune and return older plants to the same size pot, adding fresh potting soil. Prune stem tips each spring to maintain a neat shape. Remove spent flowers to encourage more blooms. When blooming slows down on older plants, propagate new plants and discard.
Propagation: Take stem tip cuttings in spring.
Pests: Spider mites often attack plants in hot, dry conditions, and aphids, whiteflies, and thrips are other possible pests.
Recommendations: The Florida Series includes plants of various flower colors that adapt more readily to seasonal changes and cooler winter temperatures. '**Florida Summer**' has yellow flowers; '**Florida Flame**' is red; '**Florida Passion**' bears coral blooms; and '**Florida Sunset**' has orange ones. '**Lutea**' has deep yellow flowers.

Croton (Codiaeum variegatum pictum)

Features: Leathery leaves in exotic colors
Size: 1–4'H × 1–2'W
Light: Bright
Temperature: 60–85°F
Water: Barely moist

Description and uses: This showy shrub is a wonderful addition to any houseplant collection. The 3- to 18-inch-long leaves can be covered with spots, stripes, or irregular bands of red, pink, orange, yellow, white, and green. A single specimen is lovely when backlit by a sunny window or as a

Croton (Codiaeum variegatum pictum)

Croton (*Codiaeum variegatum pictum* 'Red Iceton')

focal point in a houseplant grouping.
Care: Consider a croton if you have the necessary bright light conditions. Plants in lower light have disappointing leaf color and smaller new leaves. This shrub enjoys spending the summer outdoors in dappled shade, but it needs a gradual 3-week adjustment to the lower light indoors. Avoid exposure to cold drafts. Keep the soil lightly moist at all times. Croton likes high humidity. In spring and summer feed with balanced houseplant food. Keep the plant slightly root bound to control its size. Crotons are often sold more

than one plant in a pot to increase fullness. Separate and repot in spring after about a year, if desired, using good fertile potting soil. Crotons often grow more than 6 feet tall outdoors, but can be kept at 3 to 4 feet indoors with regular pruning. The sticky white sap is slightly toxic; wear gloves when grooming plants. Regular pinching encourages well-branched, fuller plants, but older crotons still often become bare at their base. When a plant becomes tall and lanky, cut off the top and root it

Croton (*Codiaeum variegatum pictum* 'Andrew')

like a stem tip cutting. It is normal for older leaves to drop off, but plants also shed leaves if they are too cool, too wet, or too dry. Wipe leaves often with a damp cloth to keep them glossy or give them a shower occasionally.

Croton (*Codiaeum variegatum pictum* 'Mamey')

Crown cactus (*see Cactus, crown*)

Propagation: Take stem tip cuttings in spring.
Pests: Mealybugs, scale, and spider mites are possible problems.
Recommendations: 'Lauren's Rainbow' has ribbonlike, emerald green leaves with a golden midrib. 'Goldfinger' and 'Gold Star' have narrow gold-variegated leaves. 'Red Curl' has unusual contorted corkscrewlike leaves.

Crown-of-thorns (*Euphorbia milii*)

Features: Blooming, semisucculent plant
Size: 6–36"H × 6–24"W
Light: Bright to intense
Temperature: 65–75°F
Water: Moderately dry

Description and uses: This plant has thick gray-brown stems armed on all sides with sharp spines. Clusters of bright green leaves appear on new growth, eventually dropping off and leaving the stems bare, resulting in a living sculpture. Tiny yellow flowers are surrounded by showy bracts that last for several weeks. They appear year round in good light or early spring through late summer if light is limited. Red is the most popular color, but bracts can also be yellow, pink, peach, or white. Crown-of-thorns grows well in a sunny south or west window. It can tolerate the neglect often found in offices. The plant is poisonous if eaten, and the sap can cause skin irritation in some people. Wear gloves when handling it and do not allow children and pets to chew it.
Care: Give crown-of-thorns bright light, 3 to 4 hours of sun a day if possible. It will grow in lower light but will flower less. It tolerates a wide array of temperatures, from 50 to 90°F, and it thrives in dry air. Feed in summer using a balanced all-purpose plant food. Allow the soil to dry to within 1 inch of the surface between waterings. Leaves turn yellow and drop if the soil is too moist. Repot every 2 years in spring using a light, fast-draining medium such as cactus mix. Without regular pruning the plant maintains leaves

Crown-of-thorns (*Euphorbia milii*)

only at its stem tips. If the plant becomes overgrown and leggy, prune it back by half in late spring.
Propagation: Take stem tip cuttings. Dip them in warm water to stop the latex sap from bleeding and allow them to dry for 24 hours before planting.
Pests: No major pest problems affect crown-of-thorns.
Recommendations: 'Short & Sweet', 'Georgusis 1', and 'Koeninger's Aalbaumle' are compact varieties.

Cryptanthus (*see Earth star*)
Crystal anthurium (*see Anthurium*)

Ctenanthe *(Ctenanthe amabilis)*

Features: Herringbone-pattern leaves
Size: 12–18"H × 12–18"W
Light: Medium
Temperature: 65–80°F
Water: Evenly moist

Ctenanthe (*Ctenanthe amabilis* 'Tricolor')

Description and uses: Like prayer plant *(Maranta)* beautiful ctenanthe is a compact plant with strikingly patterned leaves that come off the canelike stems at right angles, creating a layered effect. The leaves reach 6 to 9 inches long and 2 inches wide and are oval-oblong and blunt ended. Bars of contrasting or muted coloring follow the main leaf veins in herringbone fashion, and undersides are gray-green. This is an excellent choice for a large Wardian case, where its high humidity requirements can be met. It also looks attractive displayed on a coffee table, where the leaves can be viewed from above. This is the same plant as *Stromanthe amabilis*.
Care: Give plants medium light year round. Excess sun can cause leaf scorch. Normal room temperatures are good for growth, but plants like high humidity. Avoid cold drafts. Water moderately at all times, allowing the top inch of soil to dry slightly between waterings. Feed early spring to late fall. Repot when necessary into a peaty potting mix in late spring or summer.
Propagation: Divide overcrowded clumps as plants begin to make new growth in spring.
Pests: Possible problems include mealybugs, scale, and spider mites.
Recommendations: **'Greystar'** has silvery upper leaf surfaces with contrasting dark green veins and stalks. Leaf undersides are dark purple. **'Golden Mosaic'** has deep green leaves marked with paler green and creamy yellow streaks and patches.

Cuban oregano *(see Plectranthus)*
Cuphea *(see Cigar plant; Mexican heather)*
Cycas *(see Sago palm)*
Cymbidium orchid *(see Orchid, cymbidium)*
Cyperus *(see Papyrus, dwarf)*
Cyrtomium *(see Fern, Japanese holly)*

Dancing lady orchid *(see Orchid, dancing lady)*
Date palm *(see Palm, pygmy date)*
Davallia *(see Fern, rabbit's foot)*
Deer's foot fern *(see Fern, rabbit's foot)*
Dendrobium orchid *(see Orchid, dendrobium)*

Desert rose *(Adenium obesum)*

Features: Swollen stem base; bright flowers
Size: 12–36"H × 6–12"
Light: Bright to intense
Temperature: 75–85°F
Water: Moderately dry

Description and uses:
Desert rose has thick gray stems and leathery spirally arranged leaves clustered near the tips of the shoots. The plant produces pink, red, white, or bicolor flowers in spring. In warm conditions flowers continue into fall. The unusual shape of the plant base (caudex) in older plants gives desert rose an otherworldly appearance.

Desert rose (*Adenium obesum*)

Care: This succulent plant performs best with full sun in winter and bright light in summer. Grow it in a cactus mix. Allow soil to dry between waterings. Water sparingly in winter but avoid total dryness as that will force dormancy. Avoid wetting foliage. Grow in a relatively small pot, preferably clay. To create a larger caudex, raise the plant to expose some of the roots with each repotting. This technique is effective for plants started from seed, but not those grown from a cutting. Apply plant food only when soil is moist to avoid leaf burn. Use balanced food every 3 months during rapid growth. Use a high-phosphorus food to encourage enlargement of the caudex. The sap can irritate skin and eyes. Wear gloves and goggles when working with plants. All parts of the plant are poisonous if ingested. Do not allow children or pets to chew plant parts.
Propagation: Take cuttings in spring. Allow cuttings to dry before planting in slightly moist soil. Sow seed in a sandy soil mix such as cactus mix.
Pests: Mealybugs and scale can occasionally be problems. Spider mites may appear in hot, dry conditions.
Recommendations: **'Ruby'** has deep ruby-red flowers with a white throat. Grafted plants can have several colors of flowers on the same plant. Variegated forms are diverse; some leaves are almost white while others have only a white edge.

Delicate maidenhair *(see Fern, maidenhair)*
Delta maidenhair fern *(see Fern, maidenhair)*
Devil's backbone *(see Kalanchoe)*

Devil's backbone (Pedilanthus tithymaloides)

Features: Zigzag stems
Size: 6–36"H × 6–12"W
Light: Bright
Temperature: 70–80°F
Water: Barely moist

Description and uses:

The distinctive zigzag stems give this plant the common name of devil's backbone. It can reach 36 inches tall but usually stays smaller in a pot. The variegated form is most commonly grown. It is also known as *Euphorbia tithymaloides*.

Devil's backbone (Pedilanthus tithymaloides)

Care: Give devil's backbone bright light and treat it as other succulents. It is a member of the euphorbia family and, like its relatives, produces milky sap. Avoid handling, ingesting, or getting the sap in eyes. Use gloves when handling the plant if you are sensitive to the sap and keep the plant out of reach of children and pets. Grow devil's backbone in well-drained potting mix. Allow soil to dry between waterings. The plant tolerates dry conditions but if the soil becomes too dry, it will drop its leaves. Apply balanced food during growth. Remove stems at the soil line to shape the plant or to make cuttings. Repot in spring as needed.
Propagation: Stem cuttings are the easiest method to propagate devil's backbone.
Pests: Few problems are severe on devil's backbone. Occasional spider mites or mealybugs may develop when the plant is environmentally stressed.
Recommendations: 'Variegatus' is the most desirable form with attractive cream and green leaves, sometimes including pink. Coloration becomes more intense in cool conditions.

Devil's ivy (see Pothos)

Dieffenbachia (Dieffenbachia spp.)

Features: Bright green variegated leaves
Size: 1–6'H × 1–3'W
Light: Low to medium
Temperature: 65–80°F
Water: Evenly moist

Description and uses:

This tropical beauty has a canelike stem and arching pointed leaves up to 12 inches long, usually marbled with white or cream. It gets one of its common names, dumb cane, from the toxic sap in the leaves and stems that causes tongue numbness and swelling when chewed by humans or pets.

Dieffenbachia (Dieffenbachia seguine)

Dieffenbachia works well in many settings, ranging from specimen use where the large leaves provide a tropical architectural accent to blending into a mixed grouping of foliage plants. Place several plants in a pot if you want a shrubbier appearance. This plant is effective at removing indoor air pollutants.

Dieffenbachia (Dieffenbachia maculata)

Care: Dieffenbachia prefers medium light but tolerates lower light levels. Turn plants regularly to ensure growth fills in evenly on all sides of the plant. High humidity is beneficial, but plants tolerate some dryness. Ideal temperatures are in the 80s during the day down to 65°F at night. Avoid drafts. Allow the soil to dry slightly between waterings. It is not a heavy feeder. Use a foliage plant food several times in summer. Leaf tips turn brown if the air is too dry, light levels are too low, or plants are overfed. Repot every 2 years in spring into a high-quality potting soil. Wash or dust leaves regularly. Lower leaves naturally turn yellow and drop as they age. The result is a bare trunk with tufts of leaves at the top. Regenerate older

Dieffenbachia (Dieffenbachia 'Tropical Tiki')

plants by cutting them back close to the soil. Leave at least one node; new growth will start there.
Propagation: Use the upper portion of a plant with a bare trunk as a stem tip cutting. Cut the bare cane into 4-inch sections and place on potting mix as stem cuttings. Or air layer the plant. Once roots are produced remove and pot up the rooted stem tip.
Pests: Possible problems include mealybugs, scale, and spider mites.
Recommendations: *D. amoena* and *D. maculata* (also called *D. picta*) are all similar to *D. seguine* and are also sold as dumb cane. Many modern hybrids have been selected for their compact, bushy growth habit, staying 1 to 3 feet tall, and their showy variegation. *D. s.* 'Amoena' is the largest cultivar, with leaves to 24 inches long. *D. ×bausei* has yellow-green leaves with dark green and white patches and dark green edges. *D. oerstedii* has green leaves with a white midrib. 'Bali Hai' has bright green and white upward-pointed leaves. 'Hilo' has dark green leaves and a white midrib. 'Vesuvius' has boldly spotted sword-shape leaves. 'Tropic Snow' has pale green and cream variegation on extra large leaves. 'Exotica' has leaves that are more cream colored than green.

Dionaea (see Venus flytrap)
Disocactus (see Cactus, rattail)
Donkey's tail (see Burro's tail)

Dracaena *(Dracaena* spp.)

Features: Narrow arching leaves; some with colorful striping
Size: 1–10'H × 1–3'W
Light: Medium to bright
Temperature: 65–75°F
Water: Barely moist

Compact Janet Craig dracaena *(Dracaena deremensis* 'Compact Janet Craig')

Description and uses: Dracaenas are a large group of popular foliage plants. Most have a strong upright form with long, straplike leaves variegated with white, cream, or red and clustered at the top of the stems. Some are shrubbier. Use young plants on tabletops. Larger plants require floor space, where they make striking specimens or work well in foliage groupings. They are popular in offices and interior plantscapes. All dracaenas are good at removing indoor air toxins.

Warneckii dracaena
(Dracaena deremensis 'Warneckii')

Care: Dracaenas grow well at average room temperatures but do not like cold drafts. Give plants medium to bright light for best foliage color. They tolerate lower

Madagascar dragontree
(Dracaena marginata)

Corn plant *(Dracaena fragrans* 'Massangeana')

light levels. Avoid direct sun which can cause leaf scorch. Allow the soil to dry slightly between waterings. Avoid overwatering, which can lead to root rot. Average humidity is fine. Feed plants spring through summer using a balanced houseplant food. Repot young plants every 2 years, waiting 3 years for older plants. Use standard potting mix. Lower leaves may drop if plants are exposed to a sudden change in environment. Maintain plants at less than 6 feet by lopping off the top of the plant. Within

Tricolor dracaena *(Dracaena marginata* 'Tricolor')

weeks a pair of new shoots will appear just below the cut. Wash plants regularly to remove dust.

Propagation: Cut cane sections into 6-inch pieces and root them as stem cuttings.

Pests: Insect pests of dracaena include spider mites, mealybugs, and scale.

Recommendations: Many species and cultivars are available. **Janet Craig dracaena** *(D. deremensis* 'Janet Craig') has dark green, shiny leaves. It has been shown to be the most effective dracaena for absorbing chemical toxins from the air. **'Warneckii'** has narrow leaves with thin white stripes along the edges.
   Mass cane *(D. fragrans)* has leaves that are longer and broader. It is often grown as an interesting specimen with bare woody stems that have been topped to produce clusters of foliage on short stalks that sprout from just

Lemon Lime Dracaena
(Dracaena deremensis 'Lemon Lime')

Song of India *(Dracaena reflexa)*

below the cuts.

Corn plant (*D.f.* 'Massangeana') is the more commonly grown variegated selection with a broad yellow band down the center of each leaf. It grows to 6 feet tall.

Madagascar dragontree (*D. marginata*) has narrow leaves with a red margin that grow in tufts at the top of gray woody stems. It needs high light and humidity to do well.

Rainbow plant (*D.m.* 'Tricolor') is a popular pink- and cream-margined selection.

Song of India (*D. reflexa*) has dark green leaves with broad cream edges. Plants are shrubby and tend to grow at odd angles. Regular pruning is needed to keep plants from growing into small trees. It is also sometimes sold as *Pleomele reflexa*.

Lucky bamboo (*D. sanderiana*) has an upright growth habit that can be trained into spiral shapes with leaves well spaced on lanky stems. It is best in moist soil but will grow in water alone. Add new water every two weeks.

Ribbon plant (*D. sanderiana* 'Variegata') has a prominent white edge on its leaves. It is sometimes grown in terrariums.

Gold dust dracaena (*D. surculosa*) is smaller and shrubbier and has broad leaves brilliantly spotted with yellow or cream. It needs good light and moist soil. It is slow growing, rarely reaching more than 2 feet in height. 'Florida Beauty' is a cultivar with more prominent variegation.

Ribbon plant
(*Dracaena sanderiana* 'Variegata')

Gold dust dracaena
(*Dracaena surculosa* 'Florida Beauty')

HERE'S A TIP...

Leaf tips of dracaena may brown when the humidity is low or if the soil dries excessively. Cut the brown tip at an angle to maintain the lancelike leaf shape and keep the plant attractive.

Drop tongue (see *Homalomena, heart-leaf*)
Dumb cane (see *Dieffenbachia*)
Dwarf bamboo (see *Bamboo, dwarf*)
Dwarf banana (see *Banana, dwarf*)

Dwarf papyrus (see *Papyrus, dwarf*)
Dwarf pomegranate (see *Pomegranate*)
Dyckia (see *Pineapple dyckia*)
Dypsis (see *Palm, areca*)
Dizygotheca (see *Schefflera*)

Earth star (*Cryptanthus bivittatus*)

Features: Star-shape striped leaves
Size: 1–2'H × 4–8"W
Light: Bright
Temperature: 65–70°F
Water: Barely moist

Earth star (*Cryptanthus bivittatus*)

Description and uses: Earth star is a popular grownd-dwelling bromeliad grown for its decorative stiff leaves that often have wonderful markings or stripes in rose-red and green tones. Flowers are insignificant. Use earth star in a dish garden or a terrarium. Or try it in a decorative hanging basket or mounted on bark.

Care: This shallow rooted plant can be grown in well-drained potting soil or mounted on a slab of wood. Its life cycle, like all bromeliads, includes reaching maturity and flowering, then dying. Don't be discouraged by that because the foliage lasts a long time and it produces offsets that can be divided to start new plants at flowering time. Earth star is a light feeder. Use half strength plant food monthly during spring and summer. This is one plant that appreciates water splashed on its foliage each time that you water. Bright light brings out best foliage color, though excess light bleaches colors.

Propagation: Remove and pot up offsets after the central mother plant dies back after flowering.

Pests: Pests are rare on earth star, but it occasionally gets scale insects or mealybugs.

Recommendations: 'Pink Starlite' has deep pink edges and a dark green center.

Easter lily cactus (see *Cactus, Easter lily*)

Echeveria (*Echeveria* spp.)

Features: Succulent leaves; geometric plant shape
Size: 2–6'H × 2–18"W
Light: Bright to intense
Temperature: 65–75°F; 50–60°F in winter
Water: Moderately dry

Description and uses: Echeveria is an appealing succulent plant with plump leaves, often gray-green, sometimes fuzzy, with red tips. It forms a tight rosette or other decorative pattern. Those less than 6 inches in diameter are useful on a windowsill or in a cactus garden. Others with leaves to 18 inches long make effective specimen plants in bright light.

Care: Give echeveria the brightest light you can

Echeveria (*Echeveria elegans*)

Echeveria collection (*Echeveria* spp.)

provide. Full sun is ideal. Water well during spring and summer but allow to dry before watering again. In winter water just enough to keep plants from shriveling. If in doubt about watering, don't. Excess water will cause rot. Use half strength plant food only twice during growth for established plants. Grow in well-drained cactus mix. Repot in spring when plants outgrow their pot.

Propagation: Offsets are the quickest and easiest way to start new plants. Leaf or stem cuttings also root easily.

Pests: Root rot, mealybugs, and root mealybugs are potential problems.

Recommendations: Hen-and-chicks (*E. elegans*), also known as *Cotyledon elegans*, forms mats of 4-inch-diameter rosettes. It has stolons and grows many offsets called chicks. **Molded wax agave** (*E. agavoides*), also sometimes named *E. yuccoides, E. obscura,* or *Cotyledon agavoides,* forms clumps of 8-inch-diameter rosettes. *E. agavoides prolifera* forms clumps of red-tipped leaved 8-inch rosettes. **Painted lady** (*E. derenbergii*) has red-edged or tipped green leaves in 2-inch-diameter rosettes. It is also known as baby echeveria. **Hen-and-chicks** (*E. ×gilva*) forms small gray-green clumping rosettes. **Rosy hen-and-chicks** (*E. pulvinata*) has 2-inch fuzzy red-tipped leaves. Mature plants can have stems 12 to 18 inches tall. It is also known as plush plant and *Cotyledon pulvinata*. **E. runyonii** has clumping or solitary 5-inch-diameter rosettes. **Mexican firecracker** (*E. setosa*) slowly forms nearly stemless, hairy-leaved rosettes, 3 to 6 inches in diameter. It is also known as firecracker plant.

Echinocactus (*see Cactus, golden barrel*)
Echinocereus (*see Cactus, hedgehog*)
Echinopsis (*see Cactus, peanut; Cactus, Easter lily*)
Egyptian star flower (*see Pentas*)
Elatostema (*see Watermelon begonia*)

Elephant bush (*Portulacaria afra*)

Features: Miniature jade tree look-alike
Size: 6–36"H × 6–36"W
Light: Bright to intense
Temperature: 65–75°F; 55–65°F in winter
Water: Moderately dry

Description and uses: Small, plump, ¾-inch-long dark green leaves contrast with red-brown stems on a succulent treelike plant. Though it can grow to 12 feet tall in nature, it is easily trimmed and shaped to houseplant size. It makes a

good bonsai subject with few problems. It's said that elephants enjoy eating this shrub, which is the source of its common name.

Care: Provide elephant bush with bright light or a sunny window. Grow it in well-drained cactus mix. Allow soil to dry between waterings; water sparingly in winter. Resume the normal watering schedule when new growth appears in spring. Use balanced plant food during

Elephant bush (*Portulacaria afra* 'Variegata')

spring and summer. Avoid planting elephant bush directly into a decorative container without drainage holes. If you would like to use a decorative container, double pot, placing the growing pot on top of stones inside the decorative container. Prevent the growing pot from sitting in water because elephant bush is susceptible to root rot. Elephant bush is fast growing so pinch growing tips frequently to maintain a compact shape. Repot in spring in cactus mix.

Propagation: Stem cuttings root readily. Use clippings from pruning to start new plants. Elephant bush also will develop a new plant from a leaf cutting, though it will take longer to develop into a full-size plant.

Pests: Root rot, mealybugs, or soil mealybugs are the most common pests.

Recommendations: Variegated forms are available with white striping in the leaves.

Elephant foot tree (*see Ponytail palm*)
Elfin herb (*see Mexican heather*)
Emerald fern (*see Asparagus fern*)
Encyclia (*see Orchid, clamshell*)

English ivy (*Hedera helix*)

Features: Trailing plant with lobed leaves
Size: 6–12"H × 6–72"W, trailing
Light: Medium to bright
Temperature: 55–70°F
Water: Evenly moist

Description and uses: This versatile foliage plant's dainty demeanor makes it suitable for use in hanging baskets or pots. It is among the best houseplants for training on topiary forms or using as a groundcover beneath larger houseplants. Place it on a mantel or shelf where the stems can hang down. The stems can grow quite long but are easily

English ivy (*Hedera helix*)

controlled with pruning. English ivy is good for removing indoor toxins.

Care: This plant needs moderate light in summer and bright light in winter. Variegated types may revert to all green in insufficient light. English ivy likes average to high humidity

Needlepoint English ivy
(*Hedera helix* 'Needlepoint')

and average to cool room temperatures, ranging from 50 to 70°F, with a 10-degree drop at night. Feed in spring and summer with a high-nitrogen foliage plant food. Allow the soil surface to dry between waterings, but do not allow plants to dry out completely or remain in waterlogged soil. Repot when roots show through drainage holes using standard potting soil. Ivy stems need help to grow up a support or over a moss-filled topiary form. Tie or pin them to the support or wind them around thin supports such as wires. Some people develop dermatitis from exposure to ivy's sap and the leaves are poisonous if eaten.

Propagation: Stem tip cuttings easily root in damp perlite. Stems root where they touch the soil surface, so layering is a simple means of starting new plants.

Pests: English ivy is susceptible to spider mites, especially when humidity is low. Thoroughly wash plants once a month with cool water to discourage infestations. Isolate infested plants and prune out affected areas. Discard badly infested plants. Scale and mealybugs are also potential problems.

Variegated English ivy (*Hedera helix*)

Recommendations: Hundreds of varieties of English ivy are available, including many with small, finely cut leaves, which are called needlepoint ivies, and many with interesting leaf variegation. **'Ovata'**, also known as **'Mein Hertz'**, has leathery, unlobed leaves. **'Eva'** has purple shoots and white-margined leaves. **'Midas Touch'** has green- and yellow-variegated foliage.

Algerian ivy (*H. canariensis*) has larger, glossy leaves and likes warmer temperatures. **'Variegata'**, also known as **'Gloire de Marengo'**, is a popular white-variegated form.

Algerian ivy (*Hedera canariensis* 'Variegata')

Episcia (*Episcia* spp.)

Features: Showy foliage; flowers
Size: 6"H × 6–24"W
Light: Medium to bright
Temperature: 70–80°F
Water: Evenly moist

Episcia (*Episcia dianthiflora*)

Description and uses: This African violet relative, also known as flame violet, has short-stemmed rosettes of large, shiny, slightly downy leaves. Leaf color can be green, copper, purple, or pink overlaid with metallic colors and is often purple underneath. Plants produce numerous trailing or hanging stolons along which appear smaller plants, or offsets. Inch-wide flowers are produced in leaf axils in summer. They can be white or shades of red, yellow, orange, pink, or lavender and have a white eye. Flame violet is frequently used in hanging baskets, where plants can trail. Its love of high humidity and its small size make it perfect for terrariums. It also works well in mixed-basket plantings.

Care: Plants need medium to bright light. Low light causes spindly and weak growth. It does well under fluorescent lights. Medium light produces good foliage, which is enough for many growers. Brighter light is needed for flowers. Episcia does not like cold temperatures. Water as needed to keep soil evenly moist. To prevent brown water spots on foliage, avoid splashing cold water on the leaves. Episcia requires high humidity. Leaf edges roll or die back in dry air. Use all-purpose plant food during growing season. Plants like to be somewhat pot-bound. When repotting is needed, use a peaty African violet mix.

Propagation: Remove and root offsets or layer them. Division or leaf cuttings are other methods used to propagate episcia.

Pests: Crown rot develops if the soil is kept too wet. Mealybugs or aphids are possible problems as well.

Recommendations: Many selections of episcia have been made for foliage texture and color. **'Cleopatra'** has beautiful pink, white, and light green leaves. It needs more light to grow because of low chlorophyll content in leaves. **'Fire 'n Ice'** has green and silver-veined leaves and red flowers. **'Kiwi'** has metallic rose foliage with dark veining and orange flowers. **'Chocolate Soldier'** has silver leaves blushed with pink and chocolate brown margins. Flowers are bright orange. **'Alice's Aussie'** has shimmering pink foliage dashed with chocolate brown and orange-red flowers. **'Silver Skies'** is a very compact silver leaf plant.

E. dianthiflora (formerly classed as *Alsobia dianthiflora*) has small rosettes of velvety dark green leaves and white-fringed flowers with purple spotting.

E. repens has heavily embossed leaves that are dark or bronze-green with silver markings along the veins. Flowers are rosy red with deep red throats.

Euonymus, Japanese *(Euonymus japonicus)*

Features: Glossy green or variegated leaves
Size: 1–6'H × 1–4'W
Light: Medium to bright
Temperature: 55–75°F
Water: Evenly moist

Dwarf Japanese euonymus *(Euonymus japonicus* 'Microphyllus'*)*

Description and uses: This well-branched shrub has small, glossy green leaves that provide a beautiful backdrop for showier flowering plants. Its tidy growth habit lends itself to restricted spaces, where it can be pruned to grow upright. It is ideal for a cool room or hallway. Because it tolerates drastic pruning, it is a prime choice for topiaries and bonsai. Tiny-leaf varieties are great in terrariums, dish gardens, and mixed baskets.

Care: Japanese euonymus is easy to grow provided you give it adequate moisture, cool temperatures, and ample light. It likes medium to bright but indirect light in summer. In winter it requires 3 to 4 hours of direct sun. Keep the soil evenly moist; at lower temperatures allow the soil to dry between waterings. Feed only in summer. Plants resent being pot-bound. Repot every spring using a peat-based mix. Plants respond well to pruning, which can be done at any time. You can easily maintain Japanese euonymus at 1 foot tall and wide with frequent pruning. Pick off yellow leaves as they appear.

Propagation: Take semihardwood stem cuttings in late spring. It may take up to 6 weeks for cuttings to root.

Pests: Powdery mildew, scale, mealybugs, and spider mites can be problems, especially on stressed plants.

Recommendations: Several cultivars have been selected for leaf size and variegation. **'Aureus'** has gold-splashed, dark green leaves. **'Microphyllus Variegatus'** has bright green, white-margined leaves and only grows to 18 inches tall. **'Albovariegatus'** has tiny leaves splashed with white.

Euphorbia milii *(see Crown-of-thorns)*	**False heather** *(see Mexican heather)*
Euphorbia trigona *(see African milk tree)*	**False holly** *(see Osmanthus)*
European fan palm *(see Palm, European fan)*	**False philodendron** *(see Peperomia)*
False African violet *(see Streptocarpus)*	**False sea onion** *(see Pregnant onion)*
False aralia *(see Schefflera)*	**Fan palm** *(see Palm, European fan; Palm, Chinese fan)*
False bird-of-paradise *(see Heliconia)*	

Farfugium *(Farfugium japonicum)*

Features: Shiny green leaves splashed with yellow
Size: 1–2'H × 1–2'W
Light: Medium to bright
Temperature: 55–75°F
Water: Barely moist

Farfugium *(Farfugium japonicum)*

Description and uses: Farfugium is often grown outdoors as a perennial in warm climates but also makes a bold statement as a houseplant that tolerates low light. It was a favorite during the Victorian era in homes without central heating. It does well with cool night temperatures. The plant grows in clumps and holds its large round or kidney-shape leaves aloft. The wavy or serrated leaf margins and yellow spots accent the daisylike yellow-orange flowers that bloom profusely in summer if light is adequate. Most cultivars have variegated leaves marked with ivory or yellow and sometimes pink. It used to be classified in the genus *Ligularia* and is sometimes sold as *Ligularia tussilaginea* or *Farfugium tussilagineum*. It is also commonly called leopard plant, a reference to the splotched foliage of some varieties.

Care: Farfugium needs to be watered well, then allowed to dry slightly between waterings. Never allow it to dry significantly or be left soggy. Both extremes will cause problems. Grow it in fertile potting soil that drains well. Repot in spring as needed. Remove spent flowers to encourage additional bloom, though some people prefer to cut the flowers off and just enjoy the dramatic foliage.

Propagation: Divide clumps in spring.

Pests: Farfugium is relatively pest free but is susceptible to root rot in soggy soil.

Recommendations: Leopard plant (*F. j.* 'Aureomaculata') has large leaves, up to 18 inches wide, splashed with yellow flecks and spots. **'Kagami Jishi'** has yellow-spotted crested leaves. **'Kin Kan'** has leaves with creamy white edges.

Fatsia, Japanese *(Fatsia japonica)*

Features: Shiny green leaves, sometimes splashed white
Size: 1–10'H × 1–10'W
Light: Low to medium
Temperature: 50–65°F
Water: Evenly moist

Description and uses: Japanese fatsia is a fast growing tropical shrub with large, deeply lobed leaves of shiny green. The woody stems are sparsely branched, creating an open effect with time. Leaves can be as large as 18 inches in diameter and deeply divided into seven to nine lobes. This foliage plant is tolerant of many environmental extremes including low light and low temperatures. Mature plants need plenty of room. It makes an excellent backdrop plant

Fatsia *(Fatsia japonica)*

Bird's nest fern *(Asplenium nidus)*

in a foliage grouping or can be used as a large specimen in a corner or cool entryway.

Care: This durable plant does best in a cool, well-ventilated location with medium light, but adapts to average temperatures and low light. Plants are more open when grown in low light. It likes temperatures below 65°F and tolerates drafty spots such as near a sliding glass door or in an entryway. Water as needed to keep the soil evenly moist. Wash the leaves regularly. Feed plants in spring and summer with a foliage houseplant food. Leaves turn yellow if plants are overwatered or too hot. Repot as needed using any good potting soil. To keep plants full and shrubby, pinch out the tips regularly to promote branching. By pruning you can maintain Japanese fatsia at 3 to 4 feet tall and wide. Trim back large plants by half in spring if they look gangly or have misshapen leaves.

Propagation: Take stem cuttings in spring or summer. Air layering is effective for large plants that have developed a woody stem. You can also start small plants from seed.

Pests: Spider mites are common and, mealybugs, scale, and thrips are possible pests. Overwatering may lead to root rot.

Recommendations: 'Moseri' is a compact, slow growing selection. **'Albo-marginata'** and **'Variegata'** have leaves splashed with creamy white.

Felt bush *(see Kalanchoe)*
Felt plant *(see Kalanchoe)*

Fern, bird's nest *(Asplenium nidus)*

Features: Vase shape; wavy, broad fronds
Size: 6–18"H × 6–18"W
Light: Medium
Temperature: 55–75°F
Water: Evenly moist; barely moist in winter

Description and uses: This fern's common name comes from the hairy central crown, which resembles a bird's nest. It is easier to grow than many other ferns and does well in most home environments. Bird's nest fern adapts moderately well to drier air but thrives in higher humidity such as that found in a bathroom. It has a shallow root system, growing in the crotches of trees in its native habitat. You can grow small plants on driftwood or other decorative wood slabs.

Care: Maintain moderate soil moisture year round, but avoid getting water in the bird's nest. Feed spring through

fall using a balanced plant food. Although it tolerates drier air than most ferns, it needs high humidity to thrive and look its best. Plant it in a mixture of peat moss and potting soil. Outer fronds often turn brown with age. Simply cut them off with a scissors. Fronds may bleach out in excess light. Keep plants away from drafts, which can cause the fronds to curl. Clean fronds regularly to reduce dust buildup. Repot every 2 years in late winter, just before new growth starts.

Propagation: Divide the root ball or start new plants from spores.

Pests: Possible problems include fungal leaf spots, scale, aphids, and mealybugs. Do not confuse spore cases with scale insects.

Recommendations: 'Antiquorum' and **'Osaka'** are two selections with fronds that are ruffled on their edges.

Fern, Boston *(Nephrolepis exaltata)*

Features: Arching green fronds
Size: 1–3'H × 1–4'W
Light: Medium to bright
Temperature: 60–75°F
Water: Evenly moist

Description and uses: A well-grown Boston fern has a lush, rich appearance. Its arching form and long, frilly dangling fronds make it especially suited to hanging baskets, but it also looks great on a pedestal. A humid, well-lit bathroom is the ideal spot for Boston fern. Plants produce thin, fuzzy green stolons that root and form new plants at their tips. Cut them off if you find them

Boston fern *(Nephrolepis exaltata 'Bostoniensis')*

unattractive. Boston fern is good at removing air pollutants and increasing household humidity levels.

Care: Boston fern does well in medium to bright indirect light and average home temperatures. It needs high humidity, especially if grown at temperatures above 70°F. Keep the soil moist, but not soggy. Feed with foliage plant

Dallas fern (*Nephrolepis exaltata* 'Dallas')

food. Boston fern often needs annual repotting; use a peaty soil mix. Root pruning at the time of repotting helps maintain plant vigor. Divide the plant to maintain its size and start new plants. It is natural for some leaflets to drop. Take plants outside when conditions permit and shake them to dislodge the loose leaflets and reduce the mess indoors. Prune out brown fronds.

Propagation: Crown divisions may need to be cut apart with a knife. The species can also be propagated from spores, but division is needed to maintain characteristics of named varieties.

Pests: Root rot, scale, and mealybugs are possible problems.

Recommendations: **'Fluffy Ruffles'** is a small plant with finely divided curly fronds.

Dallas fern (*N.e.* 'Dallas') is compact, with fronds about half the length of the species. It is tolerant of drier air and lower light.

'Golden Boston' has golden yellow fronds.

Erect sword fern (*N. cordifolia*) has numerous fronds that stand more upright than Boston fern.

Kimberly Queen (*N. obliterata*) is less sensitive to low humidity. It is also good at removing indoor toxins.

Kimberly Queen fern (*Nephrolepis obliterata* 'Kimberly Queen')

Fern, brake (*Pteris* spp.)

Features: Feathery foliage; upright growth habit
Size: 1–2'H × 1–2'W
Light: Medium to bright
Temperature: 55–75°F
Water: Evenly moist

Brake fern (*Pteris cretica* 'Mayii')

Description and uses: Cretan brake fern (*P. cretica*) produces clumps of fronds from short underground rhizomes. The solid green, branching fronds grow upright and then arch over at their tips. Each slightly serrated leaf grows about 12 inches long and 8 inches wide and has up to four pairs of leaflets and a single terminal leaflet. Because Cretan brake fern is not as arching as other ferns, it looks nice when viewed from above and is better suited to a tabletop than a

Sword brake fern (*Pteris ensiformis* 'Silver Lace')

hanging basket. It is also known as table fern.

Care: Best growth is in medium to bright, indirect light. This fern prefers cool to medium temperatures. High humidity is best. Keep the soil evenly moist but not soggy. Leaves brown on the edges and curl if the plant is in low humidity or gets too little water. Feed in summer with a foliage plant food. Cretan brake fern is a vigorous grower and usually needs annual repotting. Use a peaty planting mix. Cut away the older outer fronds if they become shabby looking.

Propagation: Propagate by carefully dividing plants or by planting spores.

Pests: Scale insects, spider mites, and mealybugs could be problems on brake fern. Fronds will be damaged if sprayed with horticultural oil.

Recommendations: **'Albo-lineata'** is a low growing selection with wide fringed leaves with a bold, lighter green stripe along the midrib of each leaflet.

Sword brake (*P. ensiformis*) has medium green triangular blades up to 14 inches long.

Silverleaf fern (*P. e.* 'Victoriae') has finely divided fronds with a silver band down the middle.

Silver brake (*P. argyraea*) has dark green fronds with a broad silver stripe in the center.

Fern, button (*Pellaea rotundifolia*)

Features: Round leaves; black stems
Size: 6"H × 6–24"W
Light: Medium
Temperature: 55–75°F
Water: Evenly moist

Button fern (*Pellaea rotundifolia*)

Description and uses: Although a true fern, button fern more resembles a low growing groundcover. The leathery fronds, which can grow 12 inches long, arch downward and spread out more like the stems of a trailing plant. The black stems set off the glossy green foliage nicely. Button fern is shallow rooted and can grow in a small pot. It is an excellent choice for terrariums.

Care: Button fern grows best in medium light. It likes average to high humidly. Keep out of drying winds and drafts. Keep the soil moist at all times. Feed in summer with foliage plant food. Repot annually into a moisture-retentive peaty potting mix. Remove brown fronds, which should be few if the plant is grown well. Shower regularly to keep spider mites at bay.

Propagation: Propagate by dividing the rhizomes in spring or by growing from spores.

Pests: Scale or spider mites can be problems.

Recommendations: **Purple-stemmed cliff brake** (*P. atropurpurea*) has purple stems on its fronds.

Sickle fern (*P. falcata*) has more upright fronds.

Fern, crocodile *(Microsorium musifolium)*

Features: Veined fronds prominent wide rhizome
Size: 1–3'H × 1–3'W
Light: Medium
Temperature: 70–80°F
Water: Evenly moist

Crocodile fern *(Microsorium musifolium)*

Description and uses: In the wild, crocodile fern climbs trees with its large creeping rhizomes. Those rhizomes become a prominent feature as the plant ages. It grows to about 3 feet tall and can spread with time. The fronds are thin with prominent veins. It can be used as a table fern or grown in a hanging basket. It is also known as alligator fern and *Polypodium musifolium*.

Care: Crocodile fern responds well to high humidity, but tolerates lower humidity than most ferns. Use a well-drained fertile soil. As the fern matures and the rhizome starts to emerge, transfer the plant into a larger pot to avoid having to disturb the decorative rhizome for some time. Water or mist the rhizome regularly to keep it moist. Keep the soil evenly moist, never soggy, and use foliage plant food during the growing season. Reduce watering in cooler temperatures. Give it medium light; position it near a sunny window.

Propagation: Propagate crocodile fern from spores, by division, or by taking cuttings of rhizome sections. You can also layer it by pinning down rhizomes on moist soil.

Pests: Spider mites may develop in dry, warm conditions.

Recommendations: 'Crocodyllus' is most common.

Fern, Japanese holly *(Cyrtomium falcatum)*

Features: Dark green leathery fronds
Size: 24"H × 24"W
Light: Medium
Temperature: 65–80°F; 50–65°F in winter
Water: Evenly moist

Japanese holly fern *(Cyrtomium falcatum)*

Description and uses: Japanese holly fern is one of the most forgiving ferns, tolerating lower humidity and lower temperatures than most ferns. Its leathery dark green leaflets have toothed edges, resembling holly leaves more than fern fronds, and the plant grows in a stiff, erect form that gives it a shrubby look. It is tolerant of cool temperatures and cold drafts, so it is a good choice for entryways or cool porches. Japanese holly fern enjoys spending the summer outdoors in a shady spot. It is often grown as a shade-tolerant groundcover in warm climates.

Care: This fern does best in medium light but tolerates periods of low light. Temperatures of 65 to 80°F in spring and summer are ideal, followed by cooler conditions in fall and winter. Japanese holly fern likes even moisture but tolerates occasional drying. Fronds have a thick cuticle layer (waxy coating) that protects this fern from dry air, but it prefers medium to high humidity. Feed in spring and summer with a balanced houseplant food. Repot annually in early spring. When repotting make sure the crown sits slightly above the soil line. Divide plants every 4 to 5 years. Keep the glossy leaves clean by rinsing them from time to time in a warm shower. Remove yellow or damaged fronds as they appear.

Propagation: Divide older plants in spring or start new plants from spores.

Pests: Thrips can be a problem, along with mealybugs and scale.

Recommendations: Fringed holly fern (*C.f.* 'Rochfordianum') is a popular form with numerous and more deeply cut leaflets with fringed margins.

Fern, kangaroo paw *(Microsorium diversifolium)*

Features: Attractive fronds; fuzzy rhizomes
Size: 20–30"H × 15–20"W
Light: Medium
Temperature: 70–80°F
Water: Evenly moist

Description and uses: Kangaroo paw fern is a semitropical fern from Australia. Use it as a table fern or in a hanging basket. As it matures the plant produces "kangaroo paws," fuzzy rhizomes that grow over the edge of the pot. The fronds are shiny green and triangular shape with deep cutouts. It is also known as kangaroo foot fern and *Phymatosorus diversifolius*.

Kangaroo paw fern *(Microsorium diversifolium)*

Care: Grow kangaroo paw fern in a well-drained peaty mix. Keep it evenly moist though never soggy. Use foliage plant food in spring and summer. Keep the rhizome moist. Kangaroo paw fern needs a bit more light than most ferns and appreciates a sunny window. It can tolerate bright light if temperatures are moderate and humidity high.

Propagation: Propagate kangaroo paw fern by division or from pieces of rhizome pinned to moist soil. It may also be started from spores.

Pests: Aphids and spider mites can be a problem in hot, dry conditions.

Recommendations: No cultivars are available.

Fern, maidenhair (Adiantum pedatum)

Features: Fine-texture, bright green leaflets
Size: 12–18"H × 12–18"W
Light: Medium to bright
Temperature: 60–80°F; 50–60°F in winter
Water: Evenly moist

Maidenhair fern (Adiantum pedatum)

Description and uses: Frilly bright green fronds are set off by the dark stems and arranged in layers in a semicircle. Mature plants are full and bushy yet fine textured. Maidenhair fern requires high humidity. Consider it for use in a bathroom or in a grouping on a large pebble tray. Small specimens are an excellent choice for a terrarium.

Care: Maidenhair fern does best in medium to bright light, but it tolerates lower light. High humidity is a must. Grow it on a pebble tray or group with other plants. Low humidity causes browning of fronds. Keep the soil moist but not soggy spring through fall. The soil can dry out a little more in winter, but do not allow the root ball to dry out completely. Feed during the growing season with general houseplant food. Repot in spring as needed when dark-colored roots appear at the soil surface. Use a regular potting soil that is moisture retentive. Trim out brown or faded fronds to keep plants attractive.

Australian maidenhair fern (Adiantum hispidulum)

Propagation: Maidenhair fern is difficult to propagate, but try separating rhizomes with one or two fronds attached or sowing spores.

Pests: Scale insects can be a problem.

Recommendations: Several species of maidenhair ferns are sold as houseplants. They are all similar to *A. pedatum* in appearance and care. The list includes **delta maidenhair** (*A. raddianum*), **Australian maidenhair** (*A. hispidulum*), **delicate maidenhair** (*A. tenerum*), **Venus-hair** (*A. capillus-veneris*), and **graceful maidenhair** (*A. gracillium*).

Fern, rabbit's foot (Davallia fejeensis)

Features: Fine-texture foliage; creeping rhizomes
Size: 12–18"H × 12–24"W
Light: Medium to bright
Temperature: 60–75°F
Water: Evenly moist

Rabbit's foot fern (Davallia fejeensis)

Description and uses: This long-lived fern has finely divided airy fronds. But even more ornamental are the furry creeping rhizomes. Rabbit's foot fern sends out succulent rhizomes that grow across the soil surface and over the sides of the pot. These rhizomes take up moisture and nutrients. This fern is an excellent choice for a moss-lined hanging basket, but it also looks nice in a broad pot where you can see the furry rhizomes.

Care: Rabbit's foot fern grows best in bright filtered light. It also does well in fluorescent light. It tolerates a wide range of temperatures but prefers night temperatures about 60°F and daytime temperatures around 75°F. Feed with a balanced houseplant food. Leaf tips turn brown if overfertilized. Water well and allow the soil to dry a bit before watering. This fern needs high humidity. Repot young plants in spring in a peaty soil mix. It is difficult to repot older plants. The succulent rhizomes are brittle and break easily. Rather than repotting refresh older plants by pushing new soil between the rhizomes when the old potting mix breaks down. Never bury the fuzzy rhizomes or they will rot. Rabbit's foot fern is sensitive to salt buildup. Soak the container in a tub of warm water in early summer to draw out excess salts. Remove yellow fronds as they appear.

> **HERE'S A TIP...**
> To start new plants of rabbit's foot fern, remove pieces of the fuzzy rhizome, place on moist potting soil, and keep moist until new roots and shoots form.

Propagation: Place pieces of the rhizome on moist soil and pin them down until they root.

Pests: Spider mites can be a problem if humidity is low.

Recommendations: Deer's foot fern (*D. canariensis*) has large, thick rhizomes and narrow triangular leathery fronds. It tolerates drier air than other species.

Squirrel's foot fern (*D. trichomanoides*) has smaller rhizomes and feathery diamond-shape fronds.

Fern, rabbit's foot (*Phlebodium aureum*)

Features: Feathery fronds; brown rhizomes
Size: 2'H × 2'W
Light: Medium to bright
Temperature: 55–75°F
Water: Evenly moist

Rabbit's foot fern (*Phlebodium aureum*)

Description and uses: This native of tropical America has thick, surface-creeping rhizomes covered with golden brown scales. The furry appearance of these rhizomes gives the plant its common names. In addition to rabbit's foot fern, it is also called hare's foot fern or bear's paw fern. The rhizomes send up young fronds that look like a bishop's crook before they open. The fronds can grow 2 feet long with a 2-foot spread. The leaf blades are cleft nearly to their winged midribs, each with up to 35 lobes. They are feathery, broad, smooth, and have a bluish cast. Rabbit's foot fern grows vigorously and is usually used in a hanging basket. This plant was formerly classified as *Polypodium aureum*, and you may still find it listed that way in many references.
Care: This fern grows well from 55 to 75°F and in medium to bright light. High humidity is essential. If surroundings are not humid, grow it on a pebble tray or in an area with a humidifier. Water evenly throughout the year, less frequently in winter; never allow the soil to dry out completely. Feed once a month during active growth using a balanced plant food. Repot every other year or as needed. The soil should be fertile, porous, and well drained.
Propagation: Divide large plants in early spring. Cut the rhizome into sections, making sure each piece has some roots and a clump of fronds. Place rhizomes horizontally half in and half out of the soil. This fern is also relatively easy to grow from spores sown on damp peat moss in late winter.
Pests: Insects rarely bother hare's foot fern.
Recommendations: 'Mandaianum' is an attractive variety with large arching silvery blue-green fronds, each with wavy, ruffled edges.

Fern, staghorn (*Platycerium bifurcatum*)

Features: Antlerlike fronds
Size: 1–3'H × 1–3'W
Light: Bright
Temperature: 60–80°F
Water: Moderately dry

Staghorn fern (*Platycerium bifurcatum*)

Description and uses: This rain forest plant makes an interesting specimen. It has a single sterile frond that sends roots into the plant's support and fertile fronds that develop from the center. The fertile fronds can be up to 3 feet long. Their terminal "antlers" are usually semierect with the divided parts drooping downward. Staghorn fern is rarely grown in a conventional container. It can be grown in a moss-filled basket, but it is usually grown on a bark slab hung on the wall. Place long fiber sphagnum moss between the flat frond and the slab, cover the fern and moss with chicken wire, and staple it to the slab or tie it to the slab using strips of pantyhose. Plants will eventually root into the bark slab. Find a spot for staghorn fern high up where the drooping fronds will not be in the way of passersby.
Care: Staghorn fern needs bright but indirect light, average to high humidity, and good air circulation. As an epiphyte it can take moisture from the air. This is seldom possible in the dry atmosphere of most homes, however. It is difficult to water these ferns in the conventional method because the shield frond often covers the surface of the moss. It is better to submerge the plant in a sink or large container for about 15 minutes every couple of days. During winter rest soak the plant less frequently, watering only enough to keep it from drying out completely. Grow it in a potting mix of equal parts peat moss and sphagnum moss or long fiber sphagnum moss, replacing

HERE'S A TIP...
Wire young staghorn fern onto a board or slab with some sphagnum moss to hold moisture. Hang the board on a wall to display the fern.

the potting mix once a year. Feed potted plants during spring and summer once a month with full strength plant food. Clean the fronds by rinsing in the shower or sink; do not rub off the fuzzy white coating on the antlers.
Propagation: Grow staghorn fern from spores, which is challenging, or by separating the plantlets, which eventually form at the base of the parent plant. A healthy mature fern can be divided, but usually only into two pieces, and each piece must have adequate roots.
Pests: Scale or mealybugs can be a problem.
Recommendations: *P. alicorne* is occasionally available.

Fiber optic grass *(Isolepis cernua)*

Features: Threadlike leaves
Size: 6–12"H × 6–20"W
Light: Medium
Temperature: 55–77°F
Water: Evenly moist

Fiber optic grass *(Isolepis cernua* 'Livewire')

Description and uses: This interesting plant has narrow threadlike leaves rising directly from a creeping underground rootstock. New leaves stand erect at first, gracefully arching downward as they age. Each cylindrical leaf, which looks more like a leafless stem, is tipped by a white to cream-color pinhead-size flower. Although not particularly interesting, the flowers can appear at any time to provide an attractive contrast to the slim green line of the leaves. A pedestal or hanging basket is an effective way to display this cascading plant. Some people wrap a plastic tube around the base to produce a palmlike effect. It is a logical choice for water gardens. Fiber optic grass is also called slender club-rush and is sometimes classified as *Scirpus cernua.*

Care: Fiber optic grass needs a brightly lit spot out of the direct rays of hot summer sun. It grows well with average warmth but tolerates 45°F in winter. At temperatures above 55°F, plants grow actively all year and require constantly wet soil. It's nearly impossible to overwater a plant growing in a warm room. If temperatures drop below 55°F for a period of time, encourage plants to take a rest by watering sparingly. Apply a balanced liquid plant food to actively growing plants once every 4 weeks. Pot it up into a slightly larger container when the tufts completely cover the surface. Split clumps once the base reaches 5 inches in diameter because young plants are more attractive than old ones, which tend to develop dead centers. To create a large hanging basket, divide the plant into smaller clumps and plant several in a hanging basket.

Propagation: Divide old plants by removing clumps from the outside, discarding the center of plant. New divisions should have at least 20 leaves.

HERE'S A TIP...
Fiber optic grass makes effective "hair" in a mixed planting topiary form if kept well watered.

Pests: Fiber optic grass seldom develops disease or insect pests when grown indoors.

Recommendations: 'Livewire' is a widely available cultivar.

Ficus *(Ficus* spp.)

Features: Durable foliage; leathery leaves
Size: 1–12'H × 1–10'W
Light: Medium to bright
Temperature: 65–75°F
Water: Barely moist

'Starlight' weeping fig
(Ficus benjamina 'Starlight')

Description and uses: Weeping fig *(Ficus benjamina)* is the most widely available plant in the genus *Ficus.* This upright woody plant is available as a single-trunk tree or a multistem shrub. The glossy green leaves are often slightly wavy. Available in a wide range of sizes, it can be used as a tabletop or floor plant. Braided trunk types are quite ornamental and make a striking architectural accent. Place weeping fig in a spot where it won't have to be moved all winter, because it resents changes in environmental conditions. It ranks high on the list for removing air pollutants and improving indoor air quality. Plants enjoy spending the summer outdoors in a shady corner of a deck or patio.

Care: Weeping fig is tolerant of most indoor environments. It can handle temperatures between 60 and 85°F, but keep it away from drafty doorways and cold winter windows. Water thoroughly and allow the soil to dry 1 to 2 inches before watering again. Feed during the growing season. Reduce feeding in autumn and winter. Repot only when necessary in late spring using good potting soil. It is easy to control a plant's size with regular pruning. Pruning encourages branching and fuller plants. Freshly cut plants exude a sticky sap that may be irritating to the skin. Leaves drop readily in response to environmental changes, including too much water, too little water, movement from one location to another, and shortening days in autumn. Leaf loss isn't a major problem for the plant, which is able to regenerate new leaves rather quickly, but it can create a mess in the home.

Propagation: Weeping fig and other tree-type ficus are difficult to

Braided trunk form of weeping fig

Rubber tree (*Ficus elastica*)

propagate. Air layer woody stems of plants that have grown too tall. Semihardwood cuttings may root with the aid of rooting hormone and high humidity. Creeping fig roots at nodes, so new plants can be started by layering stems into the soil.

Pests: All ficus are valued for their lack of pest problems. Scale is the most common insect pest.

Recommendations: **'Midnight Princess'** has long dark leaves with undulating crenate (with rounded teeth) leaf margins. **'Starlight'** has green and white leaves.

Rubber tree (*F. elastica*) has a treelike form with large stiff leaves, sometimes tinged with maroon. It is especially effective at removing formaldehyde and other chemical toxins from the air. **'Melany'** has deep green miniature leaves with brilliant burgundy overtones.

Fiddle-leaf fig (*F. lyrata*) has large leaves and grows 20 feet tall or more, making a striking architectural accent. **'Ivonne'** is a rare but beautiful cultivar with green and gray-green centered leaves surrounded by an ivory margin.

Fiddle-leaf fig (*Ficus lyrata*)

Narrow-leaf fig (*Ficus maclellandii* 'Alii')

Narrow-leaf fig (*F. maclellandii* 'Alii') is a newer selection with long, slender, drooping dark green leaves different from any other fig. It is less finicky than weeping fig but does have some leaf drop. It is available as a standard tree, a bush, and braided, growing up to 9 feet tall. It is good for cleaning the air, tolerates lower light levels, and has few insect pests.

Indian laurel fig (*F. microcarpa*) is similar to weeping fig but has slightly larger and more leathery leaves. It is less sensitive to changes in the environment.

Creeping fig (*F. pumila*) is a vining plant that has small leaves and aerial roots that will cling to walls. It requires more frequent watering than other figs. **'Minima'** has especially tiny foliage and is perfect for both terrariums and as a container groundcover. **'Snowflake'** also has tiny leaves but they are heavily variegated with white.

Variegated Indian laurel fig (*Ficus microcarpa*)

Variegated creeping fig (*Ficus pumila*)

HERE'S A TIP...

When fiddle-leaf fig grows too tall for its location, or if it loses leaves and becomes bare at its base, start a new plant by air layering a long shoot tip.

Fiddle-leaf fig (*see Ficus*)
Fig (*see Ficus*)

Fittonia (*Fittonia albivenis*)

Features: Colorful netted leaves
Size: 4–12"H × 4–12"W
Light: Medium
Temperature: 65–75°F
Water: Evenly moist

Description and uses: This charming tropical plant has dark green oval leaves overlaid with intricate and showy leaf veining in red, pink, or white tones. Forms with red or pink veination are usually classified as part of the Verschaffeltii Group, while ones with white or silver veins are placed in the Argyroneura Group. Plants are also commonly called nerve plant or mosaic plant, references to their netted veination. The leaves are 1 to 3 inches long and cover the mounding

Fittonia (*Fittonia albivenis* Argyroneura Group)

plants, which first grow upright and then over the sides of the container. Nerve plant's small size and need for high humidity make it a perfect candidate for a terrarium or bottle garden. It combines well in mixed baskets and dish gardens with other plants requiring high humidity and soil moisture, such as small ferns and prayer plant.

Care: Careful watering and high humidity are keys to success with nerve plant. Water as needed to keep the soil evenly moist but do not allow the soil to become waterlogged. Unless plants are growing in a terrarium or bottle garden, take steps to raise humidity. Plants do well under fluorescent lights. Feed monthly with a balanced houseplant food spring through summer. Repot individual plants annually in spring. Use a peaty potting soil that holds moisture well, such as African violet mix. Nerve plant needs regular pinching to keep it bushy and full. Remove the insignificant small yellow flowers as they appear because they distract from the show of leaves.

Propagation: Divide plants or propagate from stem tip cuttings in spring or summer. Stems sometimes self-layer, forming roots where they touch the soil surface. Remove those that have rooted and pot up.

Pests: Possible problems include root rot, fungus gnats, mealybugs, and aphids.

Recommendations: 'Janita' and 'Bianco Verde' have pink veining. 'Superba Red' has bright red leaf veins. 'Mini White' only grows 4 inches tall. 'Minima' (also known as 'Nana') has small leaves and white veins and is undemanding.

Fittonia (*Fittonia albivenis* Verschaffeltii Group)

Flame of the woods (see *Ixora*)
Flame violet (see *Episcia*)
Flamingo flower (see *Anthurium*)

Flaming sword (*Vriesea splendens*)

Features: Red swordlike flower; banded foliage
Size: 30–36"H × 18–24"W
Light: Bright
Temperature: 65–80°F; 60–65°F in flower
Water: Moderately dry; keep water in vase

Description and uses: Flaming sword is an attractive member of the bromeliad family. It is an epiphyte that grows in the jungle attached to a tree. Its toothed multihue leaves and a bright red sword-shape flower head remain decorative for several months, making it popular with interior decorators. The tight cluster of red long-lasting bracts remains attractive long after the small yellow short-lived flowers fade.

Flaming sword (*Vriesea splendens* 'Sherry')

Care: Flaming sword needs bright light and warm temperatures during growth. If purchased in flower, cool temperatures will keep the flower head attractive longer. After it flowers the main plant dies but produces offshoots (pups) before completely withering. Water the well-drained soil only after it dries but continually keep water inside the vase (cup formed by the leaves). Rain water is best. Change the water in the vase every 2 or 3 months. Occasionally include dilute plant food in the solution. It's unlikely you will need to repot from the small pot that comes with a flowering commercially grown plant. To encourage bloom enclose a mature plant inside a large clear plastic bag for a few weeks with a ripe apple. Ethylene gas given off by the ripe fruit triggers flowering in flaming sword.

Propagation: Remove pups and plant them in separate pots.

Pests: Scale or mealybugs can be problems.

Recommendations: *V.s.* 'Flaming Sword' and 'Major' have large flower heads. *V. carinata* has broader leaves and has red- and yellow-tipped bracts.

HERE'S A TIP...

Flaming sword can become top heavy. Place its small nursery pot inside a heavy decorative container to prevent the plant from tipping over.

Firecracker flower (see *Crossandra*)
Firecracker plant (see *Cigar plant*)
Fishtail palm (see *Palm, fishtail*)

Flowering maple

(Abutilon ×hybridum)

Features: Maple-shape leaves; bell-shape blooms
Size: 1–5'H × 1–3'W
Light: Bright to intense
Temperature: 65–75°F
Water: Evenly moist

Flowering maple (Abutilon ×hybridum)

Description and uses:

Flowering maple is a tropical shrub or small tree that is rarely without blossoms when properly cared for. The pendant five-petal, crepe paperlike red, yellow, pink, orange, or peach flowers are usually solitary and have prominent orange or yellow stamens. Plants can be trained into standards or grown in hanging baskets. White-variegated leaf selections are best grown as foliage plants because they rarely bloom. Flowering maple is an excellent conservatory plant.

Care: This fast growing plant requires regular attention to water, feeding, and pruning. Grow it in any peaty potting soil mix and keep relative humidity 30 percent or higher. It does well in regular home temperatures and can tolerate 50°F in winter. At the lower temperatures, allow the plant to dry slightly between waterings. Feed from spring through fall with a houseplant food every 2 weeks. Use an acid food every 2 months to maintain soil acidity. Prune leggy plants back by one-third in spring just before new growth begins. Pinch back stems occasionally throughout summer to promote fullness. Tall plants may need to be staked. Mature plants flower best when pot-bound, but vigorous plants may need annual repotting. Deadhead spent flowers.

Propagation: When plants are 3 to 4 years old, propagate new plants from stem tip cuttings taken in spring. Discard the parent plant.

Pests: Possible insect pests include aphids, spider mites, mealybugs, and whiteflies. Uneven watering or too much direct sun can cause blossom drop.

Recommendations: Many named cultivars are available, selected for their interesting foliage and colorful flowers. **'Kentish Belle'** has a trailing growth habit and yellow-orange flowers with pronounced pink stamens. **'Linda Vista Peach'** has two-toned flowers, salmon color inside turning to orange. **'Savitzii'** has pale bronzy salmon flowers and leaves that are almost entirely white. **'Voodoo'** has dark red flowers.

Trailing abutilon (*A. megapotamicum*) is a slender branched pendulous shrub often grown in hanging baskets. **'Variegatum'** has yellow-splashed leaves and stunning yellow and red flowers.

A. pictum **'Thompsonii'**, also known as *A. striatum thompsonii*, has yellow-spotted leaves and salmon-color flowers. It works well as a hanging basket plant.

Flying foxtail (see Chenille plant)
Forest lily (see Cape lily)
Foxtail fern (see Asparagus fern)
Friendship plant (see Queen's tears; Pilea)
Gasteria (see Ox tongue)

Geranium (Pelargonium spp.)

Features: Variety of leaves; attractive flowers
Size: 1–3'H × 1–3'W
Light: Bright to intense
Temperature: 60–75°F
Water: Moderately dry

Eucalyptus-scented geranium
(Pelargonium 'Clorinda')

Description and uses:

Scented geraniums are adaptable to indoor conditions. Their finely cut, slightly hairy leaves release various fruity or spicy scents when crushed. Scents range from chocolate to lemon to rose. A few are valued as much for their flowers as for their fragrance, but scented geraniums are usually light bloomers, producing small pink to white blooms in summer. Place a pot in a sunny kitchen window where you can reach out and rub a leaf whenever you want a touch of fragrance. The pruned leaves can be used in potpourri. **Zonal geranium** (*P. ×hortorum*) has patterned leaves with a circular color patch of zig zag lines. They grow best in bright light. **Regal or Martha Washington geranium** (*P. ×domesticum*) has larger, showier flowers and needs cool conditions to bloom. **Ivy geranium** (*P. peltatum*) has decorative ivy-shape foliage and is often used in hanging baskets. It grows best in bright light and cool conditions.

Care: Geranium does best with direct sun from a south or west window. Move plants outdoors in summer, where they'll store up energy for the winter. They grow well at average room temperatures and humidity, though they prefer cool night temperatures. Keep soil on the dry side. Water sparingly in winter. Do not allow roots to dry out completely, however. Repot annually in spring using any good potting soil. Pinch and prune regularly to maintain plant shape.

Variegated zonal geranium
(Pelargonium ×hortorum)

Cut back by half to a third in spring to encourage bushy new growth. Miniature varieties work well on cool windowsills or under fluorescent lights.

Propagation: Take 3-inch stem tip cuttings in spring after new growth appears. Or take cuttings in late summer to overwinter garden plants indoors. Allow cuttings to dry a bit before planting. Bottom heat and rooting hormone will speed rooting.

Pests: Spider mites and whiteflies are the two most serious pest problems. Fungal diseases can occur, appearing either as leaf spots or black areas on stems. Discard affected plants to avoid spreading diseases.

Regal geranium (Pelargonium ×domesticum)

Ivy geranium *(Pelargonium peltatum)*

Rose-scented geranium
(Pelargonium graveolens)

Recommendations: There are numerous species of scented geraniums. They vary in size, leaf pattern, scent, and flower color. **'Mrs. Taylor'** has red flowers and pungent lemony leaves. **'Old Spice'** smells like its namesake fragrance. **Apple-scented geranium** *(P. odoratissimum)* and old-fashioned rose geranium are large, vigorous plants. **Nutmeg-scented geranium** *(P. ×fragrans)* is a smaller selection recommended for beginners because it is easy to grow. **Lemon-scented geranium** *(P. crispum)* has smaller leaves and a more compact growth habit, staying 12 inches tall and wide. **Rose-scented geranium** *(P. graveolens)* is a vigorous grower to 3 feet tall. **Mint-scented geranium** *(P. tomentosum)* grows to 2 feet with small white flowers.

German ivy *(see Wax vine)*
Gibasis *(see Tahitian bridal veil)*
Gloxinia *(see Gift plants p. 108)*

Graptopetalum *(Graptopetalum* spp.)

Features: Succulent blue-gray leaves
Size: 2–12"H × 1–6"W
Light: Bright to intense
Temperature: 65–75°F; 55–65°F winter
Water: Moderately dry

Graptopetalum *(Graptopetalum* spp.)

Description and uses: This attractive, almost whimsical small succulent with plump leaves is difficult to describe. Its color is somewhere between lavender and blue-gray. It grows upright, but with age stems can become pendant. It rarely flowers.
Care: Grow graptopetalum in bright to intense light in well-drained cactus mix. Water well during growth but allow soil to dry before watering again. In winter give it just enough water to keep leaves from shriveling. Feed lightly, about 3 times during summer. This is a brittle plant; leaves or stems are easily broken off. Keep it out of high traffic areas. There is much confusion about its botanical name. In addition to *Graptopetalum*, you may find it listed as *Sedum* or *Tacitus*.
Propagation: To start plants from leaf cuttings, lay leaves on the surface of barely moist soil. Stem tip cuttings also root readily.
Pests: Mealybugs can be a problem. Stem rot is common if the plant is watered excessively.

Recommendations: Lavender pebbles *(G. amethystenum)* has 2½-inch-long leaves of unusual color. It is also known as jewel leaf plant.
Beautiful graptopetalum *(G. bellum)*, which is also known as *Sedum bellum* or *Tacitus bellus*, has 4-inch-wide, low-growing rosettes.
Ghost plant *(G. paraguayense)* also goes by the names mother of pearl plant and *Sedum weinbergii*. It forms 6-inch rosettes of plump leaves colored similar to mother of pearl.

Gold dust dracaena *(see Dracaena)*
Gold dust plant *(see Aucuba, Japanese)*
Golden barrel cactus *(see Cactus, golden barrel)*

Golden cane palm *(see Palm, areca)*
Goldfish plant *(see Columnea)*
Good luck plant *(see Kalanchoe)*
Graceful maidenhair *(see Fern, maidenhair)*
Grape ivy *(see Cissus)*

Guppy plant *(Nematanthus* spp.)

Features: Fish-shape flowers; glossy leaves
Size: 8–24"H × 8–36"W
Light: Medium to bright
Temperature: 65–80°F; 50–55°F winter
Water: Moderately dry

Guppy plant *(Nematanthus gregarious)*

Description and uses: This African violet relative has thick, waxy, shiny leaves, often with a bright red patch underneath. The leaves are produced along stems that arch upward and outward, eventually becoming trailing. It's an attractive foliage plant with bright-color flowers in orange, red, or yellow, sometimes striped in contrasting colors. Flowers are borne near the stem or on 8- to 12-inch wiry stems that dangle like fishing lines with a goldfish at each tip. The flowers appear sporadically throughout the year, sometimes massively in summer. Guppy plant is a natural choice for hanging baskets. A few species and hybrids that have upright rounded growth habit are better suited to tabletop use.
Care: Guppy plant likes bright to medium light away from direct sun. It also does well under fluorescent lights. Average room temperatures are fine, but it prefers 50 to 55°F in winter. Allow the soil to dry slightly between waterings. Feed with a blooming plant food during active growth. Repot only when needed, because plants bloom best when pot-bound. Prune in early spring. Avoid removing flower buds when pruning. Pinch stem tips of young plants to improve overall form. Guppy plant is sensitive to excess salts, which cause leaf tip burn and stem dieback. Flush the soil with pure water frequently to leach excess salts.
Propagation: Propagate from stem cuttings or division. To create a large basket quickly, use multiple cuttings in a large pot.
Pests: Spider mites, whiteflies, and aphids are possible pests.
Recommendations: 'Black Gold' has shiny green leaves that make a fine backdrop for its bright yellow-gold, pouchlike flowers. **'Cheerio'** is a small grower with dark-tipped yellow-orange flowers emerging from a darker

contrasting calyx. It blooms readily. **'Christmas Holly'** is a bit smaller and more upright growing than other hybrids. It has glossy green foliage and bright red flowers.

'Lemon Lime' has flowers with a white tube and lemon-yellow face. **'Marianne'** is a profuse bloomer with bright orange flowers and small dark green leaves. **'Tropicana'** has purple stems, dark green leaves, a dark maroon calyx, and yellow flowers with maroon stripes.

N. crassifolius is a large, robust species with dangling orange-red blossoms.

N. corticola is a large plant with orange-red flowers dangling on purple threadlike stems.

N. gregarious has short-stalked flowers that are orange with yellow lobes. **'Golden West'** is a selection with variegated foliage in shades of white, yellow, green, and sometimes pink.

N. wettsteinii has small leaves and is perhaps the most adaptable species.

Guzmania *(Guzmania lingulata)*

Features: Colorful flower bracts
Size: 12–30"H × 24–30"W
Light: Bright
Temperature: 65–80°F; 60–65°F in flower
Water: Moderately dry; keep water in vase

Description and uses: Guzmania is an attractive epiphytic member of the bromeliad family that grows attached to a tree in its native habitat. It has stiff, toothed glossy green leaves often accented with reddish lines. Flower bracts in bright red, orange, yellow, or purple are decorative for several months. It is frequently used in shopping malls and offices because it requires little care when in flower.
Care: Guzmania needs bright light and warm temperatures during growth, but keep it cooler when in bloom. After guzmania flowers it produces offshoots (pups), and the mother plant dies. Divide the pups from the main plant and discard the old central plant. Water the soil only after it dries but keep water inside the vase. Change the water in the vase

Guzmania *(Guzmania lingulata)*

every 2 or 3 months. Occasionally include dilute food in the solution. It's unlikely that you will need to repot guzmania. Use orchid mix or a well-drained potting soil. To encourage bloom enclose a mature plant with a ripe apple inside a large plastic bag for several weeks.
Propagation: Remove pups and plant them in separate pots after the mother plant has withered.
Pests: Scale or mealybugs can be problems. Root rot may develop if soil is too wet.
Recommendations: Try some of the Guzmania hybrids that have flower heads that last up to 6 months. **'Magnifica'** has soft green leaves with red and cream lines and scarlet bracts with white flowers.

Gymnocalycium *(see Cactus, chin)*
Gynura *(see Purple passion)*
Haemaria *(see Orchid, jewel)*
Hare's foot fern *(see Fern, rabbit's foot)*
Hatiora *(see Cactus, Easter)*

Haworthia *(Haworthia spp.)*

Features: Geometric rosettes; textured fleshy leaves
Size: 1–7"H × 1–6"W
Light: Bright to intense
Temperature: 60–80°F; 50–60°F winter
Water: Moderately dry

Zebra haworthia *(Haworthia fasciata)*

Description and uses: Haworthias have fleshy leaves that form small rosettes or grow as an upright form up to 5 inches tall. Those with a rough, warty appearance are the most amenable to life as a houseplant. Some produce flowers, but most are grown for their interesting foliage, growth forms, and textures. The smaller types are lovely grown with other succulents and cacti in a dish garden. Their fascinating shapes and leaves stand out nicely when the soil surface is covered with small stones, gravel, or sand to mimic a desert landscape.
Care: Haworthias require bright light. Most need at least 4 hours of direct sunlight a day. Turn plants regularly to maintain even growth. They grow well in the warmth and low humidity typical of most home settings, but most like a cooler winter rest period, with temperatures dropping into the 50s at night. They need a free-draining potting mixture such as cactus mix. Overwatering in winter is the most common reason for plant failure. They may shrivel if underwatered, but most recover quickly when watered. These slow-growing plants are not heavy feeders. Use a cactus plant food during their period of active growth. Repot only when they grow to within ½ inch of the pot rim or when they are so root-bound that they make no new growth.
Propagation: Plants often develop offsets that can be separated and potted. Allow the severed offsets to air dry at least a day before repotting.
Pests: Haworthia is generally pest free, but spider mites, mealybugs, soil mealybugs, and aphids may show up.
Recommendations: Narrowleaf haworthia *(H. angustifolia)* grows as a clumping succulent rosette to about 1½ inches in diameter, with leaves to 4 inches long.

Spider haworthia *(H. arachnoidea)*, also called cobweb aloe, forms an inward spiral of short pointed leaves

Windowpane plant *(Haworthia cooperi)*

with many short white hairs perpendicular to the stem. This looks like a cobweb that has formed over the plant.

Zebra haworthia *(H. fasciata)* forms a stemless clumping rosette with up to 80 leaves. It grows up to 6 inches in diameter and about 7 inches tall.

Windowpane plant *(H. cooperi)* forms a stemless clumping rosette with transparent-top leaves that allow light to penetrate. It grows up to 5 inches in diameter. It develops a red cast if provided inadequate water or too much sun.

Fairy washboard *(H. limifolia)* forms a cluster of stemless rosettes with up to 30 leaves to about 3 inches in diameter. There is a variegated form with green and yellow striped leaves.

Star cactus *(H. retusa)* forms a small 3- to 4-inch, clumping rosette of almost translucent leaves. 'White Ghost' is a rare white and green variegated form.

Hearts entangled *(see Rosary vine)*
Heavenly bamboo *(see Nandina)*
Hedera *(see English ivy)*
Hedgehog cactus *(see Cactus, hedgehog)*

Heliconia *(Heliconia psittacorum)*

Features: Exotic flowers; paddle-shape leaves
Size: 2–6'H × 1–3'W
Light: Bright
Temperature: 65–80°F
Water: Evenly moist

Parrot flower heliconia *(Heliconia psittacorum)*

Description and uses:
Most *Heliconia* species (commonly called lobster claw) are large, finicky plants that require a greenhouse or conservatory to do well indoors. Parrot flower heliconia, *H. psittacorum*, is a species that adapts well to a warm, sunny spot in the home. This clump form stays under 5 feet tall, with upright green or bronze, paddle-shape leaves rising directly from the soil. The exotic bird-of-paradise-type flowers appear in opposite rows, or sometimes in a spiral along the stem. The showiest part is the hot-colored bracts that surround the smaller flowers in shades of green, red, orange, yellow, and white. Parrot flower blooms most prolifically in summer, but flowers may appear sporadically throughout the year, bringing a tropical feel to any room. The showy bracts remain attractive for months and make an interesting addition to cut flower arrangements.
Care: Parrot flower likes bright light, with some direct sun. Keep it away from cold drafts. Keep the soil evenly moist spring to autumn, watering less in winter. Grow it with high humidity; large pebble trays can help but using a humidifier is best. Feed with an all-purpose plant food during the growing period. Repot as needed, which can be as often as once a year, using any good potting soil.
Propagation: Propagate by division of rhizomes in spring.
Pests: Dry air can lead to brown leaf edges and problems with spider mites.
Recommendations: 'Andromeda' grows to 4 feet tall and has orange-red bracts shading to pink. **'Flamingo'** has deep pink bracts and cream to pale green sepals with a black band and white tip. **'Pinky'** has pinkish red bracts with pale yellow bases. The sepals are cream colored with narrow green bands and white tips. **'Lady Di'** grows to 5 feet with dark red bracts. Sepals are light yellow with a dark green band. **'Petra'** is a prolific bloomer staying under 4 feet tall. The bracts are light red, becoming orange. The flowers are bright orange with a dark green tip.

Heliotrope *(Heliotropium arborescens)*

Features: Rough dark leaves; fragrant flowers
Size: 10–18"H × 10–18"W
Light: Bright to intense
Temperature: 65–80°F; 50–65°F in winter
Water: Evenly moist

Heliotrope *(Heliotropium arborescens)*

Description and uses: Heliotrope is an attractive small plant often grown as a bedding plant and is best considered a short lived plant indoors. The gorgeous dark green, sometimes purple tinged, foliage sets off the small flowers in purple, blue, or white. Many give off a vanilla fragrance.
Care: Give heliotrope bright light or full sun indoors to induce heavier flowering. Keep the soil evenly moist during the growing season. Feed plants with a blooming plant food. Pinch stems for a bushier plant. The plant is toxic so keep it away from children and pets. Use gloves to protect yourself when handling the plant; some people develop skin irritations.
Propagation: Start heliotrope from seed or take stem cuttings during the growing season.
Pests: Whiteflies can be a serious pest.
Recommendations: Purchase plants in flower to select for best fragrance. The straight species grown from seed is usually a good bet to have fragrant flowers. If you find a particularly fragrant one, propagate it from cuttings.

Helxine *(see Baby's tears)*
Hemigraphis *(see Red flame ivy)*
Hen-and-chicks *(see Echeveria)*
Herringbone plant *(see Prayer plant)*

Hibiscus, Chinese *(Hibiscus rosa-sinensis)*

Features: Showy, crepe papery flowers
Size: 1–6'H × 1–4'W
Light: Bright to intense
Temperature: 55–70°F
Water: Evenly moist

Description and uses:
This upright woody shrub features some of the largest blooms found on an indoor plant. The saucer-shape single or double flowers can be more than 8 inches across. The crepe paper-texture petals come in white, pink, red, yellow, and orange with many bicolor forms. Individual blooms last only 1 to

Chinese hibiscus *(Hibiscus rosa-sinensis* 'Mystic Pink' and 'Amber Suzanne')

2 days, but plants bloom intermittently from late spring to late fall, and occasionally in winter. Leaves are shiny and dark green.

Care: Hibiscus needs bright light and warmth near a south or west window. A sunroom, greenhouse, or conservatory is best. The more sun it gets, the better it blooms. Move it gradually outdoors in summer to partial sun, bringing it back inside before nights cool down to 55°F. In warm weather water as often as needed to keep the soil evenly moist. In winter allow soil to dry to within 1 inch of surface. Grow with high humidity to keep flower buds from dropping and to deter spider mites, which can be a serious problem. Feed with blooming plant food during growth. Repot annually in fall, trimming out about one-fourth of the roots before repotting. Control size by pruning the plant lightly in early summer and more aggressively in fall. Blooms form on tips of new branches (new wood), which emerge from just below where older branches are tipped back.

Propagation: Root 6-inch stem cuttings.

Pests: Buds and leaves drop off when plants are stressed but usually new ones grow quickly. Hibiscus also can be attacked by spider mites, whiteflies, aphids, mealybugs, and scale. A weekly shower is helpful in deterring spider mites.

Recommendations: **'Dragon's Breath'** features bold 8-inch red blossoms with central white swirls. **'The Path'** has bold yellow flowers with magenta centers. **'Kona'** has pink, fully double flowers. **'Molly Cummings'** is a deep red form.

Hippeastrum *(see Amaryllis)*
Holiday cactus *(see Cactus, Christmas)*
Holly fern *(see Fern, Japanese holly)*

Homalomena, heart-leaf *(Homalomena rubescens)*

Features: Attractive foliage
Size: 18–24"H × 18–24"W
Light: Low to medium
Temperature: 65–80°F
Water: Evenly moist

Heart-leaf homalomena *(Homalomena rubescens)*

Description and uses: Homalomena, native to the deep shade of South American forests, is adaptable to low-light situations. It is closely related to philodendron, and the leaves look similar. The heart-shape, 4- to 6-inch, dark green waxy leaves appear on sturdy petioles. Plants may bloom indoors, with a red spathe and a white spadex (tongue). It is slow growing, so buy a large plant for an immediate impact. It is sometimes called drop tongue.

Care: Although tolerant of low light, homalomena grows better in moderate light. If the petioles become long and weak, plants aren't getting enough light. It likes high humidity but is adaptable to lower humidity. It is not a heavy feeder. Use an all-purpose plant food once a month during its growing period. Repot as needed using any standard potting soil. Remove yellowed leaves as they appear.

Propagation: Divide offsets in spring.

Pests: Pests rarely bother this plant, but thrips, mealybugs, and whiteflies may appear.

Recommendations: **'Emerald Gem'**, perhaps the most widely grown selection, has dark green leaves. **'Queen of Hearts'** has leaves with a distinct reddish tinge. **'King of Spades'** has nearly black-green leaves. **'Purple Heart'** has glossy, deep red-purple heart-shape leaves. It requires more light than the species.

Silver shield *(H. wallisii)* has thick oblong dark green leaves mottled with yellow. It is a bit more challenging to grow, since it needs high humidity. It is good at removing indoor air pollutants.

House bamboo *(Pogonatherum paniceum)*

Features: Bamboolike foliage plant
Size: 12–18"H × 12–15"W
Light: Bright
Temperature: 60–85°F
Water: Evenly moist

House bamboo *(Pogonatherum paniceum)*

Description and uses: House bamboo is new on the houseplant scene. Although it resembles miniature bamboo, it is actually a grass more closely related to sugar cane. It is a compact bushy plant with narrow stems bearing small, bright green leaves. The foliage is thick and uniformly upright when young, and arches gracefully with age. Other common names include baby panda bamboo, golden hair grass, miniature bamboo, and miniature bamboo grass. It is also sometimes misclassified as *P. saccharoideum*.

Care: This plant needs good light, with direct sunlight for part of the day, if possible. Average home temperatures are fine. It needs medium to high humidity. It likes ample moisture. Never allow the soil to dry out completely. House bamboo is a heavy feeder. Use a foliage plant food every 2 weeks during active growth. Young plants need dividing every year. Use a peaty soil mix.

Propagation: It is easy to divide house bamboo. Simply take the root ball out and slice it into several pieces and repot.

Pests: House bamboo does not have any serious insect pests.

Hoya *(Hoya spp.)*

Features: Vining plant; fragrant waxy flowers
Size: 6–12"H × 48"W, trailing
Light: Medium (foliage only) to bright (for flowers)
Temperature: 55–75°F
Water: Moderately dry

Description and uses: Hoya is a fast growing trailing plant that has attractive foliage as well as showy flowers. The thick, smooth, shiny leaves are about 3 inches long and 1 inch

Hindu rope plant *(Hoya carnosa 'Crispa')*

wide. The waxy, sweetly scented pink or white flowers with red centers are the source of an alternate common name, wax plant. It is great for hanging baskets or trained to grow upward along a trellis. Wrap long vines around them to form a wreath. Small-leaf types can be trained into topiaries. *Hoya carnosa* is considered the easiest to grow of the clan.

Care: Hoya needs bright light for good flower formation. Cool to medium temperatures help keep the plant stocky. Keep soil on the dry side. Water only after the top ½ inch of soil has dried, even less during the plant's rest period. Overwatering can lead to leaf drop and root rot. Average room humidity is fine, though high humidity improves flowering. Feed through summer with blooming plant food. Repot infrequently; plants bloom better when pot-bound. Use well-drained soil. Allow faded flowers to fall off but don't remove the flower stalks. The plant will rebloom on the same stalk. Cut back straggly plants, sacrificing flowers for a while. Hoya stems contain milky sap. Prevent cut stems from dripping onto furniture or floor coverings.

Propagation: Start hoya by taking stem cuttings anytime during active growth or by layering shoots on the soil surface. Stems will root where they touch the soil.

Pests: Mealybugs are the most severe pest problem on hoyas. Spider mites, scale, and aphids are occasional pests.

Golden wax plant *(Hoya carnosa 'Variegata')*

Recommendations: Golden wax plant *(H. c.* 'Variegata') has creamy white variegated leaves. **Hindu rope plant** *(H. c.* 'Crispa') has weeping stems covered by tightly held convoluted leaves that resemble a rope about 1½ inch thick. **'Crispa Variegata'** has similar leaves dappled in white, pink, and green.

Beautiful hoya *(H. lanceolata bella)* has diamond-shape, nonglossy smaller leaves and soft pink to white blossoms with purple-pink centers. It is a branching plant that grows upright for about a foot and then begins to trail. **'Variegata'** has lime green variegation.

Shooting star wax plant *(H. multiflora)* has thick leaves, heavy stems, and an upright-to-spreading growth habit. **'Variegata'** has a band of white variegation along the leaf edges.

Imperial wax flower *(H. imperialis)* is one of the largest hoyas. It has thick stems and large yellow or pink flowers.

New South Wales wax plant *(H. australis)* is sought for its stocky growth and shiny succulent leaves. It seldom blooms but may develop white flowers when conditions are perfect.

Hymenocallis *(see Peruvian daffodil)*
Hypoestes *(see Polka-dot plant)*
Indian laurel *(see Ficus)*

Impatiens *(Impatiens spp.)*

Features: Colorful flowers on deep green foliage
Size: 6–24"H × 6–24"W
Light: Bright
Temperature: 65–75°F
Water: Evenly moist

Impatiens *(Impatiens walleriana)*

Description and uses: Impatiens is a popular outdoor bedding plant. The most widely grown species is *I. walleriana*. Long before it became popular in the landscape, it was handed down from generation to generation as a houseplant. Modern hybrids come in a mind-boggling array of colors—pinks, reds, oranges, purples, whites, and bicolors—and forms—dwarfs, standards, doubles, variegated, and others. It blooms constantly, both indoors and out. It is also known as busy lizzy.

Care: Although impatiens is a shade-loving plant outdoors, give it bright light indoors. It may survive with less light but it will not bloom well. It likes heat and humidity. It will grow well at normal room temperature, but avoid placing it where it will get cold drafts. Keep the potting mix constantly moist. Moisture-stressed plants readily wilt and drop their flowers and buds. Dry conditions also encourage spider mites, a common scourge of this blooming plant. Routinely give the plant a shower to wash off hidden spider mites. Pinch plants regularly to shape them and to encourage branching. Repot infrequently. Pot-bound plants bloom better.

Propagation: Take stem tip cuttings any time, but especially in late summer to preserve prized garden varieties that will die with the first frost. Cuttings root readily in water or growing medium. Impatiens may also be started from seed.

New Guinea impatiens *(Impatiens hawkeri)*

Pests: Be vigilant in watching for spider mite infestations. Whiteflies are also potential pests.

Recommendations: There are too many good cultivars to list here. Simply go to your local garden center and pick out colors and forms that suit your taste. Look for impatiens with the outdoor bedding plants.

New Guinea impatiens *(I. hawkeri)* is also suited to indoor container culture. The flowers are larger and brilliantly colored in pink, red, orange, lavender, or purple. Its green or bronze foliage is often variegated with bright patches of white, cream or yellow. New Guinea impatiens tolerates slightly cooler temperatures but also appreciates ample moisture.

Iresine *(see Bloodleaf)*
Isolepis *(see Fiber optic grass)*

Ixora *(Ixora coccinea)*

Features: Orange, red, pink, or yellow flowers
Size: 2–5'H × 2–4'W
Light: Bright
Temperature: 65–80°F
Water: Moderately dry

Ixora *(Ixora coccinea)*

Description and uses: This woody shrub has leathery leaves that range in color from bronze when young to deep green as they mature. Bright orange-red flowers appear at stem tips. Individual flowers are tubular, but they are so densely arranged that you see only the four petals. This plant blooms from a young age; rooted cuttings often show flower color. Ixora, sometimes called flame of the woods, can be tricky for beginners because it resents cold air, drafts, and being moved, but it is worth the effort, especially if you have a conservatory or garden room.

Care: This showy bloomer likes abundant light, warmth, and humidity. It must have at least 4 hours of direct sun a day and temperatures above 65°F. Grow it on a pebble tray to increase humidity. Water moderately during the growing period, allowing the top half-inch of soil to dry out between waterings. During winter water only enough to keep the soil from drying out. Feed with an all-purpose plant food during the growing season. Repot as needed using a peaty potting soil. Pinch out the tips to encourage bushiness. Prune the stems after they bloom to stimulate denser growth and more flowers. Unpruned shrubs become leggy and may need staking. Many dwarf cultivars naturally remain around 3 feet tall.

Propagation: Start ixora from softwood stem cuttings taken in early summer.

Pests: Aphids and scale are possible pests.

Recommendations: Several cultivars are available with flowers in shades of reds, yellows, oranges, and white, many with dwarf growth habits.
'Angela Busman' has salmon pink flowers and a compact growth habit. 'Frances Perry' has deep yellow flowers. 'Henry Morat' has fragrant pink flowers. 'Jacqueline' has orange-red flowers and dark green leaves.

Jacob's coat *(see Copperleaf)*
Jacob's ladder *(see Devil's backbone)*

Jade plant *(Crassula* spp.)

Features: Plump leaves; treelike form
Size: 1–6'H × 1–3'W
Light: Bright to intense
Temperature: 65–75°F; 55°F in winter
Water: Moderately dry

Jade plant *(Crassula ovata)*

Description and uses: Jade plant is a tough, popular succulent. Gnarled old specimens in front windows of businesses attest to its durability. The attractive treelike form bears plump fleshy leaves in green or silvery colors. Jade plant makes a nice windowsill or cactus garden plant when small or a specimen plant with age. Mature plants may bear pink flowers.

Care: Water jade plant well during active growth but allow the soil to dry before the next watering. Feed once a month during growth. Provide intense light and some sun if possible, though the plant does reasonably well with bright conditions. Keep jade at regular room temperatures during growth and in a cool spot, down to 55°F, in winter. Repot as needed in spring in cactus mix, but keep the pot size small relative to plant size. Use a heavy clay pot because large plants become top heavy. After repotting water sparingly until growth resumes. Prune with a razor-type craft knife to shape the plant into a tree form.

Variegated jade plant *(Crassula ovata)*

Propagation: Jade plant roots readily from stem cuttings or individual leaves. Allow stem cuttings to callus (dry) a couple of days before sticking them in a porous rooting medium. Place leaf cuttings on the surface of slightly moist soil. Leaves may root where they fall.

Pests: Mealybugs, aphids, and red spider mites may be a problem on stressed plants.

Silver jade plant *(Crassula atropurpurea arborescens)*

Jade plant *(Crassula ovata)* flowers

Recommendations: *Crassula ovata* (*C. argentea, C. portulacea*) is the most common jade plant. It can grow to 4 feet tall and 2 feet wide after many years. Variegated cream and green forms are available. **Silver jade plant** (*C. atropurpurea arborescens*) has flat silvery leaves and can grow to 6 feet tall.

Japanese aralia *(see Fatsia, Japanese)*
Japanese euonymus *(see Euonymus)*
Japanese holly fern *(see Fern, Japanese holly)*
Japanese marlberry *(see Ardisia)*

Jasmine *(Jasminum* spp.)

Features: Vining plant; fragrant flowers
Size: 1–4'H × 1–6'W
Light: Bright to intense
Temperature: 60–75°F; 40–60°F winter
Water: Evenly moist

Jasmine *(Jasminum polyanthum)*

Descriptions and uses: Jasmine is grown for its heavily scented flowers and leathery, glossy green leaves. The fragrant white flowers are produced primarily in winter and their fragrance is often strongest at night. The twining stems can be trained on a trellis or allowed to trail out of a hanging basket. Create a living sculpture by training the vines around a hoop or up a slender post.
Care: Jasmine does best with 4 hours of direct sun late spring through fall. Low light causes spindly growth and poor bloom. It tolerates less light in winter and requires cool temperatures to set flower buds. Grow it outdoors in summer and fall; move indoors after it has been exposed to 6 weeks of 40-60°F temperatures. Water to keep the soil evenly moist from early summer through fall. Allow the soil to dry slightly between waterings during winter. Improper watering causes leaves to turn yellow and drop. Apply flowering houseplant food during the active growth period. Prune aggressively and repot annually in spring using good fertile potting soil. Install some type of support when repotting. After flowers fade prune back the plants and allow them to rest for a month or more. Prune occasionally in summer to keep plants shapely.
Propagate: Take stem tip cuttings in early summer.
Pests: Mealybugs and spider mites can be serious problems.
Recommendations: Common jasmine (*J. officinale*) has highly fragrant pink-tinged white flowers on vigorous plants. It usually blooms midsummer to midfall.

Arabian jasmine (*J. sambac*) has rose-shape double or semidouble creamy white flowers that fade to purple and bloom intermittently throughout the year. It has a stronger fragrance but is easier to grow because it does not require low temperatures to flower. It does best in humid conditions. **'Maid of Orleans'** and **'Grand Duke of Tuscany'** are two popular cultivars. They respond well to hard pruning and shaping and adapt well to indoor culture.

Many-flowered jasmine (*J. polyanthum*) is similar to common jasmine, but is easier to grow. It blooms winter into spring with pink flowers.

Jasminum *(see Jasmine)*
Jewel orchid *(see Orchid, jewel)*
Justicia *(see Shrimp plant; Brazilian plume)*
Kaffir lily *(see Clivia)*

Kalanchoe *(Kalanchoe* spp.)

Features: Succulent foliage; bright flowers
Size: 6–48"H × 6–36"W
Light: Bright to intense
Temperature: 65–80°F; 45–65°F night and winter
Water: Moderately dry

Mother-of-thousands
(Kalanchoe daigremontiana)

Description and uses: The kalanchoes are a diverse group of succulent plants, some with small succulent leaves on small stems, others with large leaves on plump stems. Most are grown for their foliage although some flower in bright colors. Some produce tiny plants on the edges of their leaves. Combine kalanchoe with other succulents in dish or cactus gardens or grow in a pot on the windowsill.
Care: Succulent kalanchoes need bright light and should be kept moderately dry. The showy florist's kalanchoe needs more moisture. Keep it evenly moist in active growth and flower, but barely moist at other times of the year. Feed kalanchoe with all-purpose plant food several times during the summer. Grow in well-drained soil. Kalanchoe seldom needs repotting. Prune the flowering types only after flowering has finished.
Propagation: Kalanchoe roots readily from leaf and stem cuttings. Mother-of-thousands and chandelier plant form plantlets along leaf edges. These often drop to the soil and take root where they fall.

Chandelier plant *(Kalanchoe delagoensis)*

Pests: Root rot and mealybugs are the most common problems to develop on kalanchoe.

~~Recommendations:~~

Mother-of-thousands (*K. daigremontiana*) has plump leaves to 6 inches long. It can grow to 3 feet tall and produces tiny plants on its leaf edges. It is also called devil's backbone, good luck plant, and *Bryophyllum daigremontianum*.

Felt bush (*Kalanchoe beharensis*)

Chandelier plant (*K. delagoensis*) has succulent elongated gray-green leaves and tubular red-orange flowers. It produces small plantlets at leaf edges, particularly if the plant is stressed. It is also sometimes listed as *K. tubiflora* or *Bryophyllum tubiflorum*.

Panda plant (*Kalanchoe tomentosa*)

Felt bush (*K. beharensis*) develops leaves with a thick white blush when grown well. It can take morning sun, though it survives with less. It can grow to 12 feet outdoors but seldom becomes larger than 4 feet indoors. Keep it quite dry. It is also called felt plant.

Paddle plant (*K. thyrsiflora*) has succulent leaves that develop red margins when grown in intense light. Keep it quite dry in winter.

Panda plant, pussy ears (*K. tomentosa*) is well known for its fuzzy blue-gray leaves that invite touching. The leaves are often tipped in reddish brown. Kids love this plant that grows to about 20 inches tall.

Florist's kalanchoe (*K. blossfeldiana*) is described in gift plants on page 109.

HERE'S A TIP...

Plantlets from mother-of-thousands kalanchoe root and form new plants wherever they fall and come into contact with soil. Start new plants to share with friends by placing some plantlets in a container of potting soil.

Kangaroo vine (see Cissus)
Kimberly Queen fern (see Fern, Boston)
King's crown (see Brazilian plume)
Lace aloe (see Aloe)

Lace fern (see Asparagus fern)
Lace flower (see Episcia)
Lady palm (see Palm, lady)
Laurus (see Sweet bay)
Ledebouria (see Silver squill)

Lemon (*Citrus limon*)

Features: Fragrant flowers; edible fruit
Size: 1–8'H × 1–5'W
Light: Intense
Temperature: 65–75°F; 40–50°F in winter
Water: Evenly moist

Description and uses: Lemon has shiny dark green leaves and fragrant waxy white flowers that produce edible fruit when growing conditions are favorable. The plant is usually trained to a tree form but can be kept shrubby with pruning.

Care: Lemon requires intense light, regular watering, and feeding during the growing season. Use plant food formulated for acid-loving plants. Plant it in a fertile, well-drained potting mix. Pinch or prune regularly to keep trees

Lemon and Meyer lemon (*Citrus limon* and *Citrus meyeri*)

compact and bushy. In winter it needs a rest period with cool temperatures down to 40°F. During the winter rest allow the soil to dry slightly between waterings. If you can not provide an extended cool season indoors, try growing it outside until temperatures cool. A bright unheated room might also work. Give plants a shower every two weeks to keep leaves clean and help prevent pest problems.

Propagation: Start new lemon trees from stem cuttings in spring. Lemon also may be grown from seed.

Pests: Stressed lemon plants are at risk for scale insects, spider mites, and whitefly.

Recommendations: Meyer lemon (*C. meyeri*) is a compact grower that bears heavily. Prune after flowering to thin some of the crop. Remove some fruit if branches bend excessively from the weight of the fruit load.

Lime (*C. aurantifolia*) is a thorny relative that can be pruned to maintain a reasonable size for container culture.

Leopard plant (see Farfugium)
Lilyturf (see Liriope)

Lipstick plant (*Aeschynanthus radicans*)

Features: Red tubular flowers; fleshy leaves
Size: 10–20"H × 24–36"W
Light: Medium
Temperature: 60–80°F
Water: Evenly moist

Description and uses: This African violet relative, also known as *A. lobbianus*, is one of the best indoor plants for hanging baskets, thanks to its arching growth habit and showy flowers that dangle from branch tips. The tubular, paired flowers have dark purple cups encircling bright scarlet flowers. While in bud they resemble lipstick in a case. Lipstick plant blooms for a long time in medium to bright light. It blooms most heavily in fall, with sporadic bloom throughout the year. Plants have attractive foliage even when not in bloom. Blooming plants placed outside for the

Lipstick plant *(Aeschynanthus radicans)*

summer will often attract hummingbirds. **Care:** Lipstick plant likes warmth, evenly moist soil, and average to high humidity. Plants may shed leaves if temperatures are too cold and leaves turn brown when humidity is too low. Use a blooming plant food during spring and summer. Plants bloom best when pot-bound, so repot only when the root ball is so large that plants become difficult to water. Lipstick plant likes a slightly acidic soil medium, such as an African violet mix. Cut stems back to about 4 inches from the soil line when they are done blooming.

Propagation: Remove stem ends for softwood cuttings in spring. Pot several cuttings together to make a fuller plant.

Pests: Possible problems on lipstick plant are mealybugs, scale, aphids, and thrips.

Recommendations: *A. pulcher* has greenish yellow tubes from which the red flowers emerge.

Zebra vine *(A. longicaulis)* is more popular for its purple-mottled leaves than for its green and brown flowers. **'Black Pagoda'** is a hybrid with darker leaves and bright red-orange flowers.

A. hildebrandii is bushier and more upright, growing to only 8 to 10 inches. It has abundant orange flowers and is a good candidate for growing under lights.

A. speciosus has spectacular orange-yellow flowers set off by dark green leaves.

Liriope *(Liriope* spp.)

Features: Grasslike foliage
Size: 10–12"H × 12"W
Light: Bright
Temperature: 65–75°F
Water: Evenly moist

Description and uses: Although well-known as an outdoor groundcover, liriope also makes an attractive houseplant. Also known as lilyturf, it is grown for its graceful dark green grassy leaves. Under excellent conditions it may bloom indoors, with narrow spikes of dark blue to purple flowers. Dwarf and variegated cultivars are all suitable for indoor growing. **Care:** Grow liriope in bright light and keep soil moist during

Variegated big blue lilyturf *(Liriope muscari)*

active growth and barely moist during winter. Use a fertile, well-drained potting soil. It looks best pot-bound so requires only occasional repotting. Feed every few weeks during growth. Prune the whole plant back to the soil in late winter. It will put out a flush of new growth.

Propagation: Plants send out creeping rhizomes that enlarge its clump. Divide the clump by slicing through it with a sharp knife or trowel.

Pests: Thrips can be an occasional problem.

Recommendations: **Lilyturf** *(L. spicata)* is a creeping plant that may need more frequent repotting.

Big blue lilyturf *(L. muscari)* is widely available. The species has dark green leaves; its blue flowers, similar to grape hyacinths, bloom in autumn. Some cultivars have white flowers. **Variegated big blue lilyturf** has medium green leaves edged in white.

Lithops *(see Living stone)*
Little princess agave *(see Agave)*

Living stones *(Lithops* spp.)

Features: Succulent stonelike foliage
Size: ½–2"H × 1–2"W
Light: Intense
Temperature: 65–75°F, 50–60°F in winter
Water: Barely moist

Living stones *(Lithops* spp.)

Description and uses: Living stones are remarkable small stonelike plants with two thick, fleshy leaves colored various shades of gray-green and tan. They are so successful at resembling stones that they can disappear into a stone mulch. This camouflage keeps animals from grazing them in their native South African habitat.

Care: Living stones are tricky to grow but are so unusual that few can resist the challenge. They need intense light and sun to do well. Water sparingly. If your plant flowers, withhold water until after the original leaves have shriveled and replacements are in active growth. In winter allow the plant to rest at cool temperatures with almost no water. Use a cactus mix and use a pot larger than seems required, because the plant's root system is out of proportion to its aboveground size. In the wild roots grow deep searching for water. Even though living stones require intense light for best growth, they can sunburn if moved too quickly from low light to sunny conditions.

Propagation: Start new plants from seed.

Pests: Root rot from overwatering is the most common problem to affect living stones.

Recommendations: **Hall's living stone** *(L. hallii)* is green with subtle mottling.

Hooker's living stone (*L. hookeri*) is olive to gray with red or rust mottling.

Karas Mountains living stone (*L. karasmontana*) is milky gray with orange or gray mottling.

Mimicry plant (*Pleiospilos nelii*) is a close relative of living stones that has several sets of fleshy green leaves. Its growing needs are similar.

Livistona (*see Palm, Chinese fan*)
Lobivia (*see Cactus, cob*)
Lobster claw (*see Heliconia*)

Lollipop plant (*Pachystachys lutea*)

Features: Textured leaves; bright yellow bracts
Size: 1–3'H × 1–3'W
Light: Bright
Temperature: 60–75°F
Water: Evenly moist

Description and uses: The bright yellow spires of lollipop plant are comprised of successive bracts from which protrude white flowers. This fast-growing shrub has puckered lance-shape, dark green leaves that reach up to 6 inches long. Bloom is most dependable in summer, but in good light it will bloom sporadically

Lollipop plant (*Pachystachys lutea*)

throughout the year. It is one of the few indoor plants with yellow flowers.
Care: Lollipop plant needs bright light. Low light causes spindly growth and poor bloom. It flowers best in warm temperatures. Keep it above 55°F at night. It needs high humidity. Feed with all-purpose plant food according to label directions. This shrub's fast growth rate and tendency to lose its lower leaves means regular pruning is necessary. The more you prune it, the more stems it produces, and the more it flowers. Prune right after the bracts fade to ensure you don't clip off unopened flowers. Cut back an overgrown mature specimen to within 6 inches of the soil and allow it to regrow.
Propagate: Softwood cuttings taken in spring or summer are the best way to start new plants.
Pests: Spider mites, mealybugs, and whiteflies are possible pests of lollipop plant.
Recommendations: *P. coccinea* has large plumes of dazzling red flowers in green bracts.

Lucky bamboo (*see Dracaena*)
Ludisia (*see Orchid, jewel*)
Madagascar dragontree (*see Dracaena*)
Madagascar jasmine (*see Stephanotis*)

Madagascar palm (*Pachypodium lamerei*)

Features: Succulent; spiny gray trunk
Size: 1–5'H × 1–3'W
Light: Intense
Temperature: 65–75°F; 50–60°F in winter
Water: Moderately dry

Madagascar palm (*Pachypodium lamerei*)

Description and uses: This strange plant is not a true palm, but rather a succulent from Madagascar. The spiny gray trunk bears a tuft of bright green leaves, to 4 inches long, on top. In its native habitat it is highly seasonal, dropping its leaves in the dry winter. Refoliation begins during the rainy season. The white flowers are rarely seen indoors.
Care: Water Madagascar palm well but allow soil to dry between waterings while it is growing actively. When leaves start to yellow, withhold water to prevent root rot from developing. Keep the soil dry during the dormant, cool winter period and gradually begin to water after growth resumes in spring. Grow in a cactus mix. Repot every few years in spring. It is a light feeder. Use balanced plant food only during summer growth. When handling the plant wrap the trunk in several layers of newspaper to protect yourself. Keep children and pets away from the 2½-inch spines. All parts of the plant are poisonous and should not be ingested. Grow in a clay pot to avoid moisture retention and to add stability because the plant can become top heavy.
Propagation: Start new plants from seed or offsets. Allow offsets to dry for a week before potting.
Pests: Root rot is the most common problem. Occasional problems with scale, mealybugs, or root mealybugs may develop on Madagascar palm.

Maidenhair fern (*see Fern, maidenhair*)
Majesty palm (*see Palm, majesty*)
Mammillaria (*see Cactus, pincushion*)

Mandevilla *(Mandevilla sanderi)*

Features: Pink, red, or white flowers
Size: 2–10'H × 2–10'W
Light: Bright to intense
Temperature: 65–75°F; 50–60°F in winter
Water: Evenly moist

Mandevilla *(Mandevilla sanderi)*

Description and uses: Long known as *Dipladenia sanderi*, mandevilla is a woody-stemmed climber with twining stems and elliptic lustrous bright green leaves. The trumpet-shape five-petal flowers are pink, red, rose, or white with orange to yellow throats. Most are single, but a few double-flowered cultivars are available. The flowers bloom spring through autumn and may bloom into winter in a greenhouse.

Care: Flowers appear on new growth, so heavy pruning helps stimulate new blooms. Grow in a fertile, well-drained potting mix. Keep moist during growth and feed each week with blooming plant food. Mandevilla does best in high humidity. In winter keep much drier and cool. Grow in bright light with some varieties taking full sun. Repot each spring. Cut back hard at that time. All parts of this plant are toxic. Keep out of reach of children. Wear gloves when handling; the milky sap can cause skin irritation.

Propagation: Stem cuttings root fastest with rooting hormone and bottom heat.

Pests: Spider mites, whiteflies, mealybugs, and scale insects are possible pests.

Recommendations: Several species are sold but most plants grown today are hybrids.

'Red Riding Hood' has 3-inch deep pink flowers all season long.

Shining mandevilla (*M. splendens*) has heart-shape leaves with prominent veins on the reverse and has clusters of rosy flowers with deep pink throats.

M. ×*amabilis* (*M.* ×*amoena*) 'Alice du Pont' has long-lasting, trumpet-shape ice pink flowers with a darker pink throat. This high performance hybrid works well on a trellis or other structure.

Maranta *(see Prayer plant)*
Marlberry, Japanese *(see Ardisia)*
Masdavallia *(see Orchid, tailed)*
Medicine plant *(see Aloe)*

Medinilla *(Medinilla magnifica)*

Features: Drooping pink flowers and bracts
Size: 3–5'H × 3–5'W
Light: Bright
Temperature: 70–80°F; 60–65°F in winter
Water: Evenly moist; moderately dry in winter

Medinilla *(Medinilla magnifica)*

Description and uses: *Medinilla magnifica* is a well-chosen name for this plant, for it is indeed magnificent when in bloom. The drooping flower stalks, measuring up to 16 inches long, are composed of vivid pink bracts and clusters of bell-shape carmine flowers. The plant itself is striking, with woody, four-sided stems and large leathery leaves with prominent veins. It generally grows 3 feet tall and wide though it can be much larger with ideal conditions.

Care: Medinilla is one of the most difficult houseplants to grow well. It tolerates less-than-ideal conditions if the air remains reasonably warm and can remain in bloom for months, from spring through summer, but then tends to enter into a long decline that ends in the compost pile. This plant needs extremely high humidity. It fares well in a tropical greenhouse where water condenses on the glass, but indoors you may need to use a humidifier and pebble trays. In winter it needs cool temperatures and just enough water to keep it alive. When the plant sets new buds, increase temperature and watering. Remove yellowed leaves and faded flowers; prune after flowering. Wash the leaves periodically to maintain their shine.

Propagation: Start new plants from softwood cuttings or by air layering woody stems.

Pests: Dry air causes leaf dieback and gradual decline. Spider mites and scale insects are possible pests.

Mexican heather *(Cuphea hyssopifolia)*

Features: Small lavender flowers
Size: 6–24"H × 6–24"W
Light: Bright
Temperature: 65–75°F
Water: Evenly moist

Mexican heather *(Cuphea hyssopifolia)*

Description and uses: This small shrub has slender stems, fine, dark green glossy leaves, and many ½-inch lavender flowers. It blooms spring through fall and sometimes in winter if light is excellent.
Care: Grow Mexican heather in bright light and keep evenly moist. Give it balanced plant food in spring and summer. Use fertile, well-drained potting soil. Cut back hard and repot each spring; continue to pinch stem tips to produce a bushy plant.
Propagation: Start new plants from stem cuttings.
Pests: Mexican heather has few serious pests. Whiteflies and aphids are occasional problems.
Recommendations: Numerous species and hybrids exist, few of which have been thoroughly tested as houseplants. Named cultivars come with pink or white flowers and variegated foliage.

    Cigar plant *(C. ignea)*, also called firecracker plant has red, slightly longer cigar-shape tubes with a purple-black mouth.

Mimosa *(see Sensitive plant)*
Mistletoe cactus *(see Cactus, mistletoe)*
Mock orange *(see Orange-jessamine)*
Money tree *(see Pachira)*

Monkey plant *(Ruellia makoyana)*

Features: Attractive foliage; rose-pink blossoms
Size: 6–12"H × 12–18"W
Light: Bright to intense
Temperature: 65–75°F
Water: Evenly moist

Monkey plant *(Ruellia makoyana)*

Description and uses: Monkey plant is one of those bonus plants that have attractive foliage and can have showy flowers. The thin velvety leaves have prominent silver veins and are olive green above and purple underneath. Plants produce trumpet-shape, petunialike pink flowers in fall and winter. Plants have an open, airy habit but may be pinched and pruned to produce denser growth. Monkey plant is a good choice for a hanging basket. Its need for high humidity makes it a good choice for greenhouses and conservatories. It is also known as trailing velvet plant.
Care: This plant needs plenty of light to do well—bright, indirect light in summer and some direct sun in winter. Plants become leggy and have sparse bloom if light is too low. Average room temperatures are fine. High humidity is a necessity. Keep the soil evenly moist while the plant is blooming, allowing it to dry slightly between waterings when not in bloom. Overwatering can lead to stem rot. Feed in summer with flowering plant food used at full strength. Pinch the growing tips regularly to keep the plant dense and to improve flower formation, which occurs on new growth. Remove faded blossoms to keep plants neat.
Propagation: Propagate monkey plant from stemtip cuttings taken in summer, boosting the success rate by using a root hormone and bottom heat. Monkey plant can also be started from seed.
Pests: Spider mites can be a problem, especially if the humidity is low, and aphids may attack the tender growing tips. Poor air circulation can lead to mildew on the leaves.

Monstera *(see Philodendron, split-leaf)*
Moon Valley friendship plant *(see Pilea)*
Mosaic plant *(see Fittonia)*
Mother-of-thousands *(see Kalanchoe; Piggyback plant)*
Moth orchid *(see Orchid, moth)*
Murraya *(see Orange-jessamine)*
Musa *(see Banana, dwarf)*

Myrtle *(Myrtus communis)*

Features: Shiny leaves; fragrant flowers
Size: 1–6'H × 1–3'W
Light: Medium to bright
Temperature: 55–75°F; 45°F in winter
Water: Evenly moist

Myrtle *(Myrtus communis)*

Description and uses: This shrub is native to the Mediterranean region. The aromatic glossy leaves are attractive enough by themselves when the plant is grown in medium light. If the plant is grown in bright, indirect light, it often produces numerous small, starry pink or white scented blossoms in late summer. Myrtle responds well to pruning and is easily trained as a treelike standard. It is also popular for topiary and bonsai because of its adaptability to shearing.

Care: Myrtle needs bright light to produce flowers, but medium light is fine to successfully grow it as a foliage plant. It tolerates cool to average home temperatures and likes about 45°F for a winter rest period. Humidity should be high. Keep the soil evenly moist. Plants may lose leaves if the soil is allowed to dry out, but may show yellow leaf tips if the soil stays wet for too long. Plants allowed to go into a winter rest period can get by with moderate watering during that time. Feed with foliage plant food during the growing season. Repot every year or two using a peaty potting soil. Myrtle naturally gets quite large, but it can be kept as small as 2 to 3 feet with regular pruning. It tolerates severe pruning all the way back to stubs and will leaf out again quickly. Heavily pruned plants produce fewer flowers.

Propagate: Semihardwood cuttings taken in early summer are the best way to start new plants.

Pests: Several insects can plague myrtle, especially when grown in low light and humidity. Watch for spider mites, scale, mealybugs, and whiteflies.

Recommendations: 'Variegata' has sharply pointed leaves with creamy white margins. 'Microphylla' has tiny leaves and grows to only 2 feet tall. It is especially good for training as a topiary.

Myrtus *(see Myrtle)*

Nandina *(Nandina domestica)*

Features: Bamboolike foliage
Size: 12–36"H × 6–15"W
Light: Medium to bright
Temperature: 65–75°F
Water: Moderately dry

Nandina *(Nandina domestica* 'Harbour Belle')

Description and uses: Nandina has jointed stems and exotic intricately colored and patterned leaflets. It's also sometimes called heavenly bamboo, though it is not a bamboo at all. Each leaf is made up of several leaflets geometrically arranged in triangles on thin leafstalks. The airy compound leaves are held primly erect at right angles from the canes. Creamy flower clusters appear in spring, followed by red berries.

Care: Grow nandina in bright light in order to bring out the best color of foliage. Plant in fertile soil mix. Water well then allow the soil to go moderately dry. It needs less water in winter. Feed monthly during its growth period with balanced food. To show this plant's best form, clip off the lower leaves to expose the bamboolike stems. Maintain size by pruning both foliage and roots or repot when roots become crowded. You can remove up to a third of the foliage.

Propagation: Nandina sends up multiple stems or canes. Divide large clumps of canes to make more plants.

Pests: Few pest problems plague nandina. Low light conditions will produce sparse growth and few flowers or fruits.

Recommendations: Many cultivars are sold, including dwarfs.

> **HERE'S A TIP...**
> If your nandina has produced berries, set it outside in early spring to feed the birds.

Narrow-leaf fig *(see Ficus)*
Nematanthus *(see Guppy plant)*
Neomarica *(see Walking iris)*
Nephrolepis *(see Fern, Boston)*
Nephthytis *(see Arrowhead vine)*
Nerium *(see Oleander)*

Nerve plant *(see Fittonia)*
Never-never plant *(see Ctenanthe)*
New Guinea impatiens *(see Impatiens)*

Norfolk Island pine *(Araucaria heterophylla)*

Features: Fine texture; branched tree
Size: 1–10'H × 1–5'W
Light: Bright to intense
Temperature: 60–75°F
Water: Moderately dry

Norfolk Island pine *(Araucaria heterophylla)*

Description and uses: Norfolk Island pine is a fast growing tree that can grow to 200 feet tall in its native habitat and can become a 10-foot-tall pot plant in good indoor conditions. It has a straight trunk with perpendicular branches arranged in whorls. It is a soft green. Use it in a high light atrium with ample space. It can survive short-term displays in dim light, such as when serving Christmas tree duty. It is also known as *A. excelsa* and *A. imbricata.*
Care: To grow well Norfolk Island pine needs several hours of sun each day. Grow in cactus mix. Water well during active growth but allow the soil surface to dry before watering again. Use foliage plant food every month during growth. It benefits from high humidity. In low light situations, branches may brown and fall off. Avoid pruning Norfolk Island pine to prevent disfiguring its conical shape. Repot only every 2 to 3 years. If you use it as a Christmas tree, remember that lights have a drying effect, so keep humidity up and carefully monitor moisture levels of the soil.
Propagation: Offsets occasionally develop at the base of the tree. These may be removed and potted up as new plants. Purchased plants may have multiple stems in one pot. These may be divided and separated. Norfolk Island pine may be started from seed.
Pests: Root rot from soggy soil and spider mites or scale are pests to watch for.

Notocactus *(see Cactus, ball)*
Oakleaf ivy *(see Cissus)*
Odontoglossum *(see Orchid, odontoglossum)*
Old man cactus *(see Cactus, old man)*

Oleander *(Nerium oleander)*

Features: Summer flowers
Size: 3–8'H × 3–5'W
Light: Bright to intense
Temperature: 70–80°F, 55–60°F in winter
Water: Moderately dry

Description and uses:
Oleander bears narrow glossy willowlike leaves on upward-growing branches. The species has single rose-red flowers. Hybrids can have clusters of often highly scented white, yellow, pink, or red flowers in

Oleander *(Nerium oleander)*

summer. Either single or double forms are available, and some varieties have yellow variegated leaves. Dwarf varieties are especially popular. Although they readily reach 6 feet tall indoors, you can keep them to 3 to 4 feet tall by pruning.
Care: The secret to success with oleander is summer heat and winter cold. Place oleander outside for the summer, then move it to a barely heated garage for the winter and greatly reduce watering. Grow it in a fertile soil mix. Water well during growth but allow the soil surface to dry moderately. In winter water sparingly, about once per month. Feed monthly during its growing period with blooming plant food. Prune hard after flowering. Repot in spring. All parts of this plant are extremely poisonous. Do not grow it where small children or pets have access. Always wear gloves when pruning to make certain you don't accidentally eat the sap. Wash tools and hands afterward.
Propagation: Start new plants of oleander from softwood cuttings or seed.
Pests: Oleander is susceptible to mealybugs outdoors. Spider mites, scale, and aphids also are possible pests.
Recommendations: 'Peachblossom' has double apricot color flowers.

Oncidium *(see Orchid, dancing lady)*
Opuntia *(see Cactus, bunny ear)*

Orange *(Citrus sinensis)*

Features: Fragrant flowers; edible fruit
Size: 1–10'H × 1–6'W
Light: Bright to intense
Temperature: 65–75°F, 40–50°F in winter
Water: Evenly moist

Description and uses: Orange has shiny dark green leaves and bears waxy fragrant white flowers. If grown in favorable conditions it will produce edible fruit. Orange trees have spiny stems.
Care: Orange needs bright to intense light, regular watering, and feeding during the growing season. Grow orange in a fertile, well-drained potting mix. Pinch or prune regularly to keep trees compact and bushy. Provide orange with a winter

Orange (*Citrus sinensis*)

rest period at cool temperatures down to 40°F. Keep soil evenly moist through the growing season, but allow the soil to dry between waterings in winter. Orange trees benefit from summering outdoors. Gradually move your plant to more intense sun outdoors. It can sunburn if moved out too quickly. Use a cotton swab to improve pollination and fruit set. Give plants a shower every two weeks to keep leaves clean and help prevent pests. Feed with citrus (acid) plant food.

Propagation: Take stem cuttings in spring to start new plants. Plants started from seed will take longer to come into bloom.

Pests: Oranges may develop scale, spider mites, or whiteflies.

Recommendations: Dwarf varieties are best for indoors.

Orange jasmine (*see Orange-jessamine*)

Orange-jessamine (*Murraya paniculata*)

Features: Attractive foliage; fragrant flowers
Size: 3–10'H × 3–6'W
Light: Medium to bright
Temperature: 60–75°F; 50–60°F in winter
Water: Evenly moist

Description and uses: Orange-jessamine is an exotic-looking plant that grows well in average household conditions. This fine-textured, medium-size shrub has a compact growth habit and a dense crown of glossy green leaves. It can be pruned to grow as a small tree. The leaves are strongly fragrant when rubbed, but the real treat comes from the heavily scented flowers. The long-lasting waxy white blooms have an intense fragrance resembling orange blossoms with a hint of jasmine. Young plants begin blooming at an early age. Orange-jessamine flowers most intensely in late

Orange-jessamine (*Murraya paniculata*)

summer and fall. Following blooming, green fruits appear which turn deep red when mature. Often grown outdoors in warmer climates, orange-jessamine adapts well to pot culture. It can also be used for bonsai.

Care: Orange-jessamine grows well in average room temperatures spring through fall, but likes cool to cold temperatures in winter. Provide medium to bright light. It tolerates low light but will not bloom. Keep the soil evenly moist. Average humidity is fine though higher humidity improves performance. Feed monthly with all-purpose plant food during the growing season. Repot annually in late winter or early spring. Remove yellowed leaves as they appear. Prune regularly to keep it bushy.

Propagation: Take softwood cuttings in early summer to start new plants.

Pests: Spider mites, mealybugs, and scale insects are possible pests of orange-jessamine.

Recommendations: 'Min-A-Min' is a hard-to-find dwarf variety that only grows about 3 feet tall and bears its first flowers when only a few inches tall.

Orchid, buttonhole (*Epidendrum* spp.)

Features: Clusters of small flowers
Size: 6–30"H × 6–12"W
Light: Bright
Temperature: 65–80°F day; 60–65°F night
Water: Moderately dry

Description and uses: Buttonhole orchids produce clusters of small flowers in the spring or fall. Some also flower at other times during the year. Flower colors include red, yellow, orange, pink, purple, and shades in between. Flowers are often fragrant. Although plants are variable, many are small and are easily grown in the house.

Care: Most *Epidendrum* species require intermediate to warm conditions similar to those

Buttonhole orchid (*Epidendrum* 'Rene Marques Flame Thrower')

found in most homes. A few of the commonly cultivated species, and reed stem types such as *Epidendrum radicans,* grow in cool conditions. Other reed stem plants are warm growing and are widely hybridized and adapted for home growing. Start plants in bright light. If foliage is dark green and plants do not flower, move to intense light. If the foliage turns red, move the plant into lower light intensity. Some Mexican species that do best in intense light develop red leaf pigmentation that makes the plants attractive even when not in bloom. During growth water well then allow plants to dry somewhat before watering again. Lift the pot to judge its weight. As the growing medium dries, pots will not be as heavy. Water the medium just before the pot dries out. In cool temperatures keep plants drier because roots rot easily. Use balanced plant food with each watering in summer; occasionally use a high nitrogen food. Grow in clay or plastic pots using small or medium-size fir bark or orchid mix. All buttonhole ferns need at least 50 percent relative humidity.

Propagation: Remove and pot up plantlets that grow on the stems of mature plants.

Pests: Root rot from overwatering, occasional spider mites, scale, and mealybugs are potential pest problems on buttonhole orchid.

Recommendations: *E. radicans* is a cool growing reed stemmed plant with elongated blooming clusters of orange to red flowers.

E. anisatum is a popular compact Mexican species with clusters of small anise-scent green flowers accented with red.

Orchid, cactus *(Epiphyllum* spp.)

Features: Large bright flowers
Size: 2–4'H × 2–4'W
Light: Medium to bright
Temperature: 70–80°F; 55–65°F winter
Water: Barely moist

Description and uses: This large epiphytic cactus can be used in hanging baskets or grown by a windowsill. Orchid cactus is known for its large red, pink, white, or purple flowers. It often blooms at night, although newer hybrids bloom during the day. These newer hybrids have been bred for larger flowers and more compact plant form.

Care: The rain forest origin of orchid cactus suggests that it needs more humidity and less sun than most cactus. Treat it more like an orchid. It needs bright light to do well but resents full sun. Avoid moving an orchid cactus

Orchid cactus *(Epiphyllum* spp.)

plant, particularly when it is in bud. Keep the plant warm in summer while in growth. At cool temperatures in fall and winter growth slows. Water well during summer but keep barely moist in winter. The semidormant state caused by cool, dry conditions in winter helps set buds for spring bloom. Maintain humidity levels above 50 percent in summer. Plants develop aerial roots if humidity is adequate. Grow orchid cactus in fertile, well-drained potting soil. Repot infrequently. Many of the stems have spines that break and scar easily. Keep the plant out of high traffic areas.

Propagation: Take cuttings with a sterile knife or pruner. Cut about 4 inches of stem just below joints and dry for one week. Stick cuttings in barely moist cactus mix. Gradually resume watering.

Pests: Root rot develops if plants are kept too wet. Occasional problems with aphids and scale may appear.

Recommendations: *E. ackermannii* hybrids have large white to purple flowers, up to 9 inches wide.

Orchid, cattleya *(Cattleya* spp. & hybrids)

Features: Large corsage-type flowers
Size: 18–22"H × 18–24"W
Light: Bright
Temperature: 70–80°F day; 60–65°F nights
Water: Moderately dry

Description and uses: Cattleya orchids are epiphytes with long, round pseudobulbs and leathery oval or sword-shape leaves that last for a season. They can produce two to fifteen flowers with a wide, tongue-shape lip. Many produce large, fragrant corsage-type flowers, others much smaller ones. Species tend to bloom once per year, hybrids twice.

Pseudobulb growth is directional, with an active lead pseudobulb with leaves and trailing pseudobulbs without foliage.

Care: Give cattleya orchid bright light. If the medium green leaves burn or turn yellow, light is too intense. Miniature types, smaller species and intergeneric hybrids, are small enough to grow on a light cart but may require brighter light. For plants in active growth, water plants often enough to keep the lead and

Cattleya hybrid orchid (×*Laeliocattleya* 'Orglades Grand T')

first trailing pseudobulbs plump, but not the remaining trailing pseudobulbs. At higher temperatures increase watering and humidity and decrease them at lower temperatures. Include a high nitrogen plant food with most waterings. After flowering allow plants to go drier for about 6 weeks. Grow in well-drained small or medium fir bark or orchid mix. Growth is best in a clay pot. Cattleya orchid benefits from high humidity; grow on a pebble tray or use a humidifier. Provide good air circulation. Repot every 2 or 3 years or when the growing media breaks down. Plants can bloom any time of year that new growth matures.

Propagation: Divide large clumps, including an active lead and 3 or 4 leafy pseudobulbs with each division.

Pests: Root rot and occasional scale or mealybugs may affect cattleya orchid.

Recommendations: *C. aurantiaca* is a strong grower with clusters of bright orange flowers.

C. mossiae is a prolific bloomer with 5-inch fragrant rose flowers.

×*Brassocattleya* is a hybrid between *Cattleya* and *Brassavola*.

×*Brassolaeliocattleya* is an intergeneric cross of *Cattleya*, *Brassavola*, and *Laelia*.

×*Cattleytonia* is a cross of *Cattleya* and *Broughtonia*.

×*Laeliocattleya* is a hybrid between *Laelia* and *Cattleya*.

Rhyncholaelia digbyana is a species widely used in hybridizing. It has given the beautiful frilly lips to many *Cattleya* hybrid blooms.

Sophronitis is a small epiphyte with bright orange or red flowers and is best known as a parent for red *Cattleya* orchid hybrids.

Orchid, clamshell (*Encyclia* spp.)

Features: Clusters of numerous small flowers
Size: 6–30"H × 6–12"W
Light: Bright
Temperature: 65–80°F day; 55–65°F night
Water: Moderately dry

Clamshell orchid (*Encyclia cochleata*)

Description and uses: Most clamshell orchids have numerous small flowers with a shell-shape face with additional petals that flare out in all directions. They are usually pale green to yellow but may come in almost any color. Flowers are often fragrant. These attractive orchids are relatively easy to grow and are adaptable to home culture. Clamshell orchids were previously classified as *Epidendrum* and may still be listed that way. Clamshell orchids differ from *Epidendrum* because of their pseudobulbs.

Care: Grow clamshell orchid in clay or plastic pots using medium-size fir bark or orchid mix. During growth water clamshell orchid well then allow it to go somewhat dry before watering again. In cool temperatures allow the plant to dry more because it is easy to rot roots. Apply balanced food with each watering; occasionally use a high nitrogen food. All types need at least 50 percent humidity.

Propagation: Divide plants, making certain to include two or more pseudobulbs (at least one with leaves) with each division.

Pests: Root rot, spider mites, scale, and mealybugs may infest clamshell orchid.

Recommendations: *E. aspera* is a compact plant with long spikes of orange and brown flowers.

E. cochleata has 3- to 5-inch-long pseudobulbs. It grows to about 30 inches tall with maroon and chartreuse shell-shape flowers most of the year. Other named selections are available with a variety of colors and flower sizes. It is a good beginner's plant.

E. cordigera prefers cooler growing conditions and bears large pink, maroon, and white flowers.

E. fragrans, with creamy white fragrant flowers with purple stripes, is another easy-to-grow clamshell orchid.

Orchid, cymbidium (*Cymbidium* spp.)

Features: Long lasting flowers, grasslike foliage
Size: 18–48"H × 12–30"W
Light: Bright
Temperature: 65–75°F day; 45–65°F night
Water: Moderately dry

Description and uses: Cymbidiums are popular, durable orchids with long lasting flowers borne above grasslike foliage. They grow from pseudobulbs with a creeping rootstalk. Most flowers are held erect over plants though

Cymbidium orchid (*Cymbidium* 'Apple Tea')

some are pendulous. Cut flower types can grow 3 to 4 feet tall and produce flowers that last for weeks in floral arrangements. The new miniature hybrids are about 18 inches tall and may bloom 3 times per year. These smaller forms are more easily accommodated in the home, either in a windowsill or under lights.

Care: Most cymbidiums need several weeks of relatively dry conditions and night temperatures of around 50°F to initiate flower spike development. Create these conditions by growing plants outside when night temperatures are cool. Look for modern hybrids that bloom well without a drop in temperature. Grow cymbidium orchid in medium fir bark or orchid potting mix. During its growth cycle water a plant well then allow it to dry moderately before watering again. After flowers fade water just enough to keep the pseudobulbs from shriveling. Feed with balanced plant food during active growth. High humidity and good air circulation are beneficial. Repot when the clump becomes too large for its pot, generally every 3 to 4 years. Dividing can delay bloom for a year or more.

Propagation: Divide and separate overgrown plants.

Pests: Spider mites and scale are occasional pests.

Recommendations: *C. Golden Elf* 'Sundust' is a popular newer hybrid with 2½-inch fragrant yellow flowers. Four to six blooms are borne on each spike. This cultivar needs no significant cool period to set flowers although it blooms best with a 10-degree drop in night temperatures. It primarily blooms in summer but can flower almost any time of year.

Orchid, dancing lady (*Oncidium* spp.)

Features: Numerous yellow flowers
Size: 6–36"H × 6–36"W
Light: Bright to intense
Temperature: 65–80°F day; 55–60°F night
Water: Moderately dry

Description and uses: Dancing lady orchids are generally epiphytes that produce pseudobulbs with leathery leaves or cane stem types. They are grown for their flower spikes with numerous little flowers. Smaller plants are often mounted on bark, though they all can be grown in pots. Flowers are usually combinations of yellow with white, brown, or green; some are fragrant.

Care: Grow dancing lady orchid in bright or intense light. At cool temperatures they can be grown in direct sun. Types with leathery leaves can tolerate more intense light. Generally an east or south window will produce good growth. Dancing lady orchid grows well at room temperature if you provide a drop in night temperatures to about 55–60°F. Keep humidity high with a pebble tray or

Dancing lady orchid (Oncidium Sharry Baby 'Sweet Fragrance')

humidifier. Grow in orchid mix or mount on a bark slab. Types with fleshy leaves or pseudobulbs need less water than thin-leaf types. Always water well then allow the top inch or two of mix to dry before watering again. Water sparingly during the plant's winter rest. Use balanced plant food during growth, occasionally supplementing with high nitrogen food.

Propagation: Divide clumps in spring.

Pests: Root rot, spider mites, and scale are possible problems on dancing lady orchid.

Recommendations: *O. splendidum* has numerous small yellow and brown flowers.

O. ornithorhynchum has arching flower spikes of fragrant pink and yellow flowers.

O. varicosum rogersii has numerous yellow flowers with brown markings.

Orchid, dendrobium (*Dendrobium* hybrids)

Features: Attractive flowers
Size: 6–48"H × 4–36"W
Light: Bright to intense
Temperature: 65–80°F days; 50–65°F nights
Water: Moderately dry

Description and uses:
Species dendrobium orchids vary dramatically, from plants a few inches tall to others several feet tall. They may be evergreen or deciduous, and range from those with small pseudobulbs to those with hanging canelike stems. Typical dendrobiums for the home will be hybrids that are 18 to 24 inches tall. Hybrids are available in white, pink, yellow, or lavender, usually with contrasting markings. The modern hybrids are less fussy about humidity if grown in bright light. They also have a short rest period and may bloom off and on throughout the year.

Care: Grow dendrobium orchid in bright light in fir bark or orchid mix. Use balanced plant food during

Dendrobium orchid (Dendrobium nobile Himezakura 'Sanokku')

periods of active growth. Water well but allow the orchid mix to dry to the touch before watering again. During winter or if the plant is grown at low temperatures, water sparingly. Soggy mix will produce root rot. Keep humidity high and provide good air circulation. Use a pebble tray or humidifier to increase humidity.

Propagation: Divide large clumps to start new plants.

Pests: Root rot, scale, mealybugs, and spider mites are problems to watch for on dendrobium orchid.

Recommendations: *D.* **'Banana Royal'** is an attractive windowsill plant with long spikes of banana yellow flowers.

D. **'Winter Frost'** is a compact plant, good for growth under lights or on a windowsill. It produces many eggshell color flowers.

Orchid, jewel (*Ludisia discolor*)

Features: Maroon leaves with silver veins
Size: 4–6"H × 4–6"W
Light: Medium
Temperature: 65–75°F
Water: Evenly moist

Description and uses: This low-growing, creeping orchid is grown for its attractive leaves that are deep maroon-red with silvery pink veining. It is a terrestrial orchid and works well in a terrarium. Flowers are white but are overshadowed by the foliage. It is also sometimes classified as *Haemaria discolor dawsoniana*.

Care: Grow jewel orchid in a well-drained soil mix. Never allow soil to become soggy. It also can be grown in long fiber sphagnum moss

Jewel orchid (Ludisia discolor)

or a mixture of sphagnum and fir bark. Jewel orchid performs well under fluorescent lights or grown several feet from a window. It needs high humidity. Feed infrequently during its growth period.

Propagation: Take stem cuttings when the plant is not in bloom or separate some of the rooted creeping stems from the main plant.

Pests: Pests are rare but occasional scale or mealybugs may develop.

Recommendations: Though technically all of the jewel orchids have the same name, some variation in leaf and vein colors exists. Some plants have white veins; leaf color varies from maroon to green. Select a plant in person or discuss variations with a mail order supplier.

Orchid, moth (*Phalaenopsis* spp. and hybrids)

Features: Moth-shape flowers
Size: 1–3'H × 1–3'W
Light: Medium to bright
Temperature: 75–85°F days; 60–65°F nights
Water: Barely moist

Moth orchid (*Phalaenopsis* 'Sedonas Make Dream Sedona')

Description and uses: Moth orchid is an epiphyte with wide, straplike leaves. It flowers on graceful, arching stems with mothlike flowers in white, yellow, pink, or deep purple. Many sport spots and stripes on the blooms. Plants can have 20 or more flowers that may last several months. They are a good choice as a gift plant.

Care: Moth orchid is easy to grow. It requires medium light and humidity. More intense light and higher humidity coupled with a 10-degree drop in night temperatures produces higher flower counts. Grow in small or medium fir bark or orchid mix. Water well during growth and allow the growing medium to dry between waterings. Take care to keep water out of the crown of the plant. Never allow the mix to go totally dry or to become soggy. When bark breaks down, repot in fresh bark or mix. Use a high nitrogen plant food during growth. Grow on a pebble tray or use a humidifier to increase humidity. After flowering use a sharp razor blade to remove the flower spike above the second or third node. This often will produce another round of flowering.

Propagation: Start new plants by removing plantlets that occasionally form on the flower spike.

Pests: Root or crown rot is the most common problem. Mealybugs may also infest moth orchid.

Recommendations: Moon orchid (*P. amabilis*) is a species that has white flowers.

P. lueddemanniana has 2-inch white flowers with pinkish stripes and is fragrant. It's a bit harder to grow.

Doritaenopsis is a hybrid between *Phalaenopsis* and *Doritis*. It is smaller than *Phalaenopsis* and works well in smaller places. It grows well in an east window or under lights. Easy to grow, it has multiple flower spikes with greater color range. It is usually a bit more expensive than moth orchid, but worth the investment.

Orchid, odontoglossum (*Odontoglossum* spp.)

Features: Dramatic arching flower spray
Size: 1–3'H × 1–2'W
Light: Bright
Temperature: 65–75°F days; 50–55°F nights
Water: Moderately dry

Description and uses: Odontoglossum orchid is native to high elevations in the Andes. It has plump pseudobulbs and produces arching sprays of 20 or more large round colorful

Odontoglossum orchid (*Odontoglossum* 'Margarete Holm')

flowers that often have contrasting spots on petals.

Care: Odontoglossum orchid is difficult to grow as a houseplant because it needs cool temperatures day and night. Keep temperatures below 75°F during the day and 55°F at night. At extremely high humidity (50 to 80 percent) slightly warmer conditions are acceptable as long as air circulation is excellent.

A greenhouse with evaporative cooling is ideal. Grow odontoglossum orchid in a relatively small pot to avoid overwatering. Odontoglossum orchid is sensitive to poor water quality; use filtered water, rainwater, or allow tap water to sit in an open sauce pan for over 24 hours before use to reduce chlorine content. Allow the orchid mix to go moderately dry before watering again. Water sparingly during winter rest. Light from an east window is good. Use a high nitrogen or balanced food during the growth cycle.

Propagation: Start new plants from division.

Pests: Root rot, scale, spider mites, or mealybugs are possible pests.

Recommendations: Hybrids ***Vuylstekeara***, ***Odontioda***, and ***Odontonia*** are slightly more adaptable to growing as houseplants.

Orchid, slipper (*Paphiopedilum* spp.)

Features: Straplike leaves; large waxy flowers
Size: 8–12"H × 8–10"W
Light: Medium
Temperature: 70–80°F days; 50–65°F nights
Water: Moderately dry

Slipper orchid (*Paphiopedilum* Satchel Paige Pappy AM/AOS)

Description and uses: Slipper orchid is a low growing terrestrial orchid with straplike leaves and large waxy flowers. Foliage can be solid green or mottled with maroon or sliver splotches. Slipper orchid is grown for its dramatic slipper-shape flowers with wide wings (sepals). Flowers may be brown, green, pink, purple, or yellow, sometimes with spots or stripes.

Care: Slipper orchid is relatively easy to grow. Types

with mottled foliage generally grow well with warm (65°F) night temperatures. Solid green types require up to 8 weeks of cool nights to induce bloom. An east window or two-tube fluorescent light fixture will provide enough light intensity to flower most slipper orchids. Maintain good air circulation. Keep humidity at 50 to 60 percent by growing plants on a pebble tray or using a humidifier. Provide a well-drained mix, yet one that retains some moisture. Grow in fine fir bark or use commercial orchid mix. During the growing season water well, then allow the growing medium to go moderately dry. After flowering allow the medium to go much drier and cease feeding. Keep water out of the crown of the plant.

Propagation: Divide plants after flowering. Cut rhizome sections with roots attached.

Pests: Root rot is common if the plant is overwatered. Spider mites, aphids, or mealybugs are possible pests.

Recommendations: *P. insigne* has pale green leaves and 5-inch yellow-brown spotted flowers. It is a fast grower.

P. ×maudiae has attractive mottled leaves with burgundy and white or green and white striped flowers.

Orchid, spider *(Brassia* spp.)

Features: Spiderlike flowers; graceful stems
Size: 8–24"H × 8–30"W
Light: Bright to intense
Temperature: 65–75°F day; 55–65°F night
Water: Moderately dry

Spider orchid (×*Brassidium* 'Lillian Oka')

Description and uses: Spider orchid grows from rather large pseudobulbs that store water and nutrients, each with two or three 8- to 12-inch-long leathery leaves. It produces yellow or cream flowers with dark brown or maroon spots and long spidery petals on arching flower stalks up to 18 inches long. **Care:** Grow spider orchid in bright to intense light in a well-drained epiphytic orchid mix. During its growth period, water well, but allow the potting mix to go moderately dry before watering again. Water sparingly during winter rest period. High humidity (50–60 percent) is best. Use balanced plant food. Spider orchid blooms better if given a 10°F reduction in night temperature.

Propagation: Divide pseudobulbs or remove plantlets that grow on pseudobulbs.

Pests: Root rot, spider mites, and scale are possible problems that may develop on spider orchid.

Recommendations: *B. maculata* has fragrant yellow flowers and is relatively easy to grow.

Orchid, tailed *(Masdevallia* spp.)

Features: Showy tailed flowers
Size: 1–8"H × 1–8"W
Light: Medium to bright
Temperature: 65–75°F days; 50–55°F nights
Water: Barely moist

Tailed orchid (*Masdevallia* Redwing)

Description and uses: Tailed orchid is a small epiphytic orchid from cool, misty cloud forests. It produces a fine root system and numerous flowers that can virtually cover the plant. Some flowers are fragrant.

Care: Keep tailed orchid cool with a drop in night temperature down to about 55°F. Maintain humidity between 50 and 80 percent by using a pebble tray or a humidifier but provide good air circulation. Tailed orchid roots need more moisture than most orchids, but they should never be soggy. Grow in fine fir bark or well-drained orchid mix. Repot the plant every year or two to prevent media from breaking down. The plant produces good foliage growth in medium light, but to flower well it needs brighter light. Water the roots well then allow them to become barely moist before watering again. Water sparingly during the plant's winter rest. Feed only during growth periods.

Propagation: Propagate tailed orchid by division.

Pests: Root rot, scale, spider mites, and mealybugs are potential pests.

Recommendations: *M. tovarensis* produces wonderful white flowers, two to three at a time on 4- to 6-inch spikes. It prefers warmer growing conditions and more moisture than other tailed orchid species.

Orchid, vanda *(Vanda* hybrids)

Features: Long lasting large flowers
Size: 1–6'H × 1–2'W
Light: Bright to intense
Temperature: 70–80°F day; 60–65°F night
Water: Moderately dry

Description and uses: Species vanda orchids are quite variable. Some have flat, straplike leaves; others have cylindrical (terete) succulent, fleshy ones. They range in size from miniatures to ones that grow to over 6 feet tall. Flowers are most frequently yellow-brown with brown markings but can be burgundy, green, orange, or white.

Care: The pencil-leaf terete types need full sun to bloom. Strap-leaf types tolerate slightly lower light levels. Grow vanda orchid in a bright south window. Medium green leaf color indicates favorable growing conditions. Because vanda

Vanda orchid (Vanda 'Robert's Delight Torblue' AM/AOS)

is a warm-growing orchid, home temperatures up to 80°F are good. Winter and night temperatures of at least 60°F are best. Vanda orchid is often grown mounted in an open, slatted wood basket or in fast draining media such as large redwood bark pieces mixed with perlite and charcoal. Water frequently but allow media to dry quickly. Because vanda orchid roots are often exposed, provide extremely high humidity (80 percent) all of the time. Large plants may be top heavy so add gravel in pots to add stability. Feed frequently in warm growing conditions but much less when conditions are cool. Repot when media breaks down. Soak first to make aerial roots more pliable.

Propagation: Remove and pot up plantlets (keikis). Root cuttings of terete types.

Pests: Root rot, scale, spider mites, and mealybugs are possible problems.

Recommendations: Look for hybrids with other small growing genera such as *Ascocentrum (Ascocenda)* and *Rhynchostylis (Rhynchovanda)*. Hybrids grow with less intense light. In addition to traditional vanda orchid colors, hybrids provide blues and reds.

Ornithogalum *(see Pregnant onion)*

Osmanthus *(Osmanthus spp.)*

Features: Shiny hollylike leaves
Size: 1–5'H × 1–5'W
Light: Medium to intense
Temperature: 50–75°F
Water: Moderately dry

Description and uses: Osmanthus is a woody shrub with shiny evergreen leaves that have the texture and shape of true holly, giving rise to its alternate common name, false holly. An individual plant may have both spiny leaves and spineless leaves, but juvenile plants tend to bear only spiny ones. False holly rarely blooms indoors. It becomes a festive focal point when decorated with red berries at holiday time. Unlike true hollies that are sold at holiday time, this holly look-alike can live indoors for decades.

Care: Osmanthus does best in bright light or full sun but is tolerant of medium light. It does fine with average humidity, but leaf dieback occurs in dry air. Keep soil on the dry side. Feed with foliage plant food only once or twice a year. Repot only every 2 to 3 years. Summer false holly outdoors in a protected spot. Pinch new growth regularly to keep plants bushy. Hard prune when needed to shape plants. Wash leaves regularly to remove dust.

Propagation: Take softwood or semihardwood cuttings in early summer, using rooting hormone and bottom heat.

Pests: Scale insects and spider mites are the major insect pests.

Recommendations: 'Variegatus' has variegated foliage. 'Goshiki' has gold-flecked leaves.

Sweet olive *(O. fragrans)* is a dense

Osmanthus (Osmanthus heterophyllus)

shrub growing 1 to 5 feet tall with narrow, toothless leaves. Care is basically the same as for false holly, but it needs higher humidity and cool winter temperatures, between 40 and 60°F. It is worth trying to grow if you can supply these conditions, because its cream flowers in fall and winter are intensely fragrant, similar to orange blossoms.

Ox tongue *(Gasteria bicolor)*

Features: Plump, spotted green leaves
Size: 6–36"H × 6–9"W
Light: Bright
Temperature: 70–80°F; 50–55°F winter
Water: Moderately dry

Ox tongue (Gasteria bicolor)

Description and uses: Ox tongue has distinctive succulent green leaves with raised white spots simulating the texture of an ox's tongue. Plant form varies from a somewhat flat rosette to an upright stem. Flower spikes bear round pinkish red flowers in spring. Small plants work well on a windowsill or combined with other succulents in a cactus garden.

Care: Grow ox tongue in a fertile cactus mix containing some organic matter. Water the soil thoroughly but allow it to dry to the touch before watering again. It flowers best when grown in bright light and given a winter rest at lower temperatures. Water it sparingly during winter rest. Feed during growth periods. Plants are brittle and leaves can snap off so keep out of traffic areas. Keep water off leaves.

Propagation: Start new plants from offsets or cuttings.

Allow cut surfaces to dry 24 hours before sticking in moist media.
Pests: Fungal leaf spot disfigures but does not kill the plant. Scale and mealybugs are also possible pests.
Recommendations: *O. bicolor 'Tilipmana'* is a small form with individual leaves only 2 inches long. It adapts well to windowsill gardening or growing under lights.

Oxalis *(Oxalis triangularis papilionacea)*

Features: Shamrock-shape leaflets; pink or white flowers
Size: 4–12"H × 4–12"W
Light: Medium to bright
Temperature: 60–75°F
Water: Evenly moist

Oxalis *(Oxalis triangularis papilionacea atropurpurea)*

Description and uses: This charming bloomer is among the easiest flowering houseplants to grow. The white or soft pink flowers are produced continuously except for a brief break in winter. The flowers are held above the triangular cloverlike leaves. It is an excellent partner in mixed baskets and other small-plant groupings. The purple-leaf types add subdued color even when not in bloom. It is also classified as *O. regnellii*.
Care: Oxalis likes bright light year round but tolerates less light. Good light intensifies leaf color in burgundy or variegated types. Hot, humid conditions may slow down flower production, as can low light levels in winter. Feed plants frequently and water well to keep the soil evenly moist. Repot when plants become crowded or if soil salts build up. Unlike other bulbous plants, oxalis does not require a period of dormancy. If the plant goes dormant from dryness or spider mite infestation, cut off all the leaves, repot the bulblike pips, and have a healthy flowering plant in a matter of weeks. Prevent soil-salt damage to roots by flushing the pots thoroughly with plenty of clean room temperature water every 2 months.
Propagate: Plant the small bulbils that you'll find when you repot plants. Divide plants at anytime. Pull apart the roots, slicing them into two or three smaller clumps. Repot and snip off any damage leaves.
Pests: Potential insect problems include spider mites, whiteflies, thrips, mealybugs, and scale.
Recommendations: *O.t.p. atropurpurea* is a popular selection with deep purple leaves that often have a metallic pink splotch in the center. **'Fanny'** has green leaves with silver margins. **'Silver and Gold'** never grows more than 4 inches tall and has fragrant yellow flowers and silver variegated leaves.

Pachira *(Pachira aquatica)*

Features: Tropical foliage; often with braided stems
Size: 1–6'H × 1–4'W
Light: Medium to bright
Temperature: 65–80°F
Water: Evenly moist

Pachira *(Pachira aquatica)*

Description and uses: Pachira is a Central American tree that grows to 100' tall in moist areas. It has large glossy green compound leaves. As a houseplant several stems may be braided together. In Asia it is considered a plant for good luck and prosperity so it is known as the money tree. It makes a good subject for bonsai.
Care: Despite its tropical, marshy origin, pachira is adaptable to home conditions. It prefers bright light but tolerates medium light, though the leaves will be smaller. Grow it in a fertile mix that is kept moist, never soggy. Feed it with foliage plant food throughout the summer. Repot every few years when media breaks down. To keep plants at a reasonable size, remove the plant from the pot, root prune, and return to the same size container with fresh media. It prefers high humidity.
Propagation: Start new plants from stem cuttings or seed.
Pests: Spider mites, scale, or aphids are possible pests.
Recommendations: No named culitvars are available.

Pachypodium *(see Madagascar palm)*
Pachystachys *(see Lollipop plant)*
Painted century plant *(see Agave)*

Palm, areca *(Dypsis lutescens)*

Features: Upright, feathery arching fronds
Size: 1–6'H × 1–5'W
Light: Bright
Temperature: 65–80°F
Water: Evenly moist

Description and uses: This majestic palm eventually develops long fronds that extend upward and arch gracefully. Each frond has several leaflets, giving the plant a feathery appearance. The lowest parts of the stem are yellow to yellow-orange. Its eventual large size restricts use in the home, but small seedlings are adaptable to many locations. Underplant large

Areca palm *(Dypsis lutescens)*

specimens with golden pothos or English ivy for added interest. Areca palm enjoys spending summers outdoors in a shady spot out of the wind. This is one of the best plants for ridding the air of chemical toxins. This plant is also sold as *Chrysalidocarpus lutescens*.

Care: Areca palm requires bright light, high humidity, and warmth. It prefers temperatures of 75°F or higher during the day and should remain above 65°F at night. If the humidity is too low, leaf tips turn brown. Overfeeding and salt buildup can also cause brown leaf tips. Keep the soil constantly moist spring and summer, allowing it to go slightly drier in fall and winter. Use a peaty yet porous mix such as Miracle-Gro Cactus, Palm & Citrus Soil. If the soil remains wet for too long, roots may rot. This palm needs only one application of a continuous-feed plant food each spring. Repot every 2 to 3 years.

Propagate: Start new plants from seeds or by division. Both techniques are difficult for home gardeners.

Pests: Spider mites can be a problem; give plants regular showers to deter them.

Palm, Chinese fan (*Livistona chinensis*)

Features: Large fan-shape leaves
Size: 4–10'H × 4–10'W
Light: Bright
Temperature: 60–75°F
Water: Evenly moist

Chinese fan palm (*Livistona chinensis*)

Description and uses: The Chinese fan palm (which is actually native to Japan) grows large fanlike leaves that can be 18 inches wide on small plants, becoming even larger as plants mature. The fan is held together by threadlike connectors. The plant is often as wide as or wider than it is tall.

Care: Grow Chinese fan palm in bright indirect light, such as through a curtained window. Provide normal room temperature growing conditions, with slightly lower night temperatures. It grows best in a soil mix containing organic matter that can retain moisture, yet never be soggy. Feed with a balanced plant food during summer growth. Repot in spring. Give plants a shower or wash leaves frequently with a soft damp cloth.

Propagation: Start new plants from seed.

Pests: Spider mites are the most common problem.

Palm, European fan (*Chamaerops humilis*)

Features: Exotic fans of gray-green leaves
Size: 4–8'H × 5–10'W
Light: Bright to intense
Temperature: 70–80°F day; 50–60°F night
Water: Evenly moist

Description and uses: European fan palm is an excellent choice if you have a large, sunny room that cools off at night. The stiff fan-shape leaves grow up to 2 feet across and have a silvery sheen. Older outer fronds wither and new ones are produced from the plant's crown. As plants age they

European fan palm (*Chamaerops humilis*)

often develop multiple trunks that grow at interesting angles. The trunks become rough and develop black hairs, giving plants a rugged appearance. European fan palm can be grown outdoors year round in southern climates. It enjoys summer outdoors in cooler areas.

Care: Ample bright light is the key to success with European fan palm, which needs at least 4 hours of direct sun each day and bright filtered light the rest of the time. When light is too low, the gaps between the fronds detract from its beauty. It thrives on warm daytime temperatures but needs cool nights. Keep soil evenly moist spring and summer, allowing soil to dry to within 2 inches of the surface between waterings in fall and winter. The easiest way to feed European fan palm is to give plants a time-release plant food in spring, followed by a balanced houseplant food once or twice in summer. Withhold plant food in fall and winter. The deep roots are fragile, so repot only when necessary, about every 3 years. Once plants are too large to repot, topdress them with fresh soil each spring. Keep fronds clean with a monthly shower or clean with a damp cloth. It is normal for ends of leaflets to split as they mature.

Propagate: Carefully cut away and transplant suckers when they are 8 to 10 inches tall.

Pests: Possible problems on European fan palm include scale insects, spider mites, and mealybugs.

Recommendations: Blue Mediterranean fan palm (*C.h. argentea*) is more silvery blue than European fan palm.

Palm, fishtail (*Caryota mitis*)

Features: Fishtail-shape, gray-green leaflets
Size: 6–12'H × 3–5'W
Light: Bright
Temperature: 65–85°F
Water: Evenly moist

Description and uses: Fishtail palm has bipinnate palm fronds—each primary leaflet is divided into secondary ones. The deeply arching fronds have an interesting tattered fishtail look to them. They can be as much as 3 feet wide. This upright plant has a medium growth rate but eventually gets quite large. It is best used as an architectural accent in a large room or entryway where it can be given plenty of room.

Care: Fishtail palm likes bright, filtered light. It likes average to warm room temperatures and average to high humidity (30 percent or above). It will not do well if the temperature drops below 55°F at night or if it is exposed to cold drafts. Keep the soil evenly moist spring through fall, allowing it to dry slightly in winter. Fishtail palm does best when slightly pot-bound. Repot young plants every year in a well-drained soil-based potting mix. Once plants reach a large size, topdress rather than repot. During active growth feed once a month. Do not feed in winter. Shower plants or clean leaves with a damp cloth to reduce dust buildup and deter spider mites.

Fishtail palm (Caryota mitis)

Propagate: Separate and plant the suckers that appear at the base of older plants. Gently pull apart suckers when they are 9 to 12 inches tall, keeping some roots attached.
Pests: Brown leaf tips and spider mites usually indicate that the air is too dry.
Recommendations: *Giant fishtail palms* (C. urens and C. obtusa) are two less-common species that grow to 12 feet or more.

Palm, lady (Rhapis excelsa)

Features: Bamboolike stems, fan-shape leaves
Size: 5–8'H × 4–6'W
Light: Medium
Temperature: 60–80°F
Water: Evenly moist

Description and uses: This slow growing palm has fans of broad dark green leaves. Plants grow low and broad rather than tall and upright. Over many years they can reach 10 feet tall. The leaf scars at 2- to 4-inch intervals give plants a bamboolike appearance. Lady palm is a good choice for a formal, easy-care plant that evokes an Oriental mood. It is one of the best houseplants for improving indoor air quality. It is also called bamboo palm and is sometimes classified as *Chamaerops excelsa*.

Lady palm (Rhapis excelsa)

Care: Lady palm tolerates a wide range of light, doing best in the filtered light from an east window but also tolerating low-light conditions fairly well. Direct sun can cause the leaves to turn yellow. It grows well at average room temperatures but can tolerate 45°F for short periods in winter. It likes high humidity. Water plants by soaking the soil, then allow it to dry to within 1 inch below the surface. In winter, allow it to dry to 2 inches deep. Feed monthly during the growing period using a standard houseplant food. Repot young plants every 2 years. When plants reach the desired size, repot only as needed to refresh soil. It is natural for lower leaves to dry and fall off.
Propagate: Separate and pot up basal stem suckers with roots attached.
Pests: Possible pests on lady palm include spider mites, scale insects, and mealybugs.
Recommendations: 'Koban' is a popular green variety. 'Zuikonishiki' has cream and green variegated leaves and usually stays less than 2 feet tall indoors. 'Tenzan' has curled leaves.

Palm, majesty (Ravenea rivularis)

Features: Large pinnate fronds
Size: 1–12'H × 1–5'W
Light: Bright to intense
Temperature: 65–80°F
Water: Evenly moist

Description and uses: Majesty palm is a fast growing palm that quickly can outgrow an indoor space unless confined by its container. If kept pot-bound it will remain a manageable size as a specimen plant for several years. The upright arching fronds to 5 feet in length give a majestic appearance. It has a reputation for being a bit finicky to grow as a houseplant, but most successful majesty palm owners find it easy to grow as long as they pay attention to watering and the plant gets plenty of light, humidity, and plant food. It is also classified as *R. glauca*.

Majesty palm (Ravenea rivularis)

Care: Unlike most other palms, keep the roots of majesty palm evenly moist. Its botanical name *"rivularis"*, meaning "by the river," provides the clue to success. Don't allow the roots to sit in water, but never allow them to dry out either. Use a heavier potting mix such as Miracle-Gro Potting Soil rather than Miracle-Gro Cactus, Palm & Citrus Soil. Provide bright to intense indoor light and high humidity. Give the plant frequent showers to remove dust and potential spider mite infestations. Move to a shady location outdoors over summer. Majesty palm grows best at warm temperatures but can tolerate some cold. (As a landscape plant it can survive frosts.) Feed it with foliage plant food only during the growing season.
Propagation: Start new plants from seed.
Pests: In dry conditions spider mites are almost certain to attack majesty palm. Scale and mealybugs may also attack it.

Palm, parlor (Chamaedorea elegans)

Features: Small palm with arching fronds
Size: 1–8'H × 1–3'W
Light: Medium to low
Temperature: 65–80°F
Water: Evenly moist

Parlor palm (Chamaedorea elegans)

Description and uses: Parlor palm has been a popular houseplant since Victorian times because its tolerates less-than-perfect conditions. It is an elegant, upright plant with straplike green leaflets on feathery fronds that grow 9 to 24 inches long. It is an excellent office plant, growing well under fluorescent lights. In the home it is great for filling an empty corner. It can get by on lower light levels than other palms. Young plants can be used temporarily in a terrarium. Parlor palm is good for removing indoor air pollutants.
Care: Although parlor palm tolerates lower light than most palms, it prefers medium to bright indirect light. Full sun will cause brown leaf tips. It also tolerates drier air than most palms, but stays healthier with higher humidity. Keep the soil evenly moist at all times during active growth, avoiding extremes. Yellowing leaves can indicate either overwatering or underwatering. Parlor palm prefers warm temperatures and does not like to be exposed to cold drafts. Spring through fall feed plants monthly. Repot young plants annually in spring; mature plants can go every other year. Use a soil-based mix that drains freely.
Propagation: Young plants are often sold with multiple plants in the pot. Carefully divide these to start new plants (Avoid damage to roots). Take offsets that develop at the base of older plants or start new plants from seed.
Pests: Spider mites, mealybugs, and scale insects can be problems if the air is dry.
Recommendations: 'Bella' is a popular compact selection easily kept under 4 feet tall for a long time.
   Bamboo palm (C. erumpens) has clumping stems that are smooth, green, and slender with prominent scars at nodes, resembling bamboo. Fronds grow up to 20 inches long and plants can reach 8 feet.
   Bamboo palm (C. seifrizii) is more delicate in appearance than the other Chamaedorea species, with its lacy leaves reaching 2 to 3 feet long on top of slender canelike stems about 4 feet tall. It is excellent for removing indoor air pollutants. It is also called reed palm.

Palm, pygmy date (Phoenix roebelenii)

Features: Long arching fronds
Size: 3–6'H × 3–6'W
Light: Medium to bright
Temperature: 65–85°F
Water: Moderately dry

Pygmy date palm (Phoenix roebelenii)

Description and uses: Pygmy date palm is tolerant of some neglect and less-than-ideal conditions. It grows large but is slow growing and rarely reaches more than 3 or 4 feet indoors. The narrow arching fronds have a thin layer of white scales on them. The short, slender stem eventually roughens as old leaf bases accumulate along its length. The bases of the leaflets are armed with sharp spines, and older trunks develop thorns. Place out of high traffic areas since fronds are prickly. Give it plenty of room so its arching fronds can be appreciated. This is one of the best palms for removing indoor air pollutants.
Care: Pygmy date palm likes warmth and bright light during its growing period but tolerates cooler temperatures and less intense light in winter. Water well then allow the soil to dry 1 inch deep. Keep drier in fall and winter. It tolerates low humidity, but spider mites can be a problem when air is dry. Use a continuous-feed plant food that includes micronutrients in spring. Do not feed in fall and winter. Repot young plants in spring as needed. Mature plants have brittle roots and are difficult to repot. Remove older fronds as they fade to reveal the interesting trunk. Wear gloves when trimming.
Propagate: Start new plants from seed or divide suckering plants with multiple stems.
Pests: Scale, spider mites, and mealybugs are possible insect problems on pygmy date palm.
Recommendations: Canary Island date palm (P. canariensis) is a larger, coarser palm with a spiky appearance and attractive, diamond-shape markings on its trunk.

Panama hat plant (Carludovica palmata 'Jungle Drum')

Features: Palmlike ridged leaves
Size: 1–8'H × 1–4'W
Light: Bright
Temperature: 65–80°F
Water: Moderately dry

Description and uses: Panama hat plant is a decorative, low growing palmlike plant with deeply ridged fan-shape leaves. It grows on short stems directly from the roots. It gets its common name from Ecuador, where immature leaves are split into small strips, boiled, and then bleached with lemon juice and used to produce Panama hats. It is also sometimes called C. panamanica or C. insignis.

Panama hat plant
(Carludovica palmata 'Jungle Drum')

Care: Grow Panama hat plant in bright light in a well-drained fertile potting mix. Allow soil to dry moderately between waterings. It needs less water in winter or if grown at cool temperatures. Keep humidity high. Feed with balanced plant food during the growing season. Repot young plants yearly in the spring. Older plants can be topdressed and maintained in a larger pot for several years. Give the plant a shower or wash leaves frequently to keep them clean and to deter pests.

Propagation: Divide offsets from the main stem in spring or start new plants from seed.

Pests: Spider mites, mealybugs, or aphids.

Panda plant *(see Kalanchoe; Philodendron)*
Pandanus *(see Screw pine)*
Paphiopedilum *(see Orchid, slipper)*

Papyrus, dwarf *(Cyperus alternifolius)*

Features: Grasslike plant with fans of leaves
Size: 2–3'H × 2–3'W
Light: Bright
Temperature: 50–85°F
Water: Wet

Dwarf papyrus *(Cyperus alternifolius)*

Description and uses: It is almost impossible to overwater umbrella plant. This vase-shape grassy foliage plant brings a stylish yet playful look to any room. Whorls of dainty leaves appear to float atop the elegant stems. Small greenish to brown flowers appear in summer. Dwarf umbrella plant is excellent for indoor water gardens or fountains. It is the same plant as *C. involucratus*.

Care: Umbrella plant thrives with its feet in water but also does fine when supplied with average moisture. Keep the saucer filled with water at all times or slip the pot into a larger cachepot and keep it soaking in water at all times. Plants grow well with medium humidity, but they like the brightest indirect light possible. A south or west window with a gauzy curtain is perfect. Umbrella plant tolerates a wide range of temperatures but does not like to go below about 45°F in winter or exposure to cold drafts. Feed with a balanced plant food in summer. Repot when a plant begins to creep out of its pot. Plants can grow in standard soil or even in water alone. Tall plants may need staking. Remove faded fronds and wipe leaves regularly with a dry, soft cloth.

Propagate: The easiest way to propagate umbrella plant is to bend a stem over and pin the bracts down on wet sand in a new pot. Clip the plantlet from the parent when it has rooted. Root cuttings may also be used.

Pests: No serious pest problems affect umbrella plant.

Recommendations: 'Gracillus' and 'Nanus' are dwarf forms growing about 18 inches tall. 'Variegatus' has bracts either striped with white or totally white. Variegation is often short lived and plants revert to green as they age. It requires brighter light than other types.

Parodia *(see Cactus, ball)*
Parlor palm *(see Palm, parlor)*
Parrot flower heliconia *(see Heliconia)*
Partridge-breasted aloe *(see Aloe)*
Passiflora *(see Passionflower)*

Passionflower *(Passiflora spp.)*

Features: Large striking flowers
Size: 4–10'H × 1–4'W
Light: Intense to bright
Temperature: 65–75°F
Water: Evenly moist

Description and uses: Passionflower is a rapidly growing vine that clings with long tendrils. The large flowers (4 to 6 inches wide) are complex and quite striking. All types produce abundant three-lobed leaflets.

Care: Give this vigorous plant plenty of space along with a trellis or other support. It needs a well-

Passionflower *(Passiflora 'Incense')*

drained fertile soil mix and to be kept evenly moist during active growth. Feed every two weeks with a flowering plant food. The plant will produce foliage but no flowers if light intensity is inadequate. Give it bright to intense light, such as in a sun room or conservatory. Prune to shape and to control size. Repot in spring when the plant outgrows its pot or the potting mix is broken down. Top and root pruning is an alternative to maintain size rather than moving the plant to a larger pot. Keep passionflower in an area with high humidity.

Propagation: Start passionflower from stem cuttings taken in spring or from seed.

Pests: Spider mites, whiteflies, and scale insects are possible.

Recommendations: *P. caerulea* has intricate purple, white, and blue flowers.

P. coccinea has showy crimson flowers with protruding bright yellow stamens.

P. vitifolia produces larger, bright red flowers.

P. 'Incense' has fragrant, wavy purple flowers.

P. quadrangularis is the popular passionfruit. It flowers but does not bear fruit indoors.

Peace lily *(Spathiphyllum wallisii)*

Features: Deep green leaves; white flowers
Size: 1–6'H × 1–5'W
Light: Low to bright
Temperature: 60–85°F
Water: Evenly moist

Peace lily *(Spathiphyllum wallisii)*

Description and uses: Peace lily is an easy-care plant that tolerates low humidity and low light levels and has consistent blooms. It has glossy, lance-shape leaves on arching stems that surround the central flower spikes. Flowers consist of a showy, spoon-shape, pure white spathe that forms a softly curved backdrop for the central column of tiny yellow flowers. Flowers normally appear in summer, but many cultivars bloom intermittently throughout the year. The dark leaves look attractive in a plain pot with a glossy finish. Peace lily excels in removal of several indoor pollutants, including formaldehyde, benzene, and carbon monoxide.
Care: Although it tolerates low light, peace lily does best in medium to bright filtered light. In low light the plant will have attractive foliage but probably no blooms. It likes warm temperatures. The plant may show injury if temperatures drop below 60°F or if it is exposed to cold drafts. Keep the soil lightly moist at all times, especially if it is growing in high light. Feed in summer with foliage plant food; overfeeding can lead to fewer flowers. Plants like to be slightly root-bound. Repot as needed in spring using a good quality potting soil. Remove yellow leaves and cut off flowering stems when the blossoms turn from white to green.
Propagation: Divide large clumps of peace lily in spring.
Pests: Thrips, spider mites, and mealybugs are the main insect pests.
Recommendations: 'Sensation' is a giant cultivar that grows to 6 feet tall and is often seen in malls. 'Supreme' is the most common type for household use. 'Lynise' has textured leaves and is a good bloomer. 'Mauna Loa' is a robust cultivar growing up to 3 feet tall.

Peacock plant *(see Calathea)*	**Pelargonium** *(see Geranium)*
Peanut cactus *(see Cactus, peanut)*	**Pellaea** *(see Fern, button)*
Pedilanthus *(see Devil's backbone)*	**Pellionia** *(see Watermelon begonia)*

Pentas *(Pentas lanceolata)*

Features: Clusters of colorful star-shape blooms
Size: 1–3'H × 1–3'W
Light: Intense to bright
Temperature: 65–75°F
Water: Evenly moist

Description and uses: Pentas or star flower is a shrubby plant with elliptic or lance-shape green leaves. It bears rounded clusters of small flowers at the stem tips and, under supplemental light, or intense natural light may bloom sporadically all year. Bloom is most abundant in spring and summer. The main species, *P. lanceolata*, has been mostly superseded by a series of denser dwarf hybrids in shades of

Pentas *(Pentas lanceolata)*

white, pink, magenta, purple, lilac, and red, most of which stay below 3 feet tall and wide and require no staking. If you can't find this plant in the houseplant section of your local garden center, look among the outdoor annuals.
Care: Most varieties prefer intense light but may do well with bright light. They can grow outdoors in summer as a garden annual. As a houseplant grow pentas in fertile potting soil and keep evenly moist during growth. Cut back slightly in watering in fall and winter. Use a flowering houseplant food regularly during summer. Pinch plants to keep them compact and to encourage branching.
Propagation: Many varieties of pentas are available from seed. If you find one you particularly like, you can propagate it from stem cuttings.
Pests: Spider mites and aphids are possible.
Recommendations: Numerous worthwhile cultivars are available. The **Star Series** comes in an array of colors.

Peperomia *(Peperomia spp.)*

Features: Foliage plant with interesting leaves
Size: 6–12"H × 6–12"W
Light: Low to medium
Temperature: 60–75°F
Water: Moderately dry

Description and uses: Peperomia is an easy-care plant that grows nicely in moderate light. Leaf shapes vary from heart-shape to narrow and pointed. Most are waxy. Some have interesting wafflelike texture. They may be green, reddish, or silvery gray with green leaf veins. Plants occasionally produce

Ripple peperomia *(Peperomia caperata)*

Teardrop peperomia (*Peperomia orba*)

Silverleaf peperomia (*Peperomia griseoargentea*)

slender flowery spikes that resemble rat's tails. Peperomia is great for tabletop use and is a nice companion in dish gardens and mixed baskets. It tolerates the low light of a north windowsill and stays small enough to fit on a desk or be used in a terrarium. **Care:** Give peperomia low to moderate light from an east or north window. It does fine with average room temperatures but likes good humidity. It does not like to be overwatered; treat it more like a succulent. Allow the soil to dry to within ½ inch of the surface between waterings. Raised scablike swellings on leaf undersides are caused by a condition known as edema and are the result of overwatering. Peperomia is also sensitive to excessive soil salts. Leach potting mix in summer to remove excess salts. Use a light potting soil to ensure adequate air around the roots. Repot in spring as needed, but keep plants in smallish pots. It is normal for older leaves to shrivel and die, but sudden leaf loss can be due to salt damage or fertilizer burn. **Propagation:** Stem tip cuttings and petiole leaf cuttings are the most common means of starting new plants. Plants with multiple stems may also be divided when they are in active growth. **Pests:** Root rot and mealybugs occasionally plague any of the peperomias.

Watermelon peperomia (*Peperomia argyreia*)

Red-edge peperomia (*Peperomia clusiifolia* 'Rainbow')

Recommendations:

Watermelon peperomia (*P. argyreia*) is a smaller species, growing 6 to 8 inches tall, with arching stripes of silver-gray on the nearly elliptical leaves. It is also known as watermelon begonia although it is not related to begonias.

Ripple peperomia (*P. caperata*) has deeply textured 1-inch-wide green leaves. **'Emerald Ripple'** is the standard green-leafed variety. **'Green Valley'** is widely grown, with green and white puckered leaves. **'Red Luna'** has reddish leaves. **'Metallica'** has leaves marked with silvery gray. **'Lillian'** has deep green leaves topped by white flower spikes in late summer. **'Tricolor'** has smaller leaves that have broad white borders.

Parallel peperomia (*P. puteolata*) trails with leathery green with yellow leaves to 4 inches long.

Trailing peperomia (*P. scandans*), also called false philodendron, has small oval leaves on trailing stems when young; they are more upright later.

Baby rubber plant (*P. clusiifolia*) grows about 8 inches tall with branching red stems. The thick fleshy

Baby rubber plant (*Peperomia obtusifolia* 'Variegata')

Jayde peperomia (*Peperomia polybotrya* 'Jayde')

Japanese peperomia
(*Peperomia japonica* 'Green Valley')

leaves have red margins. It is also known as red-edge peperomia. **Silverleaf peperomia** (*P. griseoargentea*) grows to 6 inches in height and has metallic silvery green leaves with a slightly rippled texture. **Baby rubber plant** (*P. obtusifolia*) is more upright growing and has large rounded, waxy, deep green leaves. '**Variegata**' is gold and white variegated. '**Sensation**' has gold-splashed waxy leaves on purple stems.

Teardrop peperomia (*P. orba*) is rarely seen as a species, but there are several dwarf varieties available. '**Astrid**', also known as '**Princess Astrid**', is a bushy, branching plant with red-spotted stems and spoon-shape, light green, downy leaves. '**Pixie**' stays about 6 inches tall and wide.

P. polybotrya '**Jayde**' is a new hybrid selection with shiny round leaves up to 4 inches in diameter. It grows up to 18 inches tall with tight overlapping concave leaves. **Japanese peperomia** (*P. japonica*) is a trailing plant with oval leaves and rippled texture. '**Green Valley**' makes an attractive hanging plant.

HERE'S A TIP...
Baby rubber plant leaves are smooth and succulent. Keep them bright and shiny by cleaning them with a soft cloth.

Persea (*see Avocado*)

Persian shield

(*Strobilanthes dyerianus*)
Features: Showy foliage
Size: 1–4'H × 1–3'W
Light: Bright
Temperature: 60–75°F
Water: Evenly moist

Description and uses:
This erect, well-branched, fast growing shrub has showy foliage. Its large lance-shape leaves are heavily marbled with rich purple and highlighted with iridescent silvery pink markings above and deep wine red below. Older plants

Persian shield (*Strobilanthes dyerianus*)

produce pale blue funnel-shape flowers just before going into decline. To help delay the decline, pinch off flower buds before they open. Persian shield does well as an outdoor potted plant in an area with partial shade. Indoors it is a nice addition to foliage groupings and it makes a wonderful greenhouse or conservatory plant.

Care: Persian shield likes bright light all year long. Normal room temperatures are fine, but no lower than 55°F. Keep soil evenly moist during active growth, reducing water and allowing plants to go moderately dry in winter. Plants need high humidity. Use an all-purpose plant food during the growing period. In early fall take softwood cuttings and start new plants to overwinter indoors. Pinch and prune as needed to improve the shape and to prevent lankiness. If plants summer outdoors, they can be moved into larger pots. In fall cut back hard and move indoors.

Propagation: Start fresh stem cuttings every year to replace older plants that have grown unattractive.

Pests: Dry indoor air causes leaf dieback. Spider mites are possible pests.

Peruvian daffodil (*Hymenocallis narcissiflora*)

Features: Ornate, fragrant spidery flowers
Size: 18–30"H × 8–15"W
Light: Bright
Temperature: 70–80°F; 60–65°F in winter
Water: Evenly moist

Description and uses:
Peruvian daffodil grows from a bulb. It can be purchased as a growing plant, sometimes in flower, or as a dormant bulb prepared to grow and flower. Plants have long bright green straplike leaves. The ornate fragrant flowers are 4 inches across, each centered with a daffodil-type white and green trumpet surrounded by a halo of long curly petals. Plants retain their foliage color and

Peruvian daffodil (*Hymenocallis narcissiflora*)

silhouette for months before and after flowering.

Care: Plant new bulbs with necks just above soil level in rich potting mix. Like amaryllis and other lilies, Peruvian daffodil requires ample water and fertilizer to bloom; after a brief rest period, can bloom repeatedly for years indoors. The bulb may not go totally dormant but goes through a resting period. Be careful about watering during that time and only give enough water to keep leaves from shriveling. When in doubt do not water. Wash leaves every couple of weeks. In growth it does best in high humidity. Dry air and cool temperatures are fine during dormant times. As the plant comes out of its rest period and new growth starts, resume the regular watering and feeding schedule.

Propagation: Remove bulb offsets that develop on mature bulbs and plant them individually.

Pests: Root rot from overwatering is the most common problem. Few pests affect it.

Phalaenopsis (*see Orchid, moth*)

Philodendron (*Philodendron* spp.)

Features: Vining, glossy leaves
Size: 1–10'H × 1–6'W
Light: Low to bright
Temperature: 60–80°F
Water: Moderately dry to evenly moist

Heart-leaf philodendron
(Philodendron hederaceum oxycardium)

Description and uses:

The heart-leaf philodendron *(P. hederaceum oxycardium)* syn. *(P. scandens oxycaridum, P. oxycardium, P. cordatum)* is a durable foliage plant that has long been the backbone of indoor gardening. Its slender stems carry heart-shape leaves up to 4 inches long. Leaves are slightly bronze and almost transparent when new, but quickly become deep green. It is easy to grow, easy to propagate, and adapts well to almost any indoor setting. Small specimens are popular in dish gardens and mixed baskets. Its low light tolerance makes it a good choice for bookshelves and for draping over the sides of a large piece of furniture. The vining stems will eventually attach themselves to a post or moss pole with aerial roots, but they need help getting started. Leaves are poisonous to pets and people if eaten in large amounts. All philodendrons rank high for improving indoor air quality.

Care: The heart-leaf philodendron likes moderate light but has a good tolerance of low light, especially in winter. Allow the soil to become slightly dry between waterings but never allow it to dry out completely. Repot every other year using well-drained fertile potting soil. Keep young plants compact and bushy by pinching back stems from time to time. The papery sheaths that cover leaf buds can be snipped out after they turn brown. Some people get an itchy rash from the sap, so work with gloves and keep sap off skin.

Propagation: Plants are easy to root from stem tip cuttings.
Pests: Possible insect pests include mealybugs, aphids, and spider mites.
Recommendations: Several yellow-leaf and variegated

Velvet-leaf philodendron
(Philodendron hederaceum hederaceum)

forms of heart-leaf philodendron are available, including **'Aureum'**, **Variegatum'**, and **'Golden'**. These grow best in cooler conditions and brighter light, because warmth and low light can cause the yellow tones to revert to green.

Several **hybrid philodendrons** have been developed. These are usually clump-forming plants with attractive glossy foliage. Some eventually begin to climb and will need support or cutting back. **'Black Cardinal'** has glossy, deep purple leaves. **'Moonlight'** has pointed leaves in bright chartreuse green, darkening to lime green. **'Prince of Orange'** has coppery orange new leaves that fade to pale green.

Red-leaf philodendron *(Philodendron erubescens)*

Velvet-leaf philodendron *(P. hederaceum hederaceum)* syn. *(P. scandens micans)* is a graceful plant with a velvety leaf texture with bronze tones on the new foliage.

Red-leaf philodendron *(P. erubescens)* is a vining species with reddish purple stems and shiny, dark green upper leaf surfaces and coppery red leaf undersides. A pillar-grown specimen is a good choice for entryways and corners.

Splitleaf philodendron, or lacy tree philodendron *(P. bipinnatifidum)* syn. *(P. selloum)*, has deeply cut green leaves that

Splitleaf philodendron *(Philodendron bipinnatifidum)*

Xanadu philodendron *(Philodendron 'Xanadu')*

Elephant ear philodendron
(Philodendron domesticum)

arise from a central crown. It is a nonclimbing type, starting out upright but gradually assuming a more relaxed posture up to 6 feet wide. Long, ropelike aerial roots are produced near the base of the plant. Tuck these roots back into the pot or wind them around the soil surface on top of the container. These aerial roots can be cut back when repotting. Tree philodendron is a good floor plant but needs plenty of room to sprawl.

Xanadu philodendron (*P*. 'Xanadu') is a clumping plant to about 3 feet tall and wide. It takes bright light and needs feeding in summer. It does not form aerial roots.

Elephant ear philodendron (*P. domesticum*) syn. (*P. hastatum*) is a climbing plant with large, to 2 feet long, spade-shape medium green glossy leaves. It does well in medium to low light. Allow it to go moderately dry between waterings. It is a bit coarse so is best if massed with other plants. It can climb quite high on pillars or other forms if given the opportunity. It is also called spade leaf philodendron.

Birds-nest philodendron (*P. imbe*) has 8-inch-long papery, arrow-shape leaves.

Fiddle-leaf philodendron (*P. bipennifolium*) has lobed leaves to 10 inches long. It loves humidity, does well in medium light, and will climb given the chance. It is also known as panda plant and *P. panduriforme*.

Fiddle-leaf philodendron
(Philodendron bipennifolium)

HERE'S A TIP...

Grow heart-leaf philodendron on a moss pole for an upright accent. Pin the trailing stems to the pole until they root into the support.

Philodendron, split-leaf (*Monstera deliciosa*)

Features: Deeply cut, large glossy leaves
Size: 2–10'H × 2–10'W
Light: Low to bright
Temperature: 60–75°F
Water: Evenly moist

Split-leaf philodendron (*Monstera deliciosa*)

Description and uses: A well-grown split-leaf philodendron, also called the Swiss-cheese plant, is a handsome, dramatic specimen. The dark green heart-shape leaves can grow up to 3 feet wide with deeply cut incisions that go almost to the central vein. Plants also tolerate low light and humidity, but their growth will not be as interesting. This climbing plant sends out aerial roots that anchor the plant to a tree or pole. When grown upward on a moss or bark pole, it becomes a strong architectural accent. It is an ideal floor plant for large spaces and can be used as a room divider. The leaves and stems are toxic and the sap can cause dermatitis in sensitive individuals, so it is not a good plant in homes with small children. *Monstera* produces a fruit that is edible when mature. It is occasionally available in specialty markets. Immature fruit has needlelike crystals that will irritate the mouth.

Care: Split-leaf philodendron tolerates low or moderate light but does best in bright light. Plants grown in low light will be smaller and lack the perforations that make this plant interesting. It also tolerates low humidity but does better with average to high room humidity. Water to keep the soil mix slightly moist but water less in winter. Feed in summer with foliage plant food. Plants respond to annual repotting. Give plants a pole for the aerial roots to grow into. Train aerial roots that form on the lower part of the stem to grow into the container soil for additional support. Wash leaves or give plant a shower to keep leaves clean and help prevent pests.

Propagation: Start new plants from stem cuttings or by air layering large plants.

Pests: Mealybugs, scale, whiteflies, and spider mites are all potential problems on split-leaf philodendron.

Recommendations: 'Variegata' has creamy white patches and 'Albovariegata' has white patches. These variegated types often revert to all green as plants get older.

Phlebodium *(see Fern, rabbit's foot)*
Phoenix *(see Palm, pygmy date)*

Piggyback plant (*Tolmiea menziesii*)

Features: Fuzzy leaves supporting little plantlets
Size: 6–12"H × 12–18"W
Light: Medium to bright
Temperature: 60–75°F; 50–65°F in winter
Water: Moderately dry

Piggyback plant (*Tolmiea menziesii*)

Description and uses: This fast grower gets its common name from its fascinating habit of producing plantlets on older leaves. Each plantlet grows on the upper surface of a leaf at the junction of the leaf and its stalk. The plantlets weigh down the slender leafstalks, giving the plant a trailing appearance. Piggyback plant is usually grown in a hanging basket but also makes a nice pedestal plant. It has a refreshing green color that looks nice with darker colored plants or a dark container. The leaf and stem hairs can cause minor skin irritation; wear gloves when working with piggyback plant. It is also known by the descriptive names "mother-of-thousands" or "youth-on-age."

Care: Piggyback plant likes medium indirect light. Full sun can cause leaf tips to burn and too little light makes plants leggy. Cool to average temperatures are fine. It likes a cool period in winter, tolerating temperatures down to 45°F. Keep the soil slightly moist at all times if plants are growing in bright light. Plants grown in medium light can go drier. It needs moderate humidity. Low humidity causes leaf margins to brown. It is not a heavy feeder. Use an all-purpose plant food several times during active growth. Repot annually. If older plants start to look tired, divide or take leaf cuttings.

Propagation: Peg attached plantlets into potting mix. Wait until the parent leaf withers to cut it away from the newly rooted plantlet. Full plants may also be divided.

Pests: Possible pests of piggyback plant include spider mites, aphids, and mealybugs.

Recommendations: 'Taft's Gold' has green leaves mottled with cream to yellow to gold tones.

Pigtail flower (*see Anthurium*)

Pilea (*Pilea* spp.)

Features: Variegated and/or textured leaves
Size: 1–12"H × 3–12"W
Light: Medium to bright
Temperature: 60–75°F
Water: Barely moist

Aluminum plant (*Pilea cadierei*)

Description and uses: *Pilea cadicrei*, aluminum plant, is a well-known pilea suitable for indoor growing. It has quilted green leaves that appear to have been decorated with silver paint. Young stems are tinged with pink, while older ones become slightly woody. Aluminum plant is a staple in mixed baskets. Also consider it for hanging baskets. Create a miniature "palm tree" for your terrarium by growing a single stem with the lower leaves pinched off. It makes a good windowsill plant.

Care: This foliage plant likes medium to bright light from an east or west exposure and moderate to high humidity. Do not allow roots to stand in water. Keep it away from cold windows. Leaves often develop brown splotches if they get wet. They also drop off if the soil is too wet or if plants are too cold. Repot annually in spring. Aluminum plant can become leggy, especially in lower light. Pinch the plant in early summer to stimulate the production of new branches.

Propagation: Stem tip cuttings are easily rooted in spring or early summer.

Pests: Root rot, spider mites, and aphids may be problems.

Moon Valley friendship plant (*Pilea involucrata* 'Moon Valley')

Artillery plant *(Pilea microphylla)*

Baby's tears *(Pilea depressa)*

has creeping succulent stems that hold small, glossy green ½–¾-inch rounded leaves; both sides are hairy. It is completely different from the plant by the same common name that is a lawn and garden weed.

Baby's tears *(P. depressa)* is a small creeping plant which will root at any node that touches the soil. It is also known as shiny creeping charley.

Recommendations: '**Minima**' is a compact selection of aluminum plant often used in dish gardens and terrariums.

Friendship plant *(P. involucrata)* is compact, with thick clusters of broad leaves that are yellow-green with a coppery sheen above and have a rich, velvety texture. '**Moon Valley**' is taller and more upright, with larger, corrugated leaves that are fresh green with deep purple veins. Avoid wetting leaves to avoid black staining.

Artillery plant *(P. microphylla)* has arching, upright green stems and tiny, fleshy apple green leaves. It gets its common name from the tiny flowers that "shoot" pollen. '**Summer Snow**' is a small-leaved, mounding selection with beautiful

Norfolk friendship plant *(Pilea spruceana 'Norfolk')*

variegation that intensifies with the amount of light received.

Friendship plant *(P. spruceana)* has wrinkled leaves to 3 inches long. '**Silver Tree**' has bronze leaves flushed silver. '**Norfolk**' has larger leaves in deep bronze and bright silver markings.

Creeping Charlie *(P. nummularifolia)*

Creeping Charlie *(Pilea nummularifolia)*

Pincushion cactus *(see Cactus, pincushion)*

Pineapple *(Ananas comosus)*

Features: Stiff silvery foliage; fruit
Size: 2–3'H × 2–3'W
Light: Bright to intense
Temperature: 70–80°F; above 60°F in winter
Water: Barely moist

Description and uses: Pineapple has tropical looking straplike leaves that form a distinctive large rosette. The rigid leaves have spiny edges that can damage skin and snag curtains or upholstery. Two-year-old plants can produce a pineapple fruit that lasts several months. However it will not be as flavorful as commercial fruiting varieties. Sometimes smaller varieties can be purchased in fruit. Plants benefit from summering outdoors.

Care: Pineapples do best in full sun or bright light, though plants in fruit can be maintained in less light. Once a plant

Dwarf pineapple *(Ananas comosus)*

flowers and fruits, the rosette dies over several months but usually sends up several offsets first. Keep plants barely moist and feed several times during growth.

Propagation: Remove offsets (pups) and pot up individually.

Pests: Occasionally mealybugs infest pineapple.

Recommendations: *A.c. variegatus* has yellow banding on the leaves.

'Nana' is a much smaller form, to about 2 feet tall, and better suited to window sills.

HERE'S A TIP...

Growing a pineapple from the fruit:

Growing a new plant from a pineapple top is fun for all. Start with a ripe fruit with leaves in good condition. Cut or twist off the top, removing any remaining fruit. Remove 3 or 4 bottom leaves to reveal part of the stem. Place the bare stem in slightly damp soil. Support the cutting until new growth is evident. Enclose the cutting in a large plastic bag and keep out of direct sun until the top is rooted.

Pineapple dyckia *(Dyckia brevifolia)*

Features: Many stiff leaves and rosettes
Size: 9–18"H × 9–18"W
Light: Bright to intense
Temperature: 70–80°F; 50–55°F night
Water: Moderately dry

Description and uses: Pineapple dyckia is a succulent terrestrial bromeliad with small orange flowers in summer. It has stiff medium green leaves with spiny edges. The 4- to 8-inch-long leaves form a dense rosette. It is a tough plant that tolerates neglect as long as it has adequate light.

Care: Pineapple dyckia grows best in full sun, although it is

Dyckia *(Dyckia marnier-lapostollei)*

adaptable to bright light. Grow it in average home temperatures with a 10-degree drop at night. Using a well-drained fertile potting mix allows the soil to moderately dry between waterings. Water sparingly, especially at low temperatures. Feed with a foliage plant food during active growth. Spines on leaf edges are sharp. Wear protective gloves when handling the plant.

Propagation: Remove and pot pups that develop at the base of the plant.

Pests: Pineapple dyckia is relatively pest free.

Recommendations: *D. marnier-lapostollei* has silvery gray recurved foliage and remains under 1 foot in diameter.

Pineapple lily *(Eucomis bicolor)*

Features: Pineapplelike flower
Size: 10–24"H × 12–18"W
Light: Bright
Temperature: 70–85°F; 45–50°F winter
Water: Moderately dry

Description and uses: Pineapple lily grows from a large bulb. It has distinctive, gently scalloped light yellow-green leaves that hug the soil and a sturdy stalk that is yellow-green, sometimes with maroon spots. When the papery flowers bloom at the top, you'll

Pineapple lily *(Eucomis bicolor)*

know how the plant got its name. The blossoms evoke pineapple, clustered in a vase shape of pale green stars below stiff darker green bracts. The flower head ages gracefully, forming purple seed capsules that last for weeks.

Care: Plant new bulbs with the pointy ends just sticking out of the soil, but wait to water and fertilize until growth appears. During active growth water well then allow to go moderately dry before watering again. Use a balanced food during growth. After flowering keep in a cool (45–55°F) and dry space. Repot every other year in well-drained potting mix.

Propagation: Pineapple lily starts readily from seed but will take several years to reach blooming size. Bulbs produce offsets which may be separated from the mother plant and potted up.

Pests: Pests are rare on pineapple lily.

Pink quill *(see Tillandsia)*

Pinwheel plant *(Aeonium arboreum)*

Features: Succulent rosette on elongated stem
Size: 6–36"H × 4–8"W
Light: Bright to intense
Temperature: 70–80°F; 50–55° winter
Water: Moderately dry

Description and uses: Pinwheel plant forms a small succulent treelike plant 6–36 inches tall with 4- to 8-inch-diameter rosettes of overlapping succulent leaves on top. As the stem elongates, lower leaves drop off, creating a trunklike effect. When a rosette produces flowers, it too then dies.

Care: Critical elements for success with pinwheel plant include plenty of light, direct sun in summer outdoors, a winter rest period with temperatures close to 50°F, and only enough water to keep the roots from dying.

Purple pinwheel plant (*Aeonium arboreum*)

During winter leaves can shrivel, but with spring warmth and water, growth will resume and the foliage will be replaced. Repot annually in fertile, well-drained potting mix. Feed occasionally with balanced foliage plant food.

Propagation: Start new plants from stem or leaf cuttings. Allow either to callous (dry) a few days before planting.

Pests: Mealybugs occasionally appear in shriveled leaves in early spring.

Recommendations: *Aeonium arboreum atropurpureum nigrum* 'Schwarzkopf' has open rosettes of purple-black leaves.

Variegated pinwheel plant (*Aeonium arboreum*)

Piper (*see Black pepper vine*)

Pittosporum, Japanese (*Pittosporum tobira*)

Features: Deep green foliage
Size: 1–8'H × 1–3'W
Light: Medium to bright
Temperature: 50–70°F
Water: Barely moist

Description and uses: Gardeners in warm climates will recognize Japanese pittosporum as a common landscape plant. This slow growing shrub's main attraction is its glossy, leathery, whorled dark green leaves, which resemble those of a rhododendron. If conditions are right, highly fragrant flowers appear in late winter or early spring, filling a room with the scent of orange blossoms. The flowers are produced in dense terminal clusters and start out creamy white and age to yellow. Japanese pittosporum does well in a garden room with lots of light and cool temps. It grows slowly so purchase a large enough plant to suit your needs. It is often used for bonsai.

Care: If flowers are a priority, provide Japanese pittosporum with bright light and cool to cold temperatures. If nice-

looking foliage is all you are after, medium light and average room temperatures are fine. Average humidity is fine for Japanese pittosporum. Allow the potting mix to dry slightly between waterings. Japanese pittosporum is not a heavy feeder. Use an all-purpose plant food during the growing period. Repot only when needed. Prune it after flowering in spring to maintain the desired shape and size.

Japanese pittosporum
(*Pittosporum tobira* 'Creme de Mint')

Propagation: Propagate Japanese pittosporum by taking semihardwood cuttings and using a rooting hormone. Plants can also be air layered.

Pests: Spider mites, mealybugs, and scale insects are possible pests of Japanese pittosporum.

Recommendations: 'Variegata' is commonly available for indoor use. Its leaves are grayish green with a variable white margin. 'Creme de Mint' is another variegated form. 'Compactum' is a dwarf variety commonly available for outdoor use but well suited to indoor culture.

Platycerium (*see Fern, staghorn*)

Plectranthus (*Plectranthus* spp.)

Features: Trailing plant with scalloped leaves
Size: 6–18"H × 6–36"W
Light: Medium
Temperature: 60–75°F; 50–65°F in winter
Water: Barely moist

Description and uses: Swedish ivy (*Plectranthus verticillatus*) is the most commonly available plant in this family. It is native to South Africa and Australia, not Sweden (where it was first popularized). And it's more closely related to mint than ivy. Nevertheless it is a popular, easy-to-grow plant that is great for beginners. Its cascading stems studded with glossy rounded, scalloped-edge leaves make it primarily a

foliage plant. But it often blooms in late spring or early summer with tiny white or pale mauve blooms on short spikes. Most people pinch off the flower spikes. Swedish ivy is an ideal plant for hanging baskets. It used to be classified as *P. australis*.

Care: Give Swedish ivy moderate light year-round and

Swedish ivy (*Plectranthus verticillatus*)

Purple-leaved plectranthus
(*Plectranthus purpuratus* 'Mona Lavender')

average to cool temperatures. It tolerates cold conditions down to 40°F for short periods in winter. Average humidity is fine. Water to keep soil slightly moist at all times but avoid overwatering, which can lead to stem rot. Use an all-purpose plant food during the growing season.

Repot as needed in spring or midsummer using any good well-drained potting soil. If space is limited prune the plant back by half in fall and rest it in a cool place until late winter. Water just enough to keep the plant from shriveling and protect from freezing temperatures. The plant will recover quickly when brought into a warm room and given good spring care. Pinch stem tips to encourage the plant to develop new branches. Prune back individual branches anytime; severe pruning will not harm this plant.

Propagation: Start new plants regularly from stem tip cuttings.

Pests: Mealybugs, whiteflies spider mites, and root rot are the main problems this plant faces.

Recommendations: 'Variegata' is a common selection with medium green leaves with white markings along the edges.

Cuban oregano (*Plectranthus amboinicus*)

Green and gold variegated forms are also available.

Purple-leaved plectranthus (*P. purpuratus*) has velvety dark purple-green leaves with dark purple undersides and purple stems. Lavender flowers appear if conditions are right. 'Mona Lavender' is a showy form with reliable bloom often used in containers and mixed flowerbeds outdoors.

Cuban oregano (*P. amboinicus*) has thick, succulent, hairy gray-green leaves edged in white. When stroked the leaves give off an herbal scent. It is used as a culinary plant in some countries.

Candlestick plant (*P. coleoides* 'Variegatus') is a shrubbier plant with frilly fuzzy, white margined leaves. It grows more upright initially, but with age develops arching stems that become long and trailing.

Silver plectranthus (*P. oertendahlii*) is also known as silver spurflower and royal charlie. It has large (to 4" wide) scalloped leaves with a tracery of silver over medium green with a purplish underside. **'Emerald Lace'** is widely available. It is also used outdoors in container plantings and hanging baskets.

Silver plectranthus
(*Plectranthus oertendahlii* 'Emerald Lace')

Pleioblastus (*see Bamboo, dwarf*)

Plumbago (*Plumbago auriculata*)

Features: Pale blue flowers
Size: 1–3'H × 1–3'W
Light: Intense
Temperature: 65–75°F; 50–65°F in winter
Water: Evenly moist

Description and uses: Plumbago is grown for its abundant pale blue flowers that can appear nonstop from spring through fall. It is often grown as a landscape plant in warm climates. Although a climber in the wild, in pots it is usually grown as a shrub or a trailer. The spoon-shape leaves are green, sometimes grayish. Plumbago is slow growing, so buy a large plant if you want it to flower the first year.

Candlestick plant (*Plectranthus coleoides* 'Variegatus')

Plumbago (*Plumbago auriculata* 'Imperial Blue')

Care: Provide plumbago with intense indoor light to keep it in bloom. Water thoroughly and allow the soil to dry only slightly between waterings. Prune the trailing stems as needed to maintain desired shape and size. Feed during the growing season with flowering plant food. Yellow leaves may indicate a lack of manganese.

Propagation: Start plumbago from stem tip cuttings or from seed.

Pests: Spider mites, whiteflies, and mealybugs are possible pests of plumbago.

Recommendations: *P. a. alba*, with pure white flowers, is a popular variety. **'Royal Cape'** bears cobalt blue flowers.

Plume asparagus *(see Asparagus fern)*
Plumose fern *(see Asparagus fern)*

Podocarpus *(Podocarpus macrophyllus)*

Features: Feathery deep green leaves
Size: 1–8'H × 1–3'W
Light: Medium to bright
Temperature: 55–75°F
Water: Evenly moist

Podocarpus *(Podocarpus macrophyllus* 'Pringles Dwarf'*)*

Description and uses: Podocarpus grows naturally as a tree but grows slowly and responds well to pruning, making it a good indoor shrub. The dark green foliage contrasts well with the cinnamon-color bark. The well-branched stems are upright, but the branches tend to drop as they age. A large podocarpus is a great architectural plant for a cool space with bright light, such as an entryway. It is a good candidate for bonsai. Buddhist pine and yew pine are other common names for it.

Care: Podocarpus maintains its attractive foliage if given medium to bright light and average to cool temperatures. It tolerates low humidity. Keep the soil evenly moist during the growing season, allowing it to dry between waterings during winter dormancy. Feed in summer with foliage plant food or only once a year if the plant is as large as you want it. Repot only when the plant outgrows its pot. Prune only if you want it to have a more bushy form. Podocarpus may need staking as it gets taller. Insert a dark-colored stake close to the trunk and tie the trunk to the stake with soft dark brown jute. Give the plant monthly showers.

Propagation: If you enjoy a challenge, propagate podocarpus from stem cuttings. Use rooting powder and bottom heat.

Pests: Watch for spider mites, scale, and mealybugs.

Recommendations: 'Maki' is a popular indoor cultivar with a denser growth habit and a whitish tinge to the new growth. **'Pringles Dwarf'** remains small, making it a good choice for growing indoors.

Pogonatherum *(see House bamboo)*

Polka-dot plant *(Hypoestes phyllostachya)*

Features: Appealing pink-spattered leaves
Size: 10–20"H × 10–12"W
Light: Bright
Temperature: 60–75°F
Water: Evenly moist

Description and uses: Once thought of as a rangy, open plant with dark green leaves spotted with pink, this plant has benefited greatly from recent breeding efforts. Newer compact selections have bold speckles of bright pink, red, or white that may cover more than half the leaf's surface. Polka-dot plant is excellent grouped with ferns and other foliage plants, where it benefits from increased humidity. It is small enough for tabletop and terrarium use. It is often used as a bedding plant outdoors.

Care: Compact growth and best leaf color come from bright light or filtered sun. Keep the soil lightly moist at all times. Plants like high humidity. Feed with balanced food. Pinch back stems regularly to keep plants bushy. The terminal spikes of tiny magenta to lilac flowers that appear from late summer to winter only detract from the foliage and should be pinched off. Leaves turn yellow and drop off if plants are overwatered.

Propagation: Start seeds at any time to keep supplies of this short-lived plant around. Stem tip or root cuttings are also possible, although they are often slow to root.

Pests: Powdery mildew, whiteflies, spider mites, and scale are potential problems.

Recommendations: **Splash Select** and **Confetti** are two series widely available as seedlings in spring. In addition to the traditional pink-speckled forms, both series have varieties with deep rose, red, and white variegations. In the

Polka-dot plant *(Hypoestes phyllostachya)*

red forms the green parts of the leaves are blushed with deep burgundy. **'Splash'** has brighter and larger pink splashes on its dark green leaves. **'Vinrod'** has rich wine red leaves marked with pink splashes. **'Wit'** has dark green leaves marbled with white.

Polypodium (see Fern, rabbit's foot)
Polyscias (see Aralia)

Pomegranate, dwarf (Punica granatum nana)

Features: Scarlet flowers; red fruit
Size: 12–24"H × 12–24"W
Light: Bright to intense
Temperature: 70–80°F; 50–60°F winter
Water: Evenly moist

Dwarf pomegranate (Punica granatum nana)

Description and uses: Pomegranate was one of the earliest cultivated fruits in ancient Persia. Some suggest it may have been the "apple" in the Garden of Eden. *Punica granatum nana* is a natural dwarf form of that historic plant. It is popular as a bonsai because its flowers and fruits grow in proportion to the size of the plant. Dwarf pomegranate has narrow, shiny dark green leaves. In early summer, but also sporadically throughout the year, it produces showy scarlet flowers. They form edible 2-inch reddish fruits. Several cultivars are available with various flower colors or double blooms. The plant is surprisingly easy to grow indoors.
Care: Standard pomegranate is a deciduous tropical tree that drops its leaves during cool dry winter conditions. You can mimic those conditions for the dwarf one, keeping it cool and dry during winter, allowing leaves to drop, or you can maintain higher temperatures and regular watering to keep it green. Always adjust watering to temperatures. If you give it warm temperatures all year, it may not flower, so a drop in night temperatures can help. Use a fertile well-drained potting mix and feed monthly during growth. At a small size allow only a very small number of fruits to develop; you may have to support those stems. It blooms best when pot-bound.
Propagation: Start dwarf pomegranate from seed or from softwood stem cuttings.
Pests: Spider mites, whiteflies, mealybugs, and scale insects are possible pests.
Recommendations: Avoid nondwarf cultivars indoors.

Ponytail palm (Beaucarnea recurvata)

Features: Swollen stem base; recurved foliage
Size: 1–10'H × 1–4'W
Light: Bright
Temperature: 65–75°F; 50–55°F winter
Water: Moderately dry

Ponytail palm (Beaucarnea recurvata)

Description and uses: Despite its palmlike look, ponytail palm is not a true palm. It is a succulent, native to arid areas in Mexico, and its bulbous lower trunk serves as a water reservoir. The long narrow leaves emerge from a central growing point similar to a ponytail, giving it a strong architectural look. It is usually grown as a specimen plant, either on a table or on the floor, depending on its size. It tolerates cold temperatures and can be used in entryways. It is long lived—30 years or more—and slow growing. Large plants are heavy and difficult to move. If you want to move it from room to room or outdoors for the summer, place the pot on a wheeled platform. It is also sometimes classified as *Nolina recurvata*.
Care: Ponytail palm is easy to grow, requiring little attention most of the year. The biggest challenge is avoiding overwatering, especially in winter. From spring through fall, water when the top 2 inches of the soil feel dry. In winter water only occasionally. Brown leaf tips and stem rot are signs of overwatering. It does fine with low humidity. In spring and summer, feed plants monthly with a balanced houseplant food. Do not feed in fall or winter. Use a fast draining soil mix, such as a cactus mix. Repot when the bulbous stem is within about 2 inches of the pot diameter. Regular cleaning of the leaves is helpful in preventing spider mite infestations.
Propagation: Small plants are often sold with several in a pot. Divide these and grow individually.
Pests: Watch for occasional spider mite infestations.

Portulacaria (see Elephant bush)

Pothos *(Epipremnum aureum)*

Features: Vining, attractive foliage
Size: 1–8'H × 1–4'W, trailing
Light: Low to bright
Temperature: 60–75°F
Water: Moderately dry

Golden pothos *(Epipremnum aureum)*

Description and uses: This vigorous, low-maintenance vine has glossy heart-shape leaves marbled with yellow, cream, or white. The long stems can reach 8 feet or more if left untrimmed. It is one of few foliage plants that doesn't lose color variation in low light. Hanging baskets are the logical use for pothos, but it can also be trained to grow upward. It is a popular office plant, growing well under fluorescent lights and surviving periods of neglect. Plant several small plants under taller plants such as weeping fig to camouflage their bare trunks. It ranks high for removing indoor toxins. It goes by various common names, including devil's ivy and philodendron, although it is not a true philodendron. Botanically it is sometimes classified as *Scindapsus aureus* or *Pothos aureus*.

Marble Queen pothos
(Epipremnum aureum 'Marble Queen')

Care: Pothos survives in a wide range of light conditions, but moderate to bright light is best for keeping the variegation strong. Plants survive low light but growth may become spindly. It grows fine with average temperatures and humidity.

Satin pothos *(Epipremnum pictum)*

Allow the soil to dry out a bit before watering. Feed spring through summer using balanced plant food. Repot annually in spring into a slightly larger pot using a well-drained potting soil. Larger plants can stay in the same pot if they are pruned back regularly. For a denser effect try planting seven or more cuttings together in a pot or train multiple vines on a plant stake. Pothos is toxic and should not be ingested; keep away from children and pets.

Propagation: Plants root readily from stem cuttings of newer shoots. Start in potting mix or root cuttings in water.

Pests: Pothos is susceptible to root rot, bacterial leaf spot, spider mites, scale, and mealybugs.

Recommendations: 'Marble Queen' is heavily variegated with white. 'Golden Queen' has more yellow than green. 'Neon' has nearly chartreuse leaves.

Satin pothos *(E. pictum)* is a smaller less vigorous plant, with attractive silver markings on satiny, deep green leaves.

Prayer plant *(see Ctenanthe)*

Prayer plant *(Maranta leuconeura)*

Features: Colorful, satiny folding leaves
Size: 1–2'H × 1–2'W
Light: Medium
Temperature: 60–75°F
Water: Evenly moist

Description and uses: Prayer plant has beautiful satiny leaves with purple undersides. The leaves fold up in response to darkness; light causes them to resume their horizontal position. The plant produces small white flowers when grown in a greenhouse, but it rarely blooms as a houseplant. Grow it in a shallow container or combine it with other foliage plants for a tabletop garden, where it benefits from the humidity of neighbors. It can also be used in hanging baskets. Prayer plant is rated good for cleaning indoor air.

Green prayer plant (Maranta leuconeura kerchoveana)

Care: Give plants moderate light from a north or east window or provide fluorescent lighting. Average home temperatures are fine, but keep plants out of cold drafts. Average to high humidity is best. Use an all-purpose plant food sparingly during the growing season. Leaf edges turn brown or entire leaves dry up in dry air or excess light. Overwatering leads to root rot, especially in winter. Plants benefit from a semidormant period in winter, resulting in a flush of new leaves in spring.

Propagation: Divide in spring by cutting the roots into large chunks.

Pests: Watch for mealybugs, scale, and spider mites.

Recommendations: Several varieties are available that are quite different from the species. **Green prayer plant** (*M. l. kerchoveana*), also called rabbit tracks, has square brownish marks between the leaves. **Silver prayer plant** ('Massangeana') has blackish green leaves with silvery gray midribs. **Herringbone plant** (*M. l. erythroneura*), also called red prayer plant, is a popular selection with bright red leaf veins set off nicely by multicolored green leaves that have purplish undersides.

Herringbone plant (Maranta leuconeura erythroneura)

Pregnant onion (*Ornithogalum longibracteatum*)

Features: Onionlike bulb; white flowers
Size: 6–36"H × 4–30"W
Light: Bright
Temperature: 60–75°F
Water: Moderately dry

Description and uses: This novelty houseplant was popular during Victorian times. It derives its name from its aboveground onionlike bulb that can grow up to 4 inches in diameter and produces offsets just under its semitransparent skin, causing it to bulge outward. The straplike semisucculent leaves reach up to 36 inches in length, arching gracefully away from the bulb. They are fragile, so keep plants out of traffic. Show off pregnant onion's bulbils, the "multiple pregnancies," by occasionally peeling off a few layers of drying skin. Plants readily produce a tall (up to 3 feet), weak-stemmed flower stalk with numerous star-shape white flowers with greenish stripes on the outside. Plants usually flower from May to August and there may be as many as 50 to 100 flowers per stalk. Most parts of pregnant onion are toxic, and dermatitis is a problem for some people while handling them. It also goes by the common name of false sea onion and is sometimes classified as *O. caudatum*.

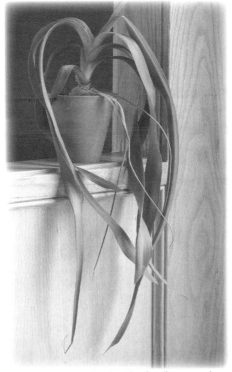

Pregnant onion (Ornithogalum longibracteatum)

Care: Pregnant onion is an easy-to-grow, adaptable plant, growing happily in a pot for many years in well-drained soil. It prefers some direct sun but scorches in sunny, hot, dry locations. Average room temperatures and humidity are fine. Allow plants to dry moderately between waterings. However if the soil dries too much, the plant will go dormant. Use an all-purpose plant food during the growing season. It is not a heavy feeder and does not require feeding in winter. Repot after flowering, covering only the base of the bulb with potting mix.

Propagation: Peel off a few layers of the skin and break the offsets loose. They root readily when inserted into potting mix. Plants can also be propagated by seed.

Pests: Possible insect pests include spider mites, whiteflies, mealybugs, and scale.

Pteris (*see Fern, brake*)
Punica (*see Pomegranate, dwarf*)
Purple false shamrock (*see Oxalis*)
Purple heart (*see Tradescantia*)

Purple passion *(Gynura aurantiaca* 'Purple Passion')

Features: Fuzzy purple leaves
Size: 10–20"H × 10–20"W
Light: Bright
Temperature: 60–75°F
Water: Evenly moist

Purple passion *(Gynura aurantiaca* 'Purple Passion')

Description and uses: This old-fashioned foliage plant, also known as purple velvet plant, has been a favorite houseplant for many years. It is a rapid grower with stems that can reach 20 inches. The stems are crowded with dark green leaves covered with soft purple hairs. It is well suited for a hanging basket. Use it to add color contrast to foliage groupings. It is sometimes listed as *G. sarmentosa*.

Care: Purple passion is easy to grow as long as it gets adequate light. The brighter the light, the more intense the purple leaf color. It likes average humidity and room temperatures but tolerates cooler conditions (down to 55°F). Keep the soil lightly moist at all times, avoiding extremes in soil moisture. The plant wilts quickly when dry but recovers well with a good soaking. Overwatered plants are susceptible to root rot, especially in cooler temperatures. Avoid splashing water on the leaves when watering because leaves develop dark patches where water remains for a long period. Feed during the spring and summer with a balanced houseplant food. Pinch out stem tips regularly to keep plants dense and attractive. Older plants produce unpleasant-smelling orange flowers. Most people choose to clip them off. New growth and young plants show best color; renew, prune, or propagate frequently.

Propagation: Start new plants from stem cuttings.
Pests: Aphids and mealybugs are potential problems.
Recommendations: The cultivar **'Purple Passion'** is the standard plant. The species is seldom available. **'Variegata'** has striking patterns of white, pink, and cream on the dark green leaves.

Purple waffle plant *(see Red flame ivy)*
Pussy ears *(see Kalanchoe)*
Pygmy bamboo *(see Bamboo, dwarf)*

Queen's tears *(Billbergia nutans)*

Features: Pendant flowers
Size: 12"H × 18"W
Light: Bright
Temperature: 65–75°F
Water: Moderately dry; water in vase

Queen's tears *(Billbergia nutans)*

Description and uses: Queen's tears is a durable plant that takes some abuse. It's a terrestrial bromeliad with narrow vases that are dark green outside, light green with creamy spots inside. It can produce hanging clusters of flowers almost any time of year.

Care: Keep water inside the vases and allow the soil mix to go moderately dry between waterings. Feed monthly. Encourage a mature plant to flower by enclosing the entire plant in a large plastic bag (dry cleaner type) with a ripe apple for 7 to 10 days. Drain water out of vases during this process to avoid too much humidity inside the bag. Plants will flower about 2 months later.

Propagation: Divide new shoots (offsets) with some roots attached. Pot them into individual containers.
Pests: Scale is an occasional problem on queen's tears.

Rabbit's foot fern *(see Fern, rabbit's foot)*
Rabbit tracks *(see Prayer plant)*
Radermachera *(see China doll)*
Rattail cactus *(see Cactus, rattail)*
Ravenea *(see Palm, majesty)*
Rebutia *(see Cactus, crown)*

Red flame ivy *(Hemigraphis alternata)*

Features: Textured maroon leaves
Size: 6–12"H × 6–18"W
Light: Medium
Temperature: 60–80°F
Water: Evenly moist

Purple waffle plant (Hemigraphis alternata 'Exotica')

Description and uses: This mounded foliage plant has fleshy wine red stems that creep or trail, depending on the container shape. New growth is upright at first and then bends at the base, rooting as it creeps. The oval- to heart-shape, scalloped leaves have an attractive combination of metallic violet above and wine red underneath. The numerous small white flowers appear on terminal spikes in summer. They show up beautifully against the shiny metallic purple background. Red flame ivy looks best in a hanging basket where its stems arch downward and hide the container. It also makes a nice pedestal plant. It is sometimes classified as *H. colorata*.

Care: Red flame ivy needs medium light to maintain the red leaf color, but no direct sunlight. Low light causes spindly, pale growth, but too much light can also cause plants to decline. Average to high temperatures are fine, but keep plants away from cold drafts and drying winds. Keep the soil evenly moist at all times. Leaf edges turn brown if the soil is too dry, and overwatering leads to crown rot. Feed in summer using an all-purpose food. Repot annually. Prune branch tips regularly to keep plants full. Cut back leggy plants severely to rejuvenate them.

Propagation: Take stem cuttings at any time of year.

Pests: Crown rot, whiteflies, mealybugs, and spider mites may be problems.

Recommendations: Purple waffle plant (*H. a.* 'Exotica') is a popular hybrid with larger, more puckered leaves that have a deeper purple sheen and are deep red underneath. **'Red Equator'** has small metallic green leaves with red underneath and a more compact growth habit.

Rosary vine *(Ceropegia linearis woodii)*

Features: Heart-shape leaves; trailing stems
Size: 2–12"H × 4–18"W; vining
Light: Bright to intense
Temperature: 65–80°F
Water: Moderately dry

Description and uses:
Rosary vine is an endearing small, colorful succulent. The thin vine suspends dark green and silver marbled heart-shape leaves. Greenish flowers with purple accents grow on short connecting stems. Small bulblike swellings (bulbils) grow on the stems at the leaf axils. Rosary vine makes an attractive small hanging basket that

Rosary vine (Ceropegia linearis woodii)

can be maintained at 4 to 5 inches in diameter with stems dangling to 12 inches. The plant is also called string of hearts and is sometimes classified as *C. woodii*.

Care: Rosary vine is an adaptable plant. It prefers well-drained soil but tolerates heavier soils. It likes bright to intense light but tolerates less. Water well and allow plants to go moderately dry before watering again. Feed monthly during growth. Prune the trailing stems to maintain plants at the desired width and length.

Propagation:
The easiest way to start new plants is to layer stems on soil until they root. Separate or divide rooted stems. Plants may also be started from seed, tubers, or cuttings; allow cuttings to callus for a day or two before planting.

> **HERE'S A TIP...**
>
> "Beads" form along the stem of rosary vine. Use them to propagate new plants by resting them on the soil and keeping them moist until new roots and shoots form.

Pests: Watch for occasional mealybug infestations.

Sago palm (Cycas revoluta)

Features: Exotic arching fronds
Size: 1–5'H × 1–4'W
Light: Medium to intense
Temperature: 55–80°F
Water: Moderately dry

Sago palm (Cycas revoluta)

Description and uses: Despite its appearance and common name, sago palm is not a true palm. The leaves may have a feathery palmlike appearance, but they are actually quite stiff. They emerge from the center trunk, arching outward. Each leaf is up to 3 feet long and is divided into many 3- to 6-inch needlelike leaflets. The domed, pineapplelike trunk has a rusty, felted covering. Sago palm is extremely slow growing, often producing only one leaf per year. The thick rough trunk is only found on mature plants. The shiny fronds appear tough but are quite easily damaged. Since so few new leaves are produced, any damage remains visible for a long time. Keep sago palm out of high traffic areas so fronds won't be broken or damaged. Leaves are toxic if eaten.
Care: Although sago palm tolerates medium light, it won't grow much without bright to intense light. It tolerates low humidity and temperature extremes but not waterlogged soil. Allow the soil to dry out between waterings. Give more water when new leaves are unfurling. Old leaves may turn yellow from overwatering. Feed only once in spring and once in summer, even less if it's grown in low light. Repot only when the base covers more than two-thirds of the entire surface of the potting mix. Be sure to use a well-drained mix. Remove old fronds when they turn brown.
Propagation: Separate offsets that grow at the base or along the sides of mature plants. This works best in winter when top growth is slowed. Remove all the leaves and set it aside to dry for a week. Then plant it in a cactus mix with half the offset below the soil level. Keep quite dry until the plant shows new growth.
Pests: Sago palm is relatively pest free but keep an eye out for scale and spider mites.

Saintpaulia (see African violet)
Sansevieria (see Snake plant)
Sapphire flower (see Browallia)

Saxifraga (see Strawberry begonia)
Scadoxus (see Blood lily)
Scilla (see Silver squill)

Schefflera (Schefflera spp.)

Features: Large glossy leaves
Size: 1–8'H × 1–6'W
Light: Medium to intense
Temperature: 60–75°F
Water: Evenly moist

Umbrella tree (Schefflera actinophylla)

Description and uses: *Schefflera actinophylla* is a widely grown, treelike foliage plant. Its leaves are made up of glossy green leaflets to 10 inches long that are attached like the sections of an umbrella, giving it the common name umbrella tree. It is also known simply as schefflera. Plant several in a pot for a fuller appearance. Umbrella tree is good for improving air quality. It is sometimes listed as *Brassaia actinophylla*.
Care: Schefflera does best in bright filtered light or indirect light from fluorescent lights and light colored walls, but it will tolerate low light for short periods. It may shed leaves if subjected to cold drafts or blasts of hot air from heating vents. Average humidity is fine. Allow some drying in the top inch of soil between thorough waterings. Leaves droop if the soil is too dry. Use an all-purpose plant food during the growing period.

Dwarf schefflera (Schefflera arboricola)

Keep drier and do not feed in winter. Repot young plants each spring using a peat-based potting mix. Keep leaves glossy by cleaning them regularly with a soft damp cloth.
Propagation: Air layering is the best method to propagate schefflera. Separate and divide multiple young plants growing together in a single container.
Pests: Spider mites, mealybugs, and scale are possible pests.
Recommendations: 'Amate' has extremely shiny leaves, is more resistant to spider mites, and stays

False aralia (Schefflera elegantissima)

compact even in low light.

Dwarf schefflera (*S. arboricola*) is a bushier plant with smaller leaflets, only about 4 inches long. There are many variegated forms and some with slightly ruffled leaf edges. **'Green Gold'** has leaves splashed with yellow. **'Luciana'** has all green leaves and grows to 6 feet. **'Compacta'** and **'Pittman's Pride'** are compact forms.

False aralia (*S. elegantissima*) looks quite different from other scheffleras. It has narrow, dark green, saw-tooth-edge leaves. They emerge copper color and turn dark blackish green. It can grow to 6 feet tall indoors and has a lean, upright form with leaves held almost horizontally. It resents environmental changes, often shedding leaves if moved. False aralia is great in foliage groupings, especially with plants with lighter colored or variegated leaves. It is often classified as *Dizygotheca elegantissima*.

HERE'S A TIP...
Scheffleras may get leggy but are easy to contain by cutting back. They will take severe pruning if necessary to get them back to an attractive shape.

Schlumbergera *(see Cactus, Christmas)*
Scindapsus *(see Pothos)*
Scirpus *(see Fiber optic grass)*

Screw pine *(Pandanus tectorius 'Veitchii')*

Features: Saw-tooth leaves
Size: 2–8'H × 2–4'W
Light: Bright to intense
Temperature: 65–80°F
Water: Moderately dry

Description and uses: Screw pine has interesting foliage that more closely resembles a pineapple than a pine, as its name implies. This tough, long-lived plant adapts well to life in homes and offices, but it needs plenty of elbowroom. The arching strap-shape leaves, which can grow to 36 inches long, have serrated edges that can slice through the skin of unsuspecting passersby. The variegated foliage is arranged in spiraling ranks similar to the frets on a screw. Plants send out aerial roots, which are used to stabilize plants in wind in their native habitat. Keep the spiny leaves away from traffic areas and small children. It is sometimes classified as *P. veitchii*.

Care: Screw pine likes bright light, ideally at least 3 hours of direct sun a day. Without enough light the plant loses much of its interesting variegation. It tolerates high temperatures

Screw pine *(Pandanus utilis)*

and enjoys spending summer outdoors in partial shade. It survives with average humidity but is better in high humidity areas. Water sparingly, allowing the soil to dry before watering. Feed with all-purpose plant food only during the growing period. Push aerial roots into the soil as they appear. Some people develop a skin irritation when handling the plant so handle carefully and wear gloves.

Propagation: Cut off basal suckers when they are about 6 inches long and root them like stem cuttings. Plants can also be grown from seed.

Pests: Spider mites and scale can be problems.

Recommendations: **'Compacta'** has leaves only 15 to 24 inches long with more pronounced striping. New growth of **'Verde'** starts out milky white, turns lime green, and matures dark green.

P. utilis has solid green leaves with burgundy edges.
P. sanderi has yellow stripes.

Sedum *(see Burro's tail)*

Selaginella *(Selaginella kraussiana)*

Features: Feathery, mossy foliage
Size: 2–6"H × 4–8"W
Light: Medium to bright
Temperature: 70–80°F
Water: Evenly moist

Description and uses: This primitive mossy plant is related to ferns. It is popular as a terrarium plant. Bright green trailing spike-moss, *S. kraussiana*, is the most popular species. It forms dense spreading mats of trailing stems with feathery foliage. It is also sometimes known as spreading club moss.

Care: Grow selaginella in a warm, humid area with medium light. An enclosed growing area such as a terrarium is best. Plants in a warm, dry living room will not survive long. Keep it moist in a fertile, well-drained soil. Feed lightly when the plant is in active growth. Trim to keep the plant at the shape and size desired.

Spreading spike-moss
(Selaginella kraussiana 'Aurea' and 'Brownii')

Propagation: Most selaginallas self-layer, forming new roots where stems touch the soil. They also start readily from stem cuttings or divisions.

Pests: Dry air causes leaf dieback and browning. Spider mites and aphids are possible pests.

Recommendations: *S.k.* **'Aurea'** is similar, but is chartreuse green. *S.k.* **'Brownii'** forms a dense, tiny cushion of green only 2 inches tall, growing to 6 inches wide.

Resurrection fern *(S. lepidophylla)* is the most unusual species. It is usually sold as a rolled-up ball of apparently dead foliage. Soak it in water, though, and the ball unfurls to reveal a flattened rosette of green, scale-covered stems.

Senecio *(see String-of-beads; Wax vine)*

Sensitive plant (Mimosa pudica)

Features: Leaves fold up when touched
Size: 12–30"H × 16–36"W
Light: Bright
Temperature: 70–80°F
Water: Evenly moist

Sensitive plant (Mimosa pudica)

Description and uses:
Here's a plant that is grown for the sheer fun of stroking it. It's not particularly attractive and rarely survives more than a year, but its fascinating habit of folding together its finely divided leaflets within a few seconds of being touched makes it a pleasure to own. Kids of all ages love it. The plant reaches its peak size in just 3 or 4 months from germination. Sensitive plant flowers readily, with small pink, fuzzy, powderpuff flowers.

Care: Sensitive plant needs warm, humid conditions and performs best in a greenhouse, though it is tolerant of bright indoor conditions. It is short lived even in the best of conditions. Keep evenly moist in a fertile potting mix. Feed several times during summer growth.

Propagation: Start new plants from seed. Pour boiling water over seed before planting to crack the hard seed coat.

Pests: Spider mites can be a serious problem. Leaf scorch from drafts and dry air is also common.

Shell Ginger (Alpinia zerumbet 'Variegata')

Features: Green and yellow striped leaves
Size: 3–5'H × 3–5'W
Light: Medium to bright
Temperature: 65–75°F
Water: Evenly moist

Variegated shell ginger
(Alpinia zerumbet 'Variegata')

Description and uses:
Shell ginger has vivid colors and strong lines, making it a showy addition to any bright room. Upright canes hold graceful, but tough, sword-shape foliage for architectural interest. Wash leaves occasionally with tepid water. Its rhizome has ginger fragrance but lacks culinary usefulness. The "shell" part of its common name comes from the shape of its flowers, which are seldom produced indoors.

Care: Shell ginger performs best in bright light and benefits from summering outdoors. If moved gradually to more intense light, it can handle full sun. It likes high humidity but is tolerant of less. Grow it in a rich potting soil. Keep the soil evenly moist during active growth. Keep it a bit drier in winter but do not allow it to dry completely. Leaves roll in on themselves if the soil is too dry. Feed during spring and summer with a foliage plant food. Repot annually, or divide when the pot is crowded, removing any dead stems from the center of the pot. Increase the pot size if you want your plant to grow larger.

Propagation: Divide shell ginger in spring, making certain that each division has a piece of rhizome and a shoot.

Pests: Shell ginger is virtually pest free. Leaf edges turn brown if the soil becomes too dry.

Recommendations: 'Variegata Dwarf' is less widely available but grows to only 1 foot tall and has the same green and yellow variegation, making it an excellent choice for container culture.

Shrimp plant (Justicia brandegeeana)

Features: Pendant flowers and bracts
Size: 1–3'H × 1–2'W
Light: Bright to intense
Temperature: 60–75°F
Water: Evenly moist

Shrimp plant (Justicia brandegeeana)

Description and uses: This interesting plant is at the top of the list for long-time bloom. It is a woody, branching shrub with dark green, slightly hairy leaves. The true flowers are white and protrude from the showy bracts, resulting in unusual blossoms that resemble pale pink, chartreuse, or yellow shrimp. Shrimp plant is a fast grower with an upright habit that responds well to a hard pruning. The 3- to 5-inch-long flowers spikes are produced throughout the growing season, which may be all year if conditions are right. It is great in a hanging basket where the interesting flowers can be viewed at eye level. It is also sometimes listed as *J. guttata* or *Beloperone guttata*.

Care: Shrimp plant grows well at average room temperatures and humidity. It requires bright light with some direct sunlight for good bloom. Water well during growth but reduce the amount of water at cooler temperatures. Feed with a flowering plant food during the growing season. To keep plants shapely and less than 3 feet tall, cut away up to half the top growth in early spring and repot in peaty potting soil. Pinch regularly to maintain a nice shape. Keep in mind that it produces flower buds all year, so pinching may remove some flower buds. Low light causes spindly growth and poor bloom.

Propagation: Shrimp plant roots easily from softwood cuttings taken in spring.

Pests: Spider mites and whiteflies can be pests.
Recommendations: 'Variegata' has white-mottled leaves and shrimp pink bracts. 'Pink Parfait' has glossy green leaves with a metallic shine, making it especially attractive when not in flower. 'Chartreuse' and 'Fruit Cocktail' have lime-colored bracts, accented by bright red flowers. 'Yellow Queen' has bright yellow bracts.

Brazilian plume (*J. carnea*), also known as King's crown, is a much larger plant with leaves up to 8 inches long and massive terminal spikes of rose-pink flowers, usually in spring. It requires higher humidity than shrimp plant and is better suited to conservatory or greenhouse culture.

Silver shield (*see Homalomena, heart-leaf*)

Silver squill (*Ledebouria socialis*)

Features: Silver with green-splotched leaves
Size: 4–6"H × 4–6"W
Light: Bright
Temperature: 55–65°F
Water: Moderately dry

Silver squill (*Ledebouria socialis*)

Description and uses: Silver squill is an attractive small bulbous plant from South Africa. The main reason to grow it is the silver-gray leaves with green splotches. Flowers are small, bell shape, and greenish white. It is also known as *L. violacea* and *Scilla violacea*.
Care: Silver squill requires cool and bright growing conditions. It performs best at temperatures below 65°F. It flowers in winter if given enough light. Grow it in a peat-based potting mix but add about one-third by volume additional sand or perlite to provide additional drainage. Allow the soil mix to go moderately dry between waterings. Reduce the amount of water after the plant flowers to induce a rest period. Begin feeding the plant after it resumes more active growth.
Propagation: Divide clumps of bulbs to start new plants.
Pests: Few pest problems affect silver squill.

Silver vase plant (*Aechmea fasciata*)

Features: Silvery foliage; pink bracts
Size: 15–30"H × 12–24"W
Light: Bright
Temperature: 65–75°F
Water: Barely moist; water in vase

Description and uses: Silver vase plant is the most popular member of the bromeliad family. Its attractive gray-green foliage, nicely splotched in silver, is arranged in a spiral urn shape, giving it the common name. It is an epiphyte that grows in the jungle attached to a tree. The leaves are stiff and spiny along the edges with a blunt tip with a thorn. The long lasting pink bracts with short-lived small blue flowers contrast well with the foliage and make the plant decorative for several months. It's a deservedly popular plant with interior decorators.

Sliver vase plant (*Aechmea fasciata*)

Care: Silver vase plant needs bright light and warm temperatures during growth. When in flower cool temperatures will help maintain the decorative bracts for a longer time. After silver vase plant flowers, the central flowering plant dies but new offshoots or pups develop at the base of the mother plant. Water the soil only after the surface dries but keep water inside the vase at all times. Rain water is best. Change the water in the vase every 2 or 3 months. Occasionally include dilute plant food in the solution. It's unlikely that you will need to repot silver vase from the pot that comes with a flowering commercially grown plant. However, divide and repot the pups to start new plants. To encourage bloom of pups that reach mature size,

HERE'S A TIP...
You can induce a silver vase plant to flower by putting an apple or other ripening fruit in a plastic bag with a mature plant for several weeks.

enclose the plant with a ripe apple inside a large clear plastic bag for a few weeks.
Propagation: Remove pups and plant in separate pots.
Pests: Scale and mealybugs can be problems.

Sinningia (*Sinningia* spp.)

Features: Bell-shape or tubular flowers
Size: 1–24"H × 1–18"W
Light: Medium to bright
Temperature: 65–80°F
Water: Evenly moist

Description and uses: Sinningias usually have hairy, elliptical leaves and tubular or bell-shape flowers. Their tubers help distinguish them from other gesneriads (African violet family), most of which have fibrous roots or rhizomes. Miniature sinningias have short-stem rosettes 2–8 inches in diameter. The flowers come in purple, pink, red, salmon, white, and bicolors. The plants produce new shoots even before the previous ones have faded. Microminiatures are 1 inch tall and wide and can grow in a thimble. They

Brazilian edelweiss *(Sinningia canescens)*

produce tiny tubular flowers throughout the year and rarely go dormant.

Care: Miniature sinningias tolerate medium light and grow best on a pebble tray or other location where humidity is high. Microminiatures need exceptionally high humidity and are best grown in a terrarium. Grow all sinningia species in a well-drained African violet mix. Keep the soil evenly moist during growth and feed regularly with African violet food. To keep microminiatures growing, remove damaged leaves and spent flowers to prevent them from producing seed. Miniatures usually go dormant after a significant flowering cycle. Gradually withhold water. When top growth has died, cut, do not pull, it off the plant and tuber. Store dormant tubers in the pot still in the soil mix. At this time keep the soil dry, adding only a few drops of water at a time to keep tubers from shriveling. Repot when new growth resumes.

Propagation: Start new sinningias from leaf or crown cuttings. Species may also be started from seed.

Pests: Cyclamen mites, thrips, aphids, whiteflies, and mealybugs are possible pests.

Recommendations: Cardinal flower *(S. cardinalis)* is an upright grower that produces one or more stems of bright green hairy leaves from a large woody tuber. The plant grows 12 to 24 inches tall and 12 inches wide. It produces brilliant red tubular flowers from fall through winter.

  Brazilian edelweiss *(S. canescens)* grows to 12 inches tall and wide. The stem and the leaves are covered with silvery white hairs. Tubular orange-red flowers are covered with silvery hairs. When the leaves dry up, stop watering and store the plant dry until new growth appears. Keep the tuber, which can grow quite large, halfway out of the soil.

  Microminiature sinningia *(S. pusilla)* grows about 1 inch tall and wide. Its tuber is the size of a pea. It has a number of tiny trumpet-shape purple and white flowers. Grow it in an enclosed terrarium in medium light and slightly moist, never soggy, conditions. Look for the sports **'White Sprite'**, with all white flowers and **'Snowflake'**, which has white flowers with fringed lobes.

  Florist gloxinia *(S. speciosa)*, see gift plants p. 108.

Slender club-rush *(see Fiber optic grass)*
Slipper orchid *(see Orchid, slipper)*

Snake plant *(Sansevieria* spp.)

Features: Durable foliage plant
Size: 6–48"H × 6–36"W
Light: Low to bright
Temperature: 60–85°F
Water: Moderately dry

Variegated snake plant *(Sansevieria trifasciata* 'Laurentii')

Snake plant *(Sansevieria trifasciata)*

Description and uses: Snake plant *(Sansevieria trifasciata)* is a carefree, tough succulent that grows almost anywhere. It tolerates neglect but responds nicely to good care. It is a strongly vertical plant with leathery, sword-shape leaves often marbled dark green and edged with yellow or white. It is great for beginners, but experienced houseplant growers love it for its dramatic upright form. When grown in bright light, it sends up a tall stalk of greenish fragrant flowers. The dwarf rosette varieties make nice desktop or tabletop plants. Snake plant ranks high on the list of plants that improve indoor air quality.

Care: Snake plant likes bright, indirect light spring through fall and moderate light in winter, but it tolerates low light year round. Average to warm temperatures are fine for growth, but do not allow temperatures to drop below 60°F. It grows best in average humidity, tolerating dry air but not high humidity. Water often enough to keep the soil lightly moist spring through summer, but allow the soil to become almost dry in winter. Snake plant rots if overwatered. Feed it only once a year with foliage plant food and repot only when the plant fills the pot. Wipe leaves with a cloth to maintain an attractive glossy sheen.

Propagation: Divide snake plant in spring, using a sharp serrated knife to cut through the

Birds-nest snake plant *(Sansevieria trifasciata* 'Hahnii')

Cylinder snake plant (*Sansevieria cylindrica*)

thick rhizomes. Root 3-inch leaf sections to form new plants, but note that yellow-margined varieties will not pass on any of their golden leaf color if propagated from leaf cuttings.

Pests: Insect pests rarely bother snake plant.

Recommendations: Variegated snake plant (*S.t.* 'Laurentii') is a popular variety with creamy yellow leaf margins. It grows to 2 feet tall. **Bird's nest snake plant** (*S.t.* 'Hahnii') grows about 6 inches tall in a squat rosette of dark green leaves. It has spawned several color variants, including **S.t. 'Golden Hahnii'**, with wide stripes of golden yellow leaves in a rosette, and **S.t 'Silver Hahnii'**, with silver-green leaves lightly flecked with dark green.

   S. cylindrica produces round, rigid leaves that can eventually reach 5 feet in length and over an inch in diameter. Leaves arch outward from a central crown.

Soleirolia (*see Baby's tears*)	**Spider aloe** (*see Aloe*)
Solenostemon (*see Coleus*)	**Spider flower** (*see Peruvian*
Song of India (*see Dracaena*)	*daffodil*)
Spanish moss (*see Tillandsia*)	**Spider orchid** (*see Orchid, spider*)
Spathiphyllum (*see Peace lily*)	

Spider plant (*Chlorophytum comosum*)

Features: Graceful foliage plant
Size: 6–12"H × 6–24"W
Light: Medium to bright
Temperature: 65–75°F
Water: Evenly moist

Description and uses: The well-known and much-loved spider plant is an excellent choice for beginners. Most plants available are the cultivar 'Vittatum', which has a white stripe down the center of each leaf. All-green plants are more difficult to find. This is among the best indoor plants for hanging baskets. A plant heavy with "babies" looks striking on a pedestal. Spider plant ranks high at ridding the air of indoor air pollutants.

Care: Spider plant likes average room humidity and temperatures; avoid extreme temperatures below 55°F and above 80°F. Feed in spring and early summer using a balanced houseplant food. Keep the soil lightly moist

Variegated spider plant
(*Chlorophytum comosum* 'Vittatum')

during active growth, allowing the surface to dry 1 inch deep in fall and winter. Brown leaf tips, which are common with spider plants, are due to contaminated water, usually from fluoride, to overfertilization, low humidity, or dry soil conditions. Trim damaged leaves with scissors following the leaf contour. Use rainwater or distilled water if your tap water is fluoridated. Repot young plants annually in spring using any good potting soil. Mature plants grown in 6-inch pots need repotting every 2 years. While less than a year old, plants start producing flowers and plantlets on the tips of upright arching stems. Plants flower best when they are exposed to short days and are slightly pot-bound.

Spider plant (*Chlorophytum comosum*)

Orchid spider plant
(*Chlorophytum orchidastrum* 'Green Orange')

Propagation: Propagate new plants from young plantlets; older ones with dry, callused roots do not root as easily. While it is still attached to the mother plant, sink the young plantlet into soil in smaller pots with the root buds barely covered. Use a bent paper clip to hold the plantlet in place until it roots. After roots have formed, sever the plantlet from the parent plant.

Pests: Scale can be a problem on spider plant.

Recommendations: 'Vittatum' is a common cultivar with white-stripe leaves. 'Variegatum' has the reverse variegation: cream leaves with a green central stripe.

   C. orchidastrum 'Green Orange' presents a sharp contrast to its more common cousin. With deep green lance-shape leaves 3 inches wide and 15 inches long, it more closely resembles a Chinese evergreen than a spider plant. The real attraction, though, is the glowing orange petiole and central vein. Care is similar to spider plant. Do not allow the soil to dry out and avoid temperatures below 55°F, which can cause foliage to blacken. It does not produce runners with plantlets, but forms an attractive multistem clump.

Split-leaf philodendron (*see Philodendron, split-leaf*)	**Squirrel's foot fern** (*see Fern, rabbit's foot*)
Spotted colts foot (*see Farfugium*)	**Staghorn fern** (*see Fern, staghorn*)
Spreading club moss (*see Selaginella*)	**Stapelia** (*see Carrion flower*)
Spur flower (*see Plectranthus*)	**Star cactus** (*see Cactus, bishop's cap*)
	Starfish flower (*see Carrion flower*)

Stephanotis *(Stephanotis floribunda)*

Features: Vining plant; fragrant flowers
Size: 1–12'H × 1–3'W; vining
Light: Bright to intense
Temperature: 60–75°F
Water: Evenly moist

Stephanotis
(Stephanotis floribunda)

Description and uses: A long-time favorite for wedding bouquets, stephanotis has waxy clusters of fragrant, long-lasting white flowers set against its dark shiny leaves. It blooms freely late spring until late fall, on new growth, but plants often send up a few flowers all year if given enough light. The flowers carry their sweet scent throughout the home. This climbing plant should be trained around a wire, cane hoop, or trellis that will allow the vine to grow longer without getting too tall. Unlike many climbing plants, it does not do well in a hanging basket.
Care: Stephanotis needs bright to intense light and cool winter temperatures. Plants will not bloom well in low light or if it is too warm. It does not like temperature fluctuations. Keep the soil evenly moist from March to midfall, letting it dry slightly between waterings in winter. Average humidity is fine. Use an all-purpose plant food during the growth period. Allow plants to rest during winter, because cool temperatures and reduced watering help it bloom. Repot infrequently; plants bloom best when pot-bound. Use a soil-based potting mixture. Pinch back stem tips to improve form. Maintain the vine at any height or width with annual pruning. Prune only after the main flush of flowering has ceased.
Propagation: Take 3- to 4-inch softwood cuttings in spring or early summer.
Pests: Mealybugs and scale are possible pests.

Stephanotis *(Stephanotis floribunda)* flowers

Strawberry begonia *(Saxifraga stolonifera)*

Features: Multicolor leaves
Size: 3–6"H × 3–12"W
Light: Medium
Temperature: 60–75°F
Water: Evenly moist

Description and uses:
Strawberry begonia has both a mounded and a trailing form to it. Plants grow as a ground-hugging rosette of rounded hairy leaves with silver veins and red undersides and stems. But even more interesting are the

Strawberry begonia *(Saxifraga stolonifera)*

plantlets, which are borne on thin runners (stolons) to 24 inches long. They hang like spiders dangling on silk threads. Plants may produce sprays of tiny white flowers in spring or summer, especially if the plant is allowed to rest in a cool place for a few weeks in winter. Grow strawberry begonia in a hanging basket. Young plants can be used in a mixed basket or a terrarium.
Care: This plant thrives on medium light. Average room temperature is good for growth; plants tolerate temperatures down to 45°F. Allow the soil to dry to within 1 inch between waterings. Water slightly less in winter. Plants develop rot when overwatered. Strawberry begonia needs average to high humidity. Leaves may die back if the air is too dry or too warm. Use a fast-draining potting soil. Repot each spring until the third year, when the crown becomes woody and prone to rot. If stolons become so numerous the plant appears unkempt, thin them by clipping off unwanted runners close to the plant's crown.
Propagation: It is easy to start new plants by rooting the runners. Use a bent paper clip to pin plantlets into small pots set around the parent plant. Detach and repot after roots have formed on the plantlet.
Pests: Aphids, spider mites, whiteflies, and mealybugs are all possible pest problems.
Recommendations: 'Tricolor' is an attractive selection with creamy white leaf margins delicately edged with red. It is more difficult to grow. It does best in a terrarium or greenhouse where the humidity is higher and temperatures are warmer.

Strawberry geranium *(see Strawberry begonia)*

Streptocarpus *(Streptocarpus spp.)*

Features: Colorful flowers; leafy rosette
Size: 6–18"H × 6–30"W
Light: Medium to bright
Temperature: 70–80°F, 60–65°F in winter
Water: Barely moist

Description and uses: Hybrid streptocarpus *(Streptocarpus ×hybridus)* is an endearing plant that blooms almost continuously if given the right conditions. The long, strap-shape leaves arch outward, resulting in plants that are often wider than they are tall. Leaves grow in a haphazard stemless rosette. Each leaf produces its own series of flower

Streptocarpus *(Streptocarpus 'Black Panther')*

spikes growing from the midrib. Most plants grown in the home are hybrids with showy trusses of flowers in pink, purple, white, or red, often with contrasting white or yellow throats. Miniature types are perfect blooming accents in terrariums. They are also called Cape primrose.
Care: Treat streptocarpus like a cool growing African violet, its cousin. Give this plant moderate to bright light. It does well under fluorescent lights. Keep the soil slightly moist at

False African violet *(Streptocarpus saxorum)*

String-of-beads *(Senecio rowleyanus)*

all times, but never soggy, spring through summer. Water less in winter but do not allow the plant to wilt. Use African violet food during growth. Flush the soil with plain water periodically to remove excess salts. Plants need medium to high humidity. High humidity can compensate for high room temperatures, which streptocarpus resents. Repot annually in spring using an African violet mix, scarcely covering the roots with soil. Keep on the dry side until active growth resumes. Overplanting can lead to root rot. Outer leaves shrivel and brown naturally after flower production ceases; remove them at that time.

Propagation: Grow plantlets from rooted leaf section cuttings with the midrib removed or start plants from seed.

Pests: Mealybugs, spider mites, and aphids are common pests on streptocarpus.

Recommendations: There are hundreds of cultivars in a wide range of colors. **'Black Panther'** has deep purple to almost black flowers with two gold eyes. **'Bristol's Blue Bonnet'** has blue flowers. **'Falling Stars'** is pale lavender with a white throat. **'Midnight Flame'** has dark red velvety flowers held well above the foliage. **'Little Gem'** has bright pink blooms that last for up to ten months in average home conditions.

   False African violet *(S. saxorum)* is in the subgenus streptocarpella. It produces elongated stems rather than a rosette. Leaves are fuzzy, plump, medium green, and about 1 inch long. Flowers are pale lavender. Give false African violet the same treatment as other streptocarpus. With stems that trail, it works well in a hanging basket. **'Good Hope'** is a widely available streptocarpella hybrid with abundant pale blue flowers.

String-of-beads *(Senecio rowleyanus)*

Features: Succulent beads on a string
Size: 3–12"H × 3–10"W
Light: Bright
Temperature: 70–80°F; 60–70°F winter
Water: Moderately dry

Description and uses: String-of-beads' common name describes the plant perfectly. Plump, succulent "beads" (leaves) are strung together on thin stems. It is sometimes called string of pearls. It makes a unique tabletop plant or hanging basket. It is easier to handle in a small pot but it can be grown in a large hanging basket. It has white daisylike flowers with lilac tones, but is mostly grown for its foliage.

Care: This succulent thrives on neglect. Give it bright light, well-drained soil, and water it when it dries out and it will be happy. Feed string-of-beads a few times during the growing season. Stems can be brittle; keep plants out of traffic areas.

To grow it as a large basket plant, start with a large number of cuttings. Plant the cuttings close together and carefully drape elongating stems over the side of the container.

Propagation: Start string-of-beads from stem cuttings or from seed.

Pests: String-of-beads is rarely bothered by pests, but mealybugs may occasionally attack it.

String of hearts *(see Rosary vine)*
Striped inch plant *(see Tradescantia)*
Strobilanthes *(see Persian shield)*

Stromanthe, showy *(Stromanthe sanguinea 'Triostar')*

Features: Variegated leaves
Size: 8–12"H × 8–24"W
Light: Medium
Temperature: 65–75°F
Water: Evenly moist

Description and uses: Deep colors and natural animation give this plant a special appeal for the indoor garden. Like its relative, the prayer plant *(Maranta)*, showy stromanthe folds its leaves at night to reveal rosy pink to red undersides. The daytime view is grand too. Each leaf is rich emerald green, stroked with warm white, on dark green stems rising from a tight clump that fans out just above the soil surface. Mature plants may send up flower stalks of white panicles with orange-red sepals and red bracts.

Care: Stromanthe needs high humidity and is best grown in a greenhouse or with a humidifier. Give it medium light in moderate temperatures; direct sun will scorch leaves. Trim and remove any brown leaf tips that develop with scissors. It resents high and fluctuating temperatures. Grow in a fertile soil mix with good drainage. Keep the soil evenly moist and feed the plant regularly during growth. Repot it when the pot becomes crowded.

Propagation: Divide showy stromanthe in spring to start new plants.

Pests: Dry plants in low humidity invite infestations of mealybugs and spider mites. Overwatering causes stems and leaves to collapse from rot or to become diseased.

Showy stromanthe
(Stromanthe sanguinea 'Triostar')

Swedish ivy *(see Plectranthus)*

Sweet bay *(Laurus nobilis)*

Features: Glossy edible leaves
Size: 2–6'H × 1–3'W
Light: Medium to bright
Temperature: 50–75°F
Water: Moderately dry

Sweet bay *(Laurus nobilis)*

Description and use:
Bay is one of the few herbs that make a good long-term houseplant. It is a slow growing tree that can be pruned to size for indoor use. The dark green leaves are leathery, fragrant, and usable for cooking, as long as you avoid treating it with pest control products. Start with a large plant, since it will take several years to develop a bushy form. Sweet bay can be sheared into a rounded shrub or trained into a standard or a topiary tree form. Consider it for adding greenery in a cool bright hallway or porch. It is also known as bay laurel or bay.
Care: Sweet bay likes average to cool temperatures spring through fall and cool to cold conditions (down to 50°F) in winter. Bright light is required to produce good growth. It grows well with average humidity and tolerates drier air. Keep the soil moderately dry but avoid extreme dryness; leaves may drop if the soil is kept too dry. Use an all-purpose plant food sparingly during the growing season. Excess nitrogen can reduce the leaf oils. Plants require infrequent repotting. Prune lightly in any season to maintain the desired shape and height. The sap can be irritating to some people, so wear gloves when working with it. Summer the plant outdoors in a semishady spot.
Propagation: Propagation of sweet bay is difficult. Try taking semiripe stem cuttings in summer, use a rooting hormone and bottom heat.
Pests: Overwatering leads to root rot or leaf loss. Mealybugs and scale insects are possible pests. Do not use chemical insect control products if you plan to use leaves for cooking.
Recommendations: '**Aurea**' has yellowish young foliage; '**Angustifolia**' has willow-shape leaves; '**Undulata**' leaves have wavy margins.

Sweetheart vine *(see Rosary vine)*
Sweet olive *(see Osmanthus)*
Swiss-cheese plant *(see Philodendron, split-leaf)*
Sword fern *(see Fern, Boston)*
Syngonium *(see Arrowhead vine)*
Table fern *(see Fern, brake)*

Tahitian bridal veil *(Gibasis geniculata)*

Features: Small leaves; dainty white flowers
Size: 6–12"H × 6–24"W, trailing
Light: Bright
Temperature: 65–85°F
Water: Moderately dry

Tahitian bridal veil *(Gibasis geniculata)*

Description and uses:
This easy-to-grow flowering plant, also known as *G. pellucida*, tolerates a wide range of conditions, making it a good choice for beginners. Plants have small, shiny green leaves with purple undersides and airy, trailing stems. The abundant tiny white flowers resemble those of baby's breath and are borne above the mass of foliage spring through summer. Its cascading form is perfect for hanging baskets. Tahitian bridal veil is a fine houseplant, but it has become a noxious weed in Florida citrus groves and should not be grown outdoors in warmer climates.
Care: Plants need bright light to produce abundant flowers as well as to stay compact and shrubby. Allow the soil to dry to a depth of ½ inch before watering thoroughly. Average humidity is fine. Feed with foliage plant food. Plants grow quickly and usually need repotting annually. Pinch growing tips every few weeks to keep plants compact. If stems become bare and leggy, cut back to 1 to 2 inches above the soil line and allow them to resprout. Remove faded or dried leaves and flower stalks. Give the plant a solid shake, outdoors or over newspaper, to dislodge these dried plant parts.
Propagation: Plants root easily at leaf nodes from stem cuttings. Tahitian bridal veil can also be divided, slicing the dense root ball with a knife into three or four new plants.
Pests: Stem rot will develop if the soil is kept too wet. Aphids and spider mites can be problems.

Tailed orchid *(see Orchid, tailed)*
Thanksgiving cactus *(see Cactus, Christmas)*
Thread agave *(see Agave)*

Tiger jaws *(Faucaria felina tuberculosa)*

Features: Succulent leaves with white bumps
Size: 2–3"H × 2–8"W
Light: Bright to intense
Temperature: 70–80°F; 60–65°F winter
Water: Barely moist

Description and uses:
Tiger jaws is a distinctive succulent with white bumps (tubercles) on top of the triangular leaves. The toothed leaves grow in pairs. Each pair resembles a gaping jaw,

Tiger jaws *(Faucaria felina tuberculosa)*

thus the common name. An individual crown is 2 to 3 inches tall and wide. Plants eventually become multistemmed, forming a spreading cluster. Flowers resemble dandelions in shape and color.

Care: Grow tiger jaws in intense light to produce flowers. Water the soil well then allow it to dry to the touch during active growth. Keep the soil much drier during cool winters. Water just enough to keep the leaves from shriveling. Feed with balanced plant food during the growing season.

Propagation: Divide multistem clumps in spring or start new plants from seed.

Pests: Mealybugs may infest tiger jaws.

Tillandsia *(Tillandsia* spp.)

Features: Silvery foliage; colorful blooms
Size: 1–36"H × 1–12"W
Light: Bright
Temperature: 70–85°F
Water: Moderately dry

Sky plant *(Tillandsia ionantha)*

Description and uses:

Tillandsias are sometimes referred to as air plants because in their rain forest native habitat they attach to trees and seem to grow in the air. They are epiphytes. Their roots anchor plants in place but moisture and nutrients enter the plant through the leaves rather than the roots. Tillandsias vary in size from tiny 1-inch plants to Spanish moss, which can hang 6 to 10 feet down in trees. Many have scaly leaves, almost appearing silver; others have nonscaly leathery leaves. They are often mounted on bark or tree fern plaques.

Pink quill *(Tillandsia cyanea)*

Care: Grow tillandsias in bright light. Pink quill *(T. cyanea)* grows in well-drained potting mix. The mix anchors the plant in the pot and should be allowed to dry moderately between waterings. Most other tillandsias are mounted on bark or some other substrate. You can attach them with a silicon adhesive applied to lower leaves, not the root area, or use

Air plant *(Tillandsia stricta)*

flexible plant ties to attach them. With either choice roots can then grow and attach to the plaques. Soak mounted plants up to 1 hour a couple of times a week. Spray rather than soak blooming plants because they are susceptible to rot at that time. Mist mounted or potted plants daily. In spring and summer spray foliage with diluted plant food. Use rainwater or filtered water to counteract their sensitivity to water high in lime. As with other bromeliads, rosettes flower only once, produce offsets, and then die.

Propagation: Remove offsets and pot up or mount as described above.

Pests: Few pests bother tillandsias.

Recommendations: Air plant *(T. aeranthos)* has red bracts and deep blue flowers. Each plant grows to 4 or 5 inches in height and width. It slowly forms a large clump.

Air plant *(T. stricta)* is easy to grow and good for beginners. Many gray-green leaves grow closely together. It has rose red bracts and dark blue flowers. It forms a nice clump, but individual plants grow larger if separated.

Pink quill *(T. cyanea)* is often grown in pots and becomes about 1 foot in diameter. It forms a showy, flat quill-like pink paddle with purple flowers.

Sky plant *(T. ionantha)* is a scaly silver plant about 1 inch wide and tall. Most forms have some red coloration at leaf tips and form blue flowers.

Spanish moss *(T. usneoides)* is the plant that hangs down from trees in the South. It can grow in full sun or shade outdoors. Maintain small pieces in the home by spraying and soaking it regularly. Indoors it grows best in a greenhouse with high humidity.

Spanish moss *(Tillandsia usneoides)*

Ti plant (Cordyline fruticosa)

Features: Upright stems with very showy foliage
Size: 4–6'H × 1–3'W
Light: Bright to intense
Temperature: 60–85°F
Water: Evenly moist

Ti plant (Cordyline fruticosa)

Description and uses: Ti plant brings a tropical touch to any room. Although some forms are entirely green, most people opt for the varieties streaked with red, orange, or pink. The long straplike leaves emerge from a central stalk on a slender, upright plant. Mature specimens become sparser as they grow taller and naturally shed their lowest leaves. The result is a sturdy trunk topped with a cluster of colorful leaves that can be used as a large floor plant. This plant is often called good luck plant and is sometimes classified as *C. terminalis*.

Care: It can be difficult to provide the high humidity and exacting light conditions a healthy ti plant needs. Plants like bright light—4 or more hours of sun a day—to maintain good leaf color, but direct sun fades the colors. Give it too little light and variegation patterns are almost lost. Make sure plants get the high humidity they need by growing them on a pebble tray or with a humidifier. In spring and summer feed plants with a balanced food that includes micronutrients. Plants prefer evenly moist soil. Repot as needed into a regular potting soil. Plant several small plants in a single pot for a fuller look. Leach pots regularly to remove excess salts.

Propagation: Propagate ti plant by sticking 2-inch-wide stem cuttings, called "ti logs," on their sides in warm, moist potting soil. It may take several months for new roots and shoots to develop.

Pests: Brown leaf tips can be caused by low humidity or fluoride. Magnesium deficiency shows up as yellowing of older leaves, especially near edges. Spider mites, mealybugs, and scale are occasional insect problems.

Recommendations: 'Tricolor' is a popular broad-leaf form with red, pink, and cream coloring on a green base. '**Lord Robertson**' is a richly colored form with green and cream leaves with rose margins. '**Red Edge**' is a compact cultivar with broad, red-margin leaves.

Cabbage palm (*C. australis*) has longer, narrower foliage that arches outward from the plant's base.

Tolmiea (see Piggyback plant)

Tradescantia (Tradescantia spp.)

Features: Interesting foliage
Size: 4–12"H × 12–24", trailing
Light: Medium to bright
Temperature: 55–75°F
Water: Moderately dry

Striped inch plant (Tradescantia fluminensis)

Description and uses: Striped inch plant, *Tradescantia fluminensis*, is a fast growing vine that is usually available in one of its variegated forms, which have white- or cream-striped leaves. The trailing stems have prominent nodes and change direction slightly at each node, giving plants a zigzag look. Young plants are popular in mixed baskets, and older plants are hanging basket standards. It makes a good groundcover plant under larger houseplants. It is also sometimes called wandering Jew and classified as *T. albiflora*.

Care: Striped inch plant and its cousins like medium to bright light. Variegated and purple-leaf types need bright light to maintain colors. Average room temperatures are good for them. Water plants thoroughly and then allow the soil to dry until the top inch of soil feels dry. Water less in winter. Use a high phosphorus food during growth. Nip out the growing tips regularly to encourage bushy growth. Older plants become leggy and unkempt. Replace them with new plants from rooted cuttings.

Purple heart (Tradescantia pallida 'Purpurea')

Propagation: Root stem tip cuttings in spring or summer. The stiff stems root readily in water or in potting mix when nodes come into contact with soil.

Pests: Possible pests include aphids, spider mites, and mealybugs.

Recommendations: 'Albovittata' and 'Variegata' are the two most widely

White velvet wandering Jew (Tradescantia sillamontana)

Boat lily *(Tradescantia spathacea)*

available white-variegated cultivars. 'Aurea' has leaves that are almost entirely yellow.

Purple heart *(T. pallida)* is slower growing and requires less pinching. It needs brighter light to bring out the attractive deep purple leaf color. It has bright pink flowers that are short lived but attractive. It is also sometimes classified as *Setcreasea purpurea*.

White velvet wandering Jew *(T. sillamontana)* has green leaves densely covered in woolly white hairs. It has shorter, denser stems and grows upright at first but eventually becomes trailing. The magenta-pink flowers borne in summer are stunning.

Boat lily *(T. spathacea)* has striking foliage, green on top and deep purple beneath. The white bracts and flowers are cradled in leaf axils, giving it the other common names of Moses-in-the-cradle and oyster plant. **'Tricolor'** is a striking white, magenta, and green variegated form with a finer texture. Propagate by division rather than by cuttings. It is also classified as *Rhoeo spathacea*.

Tricolor boat lily
(Tradescantia spathacea 'Tricolor')

Purple wandering Jew *(Tradescantia zebrina)*

Wandering Jew *(Tradescantia zebrina)*

Wandering Jew *(T. zebrina)* is a traditional easy-care trailing plant with variegated olive and silvery foliage with purple undersides. Purple forms are also available.

Trailing abutilon *(see Flowering maple)*
Trailing spike moss *(see Selaginella)*
Trailing velvet plant *(see Monkey plant)*

Tree fern, dwarf *(Blechnum gibbum)*

Features: Attractive deeply divided leaves
Size: 30–40"H × 24–36"W
Light: Medium to bright
Temperature: 65–75°F
Water: Evenly moist; barely moist in winter

Description and uses: This small tree fern makes a wonderful specimen plant in locations typical ferns will not grow. Leaves are dark green, leathery, pinnately divided, shiny, and arranged in a rough funnel shape on the plant. It is also called miniature tree fern.

Care: Give dwarf tree fern plenty of water while it's in active growth, spring into summer. At cooler winter temperatures keep it drier, but never allow it to go completely dry. It grows well in regular room temperatures but appreciates a 10-degree nighttime temperature drop in winter. Use foliage plant food during growth. It appreciates average humidity; it does not need the high humidity levels that most ferns command.

Propagation: Start new plants from offsets or spores.
Pests: Aphids, scale, mealybugs, thrips, and red spider mites can be problems for a weakened plant.
Recommendations: 'Silver Lady' is a variety with more silvery foliage.

Dwarf tree fern *(Blechnum gibbum* 'Silver Lady')

Umbrella plant *(see Papyrus, dwarf)*
Umbrella tree *(see Schefflera)*
Urn plant *(see Silver vase plant)*

Vanda *(see Orchid, vanda)*
Veltheimia *(see Cape lily)*
Velvet plant *(see Purple passion)*

Venus flytrap *(Dionaea muscipula)*

Features: Carnivorous plant with traps
Size: 4–18"H × 3–6"W
Light: Bright to intense
Temperature: 70–80°F; 50°F in winter
Water: Evenly moist

Venus flytrap *(Dionaea muscipula)*

Description and uses: Venus flytrap is found in nature only in bogs in the Carolinas. It is a carnivorous plant bearing traps that close on flies and other small insects. It needs no plant food indoors, but you can supply it with an occasional insect. The plant dies after only a few meals, so resist the urge to stimulate the traps too often. It grows 4 to 7 leaves, 1 to 3 inches wide, depending on time of year. It can produce colonies of plants if happy.
Care: Venus flytrap is easy to grow for short periods indoors, if you can provide bright light and extremely high humidity. A terrarium is ideal. Long-term growth is more of a challenge. The plant requires cool conditions (about 50°F) to trigger and maintain winter dormancy. In summer tall stalks bearing small white flowers appear. Blooms weaken the plant, so pinch them off. Grow in pure sphagnum moss or moss and sand. Repot in spring as necessary. Remove any blackened leaves.
Propagation: Divide healthy clumps to start new plants.
Pests: Excess warmth can cause crown rot.

Venus-hair *(see Fern, maidenhair)*
Vriesea *(see Flaming sword)*

Walking iris *(Neomarica gracilis)*

Features: Plantlets on flower stems
Size: 16"H × 24"W
Light: Bright
Temperature: 70–80°F; 55–65°F
Water: Evenly moist

Description and uses: Walking iris is a tropical plant that resembles iris. It has a fan of flattened, elongated lance-shape leaves. It is described as "walking" because plantlets form at the tops of the flower stems, which then bend to the ground and take root. The plant produces attractive, scented irislike flowers in winter. The blooms are white with a brown center and curling blue petals. Flowers open in the morning and bloom for only one day but are replaced by others.

Walking iris *(Neomarica gracilis)*

Care: Grow walking iris in fertile well-drained potting mix kept evenly moist during active growth. Maintain drier soil in cool winter conditions. Give it flowering plant food during spring and summer. Plants benefit from summer outdoors. Keep the plant somewhat pot-bound, because it blooms best when its roots are confined.
Propagation: Root or layer plantlets. Divide large clumps.
Pests: No significant pests affect walking iris.

Wandering Jew *(see Tradescantia)*

Watermelon begonia *(Elatostema repens)*

Features: Trailing stems; multihued leaves
Size: 2–12"H × 12–24"W
Light: Medium to bright
Temperature: 70–80°F
Water: Evenly moist

Description and uses: Watermelon begonia is unrelated to either watermelon or begonia, but its gray-green leaves overlaid with a patch of silvery green and dark green edges resemble a tiny striped watermelon or a colorful begonia leaf. Leaf undersides have purple edges sometimes mixed with pink. The trailing stems are pale pink. Masses of tiny greenish flowers appear in the joints between

Watermelon begonia *(Elatostema repens)*

the leaves and stems. It does well in a terrarium. The foliage is dense, grows steadily all year, and trails with little guidance, a tidy choice for hanging baskets or pots placed on a pedestal. It is also classified as *E. daveauanum* and *Pellionia pulchra*.

Care: Grow watermelon begonia in high humidity. Use a fertile well-drained potting mix kept evenly moist. Feed balanced plant food in spring and summer. Pinch stems regularly for a denser plant. Repot each spring until the desired size is reached.

Propagation: Start new plants of watermelon begonia from stem cuttings.

Pests: Drafts and dry air cause leaf scorch. Spider mites may infest the plant in dry conditions.

Wax cissus (*see Cissus*)
Wax plant (*see Hoya*)
Wax flower (*see Hoya*)

Wax vine (Senecio macroglossus)

Features: Glossy heart-shape leaves on trailing stems
Size: 1'H × 1'W, trailing
Light: Medium to bright
Temperature: 70–85°F; 60–70°F in winter
Water: Moderately dry

Wax vine (*Senecio macroglossus* 'Variegatus')

Description and uses: Similar to most plants that store water in stems or leaves, wax vine thrives on benign neglect. The key to maintaining this unusual vining plant is to let it dry out between waterings. Also called Cape ivy for its origins in South Africa, the leaves look like succulent ivy foliage. In a bright sunny window, cheerful yellow daisylike blooms appear in contrast to the dense foliage. Leave plenty of space around wax vine for good air circulation and to avoid breaking its sometimes brittle trailing stems.

Care: Don't be fooled by the ivy-shape leaves. Wax vine needs to be treated like a succulent. Give it bright light and warmth. Let the soil dry between waterings, and feed it only during spring and summer growth. In winter keep it cooler and let it dry more. Grow in cactus mix; repot when the plant is pot-bound.

Propagation: Take stem cuttings when the plant is in active growth. Allow cuttings to form callus before planting.

Pests: Root rot from overwatering and mealybugs are the most common problems on wax vine.

Recommendations: 'Variegatus' is the most popular variety, grown for its variegated cream and green leaves. It resembles a waxy English ivy.

Weeping fig (*see Ficus*)
Windowpane plant (*see Haworthia*)
Yew pine (*see Podocarpus*)

Yucca (Yucca elephantipes)

Features: Sword-shape foliage
Size: 1–10'H × 1–6'W
Light: Medium to bright
Temperature: 70–80°F; 50–55°F winter
Water: Moderately dry

Yucca (*Yucca elephantipes*)

Description and uses: Yucca's narrow green leaves can be 1 to 3 feet long. They are clustered in a sharply pointed, though soft, crown along and on top of a distinctive gray-brown trunk. The plant is soft and lush compared to desert yuccas, with more and larger leaves on a faster growing plant. Mature forms are often grown with one to three trunks 3- to 5-feet tall with exposed trunks and several crowns. Young plants may be grown in a 6-inch pot with one crown of leaves at soil level. Offsets called pups form at the soil surface and, when removed, create a palmlike effect on the mother plant with a tuft of foliage at the tip of the trunk. It is also called spineless yucca and sometimes is classified as *Y. guatemalensis*.

Care: To do well long term yucca needs cool winter temperatures, down to 50°F. A bright unheated room or atrium would be a good location. Grow in cactus mix. Allow it to go moderately dry between waterings; water sparingly in winter. Move the plant outdoors in spring in a protected location. It can stay out until temperatures dip to nearly 40°F in fall. At that time move it into a cool, frost-free location until spring.

Propagation: Remove and pot up rooted offsets (pups).

Pests: Warm conditions in winter will lead to pests, particularly scale and spider mites.

Zamioculcas (*see Zeezee plant*)
Zebra haworthia (*see Haworthia*)

Zebra plant *(Aphelandra squarrosa)*

Features: Bold veined leaves; yellow bracts
Size: 10–15"H × 10–15"W
Light: Bright
Temperature: 65–80°F
Water: Evenly moist

Zebra plant *(Aphelandra squarrosa)*

Description and uses: This tropical shrub is often purchased in bloom with bright yellow flowers and bracts, but the boldly striped dark green leaves are showy in their own right. Zebra plant is often treated as a temporary plant and discarded after blooming, since it is difficult to bring into bloom again without greenhouse conditions.
Care: Zebra plant likes bright light without exposure to direct sun. Keep the soil evenly moist and maintain moderate to high humidity. Use a peaty potting soil such as African violet mix. Feed spring through fall with a high-phosphorus plant food. Repot annually in spring to refresh soil. Keep plants slightly root-bound. Clip off flowering bracts when they turn brown after blooming. Let plants rest in a cool room for about 2 months, and then move to a brighter location in late spring. Plants may rebloom in fall if given adequate light. Individual plants only live about a year but they can be propagated indefinitely. Leaves become crinkled or curled in too much light. Dry air and cold drafts cause leaf scorch or drop. Pay close attention to water needs. Plants wilt both when soil is too dry and too wet.
Propagation: Take stem tip cuttings each spring. Rooting powder encourages faster rooting. Side shoots can also be removed with roots attached and repotted.
Pests: Whiteflies, fungus gnats, mealybugs, and aphids can be problems, especially on the tender new growth.
Recommendations: 'Diana' is a popular selection with dark leaves; 'Apollo' has more pronounced venation; 'Red Apollo' has reddish tints on the stems and leaves.
  A. sinclariana has coral-color bracts and protruding pink tubular flowers that last for several weeks.

Zebra vine *(see Lipstick plant)*

Zeezee plant *(Zamioculcas zamiifolia)*

Features: Waxy upright foliage
Size: 2–3'H × 2–3'W
Light: Bright to medium
Temperature: 60–75°F
Water: Moderately dry

Zeezee plant *(Zamioculcas zamiifolia)*

Description and uses: Zeezee plant tolerates neglect and low light and still looks good. It forms a cluster of thick fleshy leafstalks that radiate upward and outward. They bear glossy elliptic leaflets, creating the effect of a palm leaf. The dark green plant eventually produces offsets that fill the pot with foliage. It is a slow grower, so purchase a large plant if you want a big specimen. The plant is toxic; keep it away from children. It is also called eternity plant because it is long lasting. Cut stems may remain green and healthy in appearance for several weeks, even without water. It is sometimes listed as *Z. lanceolata.*
Care: Zeezee plant likes bright light but tolerates low light for long periods. Let the soil dry out somewhat between waterings. It can go for long periods without any water at all. Overwatering can lead to stem rot. Low to average humidity is fine. It is not a heavy feeder. Use an all-purpose plant food during the growing period. Repot as needed using any good soil mix. Remove faded leaves as they appear. It likes spending the summer outdoors in a shady spot.
Propagation: Divide offsets from large plants. Plant the bulblets that may form in the leaf axils. Or start from leaf cuttings, which can take several months to root.
Pests: Mealybugs and scale insects are rare but possible pests of zeezee plant.
Recommendations: No named cultivars of zeezee plant are readily available.

Resources

Please call nurseries and greenhouses before planning a visit; some are open by appointment only and many are not open to the public every day of the week. Note: Canadian nurseries cannot ship plants to the United States.

Plants and seeds

Allannah's Greenhouses
Box 1342
Grand Forks, BC V0H 1H0
Canada
250/442-2552
www.alannahs.com
African violets, gesneriads, specialty geraniums, and assorted flowering tropical houseplants

Aloha Tropicals
P.O. Box 6042
Oceanside, CA 92054 USA
760/631-2880
www.alohatropicals.com
Bananas, heliconias, gingers, other tropicals

A & P Orchids
110 Peters Rd.
Swansea, MA 02777 USA
508/675-1717
www.aandporchids.com
Orchids

Cal-Orchid, Inc.
1251 Orchid Dr.
Santa Barbara, CA 93111 USA
805/967-1312
www.calorchid.com
Orchids

Daniel's Specialty Nursery
16257 Quail Rock Rd.
Ramona, CA 92065 USA
760/787-1801
danielscactus.hypermart.net
Cacti and succulents

Davidson-Wilson Greenhouses
3147 E. Ladoga Rd.
Crawfordsville, IN 47933 USA
877/723-6834
www.davidson-wilson.com
Unusual houseplants; specialty geraniums

Digital Raingardens
5922 Shadow Wood Dr.
Corpus Christi, TX 78415 USA
361/852-5063
www.raingardens.com
Houseplant seeds

Epie Acres
247 Wilson Ave.
Placentia, CA 92870 USA
714/524-0994
www.epies.net
Epiphyllum plants

E.F.G. Orchids
4265 Marsh Rd.
DeLand, FL 32724
386/738-8699
www.efgorchids.com
Orchids

Florida Plants Online
www.floridaplants.com/interior.htm
Indoor plants and supplies

Glasshouse Works
Church St., P.O. Box 97
Stewart, OH 45778 USA
740/662-2142
www.glasshouseworks.com
Tropical and rare plants

GreenDealer Exotic Seeds
P.O. Box 37328
Louisville, KY 40233 USA
FAX: 502/459-9054
www.GreenDealer-Exotic-Seeds.com/seeds/index.html
Seeds of palms, houseplants, cacti, tropicals

Grow Exotics
4604 49th St. N.
P.O. Box 49
St. Petersburg, FL 33709
727/251-9996
www.growexotics.com
Houseplants, tropicals

Harborcrest Gardens
1581-H Hillside Ave., Suite 230
Victoria, BC V8T 2C1 Canada
250/642-7309
www.harborcrestgardens.com
Tropical flowering and foliage plants and African violets

Hobbs Farm & Greenery
979 Barnestown Rd.
Hope, ME 04847 USA
207/763-4746
www.hobbsfarm.com
Houseplants; ivies

Hoosier Orchid Co.
8440 West 82nd St.
Indianapolis, IN 46278
317/291-6269
www.hoosierorchid.com
Orchids

Jungle Music Palms & Cycads
3233 Brant St.
San Diego, CA 92103 USA
619/291-4605
www.junglemusic.net
Palms and cycads

Kartuz Greenhouses, Sunset Island Exotics
1408 Sunset Dr.
Vista, CA 92085 USA
760/941-3613
www.kartuz.com
Gesneriads, begonias, flowering tropicals, subtropicals, vines

Lauray of Salisbury
432 Undermountain Rd., Rte. 41
Salisbury, CT 06068 USA
860/435-2263
www.lauray.com
Cacti, orchids, begonias, gesneriads, succulents

Lindsey Products and Services
255 E. Bolivar St., #244
Salinas, CA 93906 USA
800/384-4559
www.cabrillonets.com/calplants/
Cacti and succulents

Logee's Greenhouses
141 North St.
Danielson, CT 06239 USA
888/330-8038
www.logees.com
Tropicals and subtropicals

Lyndon Lyon Greenhouses
P.O. Box 249
14 Mutchler St.
Dolgeville, NY 13329 USA
315/429-8291
www.lyndonlyon.com
African violets and orchids

McKinney's Glasshouse
P.O. Box 782282
Wichita, KS 67278 USA
316/686-9438
Gesneriads, rare and exotic
   tropicals, supplies

Mid-Pacific Orchids
P.O. Box 4282
Honolulu, HA 96812 USA
www.midpacificorchids.com
Orchids and orchid supplies

New Leaf Nurseries
2456 Foothill Dr.
Vista, CA 92084 USA
760/726-9269
www.newleafnurseries.com
Geranium and coleus plants

Northridge Gardens
9821 White Oak Ave.
Northridge, CA 91325 USA
818/349-9798
Succulents, hard-to-find
   items

Oak Hill Gardens
P.O. Box 25
37W 550 Binnie Rd.
Dundee, IL 60118 USA
847/428-8500
www.oakhillgardens.com
Specialty plants, orchids
   and supplies

Packer Nursery
P.O. Box 4056
Kailua-Kona, HI 96745 USA
888/345-5566
www.alohapalms.com
Palms and tropicals

P & J Greenhouses
20265 82nd Ave.
Langley, BC V2Y 2A9 Canada
604/888-3274
www.geranium-greenhouses.
   com
Geraniums and fuchsias

Rainbow Gardens Nursery
   & Bookshop
1444 E. Taylor St.
Vista, CA 92084 USA
760/758-4290
www.
   rainbowgardensbookshop.
   com
Plants and books

R.F. Orchids, Inc.
28100 S.W. 182nd Ave.
Homestead, FL 33030
305/245-4570
www.rforchids.com

Rhapis Gardens
P.O. Box 287
Gregory, TX 78359 USA
361/643-2061
www.rhapisgardens.com
Lady and sago palms, grape
   ivy, ming aralias

Russell's Bromeliads
1690 Beardall Ave.
Sanford, FL 32771 USA
407/322-0864
www.russelsairplants.com
Tillandsias and other
   bromeliads

SBE Seed Co.
3421 Bream St.
Gautier, MS 39553 USA
800/336-2064
www.seedman.com
Palm, cacti, bonsai and
   houseplant seeds

Seedlings.com
15 Valley Farms
Fairfield, ME 04937 USA
www.seedlings.com/seeds/
   houseplants
Houseplant seeds

Stokes Tropicals
4806 W. Old Spanish Trail
Jeanerette, LA 70544 USA
337/365-6998
Orders: 800/624-9706
www.stokestropicals.com
Bananas, gingers, heliconias,
   other tropicals

Sunrise Nursery
13105 Canyon View
Leander, TX 78641 USA
512/267-0023
www.sunrisenursery.com
Succulents, cacti

Tiki Nursery
P.O. Box 187
Fairview, NC 28730 USA
828/628-2212
African violets and other
   gesneriads

Top Tropicals
47770 Bermont Rd.
Punta Gorda, FL 33982 USA
941/575-6987
www.toptropicals.com
Rare plants, tropicals

William Dam Seeds
279 Hwy #8 West
   Flamborough
Box 8400
Dundas, ON L9H 6M1
   Canada
905/628-6641
www.damseeds.com
Herb seeds and plants

Plant Societies

African Violet Society of
   America
2375 North St.
Beaumont, TX 77702 USA
800/770-2872
www.avsa.org

American Begonia Society
P.O. Box 471651
San Francisco, CA 94147
   USA
www.begonias.org

American Bonsai Society
P.O. Box 351604
Toledo, OH 43635 USA
www.absbonsai.org

American Fern Society, Inc.
Missouri Botanic Garden
P.O. Box 299
St. Louis, MO 63166 USA
www.amerfernsoc.org

American Gloxinia and
   Gesneriad Society
1122 E. Pike St., PMB 637
Seattle, WA 98122 USA
aggs.org

American Ivy Society
P.O. Box 2123
Naples, FL 34106
www.ivy.org

American Orchid Society
16700 AOS Lane
Delray Beach, FL33446 USA
561/404-2000
www.orchidweb.org

Bromeliad Society
   International
6901 Kellyn Lane
Vista, CA 92084 USA
bsi.org

Cactus & Succulent Society
   of America
P.O. Box 2615
Pahrump, NV 89041
775/751-1320
www.cssainc.org

International Palm Society
P.O. Box 1897
Lawrence, KS 66044 USA
www.palms.org

Supplies

Eco Enterprises
1240 N.E. 175th St., Suite B
Shoreline, WA 98155 USA
800/426-6937
www.ecogrow.com
Growing supplies, lighting

B.C. Greenhouse Builders
A5 19327 94th Ave.
Surrey, BC V4 N4 E6 Canada
604/882-8408
Home greenhouses and
   supplies

Bonsai of Brooklyn
2418 McDonald Ave.
Brooklyn, NY 11223 USA
917/325-3954
www.bonsaiofbrooklyn.com
Bonsai trees, tools and
   supplies

Bonsai Learning Center
4416 Beattie's Ford Rd.
Charlotte, NC 28216 USA
704/392-9244
www.bonsailearningcenter.
   com
Bonsai tools and supplies

Charley's Greenhouse &
   Garden
17979 State Route 536
Mount Vernon, WA 98273
   USA
800/322-4707
www.charleysgreenhouse.com
Growing supplies,
   greenhouses, lighting

Dallas Bonsai Garden
4460 W. Walnut St., Suite 218
Garland, TX 75042
800/982-1223
www.dallasbonsai.com
Bonsai tools and supplies

Diamond Lights
1701 4th St.
San Rafael, CA 94901 USA
888/331-3994
www.diamondlights.com
High intensity lighting,
 indoor growing supplies

Gardener's Supply Co.
128 Intervale Rd.
Burlington, VT 05401 USA
800/955-3370
www.gardeners.com
Seed-starting supplies,
 organic fertilizers and pest
 controls, hand tools, and
 watering systems

GreenCoast Hydroponics
3560 State St.
Santa Barbara, CA 93105
877/694-9376
www.gchydro.com
Hydroponic supplies, grow
 lights, orchids and
 houseplants

Greenhouses.com
2385 Goodhue St.
Red Wing, MN 55066 USA
877/718-2865
www.greenhouses.com
Greenhouses

Greenhouses, Etc.
4804 Collister Dr.
Boise, ID 83703 USA
888/244-8009
www.greenhousesetc.com
Greenhouses, grow lights,
 and greenhouse accessories

Hydro-Farm
755 Southpoint Blvd.
Petaluma, CA 94954 USA
707/765-9990
www.hydrofarm.com
High-intensity lighting and
 indoor growing supplies

Indoor Gardening Supplies
P.O. Box 527
Dexter, MI 48130 USA
800/823-5740
www.
 indoorgardeningsupplies.
 com
Growing supplies

International Greenhouse
 Company
806 N. Main St.
Georgetown, IL 61846 USA
888/281-9337
Greenhouses and supplies

OFE International, Inc.
12100 SW 129th St.
Miami, FL 33186
305/253-7080
www.ofe-intl.com
Orchid supplies

The Scotts Company
800/225-2883
www.scotts.com
www.ortho.com
www.miracle-gro.com
Plant food, mulches, growing
 media, and pest controls

Texas Greenhouse Company
812 E. Northside Dr.
Fort Worth, TX 76102 USA
800/227-5447
www.texasgreenhouse.com
Greenhouses and greenhouse
 supplies

Windowbox.com
3821 S. Santa Fe Ave.
Vernon, CA 90058 USA
888/427-3362
323/277-1137
www.windowbox.com
Container gardening supplies

METRIC CONVERSIONS

U.S. UNITS TO METRIC EQUIVALENTS			METRIC EQUIVALENTS TO U.S. UNITS		
To convert from	Multiply by	To get	To convert from	Multiply by	To get
Inches	25.4	Millimeters	Millimeters	0.0394	Inches
Inches	2.54	Centimeters	Centimeters	0.3937	Inches
Feet	30.48	Centimeters	Centimeters	0.0328	Feet
Feet	0.3048	Meters	Meters	3.2808	Feet
Yards	0.9144	Meters	Meters	1.0936	Yards
Square inches	6.4516	Square centimeters	Square centimeters	0.1550	Square inches
Square feet	0.0929	Square meters	Square meters	10.764	Square feet
Square yards	0.8361	Square meters	Square meters	1.1960	Square yards
Acres	0.4047	Hectares	Hectares	2.4711	Acres
Cubic inches	16.387	Cubic centimeters	Cubic centimeters	0.0610	Cubic inches
Cubic feet	0.0283	Cubic meters	Cubic meters	35.315	Cubic feet
Cubic feet	28.316	Liters	Liters	0.0353	Cubic feet
Cubic yards	0.7646	Cubic meters	Cubic meters	1.308	Cubic yards
Cubic yards	764.55	Liters	Liters	0.0013	Cubic yards

To convert from degrees Fahrenheit (F) to degrees Celsius (C), first subtract 32, then multiply by $5/9$.

To convert from degrees Celsius (C) to degrees Fahrenheit (F), multiply by $9/5$, then add 32.

Index